Strategic Management Support Systems

Strategic Management Support Systems

Christine Fidler

Management in IS Research Group

Simon Rogerson

Centre for Computing and Social Responsibility

School of Computing Sciences
De Montfort University

London · Hong Kong · Johannesburg · Melbourne · Singapore · Washington DC

PITMAN PUBLISHING
128 Long Acre, London WC2E 9AN
Tel: +44 (0)171 447 2000
Fax: +44 (0)171 240 5771

A Division of Pearson Professional Limited

First published in Great Britain in 1996

ISBN 0 273 61418 5

British Library Cataloguing in Publication Data
A CIP catalogue record for this book can be obtained from the British Library

10 9 8 7 6 5 4 3 2 1

Typeset by Pantek Arts, Maidstone, Kent
Printed and bound in Great Britain by Clays Ltd, St Ives plc

The Publishers' policy is to use paper manufactured from sustainable forests.

CONTENTS

To Ralph – from one 'Fidler' to another!

To Anne and Jemma for your encouragement,
support and simply being there for me.

PREFACE

In the modern business environment and in the light of past computer system failures, organisations must ensure that development and support resources are focused on the computerised systems of most value. In other words, only those investments that are aligned with corporate strategy and mission should be considered, and those most valuable adopted.

This book focuses on the topic of Strategic Management Support Systems. A Management Support System (MSS) is a Computer-based Information System (CBIS) that supports management by supporting decision making and/or information handling activities. A Strategic MSS is an MSS which is aligned with corporate objectives and mission. Strategic MSS are therefore the MSS that are of most value and, by default, of most importance to an organisation. Strategic Information Systems Planning (SISP) provides the means of identifying information systems, and hence MSS as a special kind of information system, that support and enhance organisational strategy. It is therefore instrumental in the identification of Strategic MSS.

In order to understand Strategic Management Support Systems, both Management Support Systems design, development and use, and SISP concepts, approaches and application, need to be understood both individually and in combination. This book achieves this, by first focusing on the individual topics of MSS and SISP (the subjects of Parts 2 and 3 respectively). The book focuses subsequently on the integration of MSS and SISP which results in the identification of Strategic MSS (the subject of Part 4).

This book is unique in many ways. To the authors' knowledge, there is no other text that discusses both MSS and SISP concepts to the same level of treatment, and shows their integration clearly. The approaches to the MSS and SISP topics are also new. Essentially, the topic of MSS is approached from a functionality viewpoint rather than from the traditional and increasingly troublesome system type viewpoint. The functional view of MSS capabilities is considered to be most appropriate to the real needs of business and current computing environments. In the case of SISP, uniqueness is reflected in the explicit recognition and analysis of the symbiotic relationship between SISP methodologies, techniques and tools, on the one hand, and Strategic Culture Building (SCB) within the organisation, on the other. To the authors' knowledge, this is the first text to provide an explicit, structured view of how these aspects of SISP interrelate and how they are influenced by organisational context. Finally, the term Strategic MSS takes on a different and more appropriate meaning to that traditionally prescribed. Essentially, any MSS which is aligned with an organisation's corporate objectives, albeit a day-to-day operational MSS or an MSS for the support of strategic planning activities, is a Strategic MSS for that organisation.

The aim of this book is to provide a fresh perspective on part, if not all, of the IS landscape. The reader is encouraged to reflect upon the new concepts and relationships introduced. Information Systems is an applied discipline and so any book covering aspects of IS must include coverage of practice as well as concepts. Therefore, this book includes many case studies and projects that are designed to provide the reader with the opportunity to consider the practical implications of this new perspective.

Although this book would be nothing without the significant contributions made by others, the views expressed within the book are entirely the responsibility of the authors. In other words, the buck stops here!

Chris Fidler and Simon Rogerson

ACKNOWLEDGEMENTS

As is often the case, there are far too many colleagues, students, other academics and practitioners to mention all by name, who have helped to shape the ideas presented in this book. Thanks to all of you!

We would like to mention a few people by name, who have been particularly instrumental in the production of this book. Special thanks to:

- John Cushion and Kara Regan at Pitman Publishing, for their encouragement and advice in all aspects of writing this book.
- Our colleagues;
  - Adrian Larner and Richard Howley for their extremely thoughtful comments on the draft versions of this book,
  - John Platt and John Wain for help with the case studies,
  - Margaret Radford and Patrick Foster for performing, often extremely tedious, tasks on our behalf.

Our thanks are extended to several companies and their representatives for allowing us to reference and include material relating to their company's products and services, and for their general support in this venture. These include:

- Andersen Consulting; Susan Palmer Business Development Analyst, Bob Spurgeon Director Foundation Methodology Programme
- Business Link Leicestershire; Tony Grice Chief Executive
- The Boston Consulting Group; Barry N Jones Senior Vice President
- Cognos UK Ltd.
- *Computer Weekly*; John Riley Managing Editor
- Grace Dearborn; Peter J Hopkins Marketing Information Manager, Phil Johnson Director of Marketing Services
- KPMG Management Consulting; Brian Elliot, Roger C Lee Principal Consultants
- Oracle Corporation
- Pilot Software Inc.
- VNU Business Publications

PART 1

Introduction

*'We must indeed all hang together, or, most assuredly,
we shall all hang separately.'*

Benjamin Franklin

1 Introduction and Overview

CHAPTER 1

Introduction and Overview

1.1 STRATEGIC MSS: AN INTRODUCTION

With the globalisation of markets, and the increased quantity and diversity of competition that occur as a consequence, the traditional view of computer systems as a 'back room' supporting function is no longer viable in companies wishing to survive and prosper. Rather, companies must look for ways of using computerised systems to support the corporate strategy and to gain competitive advantage over rivals. Already, some companies have developed and used computerised systems successfully in the achievement of competitive advantage. Indeed, several have reaped the benefits of being the leader in a key computerised application area over a sustained period of time. Competitors have had to implement similar computerised systems just to survive.

At the same time, companies have frequently been disappointed with computerised systems. Development projects have often run over time and budget, and in many cases the resultant system has had minimal impact on the competitive position of an organisation. In addition, there are well publicised cases of computerised systems being total failures (such as those developed for the London Stock Exchange and the London Ambulance Service) due to vital factors not being properly evaluated prior to project initiation and/or due to fundamental design flaws. Failures, both publicly documented and private to the company, make corporate management sceptical of investing substantial human and/or financial resources in computerised systems without proper evaluation and justification. Management expect value for money.

These issues have implications for the methods by which computerised systems are selected for implementation, and the management of that implementation. Firstly, only investments that support the organisational objectives and mission should be adopted. The key issue, here, is the alignment of any investment with the organisation's strategy and mission. Secondly, implementation must always be planned and controlled effectively. Planning involves the selection of the most appropriate development method for the given situation.

Strategic Information Systems Planning (SISP) activities enable a company to identify an Information Systems (IS) strategy which is aligned with its corporate strategy and mission. SISP is defined as *the means of identifying application systems [i.e. IS] which support and enhance organisational strategy and provides for the effective implementation of these systems.* The mechanistic aspects of SISP methodologies, techniques and tools are complemented by the behavioural aspects of Strategic Culture Building (SCB) within an organisation. Both the mechanistic and behavioural aspects are present within any organisation, although which is most prominent depends on a variety of contextual factors.

This book focuses principally on how an organisation can develop *Strategic Management Support Systems. A Management Support System (MSS) is a Computer-based Information System (CBIS) that supports management by supporting decision making and/or information handling activities.* An MSS which is aligned with corporate objectives and mission is referred to as a *Strategic MSS.* Ensuring that a corporation's total MSS provision is aligned in this way is best achieved using SISP. The IS strategy resulting from SISP may comprise several projects, some of which concern the development and/or effective operation of MSS.

1.2 SOME KEY DEFINITIONS

In this book, the term Information System (IS) is defined as a system, which may include both computerised components (such as hardware, software, and communications capabilities) and non-computerised components (such as people, procedures and data), that delivers information. A Computer-based Information System (CBIS) is defined as an information system that is computer-based. CBIS operate within, and interact with, an environment comprised of many different types of systems, some of which may be (CB)IS.

The terms Information Technology (IT) and IS are distinguished within this book: the former is concerned with the underlying technological tools, whereas the latter is concerned with the application of these technological tools to support business activity. Earl (1987) adds a third key dimension to computerised systems provision within an organisation, known as Information Management (IM). This is concerned with the management issues surrounding the procurement, development and effective operation of IS/IT within the organisation. Earl states that elements of IS, IT and IM comprise an IS Strategy. IS Projects that result from an IS Strategy should always include IM aspects within their specification. (Indeed, an IS project may involve only IM aspects to be implemented, for example where an existing IS/IT system is already in situ but is not managed effectively.)

Finally, the acronym MSS is defined with respect to one system within Chapter 2, but will be used to mean both a Management Support System (singular – an MSS) and one or more Management Support Systems (plural – MSS). Whether one or greater than one Management Support System is being considered is determined by the context in which the acronym is used.

1.3 SUMMARY OF BOOK CONTENT

This book comprises four parts. The first part provides an introduction to, and overview of, the structure and content of the remaining parts. The second and third parts of the book concentrate on the two subjects that are key to understanding Strategic MSS: MSS and SISP respectively. The fourth part integrates the subjects of MSS and SISP to show how Strategic MSS can be identified, and provides a conclusion to the entire book.

The brief overview of each chapter is given in turn below.

Part 1: Introduction

Chapter 1: *Introduction and Overview* – This chapter provides an overview of the book, including: some basic definitions to be used throughout this book, an overview of each part and chapter, a brief justification for the approach adopted to the subject of Strategic MSS, a reader's road map through the chapters depending on individual requirements, and a description of the intended audience.

Part 2: Management Support Systems (MSS)

Chapter 2: What is a Management Support System (MSS)? – This chapter defines in detail what is meant by the term 'Management Support System' and establishes a framework for viewing MSS functionality. The framework forms the basis for the structure of Chapters 4 to 6 inclusive. In the chapter, several key terms, phrases and models are defined, including: Simon's Decision Making Model; three different, yet highly inter-related views of management; the difference between data and information, and the characteristics of good information; sources of data/information; and the differences between, and the comparative strengths and weaknesses of, individual and group decision making.

Chapter 3: Technology and MSS Opportunities – This chapter provides a history of MSS evolution, from the 1950s to the present day, from a technical perspective. Following on from this, several more recent technological advances that have already had, or are expected to have, impact on MSS provision are described, namely: client server systems; the Object-oriented (OO) paradigm and systems; the Graphical User Interface (GUI) and the Windows* environment; open systems; neural networks, multi-media and hyper-media applications and systems; Virtual Reality (VR) systems; the Internet; and data warehouses. These advances illustrate the opportunities that new technologies, in general, provide for enhancing the functionality available for use within MSS, and/or for enabling the greater integration of functionality within a particular MSS implementation. The existence of trends towards greater integration provides partial justification for the approach taken to MSS within this book (see Section 1.4 below for more detail on the approach taken).

Chapter 4: Information Handling Support with MSS – This chapter focuses on the provision of MSS functionality to support information handling activities. The functionality provided by information (document) preparation systems and information (message) communication systems is reviewed. Two approaches to information (document) preparation are described: the structure editor approach and the template (or style sheet) approach. Information communication can be provided in two ways: by explicit information (message) exchange or by information (message) sharing. Electronic mail (e-mail) and Teleconferencing (including Audioconferencing and Videoconferencing) provide support for information exchange. Joint Authoring Systems and Bulletin Boards provide support for information sharing.

Chapter 5: Passive Decision Making Support with MSS – This chapter looks at MSS functionality for passive decision making support. Passive decision making support concerns

---

* Windows is a trademark of Microsoft Corporation

the provision of information reports by MSS. An overall view of information reporting by MSS is described first. This includes an examination of the potential and actual scope of information reporting within organisations, the content of information reports and, in general terms, how information reports can be used to aid the planning and controlling activities of management. A four-part classification of MSS information reports is then proposed, based on two temporal issues: the time at which the reports are defined, and the time at which the reports are made available to management. Several available methods by which MSS allow users to request information reports are then reviewed for each classification of information reports in turn. During this review, several key MSS concepts, including drill-down, hotspots, traffic light colour coding, and data driven information reporting with 'slice and dice' capabilities, are described. Finally, several examples of MSS that provide passive decision making support are presented.

Chapter 6: Active Decision Making Support with MSS – This chapter focuses on MSS functionality for providing active decision making support. MSS that provide active decision making support allow the user(s) to analyse and manipulate information interactively during a decision making process. Interactive access to models, which are often of a mathematical nature, is key to the provision of this functionality. A large proportion of this chapter is therefore devoted to defining and categorising models, and to describing several mathematical techniques for formulating and solving mathematical models. The techniques covered include Weighted Score Technique, Linear Programming Technique (model formulation only), Decision Tree Technique, Simulation Technique and Rule-based Technique. Four techniques available for structuring group decision making situations, namely Nominal Group Technique (NGT), Delphi Technique, Brainstorming and Voting, are also reviewed.

The remainder of this chapter focuses on MSS functionality for active decision making support. Firstly, a logical architecture for an MSS that provides this functionality is presented and described. The architecture embraces the diversity and scope of MSS functionality available to provide active support of decision making. Particular types of MSS that provide active decision making support, namely Geographical Information Systems (GIS) and Decision Rooms (for group decision making), are discussed in some detail. Several examples of MSS that provide active decision making support are presented.

Chapter 7: MSS Development: Approaches and Techniques – This chapter reviews MSS development approaches and techniques. The issues of aligning MSS projects with organisational objectives and of assessing the feasibility of MSS projects are discussed. Attention then focuses on the overall development approaches, namely the traditional approach, the evolutionary approach and the hybrid approach, that can be adopted for MSS development. The most suitable development approach(es) for MSS providing (*a*) information handling support, (*b*) passive decision making support and (*c*) active decision making support, are discussed. Several MSS-specific development methodologies and techniques are reviewed. The scope and role of conventional IS methodologies and techniques within MSS development are critically analysed.

Chapter 8: MSS Summary – This chapter provides a summary of, and conclusion to, the preceding chapters in this part. The Grace Dearborn scenario illustrates and integrates many of the concepts raised in this part of the book.

Part 3: Strategic Information Systems Planning (SISP)

Chapter 9: What is Strategic Information Systems Planning (SISP)? – This chapter provides an introduction to SISP, and an overview of aspects of SISP to be covered in greater detail by subsequent chapters. The evolution of the role of IS/IT within organisations in general, from support to strategic, is described. The importance of, and key factors in, maintaining alignment between IS, corporate mission and organisational strategy, are discussed. SISP is proposed as the vital link between corporate mission, organisational strategy and IS strategy. A definition of SISP is proposed, which captures the mechanistic aspects of the process supported by SISP methodologies, techniques and tools, and promotes Strategic Culture Building (SCB). A review of the inter-relationships between both mechanistic and behavioural aspects of SISP/SCB is provided, and related to the nature of organisations within which strategic activity may occur.

An overview of the likely participants within a SISP activity, relative to the focus of the IS strategy, is presented. Finally, a brief introduction to some of the key methodologies, techniques and tools proposed for use within SISP is given. A three-layered view of SISP methodologies, techniques and tools is described.

Chapter 10: SISP Methodologies, Techniques and Tools – This chapter focuses on SISP methodologies, techniques and associated tools in more detail. Firstly, two key SISP techniques are explained: the Five Forces Model, and the Strategic Relevance and Impact Grid and its variations. These illustrate the ways in which SISP techniques facilitate the identification of potential IS projects. Four SISP methodologies are described in varying degrees of detail: the CSF methodology as a publicly available methodology, and the Andersen Consulting, KPMG and Boston Consulting Group approaches as proprietary SISP methodologies.

Chapter 11: How to Perform a SISP Exercise – This chapter looks at how a SISP exercise should be approached in practice. The factors that influence the success of a SISP exercise are first reviewed. One of the most important factors is the composition of the SISP team, and this is discussed in detail. The decision on whether the mechanistic aspects or the behavioural aspects predominate within a particular organisational situation is then discussed. This is dependent on several organisational factors, and the resultant blend has implications for the approach taken to SISP. The decision as to which SISP methodology and techniques to apply is also described, and a technique for facilitating this decision is presented. Finally, some guidelines for undertaking a SISP exercise are provided.

Chapter 12: Business Process Re-engineering (BPR) – This chapter focuses on Business Process Re-engineering (BPR), which has received much research and practitioner attention in recent years. The BPR concept is explained, and related to SISP and SCB. Obstacles to effective BPR are reviewed. The chapter also explores two schools of thought, one that considers BPR to be IS/IT driven and the other that considers BPR to be IS/IT enabled. The level of integration and duplicity will be dependent on the influence of each school.

Chapter 13: SISP Summary – This chapter provides a summary of, and conclusion to, the preceding chapters in this part. Use of SISP in practice is illustrated through the Bristol & West and ICI case studies.

Part 4: Strategic MSS

Chapter 14: Combining SISP/SCB and MSS: Strategic MSS – This chapter ties together SISP/SCB (described in Part 3) and MSS (described in Part 2) to show how Strategic MSS can be identified. This relationship is viewed not only at the level of general SISP/SCB activities, but also with respect to particular SISP methodologies and techniques described in Part 3. Relationships also exist between SISP and MSS due to the former being a management activity and the latter supporting management. These additional relationships are also reviewed.

Chapter 15: Conclusion – This chapter provides a summary of this part and a conclusion to the entire book. The Business Link Leicestershire (BLL) case study is used to illustrate the relationship between SISP/SCB and MSS which ensures Strategic MSS are developed and used. It also provides further illustration of SISP/SCB and MSS in practice.

1.4 UNIQUE FEATURES OF THIS BOOK WITH JUSTIFICATION

This book has several unique features. Each chapter provides new insight into the current subject of interest, and new frameworks are presented and discussed.

Four key unique features are worthy of individual attention as they have served to shape both the content and structure of the entire book.

- *The combination and integration of SISP and MSS within one text.* There are several texts that discuss SISP and there are several texts that describe MSS in relative isolation. To the authors' knowledge, there is no other book that discusses both concepts comprehensively, and shows their integration clearly.
- *An integrated, functional view of MSS.* The usual approach to reviewing the topic of MSS is to separate MSS functionality into subsets, each subset of which is attributed to a particular traditional system type, such as a Management Information System (MIS), a Decision Support System (DSS), a Group DSS (GDSS), an Executive Information System (EIS), an Expert System (ES) or an Office Information System (OIS). Each system type is then reviewed in turn.

  Associating functionality with particular system types has always been problematic. There are no universally agreed definitions of the system types. Thus, each author provides a personal set of system type definitions which dictates the separation of functionality. Furthermore, the functionality attributed to two or more system types is not normally mutually exclusive. Overlaps in functionality create confusion for the reader. In addition, technological advances already facilitate, and continue to facilitate, the integration of disparate functionality. The functionality typically associated with two or more traditional systems types (although actual association depends on the set of definitions being adhered to) can be provided by one integrated MSS implementation. Finally, corporate management are not interested in what type of system is being developed: they are concerned with the provision of appropriate MSS functionality to match organisation need. For these reasons, the classical approach of MSS description (that is, by traditional system type) is not adopted in this book. Instead, the book focuses on describing the nature and scope of available MSS functionality, and on the matching of that functionality directly to organisational need.

- *The view that all MSS facilities, when aligned with corporate mission and organisational strategy, are strategic.* Frequently, a distinction is made between operational MSS, tactical MSS and strategic MSS, based on the level of management to which the MSS is applied. This book takes a different view of the term strategic within the context of MSS in that all MSS facilities, irrespective of the management level, are potentially strategic. Alignment determines whether, or not, the potential of an MSS to be strategic becomes reality. This is true for both new and existing MSS within an organisation. For example, consider an MSS that provides information to a company's management on the progress of customer orders. Traditionally, this MSS would be categorised as operational because it supports lower-level management. Customer service is one of the company's Critical Success Factors (CSFs). The MSS enables monitoring of customer service leading to the earlier rectification of problems. It is therefore aligned with corporate mission and strategy, and, for this reason, is termed a Strategic MSS within the context of this book.
- *The explicit view of IS strategy formulation as consisting of an appropriate blend of mechanistic aspects, supported by SISP methodologies, techniques and tools, underpinned by behavioural aspects concerned with Strategic Culture Building (SCB).* The book recognises explicitly the symbiotic relationship between SISP methodologies, techniques and tools, on the one hand, and SCB on the other hand. It also looks at the contextual factors surrounding a SISP exercise that may influence the blend of the mechanistic and behavioural aspects of IS Strategy formulation. To the authors' knowledge, no other text provides an explicit, structured view of how these aspects of SISP inter-relate and are influenced by organisational context.

1.5   CHAPTER FORMAT AND LEARNING APPROACH

All chapters, with the exception of this chapter and the chapters that summarise parts of the book, include:

- an introductory section outlining the content of the chapter and what the reader should understand at the end of the chapter (that is, the chapter's learning objectives)
- a summary section which recapitulates on the chapter's content
- a comprehensive reference list
- review questions to test basic understanding related to the chapter's learning objectives
- one or more project ideas to consolidate learning of key issues within the chapter.

Throughout the chapters, emphasis is placed on combining theory with practice. Many examples are used to illustrate key concepts at the point where they are described. Selected extracts from *Computer Weekly* are given at relevant points throughout the book to supplement the main text. These are presented as either viewpoints or case studies, and either provide further confirmation of the nature of, or offer a different perspective on, some previously described concept. Many of the viewpoints and all of the case studies provide practical examples of concepts raised within the chapter in which they are placed. In addition, each of the three major parts of the book provides an in-depth case study, which serves to illustrate and integrate many of the key concepts highlighted within the part.

The principal objective of the viewpoints and case studies is to stimulate reflection and debate concerning some or all of the issues raised. The deliberate absence of commentary and questions associated with these viewpoints and case studies provides freedom to the reader to determine the aspects upon which to focus attention. Tutors may wish to prescribe a particular focus of attention if considered appropriate to their respective learning objectives.

1.6 A READER'S ROAD MAP THROUGH THE BOOK

As illustrated in Figure 1.1, there are several paths through this book. Which one the reader adopts depends on personal and/or course requirements. In all cases, reading this chapter first is clearly recommended!

Essentially, the reader that is interested only in MSS, their nature and characteristics, may read Part 1 then Part 2, although the case study in Chapter 15 is also of benefit. It is recommended that Chapters 2 to 8 are read in sequence. (Chapter 3 can be omitted when the reader has a basic understanding of each of the ten technological advances listed in Section 3.1.) Alternatively, the reader who is interested only in SISP may read Part 1 and then Part 3 (Chapter 12 can be omitted), although again the case study in Chapter 15 is also of benefit. It is recommended that Part 3 is worked through in sequence. The reader who is interested in Strategic MSS needs to read all parts of the book. Although Part 1 should be tackled first and Part 4 tackled last, the reader has a choice as to the order in which Part 2 or Part 3 is tackled. For simplicity, it is recommended that Part 2 is attempted first.

Figures 1.2 to 1.4 inclusive show the individual paths for readers interested in MSS only, SISP only and Strategic MSS respectively.

1.7 INTENDED AUDIENCE

This book is suitable for use on a wide variety of courses or option modules with a Computing and Business/Management emphasis. Whilst readers are not expected to have prior knowledge of the MSS or SISP subject areas, they are expected to have some basic grounding in Computing, similar to that covered on an Introduction to Computing course module (or other equivalent learning). Readers are also expected to have some fundamental knowledge of IS development, similar to that covered within an Introduction to Systems Analysis and Design course module (or other equivalent learning). These pre-requisite modules may be found:

- on the first year of either a mainstream Computing/IS Course or a combined honours course with Computing/IS as a component
- in the first semester of an MSc or MBA course (either at higher degree or conversion level).

For these reasons, it is expected that this book will be most suited to appropriate course modules at either second or fourth year undergraduate level, or to later

Fig 1.1 Possible paths through book chapters

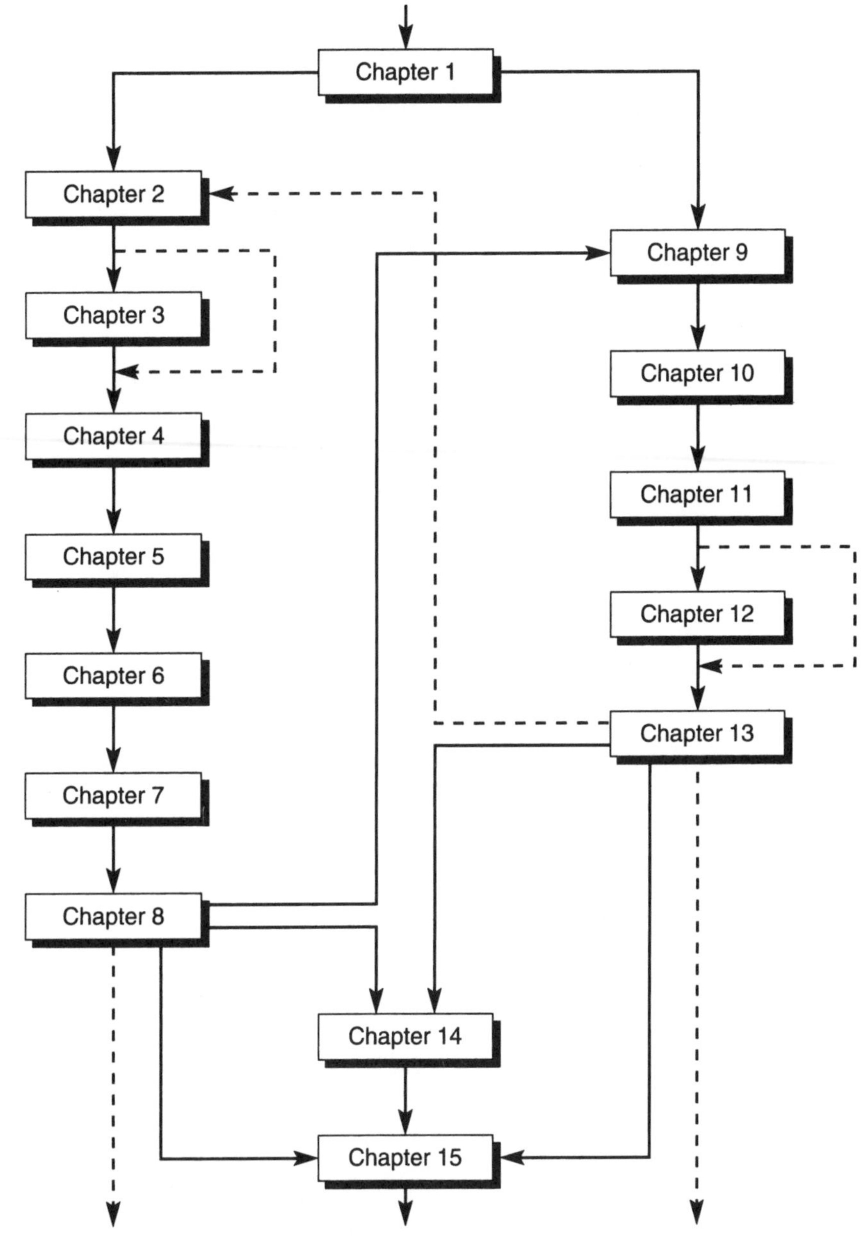

This figure shows several different paths that can be taken through the chapters of this book. The actual path chosen depends on the requirements of the reader. The dotted lines indicate less likely chapter sequences, for example where a better alternative path exists or where the omission of a chapter is possible.

Fig 1.2 Paths through book chapters for MSS readers

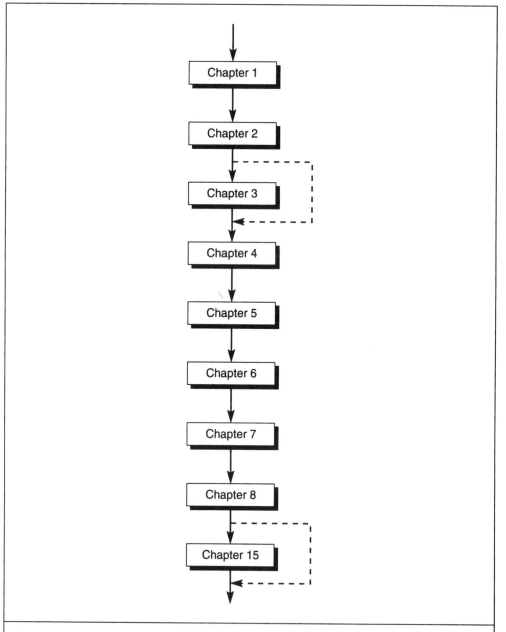

This figure shows paths that can be taken through the relevant chapters of this book should the reader be interested in MSS only. The dotted lines indicate less likely pathways. In this case, Chapter 3 may be omitted if the reader has suitable prior technical knowledge. Chapter 15 may also be omitted, although the chapter provides an overall conclusion to the book and the case study is of value to MSS readers.

Fig 1.3 Paths through book chapters for SISP readers

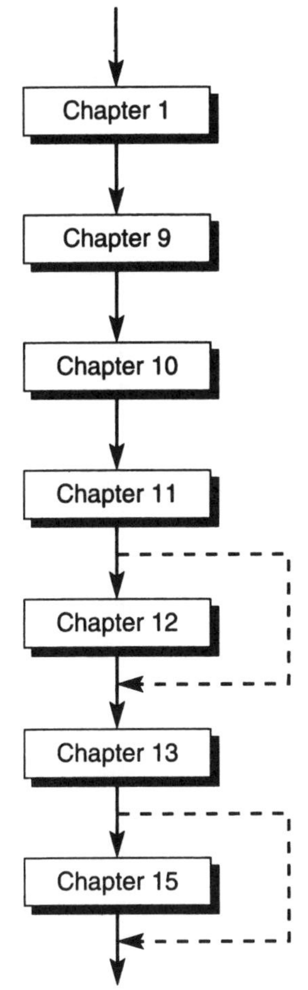

Chapter 1

Chapter 9

Chapter 10

Chapter 11

Chapter 12

Chapter 13

Chapter 15

This figure shows paths that can be taken through chapters of this book should readers be interested in SISP only. Chapter 12 can be omitted. Chapter 15 may also be omitted, although it provides an overall conclusion to the book and the BLL scenario is of value to SISP readers.

modules of Masters courses with IS/IT/IM emphasis (for example MSc Information Systems, MSc in IT and Management, MSc in Systems Analysis and Design (as a specialised topic area), MBA for IT managers, and conversion Masters in IS/IT/IM programmes). Given the unique approach to both the MSS and SISP subject areas, the book can be used not only as a core text for a particular module that focuses on Strategic MSS, MSS or SISP, but also in conjunction with other more traditional texts to present a contrasting approach for comparative purposes.

Fig 1.4 Paths through book chapters for Strategic MSS readers

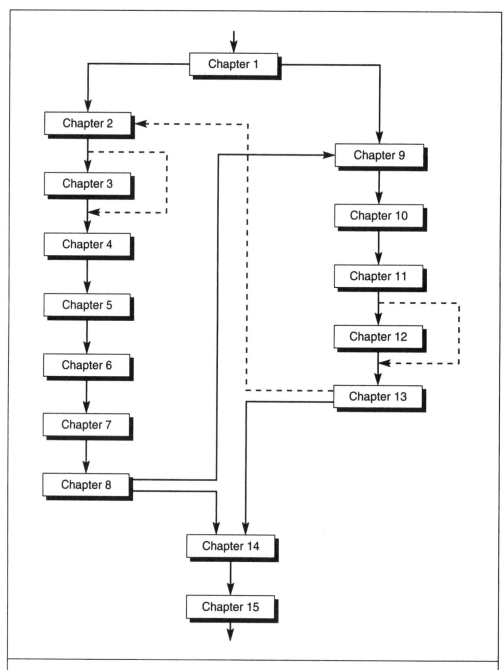

This figure shows paths that can be taken through chapters of this book by those interested in Strategic MSS. The dotted lines indicate less likely chapter sequences, for
example where a more natural alternative exists (e.g. following from Part 2 to Part 3, rather
than from Part 3 to Part 2) or where some specialist expertise is needed but not expected
of the typical reader (in the case of omitting Chapter 3).

1.8 SUMMARY

This chapter, comprising Part 1 of this book, has introduced the topic of Strategic MSS and has outlined the structure and content of the parts and chapters which follow. Some key definitions have been given, upon which subsequent chapters will draw. The unique approach to the Strategic MSS topic, and to the component topics of SISP and MSS, is outlined with justifications. A reader's road map through the book is provided and the expected audience is outlined.

To conclude, we hope you find this book refreshingly different in its approach to Strategic MSS, MSS and SISP, and that you find it not only informative and useful for your studies, but also interesting and enjoyable!

References

Earl M J (1989) *Management Strategies for Information Technology*. Prentice-Hall.

PART 2
Management Support Systems (MSS)

'The knowledge of the world is only to be acquired in the world, and not in a closet.'

Philip Dorner Stanhope, Earl of Chesterfield

CHAPTER 2

What is a Management Support System (MSS)?

2.1   INTRODUCTION

This chapter establishes what is meant by the term 'Management Support System (MSS)'. Other key concepts within the domain of MSS are also introduced. These will be drawn upon, and expanded upon, within following chapters of this book.

Three different yet complementary views of management are presented and discussed in Section 2.2. This section introduces the work of leading organisational and management theorists and associated terminology. It also provides the basis of the view adopted in this book: that information handling and decision making activities are pervasive throughout management work. This view is described in Section 2.3. MSS aim to support the information handling and decision making activities of management.

Decision making is described in more detail in Section 2.4. Several models of decision making are compared with the most commonly cited model proposed by Simon (1960, 1984). The concept of rational decision making is presented, and contrasted with the approaches to decision making actually adopted within organisations. Individual and group decision making are compared.

Information forms the subject of Section 2.5. Specifically, the nature of information is described in terms of its characteristics and potential sources. A distinction is made between data, information and knowledge.

Section 2.6 provides a definition for the term 'Management Support System' and presents a framework for viewing MSS from a functional perspective. The framework forms the overarching structure for Chapters 4 to 6 inclusive.

At the end of this chapter the reader should understand:

- *What an MSS is, and the range of functionality that an MSS may possess.*
- *Three views of management and their interrelationships.*
- *Decision making, both from a theoretical point of view and from a more pragmatic point of view.*
- *The relative strengths and weaknesses of individual and group decision making.*
- *The difference between data, information and knowledge, the characteristics of information and possible information/data sources.*

2.2   MANAGEMENT: AN MSS PERSPECTIVE

There is no universally accepted view of management. Three possible views of management are provided within this section: one that views management as an activity, one that views management as people who direct the organisation, and one that views management from a role-playing perspective. Although different in emphasis, these views are highly interrelated and complementary. Furthermore, each view provides a rich set of terminology, upon which MSS academics and practitioners draw. The following three subsections describes each of the views in turn.

2.2.1 An activity-oriented view of management

The activity-oriented view of management can be summarised by the following definition, which is indicative of the many definitions of management found within other academic texts:

> *Management is the direction of the enterprise through the planning, organising, co-ordinating and controlling of its human and material resources towards the achievement of pre-determined corporate objectives.*

Within this definition, management is seen as an activity, comprising a set of subactivities, namely:

- *Planning* – determining what needs to be done in a given situation and how it is to be accomplished, resulting in a plan of action.
- *Organising* – ensuring the organisation has the necessary structure and resources to accomplish the tasks to be undertaken.
- *Co-ordinating* – ensuring the work is facilitated, by enabling appropriate interfaces between tasks, and by providing the necessary resources to perform tasks as and when they are needed.
- *Controlling* – ensuring that the work achieved is as desired or planned, and taking action to rectify any undesirable deviations from the original plan.

Many academics have proposed similar sets of management activities to those described above. Several of these are listed in Figure 2.1. The differences between the lists can be explained in terms of variations in:

- *Assumptions* – all, except Murdick and Munson (1986), assume communication (of organisational activities specifically, and of information in general) to be pervasive within the other management activities that they propose. Lucey (1991) states that decision making takes place within all of his listed activities.
- *Detail* – some classifications are more detailed than others. For example, Timms (1967) suggests 'establishing objectives', 'planning the work of others' and 'organising' as three distinct activities. Brech (1963), however, encompasses all of these in his 'planning' activity.
- *Emphasis* – Drucker (1961) replaces 'control' with the concepts of 'self-measurement' and 'development of people'. This makes explicit his view of management as an enabling activity, rather than management as an enforcing activity. Other theorists agree with Drucker, but do not make this emphasis explicit.

The activity-oriented definition states that activities are performed in order to work towards the achievement of pre-determined objectives. Organisations can have several objectives. For example, increasing market share of a product, increasing overall profit, maintaining customer loyalty, enhancing the quality of employees' working life,

Fig 2.1 Activities of management; some classifications

Fayol (1916)
1. Plans
2. Organises
3. Co-ordinates
4. Commands
5. Controls

Drucker (1961)
1. Sets objectives
2. Organises
3. Motivates
4. Develops people
5. Measures one's own achievement

Brech (1963)
1. Plans
2. Motivates
3. Co-ordinates
4. Controls

Timms (1967)
1. Establishes objectives
2. Plans the work of others
3. Organises
4. Motivates
5. Controls work

Murdick and Munson (1986)
1. Defines organisational objectives
2. Plans
3. Organises resources
4. Initiates organisational action
5. Controls
6. Communicates organisational activities

Lucey (1991)
1. Plans
2. Motivates and leads
3. Organises and co-ordinates
4. Controls

Armstrong (1992)
1. Plans
2. Organises
3. Motivates
4. Controls

The figure provides selected lists of management activities. In overall terms, the lists are similar. Small differences between the lists can be explained in terms of the varying *detail* they provide, a change in the *emphasis* of management work that is being made explicit, and the underlying *assumptions* being made.

and simply survival, could form a subset of the objectives towards which a particular company may strive. Whilst objectives are, in the main, complementary (for instance, increasing market share may cause an increase in profit), there may be times when objectives are in conflict (for example, increasing market share may cause a degradation in employee welfare). Typically in this situation, one of the conflicting objectives is selected as the focus of current activity. Which of the conflicting objectives is selected will vary from activity to activity. As a consequence, despite their conflict, each objective is given some treatment over time. This juggling of conflicting objectives is a common part of the management activity of planning.

Management activities are regarded as working towards organisational objectives; that is, the objectives laid down by the senior management team of the organisation. However, individuals and groups of individuals, within sections, departments or divisions of a company, will also have their own objectives towards which they strive. Individual and group objectives can depart significantly from organisational objectives. There are many reasons for this departure. One possible reason is the lack of knowledge on the part of the group or individual of what the organisational objectives are. In this situation, ineffective communication of organisational objectives may be principally to blame. Unfortunately, this situation is all too common. In an empirical survey conducted by Fidler and Rogerson (1993), there is evidence that mismatches exist between top management and both division and departmental management in terms of the factors that are considered vital for success at the respective levels. Although the focus of the empirical survey was on success factors rather than objectives, the results highlight the general problem of aligning the views of groups and individuals with those prescribed for the entire organisation.

Defining management as an activity allows terms such as 'financial management' and 'personnel management' to be used, and the subactivities allow terms such as 'budget planning and control', 'financial planning' and 'resource planning and control' to become part of management terminology.

By comparing and contrasting the different planning and control systems in place within an organisation, Anthony (1965) separated management work into three basic types. These are presented in Figure 2.2. As the titles of the three types of management work suggest, the first is primarily a planning activity. The second and third types are increasingly control activities.

2.2.2 A human-oriented view of management

The human-oriented view of management is summarised by the following definition:

Management is a body of executives collectively responsible for the effective running of an enterprise.

Here, management focuses on the people that direct the organisation, rather than on the activities involved in directing the organisation. This perspective of management allows us to use terms such as 'top management', 'middle management' and 'lower management' to denote selected groups of employees at the different management levels within an organisation. Traditionally, top, middle and lower management groups are represented diagrammatically in pyramid form as shown in Figure 2.3. Within this figure, the area associated with a particular management group illustrates the relative number of employees found within that management group. Although the pyramid structure may still reflect the size of management groups within some present day organisations, its usefulness is limited. As studies have shown, contrary to Fayol's common principles of organisational structure and management (see Fayol's writings in Pugh 1984), there is no one way of organising a company and hence its management requirements. Rather, the most effective organisational and management structure for a company depends on a variety of factors, including: the characteristics of the environment in which the organisation operates (such as the nature and scope of its customers, competitors and suppliers); the management philosophy that is to be promoted (such as democratic versus authoritarian); and the nature and scope of the organisation's

Fig 2.2 Anthony's separation of management work

- **Strategic planning** – defining the objectives of an organisation, the resources required to pursue the objectives, and the policies that govern the acquisition, deployment and use of the resources.

- **Management control** – obtaining, deploying and using the resources effectively, whilst adhering to the policies for their acquisition, deployment and use, in the pursuit of organisational objectives.

- **Operational control** – assuring that specific tasks are carried out efficiently and effectively.

Anthony separated management work into three basic types: strategic planning, management control and operational control. As the name suggests, strategic planning is principally a planning activity. Control activities increase within management control work, and increase further within operational control work.

technological base. With regard to the last, the availability of MSS themselves can redistribute control over resources and decision making capabilities within an organisation. This leads to changes in management structure. Figure 2.3 provides two other representations of management group sizes, those of a diamond and an hourglass, that have been suggested to be more representative of organisations' management today. Like all generalisations, however, they should be applied with caution.

It is worth emphasising that what is meant by the terms 'top management', 'middle management' and 'lower management' may vary between organisations. One organisation may associate these terms with the formal position of management personnel within the organisation. For example, top management may comprise the Managing Director and the first line of management below him/her. Middle management comprises the divisional and department managers, and lower management incorporates everyone else below departmental management level. Alternatively, another organisation may associate management level with the types of activities that management personnel perform as described by Anthony (1965). Those personnel engaged in strategic planning activities constitute the top management team, those engaged in management control activities constitute the middle management team, and those engaged in operational control activities constitute the lower management team. Given the changes in organisational and management philosophy that have occurred in recent years, in response to market globalisation and the associated increases in competition, the divestment of responsibilities from the top few to those in the best position to perform such activities is vital to remain responsive to consumer needs (see Rosen and Kleiner 1992 for a summary of the changes needed by management in order for organisations to survive and prosper in the 1990s). As a consequence, the two approaches to categorising management personnel within an organisation into top, middle and lower management are increasingly likely to result in different groupings for the same organisation.

Fig 2.3 Diagrammatic views of management groups; the pyramid, diamond and hour-glass

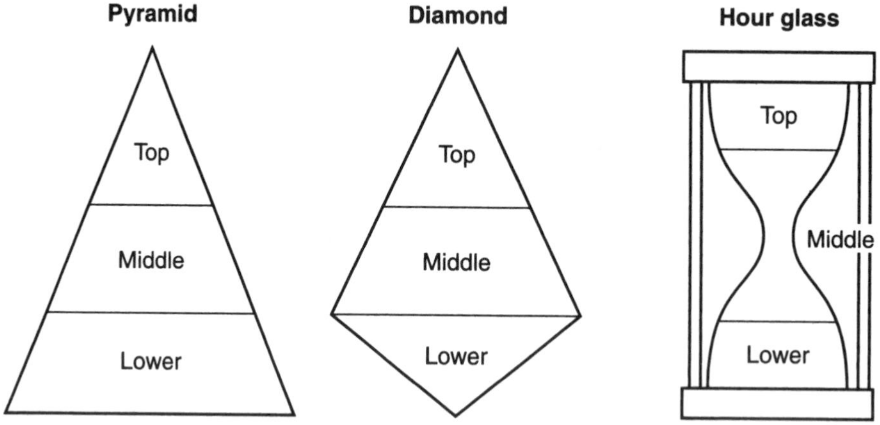

The pyramid view of management is the most commonly cited within management and organisation literature. The diamond and hour-glass views may be a more appropriate reflection of management group sizes in some present day organisations, however. These newer forms may result from the application of IS/IT within organisations. For instance, the improved access to information that IS/IT provides may enable either middle management or non-management professionals to perform some of the tasks that lower management traditionally performed (in the case of the diamond form), and top management to have direct influence, rather than indirectly through middle management, over day-to-day tasks (in the case of the hour-glass form).

2.2.3 A role-playing view of management

The third and final perspective of management concentrates on the general roles that are adopted by management personnel as they perform work. This view is commonly associated with Henry Mintzberg (1973). Based on a study of five Chief Executive Officers (CEOs), and on viewing the results of other complementary studies of management work, Mintzberg proposed a list of ten generic management roles. These were divided into those associated with interpersonal relationships, those concerned with information capture and dissemination, and those undertaken while decision making. The ten roles are presented in Figure 2.4.

Any management activity may involve a person adopting one or more roles. The predominance of particular roles being adopted by any one person will depend on the overall requirements of the management position that is held and, to some extent, on individual style and motives.

2.2.4 Links between perspectives of management

Although the activity-oriented, human-oriented and role-playing views of management have been described in isolation thus far, they are, in fact, highly interrelated and complementary. As illustrated in Figure 2.5, there are many-to-many relationships

Fig 2.4 Mintzberg's ten generic roles of management work

Interpersonal Roles – associated with relationships between the manager, the employees within his/her unit* and individuals within the unit's environment.

- *Figurehead* – representing the unit in all matters of formality.

- *Liaison* – interacting with peers and others outside the unit to gain favours and information.

- *Leader* – interacting with subordinates within the unit, for example, to issue instructions.

Informational Roles – the adoption of interpersonal roles enables the collection and dissemination of information.

- *Monitor* – monitoring information sources, both external and internal to the unit.

- *Spokesman* – disseminating selected information from inside the unit to outside the unit.

- *Disseminator* – bringing selected information into the unit from outside the unit.

Decisional Roles – the positions of authority and status, and of overseeing the available information sources, puts a person in the right context for making decisions concerning the unit.

- *Entrepreneur* – initiating change within the unit.

- *Disturbance Handler* – relieving the threats imposed on the unit.

- *Resource Allocator* – deciding where the unit should expend its available resources.

- *Negotiator* – participating in decision situations where negotiation is required.

Mintzberg's ten roles can be separated into those of an interpersonal nature, those concerned with information capture and dissemination, and those adopted within decision making activities.

* The term 'unit' is used here to mean that portion of the organisation over which the person in question has control. For instance, a shop floor supervisor's unit is that small team of people over which the shop floor supervisor has control, whereas a managing director's unit would be the entire company.

between activities and roles, activities and people, and people and roles. Take, for example, a corporate budget planning activity. When this is being performed, several people from top, middle and lower management could be involved. Each person may need to adopt several roles in the course of corporate budget planning, such as leader, monitor, spokesman, and negotiator. The spokesperson role may be required in several other activities that the same person performs, for example in both corporate budget planning and personnel hiring decisions.

Fig 2.5 The relationships between management perspectives

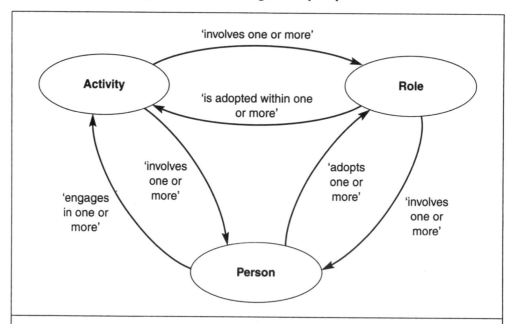

Each entity (i.e. role, activity and person) is shown as an ellipse on the above diagram. The relationships are denoted by arcs between the ellipses. There are two relationships between a pair of entities. Each relationship is of a one-to-many kind. For example, the arc from activity to role denotes the relationship "an activity involves one or more roles". In total, the relationships between activities and roles, roles and people, and activities and people are of a many-to-many kind.

To conclude this review of management, it is worth stating that this book makes no apologies for using the term management sometimes to reflect an activity-oriented view, sometimes to reflect the human-oriented view and sometimes to reflect the role-playing view. This is in line with common usage of the term. The reader will, however, be able to appreciate which view is in focus from the context in which the term is used.

2.3 DECISION MAKING AND INFORMATION HANDLING AS PERVASIVE MANAGEMENT ACTIVITIES

One of the principal reasons cited for the differences in the management activity lists presented in Figure 2.1 is the underlying assumptions made. One assumption, as suggested in Section 2.2.1, is that whilst communication of organisation activities is considered to be a separate managerial activity by some, others consider any communication of organisational activities in particular, and of information in general, to be pervasive throughout all the managerial activities that they propose. In addition, Lucey (1991) considers decision making to be pervasive throughout all managerial activities. For instance, planning involves decisions concerned with what to do and how to do it, and controlling involves decisions about whether action needs to be taken and about what form any action will take.

Mintzberg's analysis of generic managerial roles (Mintzberg 1973) also supports the argument that information communication and decision making are pervasive activities, by identifying the generic informational and decisional roles respectively. Information, to be communicated, needs to be prepared, stored and retrieved. Therefore, it is reasonable to assume that all aspects associated with information handling, not just communication, are similarly pervasive throughout management work.

What about Mintzberg's highlighting of interpersonal roles? Does this mean that human relationships are also pervasive throughout management work? Yes, this is true, but unlike the informational and decisional roles, the results of the interpersonal roles manifest themselves within the results of the informational roles (namely, the information communicated) and the decisional roles (namely, the decisions made). As Mintzberg (1973, p.58) states:

> *..the manager is an input-output system in which authority and status give rise to interpersonal relationships that lead to inputs (information), and these in turn lead to outputs (information and decisions).*

In this book, attention is focused on decision making and information handling as pervasive activities throughout management work. However, it is recognised that decision making and information handling activities are made possible only by the underlying interpersonal relationships found within a particular situation. The following two sections focus on decision making and information.

2.4 DECISION MAKING

Decision making itself is an activity which has several subactivities. The result of decision making, if effective, is a good decision. Inputs to the decision making activity include people, information, and possibly MSS and physical artefacts, such as paper documents.

To clarify what decision making entails, consider the following scenario. One of the authors of this book decided to work on a chapter on a particular Saturday afternoon. When questioned about this decision, it was established that working on the chapter was one of several alternatives that could have been chosen when considering what to do on the Saturday afternoon in question. Buying the weekly shopping was another possibility, as was watching the Saturday afternoon movie on television. There were other alternatives, such as going to see the local football match or visiting a friend, but the author was unaware of these other alternatives at the time of making the decision. Subconsciously, the author had evaluated the known alternatives against certain   factors considered to be of importance at the point of decision making. One factor was the publisher's deadline for writing the book. Other factors were the availability of food in the refrigerator and the availability of, and preference for, Sunday rather than Saturday shopping. The decision to stay home and write the chapter was the preferred alternative, since the impending deadline for book submission clearly carried significant weight within the evaluation process.

This scenario, although extremely simple, provides an insight into the subactivities of decision making.

- A situation must exist where a decision needs to be made. Within the scenario, the author knew that a decision needed to be made concerning what to do on the Saturday afternoon in question.

- The alternatives, and the factors or criteria upon which these alternatives are to be evaluated, are established. The alternatives considered will normally be only a subset of all possible alternatives. However, there must be at least two alternatives (even if they are simply yes or no) in order for decision making to take place. Furthermore, the number of factors or criteria will be only a subset of those possible.
- A method, by which the known alternatives are to be evaluated against the known factors or criteria, is identified and applied.
- On the basis of comparison, the alternative that is preferred is chosen.

The scenario involves only one decision maker from start to finish. *Individual decision making* is decision making when only one decision maker is involved. Supposing that there was another person apart from the author involved in deciding, jointly, what to do on Saturday afternoon. This additional person might not take too kindly to staying in while the author writes. In this case, a compromise may need to be reached, in that the eventual alternative chosen may not be the most favoured option for each person individually but is the most favoured option for them collectively. The joint decision making between two or more persons is termed *group decision making*.

2.4.1 Decision making models

Many models of decision making have been proposed. The decision making model presented by Simon (1960, 1984) is frequently adopted. In this model, decision making consists of three basic subactivities:

- *Intelligence* – essentially a decision finding and/or recognition activity. Searching for situations requiring decisions to be made may need to be initiated. Understanding the situation properly is paramount for effective decision making.
- *Design* – identifying the alternatives and how they will be evaluated, and performing the evaluation.
- *Choice* – selecting the best alternative from those evaluated.

Although Intelligence normally precedes Design, which normally precedes Choice, some backtracking between the subactivities is typical. This may be due to the decision situation being inappropriately formulated at the outset, which leads to backtracking from Choice or Design to Intelligence, or due to the inadequacy of any known alternative to satisfy the specified criteria, which leads to backtracking from Choice to Design in order to search for more alternatives. Take, for example, a large manufacturing company which recognises its shortfall in current hardware provision. A decision must be made as to what hardware to purchase to make good this shortfall. Two or three local IT vendors have been asked to put forward bids for tender. However, none of the eventual bids satisfy the specified operational and financial criteria. This leads to further bids for tender being invited. (In terms of Simon's model, backtracking from Choice to Design takes place.) In addition, during the second cycle of invitations to tender, the IT manager realises that the IT purchase decision is in fact not what is really required at this stage. Rather, the company needs to decide first of all what its IT strategy is before it is in a position to seek bids. (In terms of Simon's model, backtracking from Design to Intelligence takes place.)

Other models of decision making, found in the Management and MSS literature, either expand on the level of detail within each of the subactivities proposed by Simon, and/or restrict or expand the view of decision making as presented by Simon.

Fig 2.6 The relationship between the decision making views of Simon and Long

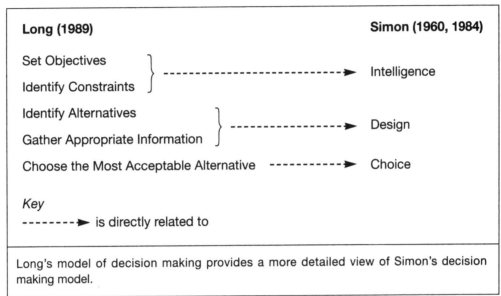

Long (1989)	Simon (1960, 1984)

Set Objectives
Identify Constraints ⟶ Intelligence

Identify Alternatives
Gather Appropriate Information ⟶ Design

Choose the Most Acceptable Alternative ⟶ Choice

Key
- - - - - - - - ➤ is directly related to

Long's model of decision making provides a more detailed view of Simon's decision making model.

For example, Long (1989) splits decision making into five subactivities as listed in Figure 2.6. As shown in this Figure, Long's subactivities can be mapped directly onto Simon's decision making model. Long's decision making model is simply more detailed than that of Simon.

Cooke and Slack (1989) view decision making as a part of an overall problem-solving process. They consider most of the Intelligence activity of Simon's decision making model as part of problem solving, not of decision making. As such they provide a more restricted view of decision making to that of Simon. Figure 2.7 highlights the relationships between the views of decision making proposed by Cooke and Slack, and Simon, within the framework of Cooke and Slack's problem-solving model.

An important issue raised by the work of Cooke and Slack is the meaning of the terms 'problem solving' and 'decision making'. Cooke and Slack clearly consider problem solving as encompassing a broader set of activities than decision making. This view is also favoured by Kroenke (1989). However, many consider these terms to be synonymous and, hence, interchangeable. Certainly within everyday speech, these terms are used very loosely.

Simon's decision making model will be adopted as the preferred model of decision making activity within this book. This is due principally to its highlighting, at a suitable level of generality, all of the principal activities that MSS aim to support but not allowing the ensuing descriptions of MSS and decision making to become too fragmented. Indeed, its simplicity with 'fitness for purpose' may be one of the reasons why Simon's model is so popular within MSS literature. The terms problem solving and decision making will be used interchangeably within following chapters, reflecting common practice in the usage of these terms.

2.4.2 Classifications of decision making situations and approaches

There are several classifications of decision making situations advocated within the MSS literature. These can be separated into two broad categories: those which classify

Fig 2.7 The relationship between the decision making views of Cooke and Slack, and Simon

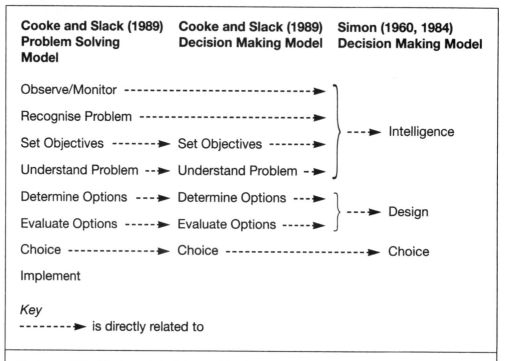

Cooke and Slack (1989) Problem Solving Model	Cooke and Slack (1989) Decision Making Model	Simon (1960, 1984) Decision Making Model
Observe/Monitor ----------------------------▶		⎫
Recognise Problem ---------------------------▶		⎬ ---▶ Intelligence
Set Objectives -------▶	Set Objectives -------▶	⎪
Understand Problem --▶	Understand Problem -▶	⎭
Determine Options ---▶	Determine Options ---▶	⎫ ---▶ Design
Evaluate Options -----▶	Evaluate Options -----▶	⎭
Choice ------------▶	Choice --------------------▶	Choice
Implement		

Key
---------▶ is directly related to

Cooke and Slack's view of decision making is more restrictive than that of Simon. Specifically, the Observe/Monitor phase (i.e. observing and monitoring for likely problem-solving or opportunity taking situations) and the Recognise Problem phase are considered to be Problem Solving activities rather than decision making activities. However, the content of the aforementioned two stages of Cooke and Slack's model form part of the Intelligence phase of Simon's decision making model.

the decision situation being addressed, and those which distinguish the ways by which decision making is undertaken within organisations.

One such classification of decision situations is that proposed by Simon (1960). A decision situation can be placed somewhere on a continuum ranging from what Simon terms 'programmed' decisions to 'nonprogrammed' decisions. Programmed decisions are those that are repetitive and routine. They are well known decisions with a defined method for identifying alternatives and evaluating them. Conversely, nonprogrammed decisions are those that are unfamiliar and novel. It is difficult to truly understand the decision and who is involved, and no suitable method exists for alternative identification and evaluation (partly owing to its fuzzy definition). Intuition and judgement on the part of the decision maker(s) are key in these situations. Gorry and Scott Morton (1971) use the terms 'structured' and 'unstructured' to mean essentially the same as 'programmed' and 'nonprogrammed'. Keen and Scott Morton (1978) developed a three-part classification of decision making situations, by allowing any decision situation between the 'unstructured' and 'structured' ends of the continuum to be termed 'semistructured'. Figure 2.8 shows how the semistructured category proposed by Keen

Fig 2.8 Types of decision situations and associated terminology

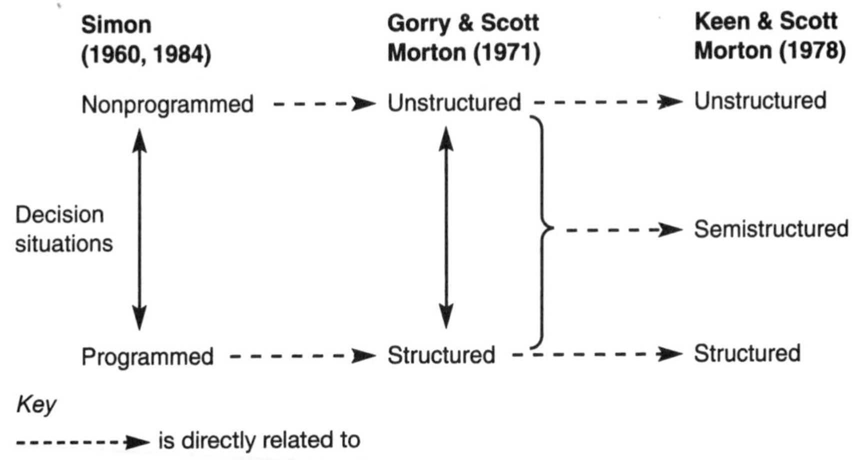

| | Simon (1960, 1984) | Gorry & Scott Morton (1971) | Keen & Scott Morton (1978) |

The diagram shows the one-to-one relationships between Simon's programmed decision situations and Gorry and Scott Morton's structured decision situations, and between Simon's nonprogrammed decision situations and Gorry and Scott Morton's unstructured decision situations. It also highlights how the semistructured decision situation category added by Keen and Scott Morton embraces the large category of decision situations, ranging from nearly structured to nearly unstructured.

and Scott Morton fits onto the programmed/structured to nonprogrammed/unstructured continuum of decision situations.

The concept of 'semistructured' decision situations is a vital one for MSS, as it is towards this broad category of decision situations that MSS are oriented. The word 'support' within the term 'Management Support Systems' implies assistance. If a decision situation is unstructured, then it is principally, if not wholly, requiring the intuition of the decision maker(s). Little assistance, if any, can be provided by computerised systems. If the decision situation is a structured one, then the decision can be performed entirely by a computerised system, as its identification and resolution can be defined in the form of a computer program. This is replacement not assistance. It is a semistructured decision situation, where some aspects of the decision making activity can be performed by a computerised system but where other aspects are left to the intuition of the decision maker(s), that is the target of an MSS. The computerised system is, in this situation, acting as a supportive tool.

Keen and Scott Morton (1978) present some typical types of decision making situations that are considered to be structured, semistructured or unstructured ones. For example, a publishing company's selection of a magazine cover has been used as a typical example of an unstructured decision: the decision is based on the intuition of the decision maker(s) with little, if any, computerised support being possible. However, with multi-media publishing packages (see Chapter 3 for a description of multi-media systems), greater assistance in this decision can now be given. A mock-up of alternative magazine covers can be provided, resulting in a form of sensitivity analysis for magazine cover selection. This puts into question the continued use of the magazine cover selection as an example of an unstructured decision. A better example nowadays might be the decision as to how to arrange music pieces for a concert programme, but even this example may have a short lifespan.

Whilst there are types of decisions that are, in general, more unstructured than others or more structured than others, care must be taken not to compartmentalise decision situations without looking at their characteristics on an individual basis. Each decision situation is unique. It has its own unique context. Take, for example, the decision situation of purchasing consumables in a company. This may be approached in an entirely different way to that of another company, despite the fact that identical consumables (such as paper, floppy disks and pens) are being considered. A company may also approach the purchasing consumables decision differently to how they approached it in the past. There are various reasons that influence the method by which people within different companies, or even different people within the same company, approach the same type of decision over time, including:

- *The policies being adhered to within the company* – policy may dictate that a certain method is used to evaluate alternatives for a particular decision, or that only a certain set of alternatives are considered. For example, a hardware purchasing decision may be restricted by company policy to only a subset of possible vendors, and that, of those tenders deemed to be satisfactory, the least costly alternative tender is always selected. Typically, this decision situation would be more easily resolved than decisions of the same type, within companies that have no such policy. Policy may also dictate whether a particular decision is made by a group rather than an individual. Group decision making is typically less structured due to the rich variety of values and beliefs being brought to bear on the decision making situation (all other aspects being equal). Group decision making is the subject of Section 2.4.3.

- *The time available within which to make the decision* – when faced with a decision situation requiring immediate resolution, there is little time for the gathering of information about alternatives, and for seeking structured ways of aiding the evaluation of alternatives. The decision making situation appears much less structured as a consequence (all other aspects being equal).

- *The experiences of the decision maker(s)* – if a similar situation has occurred before, then these experiences may be brought to bear on the current decision situation. This may make the current situation more structured (all other aspects being equal).

- *The nature of the environment in which the decision is being made* – although the same type of decision is being made, the environment can be very different. Take, for example, a company that manufactures painting overalls and a company that manufactures fashion knitwear. Both companies have to make a decision concerning how many and of what style of their products they must produce within the next week. However, the environments within which these companies operate are very different. Overall designs stay fairly static over time. Painters demand certain general standards of the overalls they purchase (for instance, they must be hard-wearing, they must cover the clothed parts of the body, and they must also be easy to clean). These standards also remain relatively stable over time. Furthermore, the number of overalls required remains relatively stable. Conversely, the knitwear fashion market is volatile. What is required, if the company is a follower rather than leader of fashion, depends on the whims of the consumers, and on the current and expected trends in fashions at that particular moment. Trends change quickly and are difficult to predict accurately. Owing to rapid change, the quantity to produce of a given style is also very difficult to assess accurately. In general terms, the overall manufacturing company's decision is much more structured than that of the fashion knitwear manufacturer's, due to the environmental characteristics (all other aspects being equal).

- *The influence of past and future decisions* – this influence may make current decisions more or less structured (all other aspects being equal). Take, for example, a company that has to make a decision on which accounting package to buy. A past corporate IT policy decision was made to purchase and support only PC Windows-based packages within the company. This decision clearly restricts the current decision situation in terms of the alternatives that can be considered. The decision is more structured in nature, owing to the previous corporate IT policy decision. Now, suppose that no such IT policy decision had been made within this company. The decision as to which accounting package to buy may still require the consideration of the likely effects of the chosen option on future decision options. For example, the decision to purchase a PC Windows-based package may limit the selection of future packages given that only one type of applications environment can be supported by the IS Department. The current decision may therefore be seen to constrain future decision options. As a consequence, fewer options may be considered in depth as viable for the present decision situation.

- *The differences between individuals undertaking the decision* – part of this could be seen as related to the aforementioned differences in experiences. However, individuals, due to their different educational experiences and social development, may adopt different approaches to decision making. For example, an individual from a scientific background may approach decision making in a more quantitative and methodical way than an individual from a social sciences background. The degree of freedom for individuals to adopt their own decision making style depends on the organisational constraints under which the individuals are working.

Approaches to decision making by groups and individuals found within organisations have been studied over many years. Typically, they are contrasted with the somewhat hypothetical *rational model of decision making*. The rational model of decision making considers decision making as:

- Seeking to achieve a maximum payoff, however payoff is defined. (From a classical viewpoint, payoff is typically equated to economic outcomes where maximum profit is the objective.)
- Taking place in an environment where there is complete knowledge of all alternatives, and of the consequences of adopting any one of the alternatives (the so-termed *condition of perfect knowledge*).
- Taking place in an environment where there is a mechanism for ranking alternatives consistently, and that the rank order mirrors the relative attractiveness of the alternatives absolutely (the *so-termed condition of perfect judgement*).

Rational decision making can occur only when the decision situation is structured. Managerial decisions, in the main, are not like this. As Harrison (1993) explains, the objectives towards which management decisions are oriented continually change. This may be due to the organisation changing rapidly in response to corresponding changes in its environment. Alternatively, the objectives may be varied and conflicting, leading to different ones being predominant at any one time. If decision making takes place over a period of time, then the objectives may even change during the decision making itself. Harrison also highlights the manager's limited information base (restricting the number of alternatives considered), and the brain's cognitive limitations in gathering and processing information (see Miller 1956). Many variables taken into account when examining alternatives are uncontrollable, so how can managers know exactly what the outcomes of a particular consequence will be? At best, they may predict certain possible values with associated expected probabilities of occurrence. Furthermore, the preferences of decision makers defy the development of a unitary formula for ranking alternatives. For example, within an MSS development decision, how should the decision maker formulate a single function that relates issues such as quality of working life, increased understanding of the business and profit? The importance of individual preferences may also vary during the evaluation period.

Ormrod (1993) provides an excellent example of how managerial decision making does not conform typically to the rational model. Reviewing the decision making activities of sixteen key managers within a UK-based hospital environment, he found inconsistencies in the factors that were being considered within decision making, even by the same individual over time. There were some prevalent factors, such as political issues and the importance of the purchasers of healthcare (i.e. the UK health authorities), but some managers were considering fewer factors in their decision making than others. Many were biased, in the factors they considered, by their previous professional and academic experiences.

An alternative and more pragmatic model, which embraces the limitations of humans to act as prescribed by the rational model, has been proposed by March and Simon (1958). Their *satisficing model* views decision making as seeking to identify an alternative that achieves some minimum level of acceptance. Decision making ceases once a suitable alternative is found. This model is true of many organisational decision making situations, particularly those involving substantial effort and time in identifying and evaluating each alternative (for example, company acquisition decisions and site selection decisions). However, many management decisions appear to blend some aspects of the rational model with some aspects of the satisficing model. Here, a subset of all possible alternatives are considered but the best of these is then selected. For instance, software evaluation decisions typically adhere to this *best of the bunch* model.

Empirical investigations have also led to certain characteristic approaches to decision making being identified within organisations. These approaches emphasise particular conditions within the organisation which led to their adoption. They all provide evidence of non-rational decision making at work.

- *Political approach.* In practice, organisational decision making situations may be highly influenced by the participants' own interests and desires. This approach to organisational decision making is particularly visible in situations where individual self-interest has exceeded the corporate interest. According to Adamski and Kleiner (1992), this political behaviour stems from a lack of alignment of the individual's view of a situation to that of others within the organisation. A principal task of management is to engender a unified corporate view that takes precedence over, or subsumes, individual views.

- *Incremental approach.* In an attempt to avoid radical change, decisions may be made which provide only a small step towards an ultimate objective. This incremental approach to organisational decision making can be very effective in situations where gradual acceptance of new concepts is possible but where a 'big bang' approach would be resisted. Changing employees' work conditions within a company, for example, might be approached in this way. Small but frequent changes hide the overall change that would have been resisted, if it had been attempted in one large programme. Another reason why this approach may be favoured is that it provides greater opportunities to evaluate changes and the evaluation of the effects of different factors. The principal difficulty with incremental decision making appears to be whether the main objective can indeed be approached in this manner. Tinkering with aspects of the current situation may be insufficient. Rather, a radical decision is needed to achieve the objective. Radical change of, rather than tinkering with, the current situation, is the essence of the original concept of Business Process Re-engineering (BPR). BPR is described in Chapter 12.
- *Garbage can approach.* In some organisational decision making situations, a ready-made solution may already exist. Indeed, solutions may initiate the search for a decision situation to which they can be applied. Great care should be taken with this approach, ensuring that a solution really fits the problem in hand, and that applying a solution does not become the end in itself rather than a means to an end. It is all too frequent that a particular solution is adopted without first understanding the nature and importance of the decision to which it is being applied. For example, many organisations in the 80s purchased IT in the vain hope that problems would emerge for which it could be used. However, many of these IT systems remained unused due to their inappropriateness to the eventual problems that arose. This approach carries a high degree of risk in its successful application.
- *Programmed approach.* Organisational decision making may be constrained by company policies. As such, the decision maker's freedom to approach the decision in the manner considered to be most applicable is restricted. This programmed approach to organisational decision making can stifle creativity and, given a highly dynamic business environment requiring flexibility and change on the part of the organisation, can lead to a wholly inappropriate decision being made.

Although organisational decision making approaches are typically non-rational, it does not mean that rational decision making is bad. Certainly, the condition of perfect knowledge and the condition of perfect judgement are useful objectives to strive towards. MSS are the very tools that can help to enhance the rationality of decisions. For example, they can aid the consideration of a greater set of alternatives for a particular decision situation, with each alternative taking less time to consider than before. MSS can provide approaches for supporting the consistent ranking of alternatives, even if the ranking involves only those criteria that are easily measured. An MSS may also provide statistical information to enable better predictions as to the probabilities of particular outcomes.

2.4.3 Group decision making

So far in this discussion of decision making, there has been little attention paid to the size and nature of the decision making body. According to Huber (1984), most corporate decisions are made by groups rather than by individuals. Furthermore, group decision making should increase as the workforce adopts a more fluid, team-oriented structure (Chorn 1991) to cope effectively with rapid change. Simon's decision making model (explained in Section 2.4.1) is suitably general to represent both group and individual decision making situations. However, each of the subactivities within this model may have added complexity due to the greater number of people involved in group decision making, as described below:

- *Intelligence* – individuals may view a decision situation in different ways. Therefore, they may disagree on what the underlying decision situation really is.
- *Design* – individuals may attach different values of importance to criteria used within alternative evaluation. They may use criteria that are not considered by others to be important. The alternatives identified by each individual may vary.
- *Choice* – owing to differences between individuals' views, choosing the preferred alternative may require active compromise and negotiation.

The principal difference between group decision making and individual decision making is that, in the former case, more than one value set is brought to bear on the decision situation whereas in the latter case only one value set is being applied. A *value set* is defined as those beliefs, expectations and views that an individual possesses. An individual's value set is shaped by that individual's experiences and background, and colours the way that individual views the world, both now and in the future. Value sets of individuals may be similar in nature. For example, the commonalty of certain aspects of individuals' value sets provides the basis for the development of a political party embracing the shared views. Very different value sets can lead to intense conflict between individuals. Differences in value sets can be seen vividly at work in the debates within the European Parliament, for example.

Groups may adopt different approaches to group decision making. Each approach may require a variation in the role that each participant plays in the decision making activity. For instance, a group may simply evaluate the recommendations made by an individual group member as to the preferred option. The individual would have prepared the case for recommendation before the group meeting. Alternatively, a group may jointly look at the decision situation, with minimal preparation having been undertaken.

Group decision making has claimed advantages over individual decision making, such as:

- *It can lead to better quality decisions being made.* More relevant alternatives and criteria, and a wider range of perspectives, can lead to a more informed decision than that undertaken by an individual alone. Groups frequently make more risky decisions than individuals as the responsibility for an erroneous decision is shared amongst the group rather than lying on the shoulders of one person. This can lead to a better outcome, as long as the risk pays off. This propensity towards greater risk taking by groups has become known as the *Risky Shift phenomenon*.

- *It facilitates decision implementation.* By involving representatives of those functions of the organisation that are expected to play a key role in the eventual decision's implementation, a sense of ownership of the eventual decision can be nurtured within all concerned. This may facilitate the ensuing implementation of the decision, both in terms of commitment and time. Indeed, failure to implement the decision reflects on those directly involved in the decision making. This fear of failure may itself create a more conducive environment for decision implementation. However, fear of failure could lead to the continued implementation of the then preferred alternative despite knowing now that the wrong decision was made.

- *It promotes creativity*. Individuals can build new ideas from the ideas of other group members, leading to more creative alternatives being formulated.

Conversely, group decision making requires *comparatively lengthy decision making meetings* (although this is offset typically by the reduced time taken to implement the eventual decision, and by the reduced time taken to gather the information necessary for informed decision making). *Risky decisions may be overly optimistic*, leading to the wrong alternative being selected. *Groupthink* is where a group forms its own shared value set which then constrains future decision making to conform with this value set. This can lead to inappropriate decisions being taken. *Dominance by one or more members over others* within the group can lead to a decision favouring the views of the dominant few.

Certain MSS are aimed at group decision making activities. Their aim is to inhibit the negative aspects, and encourage the positive aspects, of group decision making.

2.5 INFORMATION

Information is essential for effective decision making. It is used to identify situations requiring decisions to be made. It can help the search for, and generation of, decision alternatives, and can provide insight into possible outcomes and effects of selecting a particular alternative. It is through information that results of decision making are communicated to others. It is through information that decision makers gain knowledge which can then be brought to bear in both current and future decision making activities.

Knowledge is not the same as information. Knowledge is internal to each individual, whereas information is externally viewed but personally assessed (although people may agree on whether something is information). Communication forms the link between knowledge and information. For example, a report on monthly sales may be assessed as information by a Sales and Marketing Manager. It may also allow the manager to gain knowledge about the salesforce, but the report itself is information not knowledge. Written English is the language of communication in this example.

This section focuses principally on information. It establishes what information is, and examines its characteristics and sources.

2.5.1 What is information?

Information, according to the Oxford English Dictionary, is informing. When informing, one is communicating some message to some recipient (recipient, in this context, stands for one or more persons receiving the message) and that message is of value to that recipient. The information's value, with respect to the recipient, may manifest itself in many ways. For instance, it may allow the recipient to understand a current situation more clearly, or it may allow the recipient to identify decision situations, alternatives and outcomes. On the other hand, it may simply serve to enforce the urgency or importance of some issue (consider the communication of exactly the same message content twice to a manager – the content of the second message is already known but the duplication of the communication can itself create a feeling of urgency or importance). A message which has no value to its recipient is simply termed data. Although data is useless in its current form to a management decision maker (that is, by definition it has no value), data may provide the raw facts from which management information can be derived.

To summarise, information is some message that provides value to some recipient. The value of the information depends on the recipient's view of its usefulness, based on the recipient's requirements and the context within which the recipient works.

2.5.2 Characteristics of good information

Although the value of information is subjective to the individual, there are ways that messages can be made as effective as possible in their communication of the required information. Badly communicated messages can serve to diminish the value of the information contained in the message, in the recipient's eyes, or can even lead to the information appearing to be of no value, that is being viewed as data.

Aspects of communication that allow the information to achieve its greatest value possible (given its content) include the following:

● Information must be presented *in a concise and clear form*. The addition of unimportant issues may serve to hinder the recipient's focus of attention on the salient aspects. The language used to convey the information may also hinder the recipient's comprehension of the important issues. English language, for example, is well known for its ambiguity in use. The weakness of the language may also hinder expression of the salient issues. Written language, for example, cannot always convey the emphasis of a communication that gesticulation can within a face-to-face meeting situation.

● Information must be *communicated at the right time*. There is no point in conveying issues relating to a decision a day later than when the decision was made, if the message was solely meant to aid the decision making process. Indeed, that which was to convey information is now conveying data, because of its untimeliness. Too much information at the same time can also be detrimental. The recipient may suffer from so-called *information overload* due to the inability of humans to consider more than a handful of issues simultaneously.

In addition, good information should have the following characteristics in terms of content:

● Information must be *relevant to the recipient*. An irrelevant message is of no value; it is therefore data. For example, providing weekly project progress reports to the sales manager, who has no interest in these issues, is an example of data communication, not information communication. What is considered to be data and what is considered to be information to a recipient, however, depends on the current and future contexts in which the recipient works or will work respectively. Using the same example, if the projects are to lead to products for eventual sale, then the aforementioned weekly progress reports may well be, or may become, information to the sales manager.

- Information must be *accurate and complete*. Information that is inaccurate can be worse than no information at all, as erroneous decisions may be made on the basis of that information. The issue is that the information conveyed is believed to have value, even though it is actually of no value. Information that paints only a portion of the entire picture can also be misleading, resulting in ineffective decision making.

2.5.3 Organisational data and information sources

Information, or data from which to derive information, can originate from a variety of sources. With regard to an organisation, these sources can be classified as either internal or external. An internal source is one that results directly from activities performed as part of the function of the organisation. A report detailing the sales of a particular product, when it is of value to a brand manager, is an example of internal information. Sales details are generated as part of the sales department's interaction with customers. Details about the market share of a company related to other competitors, when it is of value to the Managing Director, is an example of external information. The information does not originate from corporate activities directly: rather, it is derived from data concerning both the company's position and the position of other competitor organisations. Active searching of the organisation's external environment is required to collate and summarise competitor data in order to provide the required information.

Organisational data and information can also be classified as either *formal* or *informal*. A message is considered to be formal if it is a mandatory part of the reporting requirements of the organisation. A monthly production report, which is generated by the Production Department in line with established corporate reporting procedures, is an example of formal data/information. On the other hand, a memorandum between two executives, sent because of necessity rather than because of any formalised corporate requirement, would be an informal data or information source. In the case of the formal category, the optimum situation is when all formal messages provide information. Unfortunately, this is not always achieved in practice. The reporting requirements of an organisation may not correspond exactly to the needs of management. Ackoff's seminal paper, entitled 'Management Misinformation Systems' (Ackoff 1967), was one of the first to acknowledge the failure of computerised management reporting systems to provide the right information to the right person at the right time. Although written a long time ago, the issues raised within this paper are still prevalent today (and are discussed further in Chapter 3).

By combining the external/internal and formal/informal dichotomies, a 2×2 matrix of data/information sources is derived. Figure 2.9 presents this matrix, with examples of each of the four resultant categories of sources.

Internal information can be considered to be the bonding agent that enables an organisation to function as a holistic unit. It is only through information that management can monitor progress towards organisational objectives. It is through information that organisational objectives are communicated. Without information, the organisation essentially becomes a set of disparate groups working towards their own ends rather than towards the corporate good.

Internal information allows the organisation to function as a holistic unit, but this is insufficient on its own to ensure survival and growth of the organisation. This is where external information comes into play. External information enables manage-

Fig 2.9 Classification of data and information sources with examples

	External	**Internal**
Informal	• Letter from supplier • Electronic mail from external contacts • Fax on competitor moves • Customer meetings	• Memos • Face-to-face conversations • Telephone conversations
Formal	• Minutes of formal meetings with clients • Annual corporate report of competitors	• Monthly project report • Annual budget plan • Daily production report

Data and information sources can be classified as either internal or external, and as either informal or formal. This provides a 2 × 2 matrix, shown above with illustrative examples.

ment to comprehend the strategic position of their organisation relative to its competitors, and the global trends within product markets and in society as a whole. The provision of the appropriate mix of quality internal and external information, of both informal and formal kinds, together with management's ability to act upon this information effectively, are of utmost importance to an organisation in order to survive and prosper.

MSS support the provision of management information. For example, they can provide the following facilities to support information provision:

- The preparation of information into a format suitable for the purpose for which it is intended. Facilities for combining text, graphics, tables, images, and even sound and video clips, may be required.
- The exchange of internal and external information between employees, and between the organisation and outside agencies.
- The collation and manipulation of internal data to provide information concerning key business functions.
- The provision of external data, and its combination with key internal data, to enable comparisons to be drawn concerning the company's operations and those of its competitors. An organisation may commission an external data-gathering activity from a company that provides market research services. Examples of UK-based companies offering market research services include Romtec, Business Intelligence, KPMG, KEW associates and Price Waterhouse. Alternatively, the company may initiate specific market research activities using its own market research resources. External data may also be available publicly. The UK census data collected every ten years by government provides a rich variety of statistics on households, homes and occupations. This data can then be made available to companies for a fee. Cou-

pled with previous census data, general trends in demographics, family life, job occupations and home ownership, amongst others, can be established and capitalised on by organisations that are party to this data source. Computerised external data banks may be available on disk or CD-ROM, or even on-line to those managers requiring the information on a routine basis. The Dow Jones Information Service provides up-to-date stock market data and corporate financial statistics via computer systems when needed. (For a comprehensive review of publicly available external data/information sources for UK businesses, consult Burke 1995.)

2.6 MANAGEMENT SUPPORT SYSTEMS: DEFINITION AND FRAMEWORK

In Section 2.3, decision making and information handling were identified as pervasive activities throughout management work. Sections 2.4 and 2.5 followed by describing decision making and information in detail.

In this section, the definition of MSS for this book is provided and discussed. A framework for viewing MSS from a functional perspective is then presented. This framework provides the overarching structure for Chapters 4 to 6 inclusive.

2.6.1 A definition of MSS

In this book, an MSS will be defined as follows:

> *An MSS is a Computer-Based Information System (CBIS) that supports management via support of decision making and/or information handling activities.*

There are several issues worthy of further discussion with respect to this definition.

The first issue, regarding the MSS definition, is that an MSS is defined as a Computer-based Information System (CBIS). A system, according to General Systems Theory (GST), is a set of parts (or components) that constitute a whole, thus showing properties of the whole rather than of its constituent parts (Checkland 1981). As defined in Chapter 1, an Information System (IS) is *a system which delivers information*. An IS is composed of a set of parts, which may include computer-based components (software, hardware and possibly communications capabilities), people, procedures and data, that together constitute a whole. The information provided by an IS cannot be attributed to just the computer-based components, the people, the associated procedures and data. Rather, the ability to provide information is a property of the whole IS, rather than as a consequence of any particular component's role within the IS alone. A Computer-based Information System (CBIS) is *an IS which is computer-based*. People, procedures and non-computerised data are outside of the CBIS, but interact with it. The CBIS affects, and is affected by, those elements that interact with it. An MSS, as a CBIS, is a combination of hardware, software and communications capabilities that works on behalf of management within a particular organisational context. It is management working within an organisational context that determines whether the MSS provides effective information handing and decision making support.

GST is a meta-discipline, in that the concepts advocated within GST are universally applicable to other domains of study. Organisational theory and management has applied many of the concepts of GST. For example, the control mechanisms found within organisations can be described in terms of Control Theory, which is part of GST. Both Zwass (1992) and Harry (1994) provide excellent chapters on GST concepts, and how these concepts relate to organisational structure, operations and management. This book does not devote a separate chapter to GST concepts, but will acknowledge and describe the application of these concepts as and when required.

The second issue, with respect to the MSS definition, is that an MSS is a support system, not a replacement system. As explained in Section 2.4.2, the target decision situations for MSS are those that are semistructured, where management intuition and MSS capabilities constitute the most effective combination.

The third issue, with respect to the MSS definition, is that the word management can be viewed from an activity-oriented perspective (for example, planning, organising, monitoring and controlling), a human-oriented perspective (such as top, middle and lower management), or a role-playing perspective (for example, spokesperson, leader and disturbance handler). In theory, it may be possible for an MSS to support all activities, all levels and all roles. In practice, a particular MSS will support a subset of activities, levels and roles only. This is due to a variety of constraints of a operational, technological, legal and economic nature.

The final issue to note, with respect to the MSS definition, is that the pervasive activities of decision making and information handling are made explicit within the definition.

2.6.2 A framework for viewing MSS

The MSS definition given in the previous subsection is a broad one, covering a high proportion of CBIS found within organisations with a range of possible functionality. In this section, a framework is presented for viewing MSS functionality. The principal reason for developing the framework is to provide a structure with which to organise the descriptions of MSS capabilities in Chapters 4 to 6 inclusive. The framework for viewing MSS functionality is illustrated in Figure 2.10. This provides a logical rather than a physical view of MSS. Although MSS functionality can be distinguished logically using this framework, in reality a particular MSS implementation may provide a combination of the functionality which is not so easily separated.

The principal aspects of the MSS framework are as follows:

- With regard to a certain manager, or a group of managers, a particular MSS function may exist to support principally the information handling (i.e. information preparation and information communication) activities of a particular management group (that is, one or more persons engaged in management activities). On the other hand, a particular MSS function may exist to support principally the decision making activities of that management group. It is important to note that information is actually being 'prepared and communicated' during both of these types of function. The former type is concerned principally with the preparation of documents and the exchange of information between management personnel, but the latter type is concerned with the provision of information, which involves data collation and manipulation by the MSS. This categorisation of MSS functionality into

Fig 2.10 A logical framework for viewing MSS capabilities

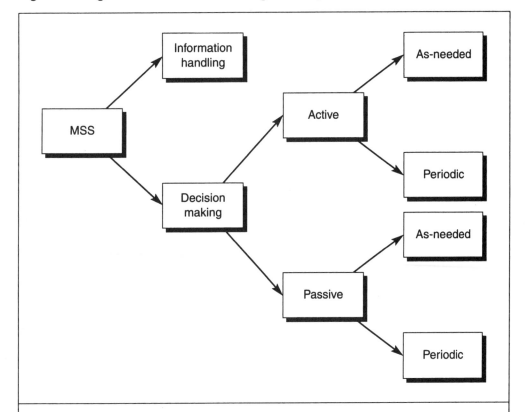

MSS capabilities can be separated into those concerned principally with information preparation and communication, and those concerned with decision making. Within decision making, support can be active or passive. Both active and passive decision making support can be provided on a periodic or as-needed basis.

aspects supporting information handling activities and aspects supporting decision making activities provides the first part of the MSS framework.

- The support of decision making activities can itself be separated into whether it is passive or active. A passive decision support capability provides information concerning the current decision making situation at some point in time. How the information is used, however, is up to the decision maker(s). Table 2.1 provides a view of passive decision making support in terms of Simon's decision making model (this model was described in Section 2.4.1). Active decision making support assists the particular process of decision making adopted by the decision maker(s) directly. Active support involves the provision of mechanisms for the analysis and manipulation of information interactively to provide greater insight into the decision situation and associated options. Table 2.1 also provides a view of active decision making support relative to Simon's decision making model. (Hereafter, the phrases 'passive decision making support' and 'passive support for decision making' are considered equivalent in meaning and will be used interchangeably. The

Table 2.1 Passive and active decision making support in relation to Simon's decision making model

Simon's Decision Making Model	Example Passive Decision Support via MSS	Example Active Decision Support via MSS
Intelligence	• Reports on aspects of business, such as production, sales, operations, personnel • Report of competitor statistics • Sales forecast report	• Interactive data analysis concerning the company's current state • Forecasting and analysing company data on an as-needed basis
Design	• Report on an alternative • Comparison reports	• 'What if' and 'what's best' analysis of data • Simulation of expected outcome and effects of a particular alternative • Ranking and scoring of alternatives interactively
Choice	• Information to confirm and justify selection of alternative	• Result of 'what's best' analysis (in Design Stage) • Results of scoring/ranking alternatives • Group negotiation support

This table provides examples of passive and active decision making support by MSS, relative to the Intelligence, Design and Choice activities of Simon's decision making model.

same is true for 'active decision making support' and 'active support of decision making'.) It is worth stating at this point that an MSS that provides passive decision making support is not inferior in its support of management activities to an MSS that provides active decision making support. Both types of support are extremely useful. There are management situations where passive decision making support is more applicable than active decision making support, and vice versa. The target management and organisational context governs the most appropriate form of support for the decision making activities in hand.

• Decision making support can be categorised by whether it is available on an as-needed basis, or whether it is available only on a periodic basis (for example, weekly, monthly, or yearly). The availability of support depends not only on the capabilities of the system to provide the support but also on the organisational context. An MSS capable of providing periodic support can never be used in any other way. However, an MSS providing facilities for use on an as-needed basis could also be used for periodic support. For example, an MSS may be able to provide decision support as-needed, but because of company policies, support by the MSS is available only on a periodic basis.

(The issue of as-needed versus periodic support is most pertinent with respect to passive decision making support, and is therefore discussed at length in Chapter 5. Most MSS providing active decision making support will be available on an as-needed basis owing to the interaction needed between the user and the MSS.)

2.7   SUMMARY

This chapter has introduced the concept of a Management Support System (MSS) as a CBIS that supports management via its support of decision making and/or information handling activities. A logical framework for viewing MSS functionality has been described. This provides the basis for organising the descriptions of MSS functionality within Chapters 4–6 inclusive. Specifically, Chapter 4 focuses on the information preparation and communication aspects of MSS functionality. Chapter 5 concentrates on MSS functionality for passive decision making support, and Chapter 6 covers MSS functionality for active decision making support.

Additionally, this chapter has also introduced key concepts and associated terminology that will be drawn upon within subsequent chapters. These include:

- The three different, yet highly complementary, views of management.
- The pervasive nature of decision making and information handling within management work.
- Simon's model of decision making, and the rational and non-rational approaches found within organisational decision making
- The aim of MSS to support semistructured decision situations.
- The relative strengths and weaknesses of group decision making and individual decision making.
- The distinction between data, knowledge and information, the characteristics of information, and possible information/data sources

References

Ackoff R (1967) Management Misinformation Systems. *Management Science* Vol 14, No 4. pp.147–56.

Adamski T and Kleiner B H (1992) The Politics of Management. *Management Research News* Vol 15, No 1. pp.19–23.

Anthony R N (1965) *Planning and Control Systems: a Framework for Analysis.* Harvard University Press, Cambridge, MA.

Armstrong M (1992) *Management Processes and Functions.* Institute of Personnel Management. Revised Edition.

Brech E (1963) *The Principles and Practice of Management.* Longman.

Checkland P (1981) *Systems Thinking: Systems Practice.* John Wiley.

Chorn N H (1991) Organisations: a New Paradigm. *Management Decision* Vol 29, No 4. pp.8–11.

Cooke S and Slack N (1989) *Making Management Decisions.* Prentice Hall.

Drucker P (1961) *The Practice of Management.* Mercury.

Fayol H (1916) *General and Industrial Management.* Pitman.

Fidler C S and Rogerson S (1993) Current IS Practices within UK-based Organizations. *Information Management & Computer Security* Vol 1, No 2. pp.13–20.

Gorry G A and Scott Morton M (1971) A Framework for Management Information Systems. *Sloan Management Review* Vol 13, No 1. pp.55–70.

Harrison E F (1993) Interdisciplinary Models of Decision Making. *Management Decision* Vol 31, No 8. pp.27–33.

Harry M (1994) *Information Systems in Business*. Pitman.

Huber G (1984) Issues in the Design of Group Decision Support Systems. *MIS Quarterly* Vol 8, No 3. pp.195–204.

Keen P G W and Scott Morton M (1978) *Decision Support Systems: an Organisational Perspective*. Addison-Wesley.

Kroenke D (1989) *Management Information Systems*. McGraw Hill.

Long L (1989) *Management Information Systems*. Prentice Hall.

Lucey T (1991) *Management Information Systems Sixth Edition*. DP Publications.

March J G and Simon H A (1958) *Organizations*. John Wiley.

Miller G A (1956) The Magical Number Seven, plus or minus Two: some Limits on our capacity for Processing Information. *The Psychological Review* Vol 63 No 2. pp.81–97.

Mintzberg H (1973) *The Nature of Managerial Work*. Harper & Row.

Murdick R G and Munson J C (1986) *MIS Concepts & Design*. Prentice Hall.

Ormrod J (1993) Decision Making in the Health Service. *Management Decision* Vol 31 No 7. pp.8–14.

Pugh D S (ed) (1984) *Organization Theory*. Penguin Books Ltd.

Rosen T S and Kleiner B H (1992) Management in the 1990s. *Management Research News* Vol 15, No 8. pp1–5.

Simon H A (1960) *The New Science of Management Decision*. Prentice Hall.

Simon H A (1984) Decision Making and Organizational Design. In Pugh D S (ed) *Organization Theory*. Penguin Books Ltd. pp.202–223.

Timms H L (1967) *Introduction to Operations Management*. Irwin.

Zwass V (1992) *Management Information Systems*. W C Brown.

Review questions

1 Describe the three views of management, and explain why they are different yet highly interrelated.

2 How does Mintzberg's view of management work support the notion of decision making and information handling activities being pervasive throughout management work?

3 Describe Simon's decision making model. Compare it with another decision making model, either one encountered within this chapter or another with which you are familiar.

4 Identify a decision you have made recently and describe it in terms of Simon's decision making model.

5 What are 'semistructured' decision situations? Why are these the target decision situations for MSS?

6 Describe why the political approach, the incremental approach, the garbage can approach and the programmed approach found within organisational decision making, are non-rational approaches.

7 List and justify three possible advantages and two possible disadvantages of group decision making (as opposed to individual decision making).

8 Describe the difference between data and information, giving real-life examples to illustrate your answer.

9 List three characteristics of information. Justify your selection.

10 From an organisational context with which you are familiar, give an example of external information, internal information, informal information and formal information. Describe how the information is used in the case of each example, and by whom.

11 Define the term 'Management Support System', and list the functionality you may expect to find within an MSS implementation.

Project idea

Within an organisation of your choice, interview one or more managers about their work. Specifically:

● Find out what decisions they have been involved in recently, and categorise each of them by whether it is a planning, organising, co-ordinating or controlling decision.

● Find out what roles, according to Mintzberg, they adopted during the course of each of their decision making activities.

● Find out which decisions involved group decision making and which involved individual decision making.

● Classify the decisions according to whether they are unstructured, semistructured or structured, and identify any computer-based support that they use within each of the decision making activities identified.

From your survey:

● Show empirically the many-to-many relationships between activity, people, and roles as illustrated in Figure 2.5.

● Critically appraise the current usage of MSS by the manager(s) you have identified.

● Can you identify any decisions that could benefit from MSS but are not currently supported? What financial, social and/or technical issues may need to be considered before any MSS to support the decision(s) you have identified could be developed?

CHAPTER 3

Technology and MSS Opportunities

3.1 INTRODUCTION

As defined in Chapter 2, MSS are *computer-based* information systems. The scope and characteristics of computing technology (hardware, software and communications capabilities) influence the MSS opportunities available to companies. However, only when the MSS opportunities presented match the needs of an organisation should MSS be exploited.

The purpose of this chapter is twofold:

- To review key aspects of computing technology and associated issues that have influenced, and/or will influence, the design and development of MSS.
- To provide justification for one of the major premises upon which this book is based: that technological advances make possible the development of seamless, integrated MSS that provide the functionality requested by management.

Section 3.2 outlines the principal advances in computing technology over the last forty years and the opportunities that these have provided for the evolution of MSS. The traditional names used to refer to specific types of MSS provision are also introduced in this section. Section 3.3 reviews some of the important, more recent technological developments that either have had significant influence on MSS design and development or are expected to be of greater significance in the future. The topics reviewed are as follows:

- Client server systems.
- The Object-oriented (OO) paradigm and systems.
- The Graphical User Interface (GUI) and the Windows Environment.
- Open systems.
- Neural networks.
- Multi-media and hyper-media applications and systems.
- Virtual Reality (VR) systems.
- The Internet.
- Data warehouses.

Although the above list of technology-related topics is by no means exhaustive, the review of these topics demonstrates the substantial opportunities that technological developments, in general, provide to MSS developers. These opportunities provide the potential for enhanced functionality provision within MSS and/or the potential for greater integration of functionality within one physical MSS implementation. Finally, Section 3.4 provides a summary of this chapter.

At the end of this chapter the reader should understand:

- *That technological advances influence the opportunities available to MSS developers for the design and development of MSS, and that keeping abreast of such advances is vital.*
- *The nature of several of the more recent technological advances, and their current and/or potential impact on available MSS functionality and/or the integration of management support services.*

3.2   A TECHNOLOGICAL HISTORY OF MSS

The first business computing resources became economically and technically feasible for large businesses in the 1950s, with the introduction of the first programmable mainframe computers. The focus at this point in time was principally on the development and operation of several large Data Processing (DP) applications (nowadays termed Transaction Processing Systems (TPS)) that were considered essential to business, such as payroll processing, and order processing and invoicing. Most applications were run periodically, for example weekly or monthly, in a batch mode of operations. They were typically developed by specialist programmers. The computers were maintained and operated by specialised technical operators, and were relatively isolated from the core functions of the business.

In the 1960s, it was recognised that data, collected as part of the DP functions, could be used to derive information for management. For example, the number of orders received per week, when compared to previous weekly totals or the totals at the same time in previous years, could be of use to the Sales and Marketing Manager for evaluating current performance. So-termed 'Management Information Systems (MIS)' were developed by many organisations to provide a set of periodic information reports to management. Early MIS operated in batch mode, providing large and often unwieldy hard copy reports that were placed on managers' desks at specified times. Eventually, on-line access to reports was possible for those companies who could afford the financial outlay. This allowed reports to run directly from an attached terminal rather than waiting for batch operations to run overnight.

The methods by which data was stored for subsequent manipulation within programs also came under scrutiny in the 1960s. The problems associated with the program-centred approach to data management (where each program creates and manipulates its own data files) led to the proposal and development of database systems that reflected a data-centred approach to data management (where data is independent of the programs that manipulate it). The first database systems were typically based on the hierarchic data structure and manipulation model. At the end of the 60s, E. F. Codd defined the underlying data structure and data manipulation method that formed the foundations of relational database systems, by far the most popular type of database system in commercial use today (see Codd's seminal paper, published in 1970). Date (1990) provides a comprehensive description of the Relational Data Model as well as summaries of other notable data models, including the Hierarchic Data Model.

Also at this time, minicomputers started to be employed within specialised functions of the organisation, such as R & D and manufacturing. However, the development and maintenance of software for business applications was still very much the province of specialist Analyst Programmers. The growth in demand for applications development and the subsequent requests for enhancement/modifications led many organisations to suffer substantial backlogs of development requests. Computer departments became seen as unresponsive to business needs.

It was also towards the end of the 1960s that Ackoff wrote his paper entitled 'Management Misinformation Systems' which told of five misconceptions that designers and developers of MIS possess with regard to management support requirements (Ackoff 1967). These misconceptions were as follows.

- The critical deficiencies under which most managers work is the lack of relevant information.
- Managers need all the information they request.
- If managers have all the information they need then their decision making will improve.
- Better communication between managers improves organisational performance.
- A manager does not have to understand how the information system works, only how to use it.

According to Ackoff, these assumptions were unfounded for the following reasons respectively:

- One of the largest problems for management is not a lack of relevant information, but rather an abundance of irrelevant information (that is, data). Condensation and filtration of information reports received is therefore key to any MIS.
- In order for managers to know all of the information types needed, they need to know all the decisions that they will face and their respective information requirements. This is seldom the case in practice. Managers will tend to err on the side of caution and request more reports than actually required 'just in case'.
- It is not a case of simply receiving the information: a manager needs to know what to do with it once received.
- Organisation performance can actually be hindered by too much communication as well as by the lack of communication (Ackoff provides an example of the Sales and Production departments of an organisation where each is cognisant of the other's tactics concerning the pricing and quantity to manufacture of a product. Each is therefore able to pre-empt the other's tactics. This led the two departments to make worse decisions for the organisation, concerning the price and the quantity of the product to produce, than would have been made had each been less aware of the other's manoeuvrings.)
- By not knowing the information source and how it was processed, the manager is less likely to use the system. (Whether managers always require complete in-depth understanding of how information is processed is debatable. For instance, some common Operations Research (OR) techniques, such as Linear Programming (described in Chapter 6), are applied within MSS. The intricacies of the Linear Programming technique are not easy to comprehend by the non-mathematical manager, and yet decisions are based on the solutions of Linear Programming models. This is because Linear Programming is a tried and tested technique. Despite not understanding the model's processing in depth, managers need to be aware of what factors have been taken into account within the Linear Programming model to judge its scope and reliability of solution.)

At the end of his paper, Ackoff proposed an MIS design methodology which centres on the identification of decision types faced by management and the formulation of their information requirements.

Like Ackoff, Michael Scott Morton concentrated his research work of the early 70s on decision making support. This research led to the development of the subject of study known as 'Management Decision Systems' (Scott Morton 1971), but was later renamed 'Decision Support Systems (DSS)'. DSS are CBIS that provide active support of management decision making, by providing interactive access to data and mathematical models. The growth of the DSS support concept was aided by the introduction of the microcomputer. The microcomputer enabled small businesses, who could ill-afford the financial outlay required for mainframe or minicomputer technology, to utilise computerised applications to support business operations. Software was soon developed for non-IS specialists to develop their own basic applications and to run applications locally. For instance, spreadsheet and word-processing software became common tools on a PC platform, the former tool enabling small but useful DSS to be developed by the user directly. (The development of applications by a non-IS professional is commonly called End-User Computing (EUC) and is mentioned further in Chapter 7.)

Fourth generation languages (4gls) soon became an attractive alternative to third generation languages (3gls) such as COBOL, for developing new business applications. 4gls provide the facilities for creating data structures to hold applications data (typically within a relational database), and for developing a suite of programs for data entry, data manipulation and information reporting. These packages started by providing their own specialised languages for data structure and manipulation. However, SQL (see, for example, Van Der Lans 1989) has become the standard data definition and manipulation language to which most 4gls adhere. In addition, screen painters and report writers have made application development within 4gls, and also 3gls, more efficient.

The discipline of Artificial Intelligence (AI) had some commercial successes in the latter part of the 1970s with the development of so-called Expert Systems (ES) for both industrial and commercial applications. The field of AI has two principal and interrelated aims, one stemming from a technical perspective and the other from a philosophical perspective:

- To provide computer systems that, in some ways, exhibit aspects of intelligent behaviour (the technical perspective).
- By the provision of computer systems, to further understand the workings of the human brain (the philosophical perspective).

ES are one of the many products resulting from the technical side of AI research. They either provide expert advice within a particular specialised area of business (for example, on whether a particular merger with a given company would be a good move for a particular organisation) or simply provide more consistent advice or recommendations on a particular subject which would require human competence rather than human specialist expertise. Other innovations from within the area of AI, such as neural networks and voice recognition systems, are also beginning to have impact on current management support provisions (neural networks are discussed further in Section 3.3.5, and voice recognition is described further in Chapter 4).

The 1970s also saw the development and growth in computer networking capabilities. A computer network is a collection of autonomous systems, typically referred to as hosts, that have the ability to intercommunicate over some form of communications subnet. Its purpose is to make all computing resources potentially available to anyone on the network irrespective of the physical location of either the resource required or the user requiring the resource. Networks can be separated into those that operate over short distances, typically confined to one or more closely sited office blocks (so-called Local Area Networks (LAN)) and those that span substantial geographical areas, typically using existing telephone lines and satellite communications for transmission (so-called Wide Area Networks (WAN)). Some of the first services provided to computer network users were electronic mail, file transfer capabilities between network users, and basic computer conferencing. These facilities were later combined with other personal productivity tools, such as word-processing and spreadsheets, to provide an integrated 'Office Information System (OIS)' for use by office workers.

Technological advances from the 1980s to the present day have expanded the possibilities for MSS provision. For example, networked computer systems with appropriate software have enabled so-termed 'Group Decision Support Systems (GDSS)' to be developed. These systems provide decision making support to groups whose members may be remotely located and/or where member involvement within the group is dispersed in time. Furthermore, so-termed 'Executive Information Systems (EIS)' have become a popular development focus for many organisations. These systems provide management with quick and easy access to information which may be derived from several internal and external data sources. The advances in communications networks and their inter-operability have been vital to EIS development. Although EIS were originally conceived as being top management tools, it is now widely recognised that all management levels can benefit from access to information through an EIS.

3.3 TECHNOLOGICAL ADVANCES: IMPACT ON MSS DESIGN AND DEVELOPMENT

Even from the brief overview of the evolution of MSS in Section 3.2, it can be seen that technological advances have offered increased potential for MSS provision. The functionality that is available to support management has increased over time. The potential for combining functionality within one integrated, seamless support system has also increased. Indeed, it is no longer the case that an organisation has to implement an MSS which functions in complete isolation from other application systems. Rather, the MSS designer can more easily 'pick and mix' the available software, hardware and communications capabilities, combining them to provide the MSS needed by the organisation.

It is this ability to 'pick and mix', which many organisations are presently exploiting, that provides part of the underlying rationale for the overall approach to MSS adopted within this book. The normal approach to describing the subject of MSS is to describe each of the traditional MSS system types (that is, MIS, DSS, EIS, OIS, ES, and GDSS) separately. This approach to MSS description has always been problematic as there is no standard set of definitions for these system types, and definitions, when proposed, do not lead to system types that are mutually exclusive in functionality (Boaden and Lockett 1991, and Fidler and Rogerson 1995, examine the problem of definitions in more detail). This leads to great discussion on the part of several academics on what constitutes one type of system and what constitutes another type of system. Yet the principal objective of any MSS implementation is to support the

Fig 3.1 The impact of technological advances on MSS provision

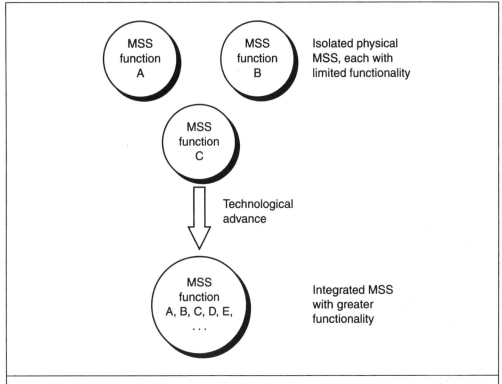

The diagram shows that technological advances have made possible the combining of functionality that traditionally was provided within separate systems. Also the functionality that can be provided within MSS continues to grow.

organisational requirements for management support. Whether it is a DSS, an ES or a hybrid system, combining ES and DSS capabilities, is not the issue for organisations. The organisational need, and the provision of an MSS with the functionality to match that need, is the principal concern.

This section describes several of the more recent technological advances with respect to MSS design and development. The ramifications for MSS provision are discussed with respect to each advance. Collectively, these advances, and others, contribute further to the facilities available to MSS developers, by enhancing the functionality available to support management and by increasing the potential for an integrated MSS provision. Figure 3.1 illustrates the impact of technological advances on MSS provision in general. Table 3.1 lists the specific technological advances to be discussed below, together with an indication of which way(s) each contributes, or will contribute in the future, to MSS provision.

3.3.1   Client server systems

Client server systems are very popular within modern business environments. In a survey provided by IDC (*Computer Weekly*, 9th June 1994), over 50% of the companies

Table 3.1 Technological advances and their individual contributions to MSS provision

Technological Advance	Contribution to MSS Provision	
	Potential for MSS Facilities Enhancement	Potential for Systems Integration
Client server systems		yes
Object-oriented paradigm and systems		yes
Graphical User Interface and the Windows Environment	yes	yes
Open systems		yes
Neural networks	yes	
Multi-media and hyper-media applications and systems	yes	
Virtual reality systems	yes	
Internet	yes	yes
Data warehouses		yes

The table shows each technical advance, and whether it increases, or is expected to increase in the future, the available functionality for MSS provision and/or the potential for integrating functionality within a physical MSS implementation.

surveyed indicated that they were either planning to use, or already using, client server systems. The growth of client server systems can be attributed to the following factors:

- The proliferation of PCs within organisations, and the desire to allow communication and data co-ordination between these PCs.
- The development of networks of sufficient reliability.
- The development of the client server model within high-powered workstation environments, such as ALTO at the Xerox Palo Alto Research Centre.
- The need for a low cost alternative for those organisations that can ill-afford the initial financial outlay required for mainframe or minicomputer systems. (Whether client server systems are low cost in on-going maintenance and support terms, however, is debatable. One survey found that client server support costs could greatly exceed those of mainframe technology (Boyle 1995).)

A client server system has several clients (typically PCs) with which the users interact. These clients are connected together by a network (typically a LAN). One or more server computers (which can also be PCs, but mainframe and minicomputer servers are possible) are also linked to the network. Whereas a mainframe system performs all the data management and processing, to the point where the output is ready to be positioned on the screen, client server systems distribute processing, data storage and systems operating tasks between the client requiring the processing and the available servers. For instance, the processing tasks between client and server(s) may be separated so that the client performs the processing for screen displays and screen management, local security, and for running local applications, whereas the server(s) perform the processing for database and other media management, and the operation of shared peripherals such as printers. In total, the Gartner group (*Computer Weekly*, 9th June 1994) identified five variant models of computer task separation within client server systems. These models are summarised in Figure 3.2. Determining the separation of computer tasks between client and server(s) depends greatly on the organisational situation, and how the particular applications software is configured. Indeed, a recent paper showed that the separation can be very important in the efficiency of applications that run on client server systems (Sargent and Miglautsch 1995).

Applications packages, stored locally on client PCs, can be used in addition to the applications available on the servers. Indeed, it is often possible to download data housed on a server into a local application, such as a spreadsheet package, for subsequent analysis and presentation of results.

Client server systems provide for incremental growth. The number of clients and servers can usually be expanded (within the network's effective range of operation), allowing businesses to start small and expand their resource incrementally. Upgrading a server requires less investment than mainframe upgrades. If the network fails, locally stored applications continue to function.

In summary, client server systems provide an alternative approach to an integrated computer resource provision, and possibly the only viable approach to smaller businesses and to those organisations with substantial PC investments. In the context of MSS, many products, with which MSS are developed, run on client server systems. Client server systems enable organisations to link together existing computer systems, enabling greater integration of an organisation's software and hardware facilities, and more effective data storage and data exchange.

3.3.2 The Object-oriented (OO) paradigm and systems

The Object-oriented (OO) paradigm is a subject of great current interest. It is influencing work in all aspects of the Systems Development Life Cycle (SDLC), from enterprise modelling to programming language development and maintenance. However, the OO paradigm is not new: it was first implemented within the SIMULA programming language in the late 60s (Birtwistle et. al. 1973). Smalltalk 80 was the first well publicised OO programming language (Goldberg and Robson 1983) and probably triggered the current wave of research interest in OO.

The OO paradigm views everything as an *object*. Instead of separating data from the processes that manipulate it, an object contains both the data pertaining to that object and the procedures that allow manipulation of the data. For example, an employee object may incorporate data, such as the employee's name, address, data of birth, year started employment and so forth, and the procedures for manipulating the data about that employee, such as 'view employee details' and 'fire'. An object belongs to an *object class*. So, for example, the aforementioned employee object would belong to an 'employee' object class. The employee object class provides a specification of the data that every employee will possess (although the data values will differ) and a specification of the procedures (a procedure in OO terminology is known as a *method*) that manipulate employee

Fig 3.2 The five variants of the client server computing model

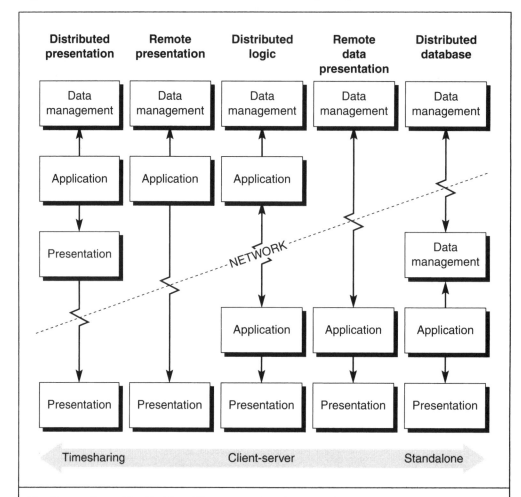

The Gartner Group identified five different ways that the processing between client and server can be configured, ranging from one that is very client-biased to one that is very server-biased. In the most client-biased arrangement, the server performs a subset of the required data management activities. The remaining data management activities, together with any applications processing and presentation of information and screen displays, are the responsibility of the client. In the most server-biased arrangement, the client simply maps the pre-formatted screen of information received across the network from the server onto the local screen display: all data management, applications processing and screen presentation preparation tasks are performed by the server.

Reprinted with permission from *Computer Weekly*, 9th June 1994

data. Classes can have superclasses, which themselves can have superclasses, and so on. Thus, a class hierarchy is formed. The specification of data and methods takes place at the most appropriate level of class definition. Objects *inherit* the data structures and methods specified by their class and all of the class's superclasses. For example, the afore-mentioned 'employee' class might have an 'employable person' superclass, which itself might have a 'person' superclass. The data and methods specified within the 'person' class will therefore be inherited by any object that is of the 'employable person' class, and, even more specifically, by any object that is of the 'employee' class.

Objects interact with each other by sending *messages*. A message is sent from one object to another and causes the receiving object to perform the method specified in the message. The receiving object returns any results. Processing a method may require the object to send several messages to other objects, for example to invoke methods for retrieving data values for return to the message-sending object for subsequent manipulation. It is through message passing and the subsequent invocation of methods within objects that processing takes place within an OO environment. Figure 3.3 illustrates the principal concepts of the OO paradigm and their relationships.

Since the development of Smalltalk 80, the OO concept has been incorporated into traditional 3gls to form hybrid languages such as C++ (Stroustrup 1983, Cox 1984, Stroustrup 1986). In addition, researchers have investigated the possibility of applying OO concepts to other computing domains, such as database systems, and systems analysis and design (see, for example, Brown's book with respect to OO database systems (Brown 1991), and the works of Rumbaugh et al. (1991) and Coad and Yourdon (1991) with respect to OO analysis and/or design).

The recent commercial interest in OO stems from the envisaged benefits that OO development may bring to companies engaged in software development. These benefits include the reusability of objects/classes between applications and the more efficient maintenance of applications. Having set up a class hierarchy with defined methods, if it is possible to reuse parts of the class hierarchy then development time will be saved. The internal workings of an object's method can be changed without impact on other objects that pass invocation messages to the object. This can lead to more efficient maintenance of OO application systems. Extensions to applications can also be made by introducing new subclasses of existing classes, at both design and programming levels of activity. This is straightforward *as long as the class hierarchies were properly designed in the first place*. Proper design is vital. Providing too flat a class hierarchy, for instance, would limit reuse and ease of extendibility. Design of an OO system therefore requires considerable time and effort, but this additional time is typically justified on the basis of the reduced time later in the SDLC.

Despite its intuitive appeal, there is currently little in the way of substantive evidence as to whether the OO paradigm fulfils its promises and under what conditions this fulfilment occurs. Even with partial success, the OO approach will remain prominent for some time: it has too much commercial backing to simply wither and die. In the context of MSS, many more recent development products embrace OO concepts to some degree. For example, developing a Graphical User Interface (GUI) using Windows-based MSS development packages (GUIs and Windows are discussed further in the following subsection) involves creating objects of pre-defined classes. For instance, creating a specific menu for an MSS application may involve creating an object of a pre-defined 'menu' class provided within the package. The menu class provides the data structures and methods that a specific menu object needs in order to function as a menu.

More transaction processing applications are expected to be developed using OO analysis, design and programming tools. More legacy software* is expected to be

---

* The term 'legacy', when used within a computing context, normally means 'something which existed previously'. Legacy software is therefore software which has already been developed. Interestingly, some prefer the term 'heritage' to 'legacy', as heritage appears to convey a more positive image of existing systems.

Fig 3.3 Object-oriented concepts and their relationships

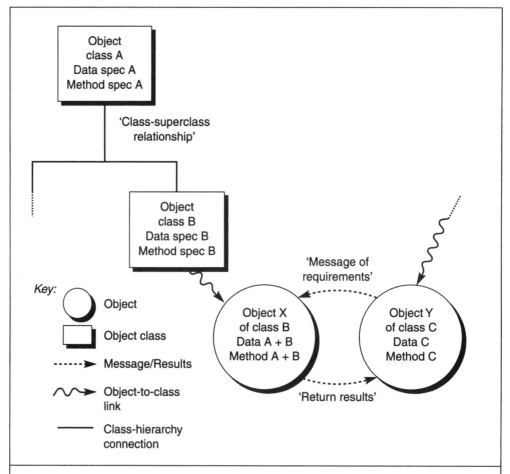

The diagram shows two objects X and Y. Object X is of class B, which is a subclass of A. Therefore, object X inherits the data structures and methods that are specified by both B and A object classes. Another object Y, of class C, may have a method that requires the sending of a message to object X. This message may invoke one of object X's methods in order to satisfy the requirements of object Y. Once the invoked method is completed by X, the results of that invocation are returned to object Y. In total, the diagram illustrates the principal concepts of the OO approach (namely, objects, classes, inheritance, methods and messages) and their interrelationships

❑ *Viewpoint*

Early adopters of object-oriented technology in the UK have scaled back their early expectations of likely benefits. In particular the prospect of re-using software objects has been downgraded. But it is early days, and most companies have less than two years experience with the technology. ■

Reprinted with permission from *Computer Weekly*, 1st June 1995

❑ *Viewpoint*

Bank fails to control object development

Swiss Bank has admitted that after three years of object development it has ended up with thousands of incompatible, spaghetti code objects.

The bank is now cleaning up its object-based applications and is imposing coporate-wide standards for its future object-oriented development.

"We're not at crisis point yet, but we could end up there," said Malcolm Dick, Swiss Bank's global head of fixed technology. "Because of the pressure to deliver object applications fast, we overlooked the fact that object technology is all about defining protocols and interfaces."

Swiss Bank is one of the most ambitious users of object technology, and in three years it has transformed itself from an organisation whose IT was almost 90% Cobol-based to one which has an enterprise-wide object-oriented IT strategy based on NeXT's Nextstep development environment.

Dick said that because object-oriented applications are between three to five times faster to develop, adopting object technology has given the bank a huge commercial advantage.

"We've had a two-year edge over our competitors. Without objects this would have been impossible," he said."For example, our traders can create a new financial instrument themselves in around 15 minutes by dynamically fitting objects together. Object technology means we can offer our clients financial products in complex areas such as derivatives, which no one else can offer."

But the enthusiastic take-up of object technology has led to the accumulation of a large number of incompatible objects. Now the bank wants to exploit the second main advantage of object technology, and achieve extensive software re-use.

But this requires all objects to be created in a disciplined and standardised fashion, with common interfaces. "We want to get to the point where we can plug-and-play with objects, so we are going to have to be more careful over the object interfaces," said Dick.

He estimates that the standardisation programme will take up to two years to complete. ∎

Reprinted with permission from *Computer Weekly*, 22nd June 1995.

embedded within OO envelopes, allowing them to be viewed as pre-defined objects and to function within an OO environment. In the light of these trends, MSS developers may need to adopt a complementary OO approach to developing MSS. Development would centre on the creation of management object classes, that provide methods for requesting data from other object classes, for analysing the data and/or for reporting information. An OO approach throughout MSS development may need to be adopted.

3.3.3 The Graphical User Interface (GUI) and the Windows environment

The target of operating systems was originally the technically literate user. However, with an increasing number of computer users being non-IS professionals, the command-based approach provided within operating systems for performing basic housekeeping functions, such as copying disks or locating files, had to be reviewed. The Apple Mackintosh PC was one of the early systems providing a more so-termed 'user-friendly' appearance for PC-based operating systems. It provided a Graphical User Interface (GUI) rather than a text-based interface. Using a mouse, operations could be invoked by pointing to, and clicking on, various icons and menu items, and by dragging icons across the screen and dropping them on special screen areas.

WIMPS (acronym for Windows, Icons, Menus and Pointing devices) GUIs are now commonplace. Windows is the most popular WIMPS GUI for users of underlying

DOS-based PCs. Nowadays, it is often the case that PC purchases include Windows as part of the deal.

Windows is a very versatile product. As well as providing users with easy access to operating systems functions, it provides applications software developers with the capabilities to develop applications with the same 'look and feel' GUI as presented within the Windows environment. It also provides useful facilities, such as Object Linking and Embedding (OLE) and Dynamic Data Exchange (DDE). OLE allows an object (such as a spreadsheet or a wordprocessed document), developed within one Windows package, to be referenced within objects developed using other Windows packages. It also permits an object, developed using one Windows package, to be amended using the same package from within the confines of another development package. Object referencing sets up a link between the object and its reference point. When the actual object is amended, all objects linking to the changed object see the changes. DDE allows the importing of data between Windows-based applications. Current development of the Windows product is focused on the provision of a truly Object-oriented Operating System (Semich 1994).

From an MSS perspective, GUIs such as Windows provide management with increased ease of access to management support applications. The Windows environment provides the building blocks for integrating package functionality for management support.

3.3.4 Open systems

Vendor systems (hardware, software or communications networks) are said to be open systems if they are compatible with other such products from different vendors. Open systems promise economic benefits for all stakeholders (vendors, customers, third party software houses, and so forth). For instance, customers can select the best tools for the business need and can more easily make changes to their product bases. Vendors can work jointly towards product innovations rather than having to 'go it alone' both in financial terms and in terms of available human resource expertise (the old adage – 'two heads are better than one' – is appropriate here).

According to Hugo (1991), open systems are soon to become a reality. This depends, to a great extent, on his definition of open systems. The situation where all computer technology is truly open will be extremely difficult to achieve, even in the long term. However, incremental improvements to the interoperability of, and compatibility between, products are certainly possible.

Standards are vital to the development of open systems. These exist for many aspects of computing technology, including:

- Operating systems standards such as UNIX and MS-DOS.
- Standards for interfacing applications programs with operating systems.
- Electronic Data Interchange (EDI) standards.
- Networking standards (for example standards for Ethernet LAN and Token Ring LAN arrangements), standards for how data is communicated across a network, and even standards for an entire network communication architecture (such as the OSI Reference Model).
- Standards for connecting computers to their associated peripherals.

Many official standards bodies exist. The British Standards Institution (BSI) and the American National Standards Institute (ANSI) operate on a country-wide basis whereas the International Standards Organisation (ISO) has world-wide influence. In theory, each may promote a different standard for the same technology, although in practice there is much liaison and co-operation between standards bodies. Typically, this leads to common standard definitions but with different labels (for example, the Ethernet LAN standard, originally developed by Xerox, is now an Institute of Electrical and Electronic Engineering (IEEE) standard and also an ISO standard). As well as officially endorsed standards, there are other so-termed *de facto* standards which have been adopted widely by the computing technology market. These are typically backed by large players in the field (for example, IBM).

Some standards are better defined than others. Standards presented in English, for example, are open to ambiguity. Formal specification languages provide less opportunity for ambiguity. Some standards have specified tests to verify conformance to the standard, whereas others do not include such test specifications.

Many companies are adopting computing technology which is considered more open in an attempt to make their IT more flexible and resilient in the light of organisational change. DHL World-wide Express (USA) is one such company: it has embarked on a project to integrate current systems and, eventually, to re-design the entire corporate IT platform (Freedman 1991). Any existing software is to be amended to conform to the official standards set for its development language. A new organisational policy has been implemented whereby all new applications software is bought 'off-the-shelf' if at all possible. The current proprietary network is being discarded in favour of one that complies with networking standards and is totally compatible with the current international network operated by DHL. There is also a move away from minicomputer to client server systems. All packages will import and export data to and from common data repositories within DHL, to allow sharing of consolidated data across applications.

Weyerhauser, a paper products manufacturer, has also made its computing provision more open. A fibre-optic network has been installed throughout the company. The IBM mainframe computers have been replaced with client server systems. PCs are available throughout the company to allow access to manufacturing data held on servers and its downloading to local PC-based software applications for subsequent analysis and reporting. Legacy systems can also be accessed across the network. In total, the new systems permit faster and better access to information to satisfy customer queries than that employed previously. This gives Weyerhauser a competitive advantage over its competitors, as well as protecting current IT investments from future changes and allowing IT to expand with minimal disruption (Ledbetter 1993).

With respect to MSS design and development, the message is simple: the more open computing technology becomes, the greater the capability for providing an integrated MSS provision to match business needs.

3.3.5 Neural networks

Neural networks are a recent commercial development from the Artificial Intelligence (AI) community (already mentioned in Section 3.2). A neural network is a computer system that comprises two or more layers of connected neurons. Neurons are simple processing units that take input signals, either provided by another neuron or from some other external input source, and produce an output signal. The output signal may then form an input to one or more other neurons in the next layer or, if the last layer is reached, form part of the output of the neural network to the user. Two neurons are connected if the output of one forms an input to the other. Neuron connections are usually called links. Within any neural network there is always an input layer (which receives the input from the user) and an output layer (which reports results to the user). Between these two layers, there may be one or more so-called hidden layers (these are hidden from the neural network user).

Neural networks have to be trained (see below for details of training requirements). The result of training is the attachment of a numeric weight to each link. When the neural network is in real-life operation, the numeric weight is used to multiply the value of the signal provided as output from the connected neuron in the previous layer to provide a weighted value. The weighted values of all the links are then aggregated to form a combined input value for the connected neuron in the current layer. The neuron then transforms the input value, using an appropriate transformation function, into the value that is output from the neuron. Figure 3.4 provides a diagram of a simple neural network with one hidden layer.

Neural networks can be categorised as being of either a feedforward type or a feedback type. The neural network presented in Figure 3.4 is an example of a feedforward neural network, as none of the outputs from the output layer of the neural network form inputs to the input layer. If this were the case, then the neural network would be classed as a feedback neural network. In many cases, feedforward neural networks are sufficient to perform the task. However, if the network is representing something that is time-dependent (that is, where the input value for a particular time period depends on the output value of one or more previous time periods) then feedback neural networks are essential. A neural network that is trying to forecast some value in the future based on previous values is a particular example of where a feedback neural network is applicable.

Training involves passing a sufficiently rich set of past cases and their results through the neural network. The neural network uses these cases and their results to configure its link weights so that, when in operation, a given input value set results in a correctly calculated output value set. Properly trained, a neural network can predict the outcomes of situations in the future. Normally, a few cases are set aside for testing the neural network's configuration just before the network is put into real-life operation.

The number of business applications of neural networks is increasing. This is being fuelled, at least in the UK, by the active support of neural network applications within business by Government. Specifically, the Department of Trade and Industry (DTI) is funding a technology transfer programme to promote and introduce the concept of neural networks, and its associated technologies, to an estimated 6,000 UK companies. Thomas Cook Holidays, described in Milton (1994), already uses neural networks to aid the matching of potential customers to particular current or potential future holiday packages. The neural network was trained using statistics of known customers and the holiday that they selected for the previous year. The preparation and training of the neural network was completed in about a day. It was then tested on some of the customer data kept back for this purpose, and was found to predict the holiday destination with over 80% accuracy. The neural network can work from incomplete and/or

Fig 3.4 A simple neural network

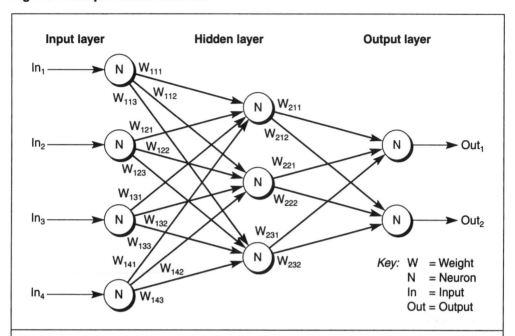

The diagram shows a simple neural network with one hidden layer. The input layer has four neurons, the hidden layer has three neurons and the output layer has two neurons. Hence, this neural network is called a {4-3-2} neural network. From training, each of the interconnections is assigned a numeric weight, which identifies the contribution of the output of the neuron on the left-hand side of the interconnection to the combined input value of the neuron on the right-hand side of the interconnection. It is the function of the neurons, together with the numeric weights, that enable a neural network to perform effectively within a given task.

imprecise customer data. It can also inform the user as to the reasons why a holiday destination was considered particularly appealing to a customer.

Neural networks are also being developed for use in Finance. The London Stock Exchange is introducing a system, which incorporates a neural network, to detect patterns of movement in financial transactions that suggest the existence of insider dealing. TSB is applying neural networks to various forecasting requirements, such as forecasting fixed interest rate movements, foreign exchange rates and insurance claims (Davidson 1994). A stock manager with Fidelity Investments uses a neural network to select the most profitable stocks, and Nestor Inc. uses a neural network to support mortgage lending decisions (Perry 1994).

With respect to MSS design and development, neural networks offer an alternative approach to active decision making support to those provided by other modelling techniques (such as those described in Chapter 6). Indeed, the forecasting system within TSB is an example of the application of neural networks to support decision making. Venugopal and Bates (1994) offer some possible neural network applications to marketing management, including segmentation of market decisions, target market decisions, sales forecasting and product test location decisions.

❏ *Viewpoint*

Barclays Bank is working on a project to use neural network technology to detect fraud as part of a data visualisation research project backed to the tune of £90,000 by the Engineering Physical Research Council. The bank is collaborating with Recognition Systems and Aston University's Neural Computing Research Group led by Professor Chris Bishop.

By displaying information about the way customers use their account in a graphical form, and comparing the patterns with previous use patterns, Barclays hopes to be able to pick out fraudulent use more easily. ∎

Reprinted with permission from *Computer Weekly*, 31st August 1995.

Neural networks provide additional and potentially very powerful capabilities to MSS developers for management support provision, in situations where the past can be used reliably to predict the future.

3.3.6 Multi-media and hyper-media applications and systems

Advances in input peripherals and storage capabilities, and in the processing power of computer systems, have made multi-media systems feasible. These systems combine different media such as text, sound and image (photographs, scanned images and video) into an integrated system. Nowadays, multi-media systems for person-to-person(s) communication (such as videoconferencing, which is described in Chapter 4) are becoming increasingly popular. In this section, attention is focused on multi-media software applications.

Within a multi-media software application, a user progresses through information items in different media formats either in a sequential manner (the application restricts the user to one pre-defined pathway through the information) or in a non-sequential manner (where the user selects the path from possibly thousands of different paths). A multi-media application that allows users choice over which path to follow at any point in time is referred to as a hyper-media application.

The programming of a hyper-media application involves the specification of nodes and links. Nodes contain information in one or more media formats. At specified points, a node's information may contain links to other nodes. When the user of the hyper-media application finds one or more links at a node, a decision needs to be made as whether to stay with the current node or traverse one of the links to another node and, thus, to other information. By selecting links to follow at appropriate points, the user develops a path through the information presented within the hyper-media application.

The most popular application of multi-media software is to Education. History education (such as learning an aspect of music history or learning about the history of an ancient building) appears to be a well suited application area. So far, little has been published on the potential role of multi-media applications in the provision of management decision making support. Some possibilities have been suggested by Mahapatra and Courtney (1992), for example, to capture and disseminate organisational knowledge and to facilitate searching through company documents. Organisational knowledge captured within a hyper-media application system would enable past decisions to be recorded to inform future decisions and to facilitate training of new company employees. Videos of meetings held, any sounds of interest (for example, the sound of a particular defect in manufacturing equipment) and any reports produced could be stored and inter-linked. Becoming familiar with a new MSS may also be facilitated through a multi-media application which provides information on how to operate and use the MSS most effectively.

3.3.7 Virtual reality systems

Virtual Reality (VR), although originally applied to the entertainments industry, is becoming increasingly viewed as an important concern for other business sectors. Many companies are developing VR applications and the Frost and Sullivan market research company expects the VR market will be worth at least $1 billion by 1997 (Cheek 1994). This upsurge in VR business is expected as better hardware becomes available to cope with the resource-intensive nature of VR, better quality software becomes available for VR applications, and business interest is heightened in the possibilities that VR may provide for competitive advantage.

A VR application provides real-time, interactive 3D graphics which one or more users can manipulate directly. Manipulation of the graphics occurs by monitoring the movements of the human body, such as head, hand and leg movements. Typically, the user wears a special helmet or eye glasses for all-around graphic display and the monitoring of head movements, and a special glove for monitoring hand movements. The helmet and gloves have sensors that relay a particular movement to the computer system, which determines the graphical image to be projected onto the screen to reflect the movement made. Treadmills are used to permit walking and to relay that movement to the computer system. Graphical updates are very resource intensive, and, as a consequence, most users of current VR applications experience a time delay between movement and graphical update.

VR has many potential business applications. The most recognised areas of application are the interrelated functions of design/construction and marketing/sales. Using VR software, designers can view the results of their designs, in terms of operation, safety and aesthetic appeal, before the designs are actualised. Dragon Exhibitions has a VR system that takes a specification of exhibition requirements from a client and provides a view of what the exhibition will look like. The client then embarks on a virtual tour of the proposed exhibition stand. Changes can be made and viewed, as the client progresses through the tour. This system ensures the client eventually receives what is really required. The client is more likely to go ahead with a contract and to continue using the service in the future (Cheek 1994).

The construction industry has also started to use VR systems. An architect's drawings of a building can be transferred onto a VR system. The architect can experiment with a design and appreciate what it would be like to reside in a building by 'virtually walking around it'. Once the design is agreed, the VR application can be used by prospective customers to gain a much better understanding of what the building offers than by looking at written plans. It is envisaged that this facility will persuade more potential customers to purchase buildings before they have been constructed.

Other example VR applications are described in Patel and Cardinali (1994). Most current applications support decisions made by professional specialists rather than by management. VR has the potential to support management decisions where high visualisation is required, either in terms of the subject of decision making or in terms of the process of decision making. With respect to the subject of decision making, visualisation of the options open to management may be very helpful. For example, supposing a decision needs to be made by a car dealer chain about which of several buildings is to be used for a new showroom. Having a VR simulation of several suitably sized buildings on offer allows management to appreciate which may be the most suitable with regard to their internal and external design. In terms of the process of decision making, VR may be able to incorporate some of the human aspects of group decision making that other technologies such as Teleconferencing (described in Chapter 4) fail to provide. With VR, meeting participants could virtually meet in a room and converse there, seeing and hearing each other as if they were located in the same place. This would create a similar effect to that expected within the MIRROR distributed meeting facility being investigated at the University of Arizona (Chappell et al. 1992), with the added bonus that VR meetings could take place at any location rather than in specially designed meeting rooms. However, before VR can be of real benefit, less cumbersome methods of tracking movements of all kinds need to exist.

3.3.8   The Internet

Of all the technological developments that have become popular over recent years, the Internet must be the one most widely spoken about. This is due to its vast potential for personal and business use. An internet (with a small i) is a collection of interconnected networks that functions as one seamless network. The Internet (with a capital i) is the name of one such internet. The Internet, sometimes referred to as the Information Superhighway, is the world's biggest computer network.

The Internet is not new. US military research in the late 60s laid the foundations for the Internet by the introduction of the ARPAnet; a network purpose built to connect organisations participating in Government sponsored research projects. The majority of ARPAnet users were based in educational establishments. The Internet grew gradually, although commercial use was not permitted until the US government issued a statement endorsing its commercial application in 1991. Since this statement was issued, growth of the Internet has been prolific, from approximately 3,000 interconnected networks in 1991 to approximately 46,000 networks at the beginning of January 1995. In 1994 alone, the number of host computers linked to the Internet doubled. The total number of Internet users is estimated to be growing by ten percent every month.

The services available through the Internet are already substantial. Not only are electronic mail (e-mail) and document transfer facilities available, but users can subscribe to user groups for sending and retrieving information on specialised topics. The World Wide Web (WWW), started in 1992 in Europe, enables information, resident on thousands of server machines throughout the world, to be accessed via the Internet through an appropriate WWW browser tool. The WWW can be described as an enormous hyper-media application system, spanning the entire Internet. A web of indices enables users to locate the information of interest.

Commercial companies are investigating how their services can be made available over the Internet. Some services are already available. For example, companies are adding to the WWW, providing information that describes their products and services. The Electronic Newstand service provides extracts of journals and magazines on-line, with an electronic means of subscription. Thousands of people access the Newstand each day. However, so far, subscription numbers have been disappointing, averaging 10 per week for each of the more popular titles. Financial companies are introducing monthly or weekly information on the Internet concerning their financial performance. The information is available free of charge as it is seen as a marketing tool. In the same vein, Sainsburys plc provides an on-line wine and price list for customers to view. On-line shopping services, where users can browse product catalogues and place orders electronically, have also been developed. However, like the Newstand, information access is substantial but solid commitments to purchase are relatively small in number so far.

Some of the current resistance to using the Internet for product ordering and for providing services can be attributed to concerns over Internet security. Although the perceived threat may be worse than the actual threat (we use the postal service, fax and telephone frequently to convey sensitive information and financial transactions, despite the fact that none of them is wholly secure), this situation has to be overcome before commerce can embrace the Internet fully as an alternative to, or even a replacement for, conventional services. Methods are needed by which financial transactions can be properly authenticated, and personal or sensitive information can be encrypted.

❑ *Viewpoint*

Firms need to be on the Net now, says report

IT departments should start setting up Internet specialist units in order to provide their companies with both the facilities and the vision needed to exploit new ways of doing business, according to new research.

Forrester Research, which has always rejected the Internet hysteria, believes that companies should nonetheless start preparing now for an Internet presence, beginning with the IT department. It also believes Internet activity will encourage and reinforce links between IT and end-users.

The Internet has been "vastly overblown as the next major sales channel," Forrester says, but it adds, "Over the next 18 to 24 months, companies must begin to offer external E-mail connections as a basic customer service. While mail is hardly a flashy application, we believe it will be a requirement of doing business."

Pioneering companies will extend parts of their systems to the outside world through developments of the World Wide Web, giving customers and suppliers access to ordering, accounting and information applications using multimedia.

This is still some way off, but there could be significant progress before the end of the century, according to Forrester director Mary Modahl.

"At present consumers are surfing the Net but no-one buys anything. A dozen pizzas a week, two or three bouquets: these are the dismal sales figures. However, the barriers that make the Internet difficult will fall within three years and the World Wide Web will soon offer businesses significant promise."

Meanwhile, IT departments need to be prepared, Forrester says. Its latest report says departments need to set up a specialised Internet group, with "professional mastery" of topics ranging from security to Internet tools, and the written and unwritten rules of the Internet, known as Netiquette.

The formation of an Internet unit in IT does not mean that companies will fall into the old problem of IT specialists dominating business use of technology and putting off end-users. Forrester says, IT will provide two critical elements: the infrastructure for exploiting the Net, and the vision to show users the potential. ∎

Reprinted with permission from *Computer Weekly*, 27th July 1995.

❑ *Viewpoint*

Cyber-cheques idea bounced round UK banks

Britain's top banks are being encouraged to join a consortium developing a system to send cheques electronically over the Internet.

The plan, the latest in a series of attempts to develop electronic commerce, is the brainchild of a US group, the Financial Services Technology Consortium, which involves seven banks including Citibank, Bank of America and the Bank of Boston, plus suppliers IBM and National Semiconductor.

The consortium believes that development of an electronic cheque will complement moves by a string of interested parties – including Microsoft, Mastercard, Visa, Mondex and personal financial software maker Intuit – to develop secure financial systems.

"Our goal is a cheque-like mechanism working on the Internet," said John Doggell, director of applied technology at the Bank of Boston.

Doggell was in London last week to discuss the proposal with British banks. The consortium is currently working with the Bank of Montreal to incorporate international input to the scheme. He said the consortium plans to demonstrate the electronic cheque concept in September or October, with a trial due next year.

The system, which incorporates digital signature standards and secure host algorithms, will support the Rivest-Shamir-Adleman security mechanism, and involves the concept of pulling a transparent wrapper around the cheque to prevent tampering. Additional encrypted security could be added, Doggell said.

The consortium insists that there will be a need for electronic cheques, despite a previous concentration on the electronic cash idea, and credit card authentication. ∎

Reprinted with permission from *Computer Weekly*, 31st August 1995.

The Internet provides several possibilities for furthering MSS design and development. It enables on-line information services to be set up, which could be used by their originating company for product and service analysis and evaluation. For example, companies have set up on-line user groups associated with their products, providing them with an easy way of evaluating customer satisfaction and gaining valuable insight into future customer needs. External information regarding competitors, and general demographic and economic trends, is also available through subscription on the Internet (Dow Jones already provides information scavenger services for users across the network as well as its traditional on-line financial information). Eventually, MSS product vendors, or possibly MSS product brokers, could provide MSS products to companies across the Internet on a limited loan basis. A contract would be established, similar to a Service Level Agreement (SLA) agreed between purchaser and provider of facilities management. Possibly of greatest use in one-off situations, this service would allow companies the opportunity to utilise the most appropriate software for a particular management support requirement, without having to purchase the software outright.

3.3.9   Data warehouses

Data warehouses are concerned with internal data access, integration and sharing. Like the Internet, the ideas behind data warehouses are not new. For instance, Information Centres (ICs) have been available within larger companies for many years. ICs perform a similar function to that expected of data warehouses; they allow users to access corporate data repositories and to extract data of interest for subsequent manipulation using packages such as spreadsheets. The principal difference between ICs and data warehouses lies with the roles that each is perceived, by management, to play within the organisation. Essentially, ICs are perceived as support services. Data warehouses, on the other hand, are perceived as being of great strategic importance to a business, enabling more informed management decision making to take place.

A data warehouse serves as the repository of all corporate data. The data is logically centralised, even though it may physically reside on several distributed computers. The data within the data warehouse can only be read; any updating is performed by the underlying Transaction Processing Systems (TPS) that feed data to the data warehouse. Programs are run at periodic intervals to extract and consolidate data from one or more TPS, and to verify that the consolidated data is internally consistent, in the required format and at the right level of detail.

Data warehouses may structure data in a multi-dimensional format, rather than just the two-dimensional, tabular format of relational database systems. (Much commercial data is more naturally represented in a format that has greater than two dimensions, although data with more than five dimensions is rare. Take, for example, an organisations' sales by product by store by month. This data is most naturally stored in a three-dimensional data format.) Users of the data warehouse can then manipulate data (but not change it) directly using appropriate software. When multi-dimensional data repositories are involved, this manipulation activity is referred to as 'slice and dice'. This term is explained in greater detail by the illustration and description provided in Figure 3.5. Taking the sales example above, a user can 'slice and dice' the data to extract the total store sales figures for a particular product of interest, for each month of a given year. This extract of the data could then be imported into a familiar spreadsheet package for graphical analysis. Figure 3.6 provides a logical view of a data warehouse's role within the organisation and its relationships with other computerised systems.

Implementing a data warehouse is rarely easy. There are technical difficulties in providing a single, consistent pool of data from many disparate data sources. Different meanings may be attached to the same business term by different business functions.

❑ *Viewpoint*

There was room for some 240 delegates at a conference on data warehousing which some 1,200 people wanted to attend earlier this year. A survey of these enthusiasts showed that a quarter (26%) were already using a data warehouse and two-thirds were considering the investment.

Most companies wanted to use warehousing as an aid to sales and marketing functions whose constantly changing interests have not been well served by traditional data processing. Traditional database query methods just cannot cope with the number-one concern of delegates: the ability to run queries on-line and interactively instead of submitting standard or laboriously constructed search statements.

The main business issue was the need to justify the significant investment the technology requires. As a close second in ranked importance was the question of finding sponsorship from senior management. ■

Reprinted with permission from *Computer Weekly*, 14th September 1995.

Fig 3.5 The 'slice and dice' approach to data manipulation

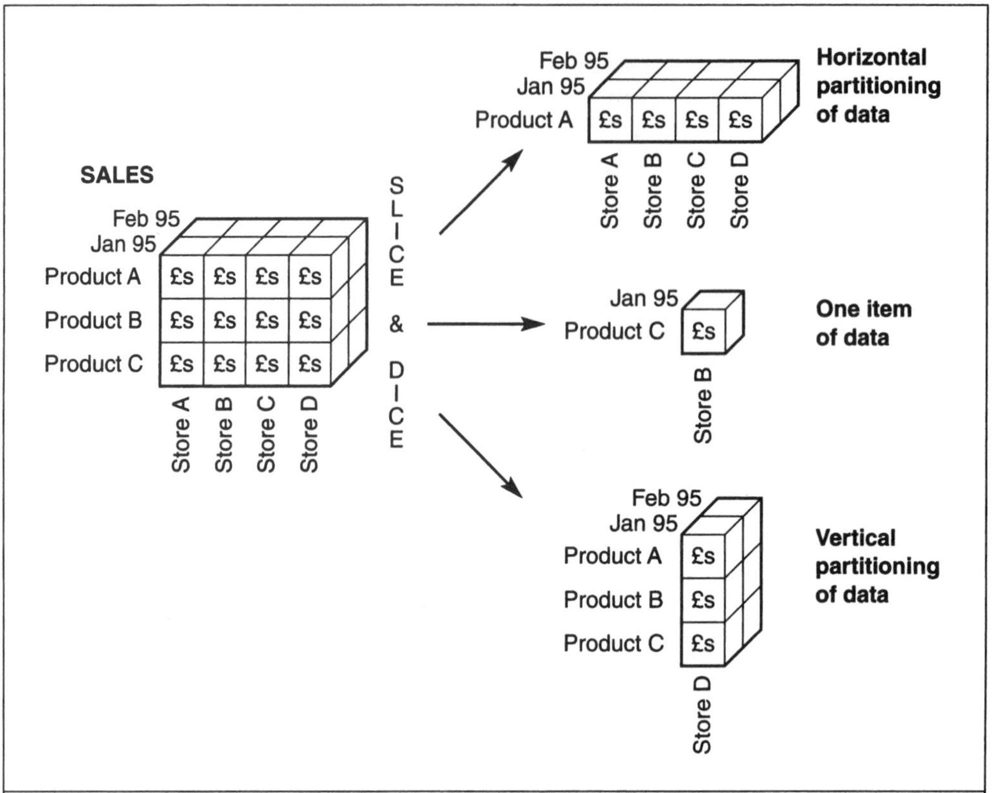

A 'slice and dice' capability allows the user to extract the required portions of multi-dimensional data quickly and easily. Take, for example, the three-dimensional sales data portrayed in the above diagram. Sales for each product, for each store and for each month are stored in £s values. Using a 'slice and dice' capability, a horizontal partitioning of the data (such as product A's sales only), a vertical partitioning of the data (for example, store D's sales) or a specific data item (such as the particular sales value for January for product C for store B) can be extracted. These are only a few of the ways that a 'slice and dice' capability can essentially 'carve up' data. Totals and counts of values can also be produced.

This can lead to differences in the data stored by the business functions with respect to the term, which have to be resolved. Social factors, such as the attitudes of departmental management to the public availability of departmental performance data in the data warehouse, may have negative repercussions on implementation activities.

One company that has managed to develop a data warehouse is British Petroleum (BP) (Warren 1994). It is considered to be successful by BP's IT management as it allows easy and rapid access to consistent corporate data directly by a large number of non-IT specialist users (over 300). The data warehouse collates data, stored in a two-dimensional format, from a variety of financial, research and development databases, and from selected TPS within the company. It integrates the data to form a separate two-dimensional relational database. The relational database acts as a consistent corporate data repository. Data extraction occurs each night to ensure the data repository is sufficiently up-to-date to be useful. Holos software, from Holistic Systems, provides a multi-dimensional data storage facility and a 'slice and dice' facility. Portions of the corporate data repository are extracted and transformed to be stored in Holos' multi-dimensional data store. BP managers can subsequently analyse the data using Holos, using the 'slice and dice' facility. Alternatively, data can be imported from the corporate data repository into local spreadsheet facilities.

Fig 3.6 The role of a Data Warehouse and its relationships with other corporate computer systems

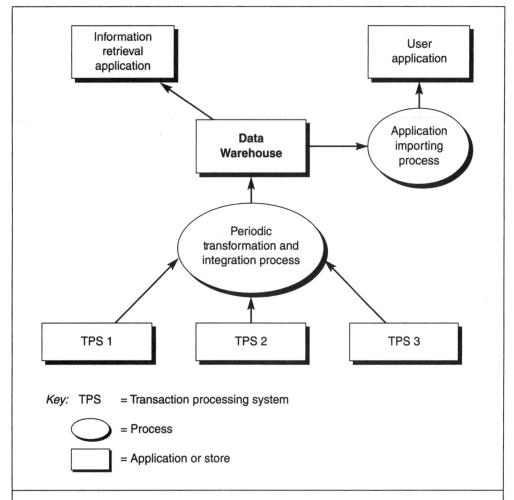

Existing transaction processing systems provide the raw data upon which the warehouse is based. This data needs to be extracted at periodic intervals, and transformed and integrated into a single consistent pool of data which forms part of the data available within the data warehouse. User applications can access this pool of data. Applications can retrieve information from it directly, using an available information retrieval facility with slice and dice capability (if the data warehouse is in multi-dimensional format). The resultant information can be copied and imported into a local application for subsequent manipulation and analysis.

Integrated data repositories, of any kind, are important to MSS provision. They provide consolidated data sets, from which data can be extracted and manipulated to provide the appropriate management support.

3.4   SUMMARY

This chapter has reviewed the history of MSS evolution from a technological perspective, and has described several of the more important recent technological advances that are influencing, or are expected to influence more significantly, MSS design and development. Technology offers MSS developers new opportunities in two principal ways: by providing greater capacity to integrate hardware, software and communications facilities, and by providing enhanced MSS functionality upon which MSS developers can draw. In all cases, technology must be matched to organisational need. All the technological advances discussed in Section 3.3 were seen to improve the opportunities available to MSS development in at least one of the two aforementioned ways.

In the years to come there will undoubtedly be other advances that will have a bearing on MSS design and development. It is a difficult yet essential task for MSS developers to keep a close watch over possibilities presented by new technologies.

Finally, this chapter has provided justifications for one of the fundamental premises upon which this book is based. From the review of MSS evolution and of several recent technological advances, there is evidence that the integration of computing technology is progressing rapidly. It is already possible to provide a physical MSS implementation which provides an integrated set of facilities in support of an organisational need, each facility of which would traditionally have been associated with a particular MSS type, such as an MIS or a DSS. Companies are embracing this opportunity for greater integration. Functionality is the key issue within modern MSS design and development. Organisational management are concerned with the functionality provided within MSS, not with how they are labelled. Determining the functionality required, and integrating systems capabilities to provide that functionality, is the principal task of MSS developers.

The remaining chapters within Part I of this book focus on the functionality available for use within MSS today, and on the approaches and techniques available to aid MSS development.

References

Ackoff R (1967) Management Misinformation Systems. *Management Science*, Vol. 14, No 4, pp.147–156.

Birtwistle G M, Dahl O-J, Myhrhaug B and Nygaard K (1973) *SIMULA BEGIN*. Auerbach Publishers Inc., Philadelphia, PA, USA.

Boaden R and Lockett G (1991) Information Technology, Information Systems and Information Management: Definition and Development. *European Journal of Information Systems* Vol 1 No 1, pp. 23–32.

Boyle B (1995) Why Client/Server can cost you dear. *Computer Weekly* July 13th Edition. p. 14.

Brown A (1991) *Object-oriented Databases*. McGraw-Hill.

(References continued on p. 75)

CASE STUDY: GLOUCESTERSHIRE CONSTABULARY

A force to be reckoned with

by Emma Mansell-Lewis

Although it seemed a commendable idea at the time, the Government's mandate that Britain's police forces must provide regular performance indicators, such as incident response times, has found many constabularies struggling to wrest the appropriate statistics from their operational systems, which were not designed to provide management information.

But Gloucestershire Constabulary had a marked advantage over other forces in that it had already developed a data warehouse to provide just this type of information and more. The development had come about through necessity as much as technological progress.

Dave Kent, the force's IT manager, explains. "The command and control system, for example. is designed to log an incident and then allocate a resource to that incident. It is not designed to collect information. Yet it holds a lot of useful information such as the length of time it takes to respond to an incident."

He adds, "There was also a need to standardise and consolidate information about people, which was located across several different systems."

The Gloucestershire Constabulary is one of 43 police forces serving England and Wales. It covers a diverse rural and urban area with a population of over half a million people. and in a typical year it will deal with more than 60.000 crimes and 170,000 incidents, ranging from cases of stray sheep to multiple road accidents.

It was back in 1992 that the force recognized the need for a tool to extract management information from its many computer applications. To fulfil this need, consultants Hoskyns were called in to provide a Management Information System (MIS).

Reveals Kent, "The objective of the MIS was to centralise pockets of information from all over the force. We wanted reporting and Executive Information System (EIS) style

facilities, not just a standard database tool. The Hoskyns solution supplied an IBM RS/6000 with an SAS database and SAS software to take data from the Command and Control systems."

Hoskyns completed its part of the project in November 1992 and at that point Sergeant Paul Collins joined the development team to initiate the next phase.

Collins says, "Information is the life blood of police work. The MIS touches on most aspects of policing in Gloucestershire, so we needed a system that could easily integrate the different computers we run."

At this stage the applications were not user friendly. With police resources stretched, the constabulary needed a system that was easy to understand and operate without the need for specialist training. and which would be relevant to all tiers of the force.

Information manager John Sproston explains, "SAS Institute helped us to develop a pilot system which allows people with little or no technical knowledge to get results using only a mouse to point and click on push buttons."

However, as Kent adds, there were some clear lessons learnt during this phase. "A project such as this should be organisation driven rather than IT driven. Perhaps at the start we approached it from the wrong direction: it has only really taken off since the user community has taken control."

He adds: "The one thing that it is absolutely critical to get right is the data model. It must reflect the way your organisation operates. For Gloucestershire Police force we are interested in persons, locations and events. We set up the data model right from the outset."

The MIS is now developing into a fully fledged data warehouse providing information for day-to-day use and strategic planning. Development is led by a user group which

▶

includes representatives of all the five Territorial Police Divisions and specialist departments.

Chairman of this user group is Superintendent David Jackson who comments, "We wanted to provide a system that could benefit our staff instead of imposing a specification from the centre which would probably be of less relevance. We have achieved this and continue to take the views and needs of users into account in designing a system to meet their needs."

Currently the system is taking information from three internal data sources and one external; a demographic feed based on census information provided by Gloucestershire County Council.

Kent insists, "We need to draw in more information from more applications. We need to improve the presentation of information to the users and then move to develop other, more sophisticated applications such as financial models."

However, Ken concedes that the project is a victim of its own success when it comes to getting the users on board. "There is a huge learning curve," he says. "It has been a long process. It is difficult for the users to envisage something they have not seen.

"The possibilities for analysis are unlimited, with more information and improved presentation with the system, but we have a big education process to undertake with the users: they want more before we can fully explain what they already have." And that, he believes, is a resources problem.

"You do need specialised users who can think laterally and are outside the IT department," he says. With this in mind, the force has recently created an information department designed to meet the needs of the users.

Even at such an early stage – with Kent maintaining that they are only 10% into the project – benefits have been attained. "We can use people more efficiently, which is absolutely key. As a police force we have always got more things to do than we can handle. But the benefit of providing consolidated information to help solve crime is considerable."

On the front line. the system provides operational managers with information about areas of greatest need. Crime Management Units can use the data warehouse to analyse crime trends and, by drawing in data such as the previously-mentioned census statistics, can diagnose the root causes of problems .

Special units such as Gloucestershire's Operation Gemini – an initiative designed to tackle burglary and car crime – can then be directed at the areas identified by the data warehouse as in need of specific attention. In this way, resources are now focused where the need is greatest.

Meanwhile, there are the performance indicators. One of the main users of the SAS-based data warehouse is the force information officer, Mandy Hutson-Smith.

In addition to developing the use of information throughout the force, Hutson-Smith is also responsible for submitting statutory reports to the Home Office on 25 different performance indicators.

She says, "The new system has considerably reduced the time I spend gathering information. Reports from the Crime Recording System, which used to take hours to produce, now take seconds."

The next move, along with increasing the data feeds into the warehouse, is to extend the user base outside the headquarters to those in operations. The potential benefits of the system in this area are great.

As deputy divisional commander at Cheltenham Police Station, Chief Inspector Ian Jones comments, "The data warehouse allows us to draw together information that was previously dotted about in different locations. We can now analyse the data and make better use of our resources at a time when they are being cut in real terms."

Kent concludes, "This is a project that will never finish. We have started small and there was a big learning curve: it took one developer a year to learn the data structure and a year to get involved in the presentation of data in a useful way to the users. Once that is achieved the benefits are exponential." ∎

Reprinted with permission from *Computer Weekly*, 10th August 1995.

References continued

Chappell D A, Vogel D R and Roberts E E (1992) The MIRROR Project: A Virtual Meeting Place, *25th Anniversary Proceedings of the Hawaii International Conference on Systems Sciences* Vol IV. pp. 23–33.

Cheek M (1994) Imagine what you could do with IT. *Computer Weekly* June 9th Edition. pp. 46–47.

Coad P and Yourdon E (1991) *Object-Oriented Analysis*. Yourdon Press.

Codd E F (1970) A Relational Model of Data for Large Shared Data Banks. *Communications of the ACM* Vol 13 No 6. pp. 377–387.

Cox B (1984) Message/Object Programming: an Evolutionary Change in Programming Technology. *IEEE Software* Vol 1, No 1. pp. 50–61.

Date C J (1990) *An Introduction to Database Systems, Volume 1* Fifth Edition. Addison-Wesley.

Davidson C (1994) At the Cutting Edge. *Computer Weekly* July 7th Edition. pp. 28–29.

Hugo I (1991) *Practical Open Systems*. NCC Blackwell.

Fidler C S and Rogerson S (1995) The Term 'Management Support Systems' comes of age. *Systemist* Vol 17 No 4. pp. 219–232

Freedman D (1991) The Open Road. *CIO* Vol 4, No 13. pp. 62–63.

Goldberg A and Robson D (1983) *Smalltalk-80; the Language and its Implementation*. Addison-Wesley.

Ledbetter R (1993) Paper Mill embraces Open Systems with Open Arms. *Manufacturing Systems* Vol 11 No 9. pp. 42–48.

Mahapatra R K and Courtney J F (1992) Research Issues in Hypertext & Hypermedia for Business Applications. *Database* Fall Edition. pp. 10–18.

Milton R (1994) IT with an IQ. *Personal Computer World* March Edition. pp. 320–324.

Patel H and Cardinali R (1994) Virtual Reality Technology in Business. *Management Decision* Vol 32 No 7. pp. 5–12.

Perry Jnr. W G (1994) What is Neural Network Software? *Journal of Systems Management* September Edition. pp. 12–15.

Rumbaugh J, Blaha M, Premerlani M, Eddy F and Lorensen W (1991) *Object-Oriented Modelling and Design*. Prentice-Hall.

Sargent G and Miglautsch T (1995) Implementing a Client/Server Decision Support System on a large Database. *Proceedings of the 13th International Conference of the Association of Management* Vol 13 No 1. pp. 215–218.

Scott Morton M (1971) *Management Decision Systems*. Harvard University Press.

Semich J W (1994) What's the Next Step after Client/Server? *Datamation* 15th September Edition. pp. 26–34.

Stroustrup B (1983) Object-oriented Languages for the Mackintosh. *ACM SIGPLAN Notices* Vol 17 No 1. pp. 42–51.

Stroustrup B (1986) *The C++ Programming Language*. Addison-Wesley.

Van Der Lans R F (1989) *The SQL Standard: a Complete Reference*. Prentice-Hall.

Venugopal V and Baets W (1994) Neural Networks & their Applications in Marketing Management, *Journal of Systems Management* September Edition. pp. 16–21.

Warren L (1994) Super Stores. *Computer Weekly* September 8th Edition. pp. 26–27.

Review questions

1 Put the following list of MSS types into order of their conception, and for each type briefly describe the catalysts that led to their development;

Decision Support Systems (DSS)
Management Information Systems (MIS)
Executive Information Systems (EIS)
Office Information Systems (OIS)

2 Identify the two general opportunities that technological advances provide to MSS developers and their organisations.

3 Which of the technological advances listed in Table 3.1 influence, or are expected to influence, MSS design and development by providing:

Greater integration of hardware
Greater integration of software
Greater integration of communications
Greater ability to access and integrate data from disparate data sources
Greater ease of use of software systems

Briefly give reasons for your choice in each case.

4 Describe several ways you believe Virtual Reality, Neural Networks and Multi-media applications systems could aid management decision making.

5 'Functionality is the key issue with modern MSS design and development.' Discuss what is meant by this statement.

Project ideas

Here are two possible projects.

1 Review the current year's publications of a popular computer magazine, such as *Computing* or *Computer Weekly*, and identify two or three technological advances that are being talked about within the Computing industry. Prepare a concise description of your chosen advance. Also write down your own thoughts on how important the advance is to MSS design and development and how it is, or could be, employed within MSS design and development. In your tutorial group, present your description and thoughts, in the same time slot as other students who have identified the same advance (if this situation exists). After each advance has been presented, a group discussion takes place leading to a consensus view of the importance and impact of the technology on MSS design and development.

2 Visit a local company and perform a review of their MSS. Ask the IT manager about general trends in the company's provision of MSS. Also ask whether any of the technological advances described in this chapter are being employed, or are expected to be employed, within the company and its provision of management support, and the reasons why, or why not. Present your findings to your tutorial group. While listening to the presentations of others, seek to identify any commonalities across the presentations concerning the trends in MSS provision and the (potential) employment of the specific technological advances within MSS. Does your group view tally with that presented in this chapter? If not, why not?

CHAPTER 4

Information Handling Support with MSS

4.1 INTRODUCTION

In Chapter 2, an MSS was defined as *a computer-based information system that supports management via support of decision making and/or information handling activities.* The purpose of this chapter is to provide an overview of the methods by which MSS can support the information handling activities of management.

Information handling involves both information preparation and communication (sub)activities. Support for information preparation concerns the design and structure of electronic documents, which may have components of several different media formats (for example, textual, graphical, scanned images, and even video clips and sound). Support for information communication activities concerns the methods by which the dissemination of information/documents, from some source point to some destination point, takes place and the methods by which computer systems can facilitate information/document sharing.

Documents, at various stages of preparation, need to be stored electronically, even if they are to be disseminated as soon as the final version is achieved. Computerised information dissemination also requires the document to be stored at certain stages between the document's source and destination. Thus, computerised document storage and subsequent retrieval are integral parts of information handling support. These topics will be touched upon briefly at appropriate points, as will the input and output peripherals that facilitate the capture of the components of a document and the presentation of documents in human-readable form respectively.

The emphasis of this chapter is on the MSS functionality that aids information handling activities. Therefore, descriptions focus principally on the capabilities provided for information handling rather than on underlying technical configurations. Reference will however be made to particular technology, including issues previously described in Chapter 3, where appropriate.

The structure of this chapter is as follows. Section 4.2 focuses on MSS information preparation support and Section 4.3 focuses on information communication support. It is worth noting that several of the software products mentioned by name in either Section 4.2 or 4.3 may support both information preparation and communication. Indeed, they may also be able to support decision making. This is to be expected, as MSS functions, rather than the physical systems, are the main emphasis of description. Finally, Section 4.4 provides a summary of the chapter.

At the end of this chapter the reader should understand:

- *The MSS functionality currently available for information preparation support.*
- *The MSS functionality currently available for information communication support.*

4.2   INFORMATION PREPARATION SUPPORT WITHIN MSS

As stated in Chapter 2, in order for information to be of maximum value, it must be:

- in a clear and concise form
- accurate and complete
- communicated at the right time
- relevant to the recipient.

The effective preparation of documents is key to ensuring that the information conveyed is clear, concise and complete. This requires thoughtful planning of the document's structure and content by the document author, or authors (when a joint document authoring activity is taking place). Decisions also need to be made regarding the choice of media to be used at specific points for conveying information. Some of the more recent document preparation systems may offer the possibilities of using image, sound and/or video media in addition to the more traditional textual, graphical and tabular forms.

Creating a document is an iterative process. Structure, content and/or media formats change as document preparation progresses. Technically, the possible ways of structuring a document and the range of media available to document authors is limited by the functionality of the document preparation system being used. However, there may be other, non-technical, reasons why document structures and the range of media are restricted beyond the limitations of the document preparation system. Organisations may have document standards to which all employees are expected to adhere. These standards may prescribe a particular structure for key corporate documents. For example, an organisation may always require 'management report' documents to have:

- a title page
- an executive summary
- one or more sections, the last section being a 'summary and conclusions' section
- a reference list if there are references to other information sources or documents
- any number of appendices.

The media to apply may also be prescribed by corporate policy or standards. For example, within formal management documents, graphics and images may be preferred to text. However, in informal documents, such as memoranda, no such restrictions may apply. Within the restrictions already placed on document preparation, individuals may also have preferences that constrain their approaches to structuring documents and use of media. Figure 4.1 highlights the ways in which factors, both technical and non-technical, can successively restrict the options available for both document structuring and media selection.

Two principal document structuring approaches have been proposed for document preparation software: the *Structure Editor approach* and the *Template approach*.

Fig 4.1 Media and structure options: influencing factors

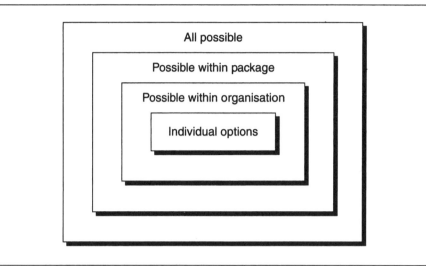

This diagram has several superimposed squares. Each square delimits an area, whose size represents, albeit simplistically, the available options for document structure and media selection. The larger the area of the square, the greater the number of options available. The diagram highlights that a document preparation system provides a subset of all possibilities for structuring a document and a subset of all media possibilities. However, the organisation may further restrict the options a document author has to structure documents and to select the medium to apply at a given time. The options may be constrained even further by the individual preferences of the document author.

The *Structure Editor approach* provides a top-down approach to document structuring. The structure of a particular type of document (for example, a progress report, a management report) is first described at the highest level of abstraction, that is at the level of the entire document. The component types found within a document of this type are then described, together with any sequencing rules between the component types, and whether any component iteration and optionality is allowed within documents of this type. Each of the component types may themselves be decomposed into other more detailed component types, together with their own sequencing, iteration and optionality characteristics. These more detailed component types may also be decomposed, and so on.

The resultant document type structure, developed through successive decomposition, has a tree-like form. Component types at the leaves of the tree provide the containers for actual document content. These component types may dictate the media that are used for component information presentation (for example, a component type specified as a text type states that instances of this component type will always be of a textual form). The designer may even complete some of the content of these most detailed component types. For example, if an executive summary is always to have the heading 'Executive Summary', then this can be defined as the content for the 'title' subcomponent type of the 'executive summary' component type of the overall document type description.

Fig 4.2 A 'management report' document structure created using a Structure Editor

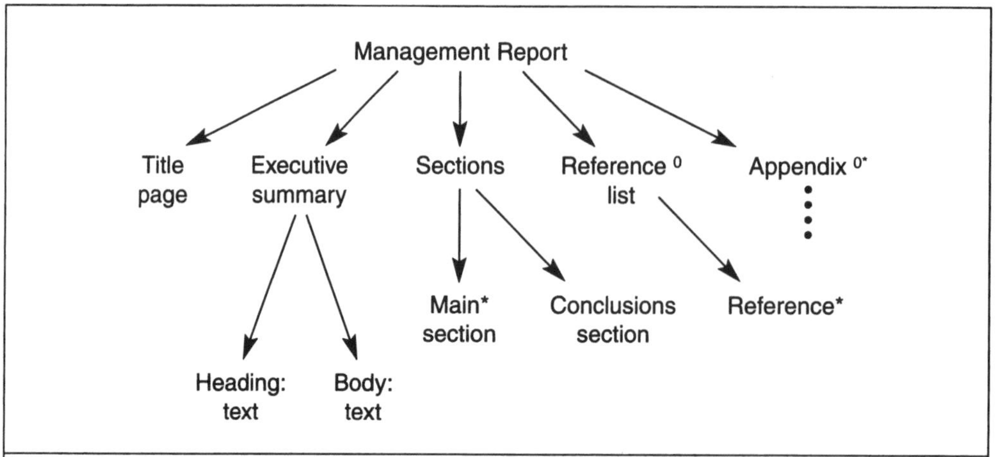

The diagram illustrates part of the structure that could be defined by a company for any document of type 'Management Report' using a Structure Editor. Any document of this type must have a title page, followed by an executive summary, followed by one or more sections, the last always being a 'Summary' section, followed by an optional reference list, followed by zero or more appendices. The executive summary will always have a title followed by the body (content) of the summary.

Figure 4.2 provides a diagrammatic view of a 'management report' document type structure which may result from using a Structure Editor approach.

Development of so-called Structure Editors was a popular research topic in the 1970s and early 1980s (see, for example, the particular work of Englebart et. al. (1973) and Walker (1981)), but this popularity appears to have diminished. The principal focus of research was the development of languages that were effective in capturing the structure of predominantly textual documents. Presentation aspects, such as page layout, font types and sizes, were not mainstream research issues. A few recent document preparation systems possess some of the characteristics of a Structure Editor approach. Outliners, for example, allow the description of documents in a tree-like form. The document can be viewed at different levels of abstraction. These levels range from an outline view of the document structure to successively more detailed levels of view, the most detailed level being that of the entire document content. Indeed, parts of the document can be seen, simultaneously, at different levels of abstraction to other parts, depending on the requirements of the individual viewing the document.

The *Template approach* to structuring documents is the preferred approach within recent document preparation systems. Document templates (also referred to as style sheets) are prepared and stored as system files. When a document is to be created based on a particular template, a copy is made of the template file. It is this copy that provides the basic structure from which the particular document is created.

A template can be as general or as specific as required. For instance, the template could be an outline of a document to the point where actual headings and numbers of sections are specified. Optionality of sections is catered for either by the deletion of redundant section(s) by the document creator or by the addition of extra sections by copying and pasting the section template provided. On the other hand, the template may simply provide a set of pre-specified paragraph styles, each associated with a particular function key. For example, a section heading paragraph style and a section body paragraph style may have been set up to facilitate standardisation and consistency in the presentation of section headings and content respectively. The document creator determines how many sections will be needed within a document and what each section's heading will be.

Lotus' AmiPro software is one of many PC-based tools that support the Template approach to document preparation. Users can add to the number of paragraph styles available within a particular style sheet (i.e. template). They can also add new personal or company-wide style sheets to the set of standard pre-specified style sheets provided by the vendor (which includes an assortment of fax, memo and letter style sheets).

The major difference between the Structure Editor approach and the Template approach is the level of restrictiveness enforced by the document preparation system. Structure editors impose very tight controls over the preparation of a document, in that deviations from its document type structure are forbidden. This may be too rigid for some organisations, where justified 'exceptions to the rule' are tolerated. Strict conformance to a document type structure may also stifle organisation creativity and learning. Templates provide guidelines for document preparation only. There is no mechanism within the document preparation system for stopping local changes to a document's structure being made. Adherence can never be guaranteed. Policies regarding the use of templates must therefore be communicated and monitored in the same way as other company policies.

Most current document preparation systems provide a document author with an identical view of the document, irrespective of whether the document is being created or whether the document has been output to a printer or whether the document is being displayed in its finished form on a screen. These document preparation systems are referred to as being WYSIWYG (acronym for 'What You See Is What You Get'). WYSIWYG capabilities were not possible within the first commercially available document editors of the 70s. Early wordprocessors, such as Vi for UNIX* systems, required document authors to embed formatting commands within documents in order, for example, to make portions of the text bold or underlined, to double space the text, and to centre the appropriate text, when output to the printer.

Sophisticated input devices enhance the capability of document preparation systems to capture information more quickly and in different media formats. For instance, Optical Character Readers (OCRs) enable pre-written text to be digitised. Most OCRs are quite good at recognising printed text, but have difficulties with the nuances of hand-written text. Voice recognition systems provide another approach to capturing text input without having to type it in at a workstation. In their current state, voice recognition systems cannot recognise natural, continuous speech, and

---

* UNIX is a trademark of AT&T

require training in order to recognise the idiosyncrasies of a user's spoken dialect. However, once trained and with clear speech, voice recognition systems have been able to reach rates of 50 to 100 words a minute (see Frampton 1994 for an overview of commercially available voice recognition systems). Image processors take a photograph or picture and digitise the image using a special purpose camera. The digitised image is stored in computer memory. It may then be edited, bit by bit, and embedded within a document. Capturing video frames and sound is also possible, although optical disk storage such as CD-ROM is often needed for the effective use of these media owing to their substantial computer memory requirements (this is particularly the case with PC-based systems). CD-ROMs provide vast storage capabilities in comparison to the more traditional magnetic disk storage devices. For instance, Long (1989) cites an example of a vendor providing an entire twenty-volume set of encyclopaedias on one CD-ROM disk.

The inclusion of video and sound within current document preparation systems, to form *multi-media document preparation systems*, is still very much in its infancy (multi-media and hyper-media applications and systems were discussed in Chapter 3). Although technically feasible, there are issues of a non-technical nature that need to be addressed before these facilities can become more widespread. Two of these issues are as follows:

- At present, most CDs are of the 'Write Once Read Many' (WORM for short) type. Current users of CDs purchase CD-ROM readers only. This allows vendors of multi-media software to maintain more control over the dissemination of their software, in that copying from CD to CD is confined to the laboratory. If organisations are preparing documents that include sound and video, then writing to CDs becomes essential. Providing organisations with writeable as well as readable CDs and associated CD writer/reader systems will place CD applications software in an identical position to software available on magnetic disks. The potential for illegal copying of software is vastly increased. (Interestingly, there are already many cases of illegal copying of CDs taking place, as mentioned in *Computer Weekly*, 21st September 1995.)
- Although it is generally felt that video and sound are very useful additions to the media types available within document preparation software systems, there is little in the way of hard evidence to confirm this position. Empirical evidence needs to ascertain the potential of multi-media document preparation systems. Evidence may sought by in-depth studies of several organisations over time in combination with more general snap-shot surveys of a larger population of companies.

Hard copies of a document may be required at various stages of preparation. There are a vast array of printers available for this purpose, differing in terms of their speed, print quality and price. For example, a laser printer is a frequent choice for organisations requiring a high quality output at a fairly rapid pace. The downside is typically the cost compared to other printer types. Colour printers are also of somewhat higher cost, but the good quality text and higher visual impact (when colour is used effectively) makes these printers attractive to many organisations. As well as adopting at least one good quality printer, companies may provide additional yet cheaper printers, such as dot-matrix impact printers, for the printing of less important documents (at least in presentation terms) such as internal memoranda and work-in-progress reports. Printers are usually shared between user workstations when operating in client server mode (client server systems were described in Chapter 3).

❏ *Viewpoint*

UK Drugs company high on document system success

UK pharmaceuticals company Zeneca is installing a client/server-based document management system to automate the vast amount of documentation demanded by drug regulatory bodies.

Zeneca will implement US specialist Documentum's Enterprise Document Management System (EDMS) as the core of its Emergent Dossier Project. EDMS will run on two Sun Sparc server 100Ls, one in the UK and one in the US and will eventually support 2,000 users throughout the world.

The new document management system replaces a variety of systems which required time-consuming compilation and validation of the entire dossier at the end of a submission project to a regulatory authority.

Instead Zeneca staff will be able to access electronically submissions in progress worldwide as they develop, greatly reducing the time required to create, approve and submit the approvals.

Achieving approval for new drugs, the supercomputing that helped design them, and the administrative software that supports their production, is one of the most stringently controlled processes in industry. The paperwork associated with getting regulatory approval is mountainous. ∎

Reprinted with permission from *Computer Weekly*, 24th August 1995.

4.3   INFORMATION COMMUNICATION SUPPORT WITHIN MSS

As stated in Chapter 2, communication requires the receipt of a message by a recipient (where the term 'recipient' embraces one or more persons), and information is said to have been communicated if the message received has value to the recipient. There are two principal approaches to information communication employed within MSS. The first approach makes explicit the transmission of some message from some location to another. The physical message transfer may require only the copying of a file from one user's file store to another user's file store on the same host computer system or server. On the other hand, the message may have to be physically transmitted across thousands of miles in order to reach its destination. However, clearly defined human roles of sender and receiver are being adopted with respect to the message, irrespective of the actual effort involved in message transferral.

The second approach to information communication creates a feeling of information sharing between users. At least from a logical perspective, a message is placed by its creator in a shared workspace. The users of the workspace are then able to view the messages created by other users. Person-to-person information communication therefore comprises the storing and sharing of messages within the common workspace environment. Figure 4.3 provides an illustration of these two approaches to information communication to aid understanding and comparison.

Current application systems that can support the visible exchange of a message between some sender and some receiver(s) are electronic mail (e-mail), Teleconferencing and Chat facilities. Joint Authoring Systems and Bulletin Boards can be used to support message sharing. These five applications systems are discussed in the following five subsections.

4.3.1   Electronic mail

Electronic mail (e-mail) systems have evolved greatly over the past twenty years. Originally available on mainframe and minicomputer systems, e-mail users were provided

Fig 4.3 The two approaches to information communication

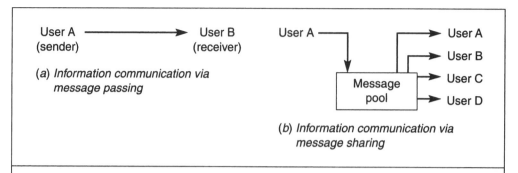

(a) Information communication via
message passing

(b) Information communication via
message sharing

This diagram illustrates the two approaches to information communication: by message passing between sender and receiver(s) and by message sharing. The diagram uses an example of User A wishing to communicate information in some way to User B. Using message passing, User A would send a message containing the information to User B. Using message sharing, User A would place the message into a pool of messages, which User B can access and view. Other authorised users can also access the pool of messages.

with basic facilities for preparing and sending messages through dumb terminals to other users of the same host computer. With the advancement of, and standardisation in, networking and the introduction of client server systems, e-mail has become an integral feature of desktop PC applications. With the appropriate e-mail facilities, users can send and receive messages both company-wide and world-wide.

E-mail usage within a company may be minimal at first, but grow rapidly once a sufficient number of employees (the so-called *critical mass*) use e-mail actively within their organisational activities. E-mail becomes a valued and standard approach to organisational communication, rather than simply an optional extra of little perceived value. Critical mass will vary between organisations, depending on a variety of contextual factors. It is also expected to depend greatly on the external communications facilities and services available through e-mail (the additional benefits of using e-mail with external connections and additional services may serve to lower the critical mass for an organisation). The relationship between critical mass and the richness of e-mail services provided is an interesting area of further research.

Present e-mail systems typically offer the following facilities to users:

● *The ability to prepare a message.* A message consists of: system-required header information (such as the message's destination(s), whether it is to be copied to any other e-mail users for information, and the subject of the message) and the actual content of the message. A special message editor allows both header information and the message content to be specified. E-mail editors can be fairly basic in their facilities: many e-mail editors allow the creation of text-based messages only. However, some e-mail systems allow users to prepare the content of messages using other more sophisticated document preparation systems. This enables documents employing other media, in addition to text, to be generated. A file created outside of the e-mail environment may need to be physically transferred to a file location recognised by the e-mail facility and embedded within a file created by the e-mail editor, which provides the system-required header information.

- *The ability to send a message to one user or to broadcast the message to several users.*
- *The ability to receive a message and to retrieve its contents.* Increasingly, messages sent through one type of e-mail software are able to be received by users of another type of software. This is due to the wider standardisation of network protocols and the increasingly open nature of systems. (Open systems were discussed in Chapter 2.)
- *The ability to store messages, both sent and received.* A received message is usually stored in a special logical 'in-tray' until read. Furthermore, users can create a personal folder for messages relating to a certain topic and direct a received message towards a particular folder for storage. Copies of messages sent are automatically stored in a special 'sent' folder.
- *The ability to forward messages received to other users* accessible through the e-mail system.
- *The ability to print and/or fax messages.*

E-mail systems may also provide the following capabilities:

- *The ability to send messages not only to those users of the same host computer or of the same LAN configuration, but also to users of different hosts and networks.* Thousands of miles may separate the sender and receiver(s). Linking the local host or network via a gateway to the Internet (described in Chapter 3) is a method by which these facilities can be provided.
- *Encryption and decryption of messages.* This facility is available when messages are sent and received within the same e-mail facility. Encryption and decryption across networks is a problem unless standards are enforced. (The Internet currently suffers from this problem are there is no controlling body to impose standard encryption/ decryption methods.)
- *Automatic notification of a message received*, possibly by the change in the colour of a mail icon, or by the flashing of a mail icon, on the receiver's screen .
- *A search facility* to enable messages either stored or not yet read to be searched by sender name, subject, date, and so forth. Search facilities may cover not only searches of header information but also searches for a specified text string within the contents of several messages.
- *Automatic or selective notifications to the sender*, when a message has been received and/or read.
- *The ability to define rules* which dictate the actions to be taken whenever some event occurs (an example of a rule could be 'to send a notification of receipt whenever a message is received from senior management'). This facility, if appropriately used, can make the e-mail system function as a basic workflow management system (Bate and Travell 1994 provide a description and review of workflow management systems).
- *An address book* of user e-mail addresses, with associated textual descriptions for easier recognition. The creation of abbreviations for user e-mail addresses may be possible by each user for personal use.

E-mail products, available commercially within the PC-LAN market, include cc:mail from Lotus Development Corporation, Mail from Microsoft Corporation, and Firstmail from Novell Inc.. A mail messaging software review in *Network Computing* (Network Computing 1994) provides a very clear comparative analysis of the functionality of these and other products. Finally, *remote e-mail* software supports users of notebook or laptop

PCs. The software stores batches of messages for later communication when the PC is connected to either a telephone line by a modem or a computer network.

4.3.2 Teleconferencing

A Teleconferencing system enables people that are geographically dispersed to participate in a meeting, during which they communicate. The way in which meeting participant's communicate depends on the technology that is being employed. For instance, with Audioconferencing facilities, participants communicate using speech alone. This facility is normally applied to meetings conducted over two sites, although Audioconferencing can be beneficial when more than two sites are involved. Each participating site can hear the issues raised by participants at other sites almost as if the meeting was taking place at one central location.

As speech is the only medium of communication within Audioconferencing, other forms of communication, such as facial gestures and general body language, are lost. Another form of Teleconferencing, which has become extremely popular, is Videoconferencing. Here, communication is in the form of integrated sound and video. It is therefore considered to be a much richer form of electronic communication than Audioconferencing. There are two principal approaches to implementing Videoconferencing within organisations. The *Room-based Videoconferencing approach* is typically implemented within larger companies. Special meeting rooms are constructed, each of which has adequate room capacity for local participation requirements (which could be any size from a small two or three person capacity to a large lecture theatre capacity). Typically, a member of the technical support staff is present in each meeting room to ensure the technology is used effectively during the meeting and that the participants do not have to be concerned with underlying technical issues. Vendors provide customised configurations of these relatively high-cost systems, such as that found within General Electric (Gowan and Downs 1994). A possible configuration is where two public TV screens are provided within each meeting room, located in front of the local meeting participants. The pictures displayed on the TV screens are typically full motion ones. These are captured by strategically placed cameras around the meeting rooms involved. Sound is captured through microphones, which may be suspended from the ceiling of the meeting rooms for better reception. The TV screens display views of the participating meeting rooms, including what is being transmitted from the local room to the remote meeting rooms. For instance, in the case of a meeting involving two rooms (this being one of the most common situations), one TV screen displays what is being transmitted from the local meeting room to the remote meeting room, whilst the other TV screen displays a view of the remote meeting room. 'Picture-within-picture' screen displays may be possible, for example to show what is being transmitted by a particular camera at a remote or local meeting room, or, in the case of a meeting involving more than two meeting rooms, to show pictures of all remote sites simultaneously.

Figure 4.4 illustrates a possible physical arrangement for Room-based Videoconferencing.

The second approach to Videoconferencing is the *Desktop Videoconferencing approach*. Here, each participant in a meeting has a personal terminal with attached camera and microphone. In a two-participant meeting, the remote participant is displayed on the local screen. If greater than two participants are involved, then the terminal may display equally sized windows on the screen, one for the image of each

Fig 4.4 A possible physical arrangement for room-based videoconferencing

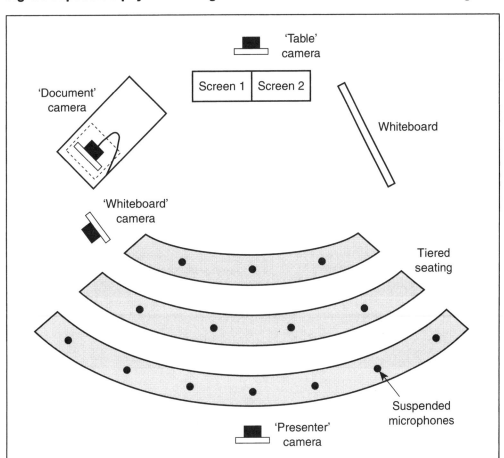

A room with tiered seating is a possible setting for this type of Videoconferencing. TV screens are placed in front of the participants within a particular room. Several cameras are required; at least one above the television screens to capture displays of the participants at the local site. There may also be a 'whiteboard' camera that focuses on the whiteboard in the room, and a 'document' camera with which document and overhead images can be captured and transmitted to remote sites.

remote participant. Alternatively, the picture of one of the participants (for example, the meeting leader or the main 'speaker' at a particular stage in time) might occupy most of the local screen, with all the other participants (apart from the local participant) displayed in smaller windows around the screen. The local participant may have control as to who is the focal participant at any point in time, and therefore who is the principal focus of the current local display.

Although full motion Desktop Videoconferencing systems are available and are increasingly popular, the freeze-frame approach (refreshed at 10 second intervals for example) is a more economical choice. Meetings involving two desktop PCs are most common.

Videoconferencing, particularly the Desktop approach, is a relatively new topic of research. A great deal of current research attention is focused on identifying the effects of Videoconferencing systems on meetings. Little, as yet, has been written about the particular effects of Desktop Videoconferencing systems. However, there are several papers that, although related empirically to the effects of the Room-based Videoconferencing approach, provide results which are applicable to both approaches. Research conducted to-date suggests that Videoconferencing is not as rich as face-to-face meetings. For example, Kydd and Ferry (1994) found that Videoconferencing systems do not always promote the same level of mutual trust and loyalty within meeting participants to that gained within face-to-face meetings. The technology also is still in its early stages: the slight delay in transmissions between sites makes the remoteness of participants visibly apparent. Full motion Videoconferencing systems are considered more effective for meeting use than freeze-frame ones. Furthermore, Videoconferencing works best when:

- Used to exchange and share information to reduce uncertainty surrounding an agreed topic, rather than within complex decision making situations, where a consensus opinion needs to be formed on some emotionally charged topic with many potential conflicting standpoints.
- Participants are previously acquainted with one another by face-to-face meetings, as rapport is already established between participants.

❑ *Viewpoint*

Open Standards set to aid videoconferencing

The Versit alliance of Apple, AT&T, IBM and Siemens is seeking to boost the growth of videoconferencing by defining and freely publishing a set of specifications to ensure that different systems can work together.

Videoconferencing is already growing fast and the Gartner Group recently estimated that sales of videoconferencing products worldwide could grow from $600m (£400m) in 1994/1995 to around $8bn by 1998.

As videoconferencing increases in popularity it is more important for different systems to work together. Leading manufacturers achieve a basic level of interoperability by conforming at least to the mandatory core of the international H.320 standard as defined by the International Telecommunications Union (ITU).

The standard, however, also includes some 200 optional features which can sometimes cause problems. The Versit group is trying to resolve the issue by publishing details of fewer than 20 options which it reckons manufacturers should follow.

Versit was formed last year to stimulate the growth of systems combining computing and communications.

For videoconferencing, Versit has published on the Internet an Implementers' Agreement which 'specifies precisely defined subsets of options and sequences of commands required for desktop voice, video and data interoperability'.

AT&T's Larry Jacobs, one of Versit's four managing directors, said "We are not trying to compete with the ITU but to add value where it is needed".

Earlier this year Versit released details of a personal data interchange specification and of a Universal Network Port based on Apple's GeoPort technology. Both can be used without fees or royalties. The first defines an electronic business card and the latter a high-bandwidth port for computers to access the full digital capabilities of modern telephone switches. ■

Reprinted with permission from *Computer Weekly*, 28th September 1995.

- Adequate training has been provided.
- Effective meeting preparation has taken place previously, including the setting of a highly focused agenda, the preparation of clear visual aids and the chairperson's personal effective preparation for the meeting.
- No more than five sites are involved, and all are utilising Videoconferencing (sites employing Audioconferencing have more difficulty in equally participating within a meeting where other sites are using Videoconferencing).
- A small number of participants (less than fifteen) are involved in an active meeting (that is, when two-way information communication exists between participants), although more participants can be accommodated when the meeting is passive in nature (where one-way information communication predominates). Meeting effectiveness decreases as the number of participating sites increases and/or as the number of participants at each site increases (in the case of Room-based Videoconferencing).
- The time of the meeting is relatively short (less than two hours) so that participants' focus of attention is maintained.

4.3.3 Chat facility

A Chat facility enables two people, remote in location, to 'talk' to one another interactively through a computer system. A user's screen is divided into two. One screen area displays the messages sent by the local user, and the other screen area displays the messages received from the remote user. All messages are echoed to the remote user as if the local user were preparing the message (that is, echoing of the message is on a letter-by-letter basis). Figure 4.5 provides an illustration of a possible Chat facility screen display.

Chat facilities provide a more interactive form of person-to-person messaging than e-mail. However, the potential for confusion exists if the receiver of a message does not wait until the sender has finished the message before responding. (This problem is akin to that experienced when normal speech is interrupted.) If interruption occurs, it can take some time to reach a point at which further effective 'chatting' can take place.

4.3.4 Joint authoring systems

Joint Authoring Systems are document preparation systems and, hence, could have been discussed in Section 4.2. However, these systems permit several people to author a document simultaneously. They all share the same information held within the document at any point on time, allowing them to view the document and comment on its content and/or structure. This information sharing provides justification for discussing Joint Authoring Systems in this section.

The normal approach to joint document authoring is to delegate the authoring of parts of the document to individuals. Each author creates his/her own part in parallel. The author of a particular part is the only person to have write access to the part: non-authors cannot change its structure and content directly, but can only annotate it. Any annotations are made available to the author for subsequent review and possible incorporation. All participants in a joint document authoring activity see the amendments made by authors immediately on their individual workstation. Interdependencies between parts of a document may be automatically monitored and authors alerted when changes in one part affect their own part(s). The delegation of document author-

Fig 4.5 A possible Chat facility screen display

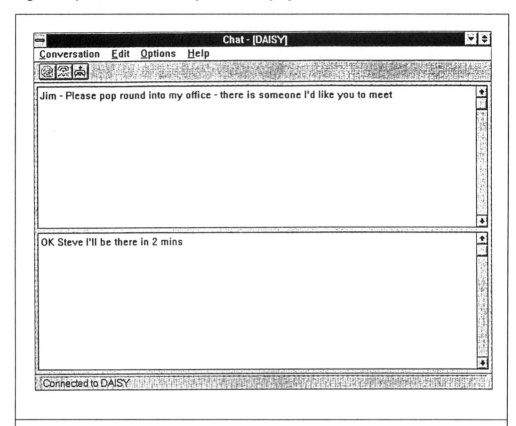

The screen is divided into two. The top screen area displays what is typed at the local terminal by Steve. The bottom screen area displays the messages as they are typed by Jim at another terminal. Chat facilities have been developed for mainframe, minicomputer and client server systems.

Reproduced with permission from *Personal Computer Magazine*, November 1992.

ship may change over time. For instance, when all parts have been developed by the appropriate individuals, total document authorship may revert to one person for overall checking and authorisation.

Joint Authoring Systems have proved beneficial in certain organisational situations. Using a Joint Authoring System has been found to quicken document development (over its production by one individual), and to encourage teamwork and team ownership of a document. A more technically complex approach to joint document authoring is where all participants in the authoring process can both view and change all parts of a document. This approach may be favoured by groups where there is prior agreement as to the document's content and where consistency in presentation style can be maintained. Minor changes, or changes of a factual nature, can be made by each participant directly on the document, without having to channel these amendments through a particular author. Research groups may find this approach beneficial:

joint papers can evolve as participants add their own ideas. However, this type of joint document authoring is inappropriate in situations where consensus as to the document's overall content and presentation style have not been established prior to the authoring process, and where individual presentation styles vary considerably. Each participant may amend the same portion of the document to reflect their personal views rather than the overall consensus of the group, leading to a state of continual amendment and re-amendment. This may also occur if no rules of presentation are laid down and each participant has their own presentation style. As a result, documents may be less than adequately cohesive and take longer to produce than if the entire document preparation had been delegated to one person at the outset.

4.3.5 Bulletin board

A Bulletin Board can be considered to be a semi-public message area. A Bulletin Board may be created to act as a platform for discussion about a particular topic, where only selected users are allowed to participate. On the other hand, public access to a Bulletin Board may be granted. Messages on the specified topic are sent to the appropriate Bulletin Board. These messages are collated into one list, which other authorised users can view and respond to as required.

4.4 SUMMARY

The purpose of this chapter was to provide an overview of the available methods by which MSS support the information handling activities of management. Information handling involves both information preparation and communication (sub)activities. Support for information preparation was the subject of Section 4.2. Within this section, two approaches to structuring documents, the Structure Editor approach and the Template approach, were described and compared. In addition, some of the input,

(Summary continued on p. 94)

❑ *Viewpoint*

Liveboard's UK debut

LIVEWORKS, a spin-off from Xerox Corporations Palo Alto Research Centre, has introduced its Liveboard system to the UK through Reflex, the Reading specialist in presentation equipment and services.

Liveboard has been available for more than a year in the US and around 150 units have been installed. It is a wardrobe-sized unit designed for use by groups working in business conference rooms.

The output of an enhanced, 486-based PC is directed, by back-projection, to a large screen which is sensitive to an infra-red pen device. The system can be used at a number of levels culminating in remote sharing of working documents and images by groups in different locations.

At its simplest, the Liveboard can be used for showing PC-based presentations and applications. A keyboard or the pen device can be used to drive applications or update figures or diagrams. The PC has the pen extensions to Windows and can handle diagrams as "ink" images. And it can handle some handwriting recognition.

The next stage is to run the Meeting Board software to turn the system into an electronic flip chart. Lists can be written onto the screen and rearranged. ■

Reprinted with permission from *Computer Weekly*, 29th September 1994.

CASE STUDY: E-MAIL MANAGEMENT

Pandora's mailbox

by Alison Classe

In the past, companies have tended to adopt electronic mail (E-mail) in a spirit of experimentation.

However, for many of them it has turned out to be not just a convenience or an executive toy but a serious tool that enables them to do business in a way they otherwise would not be able to.

Martin Telfer, IT director of leading London law firm Masons, says, "We specialise in the construction industry and there's a lot of activity in the Far East. E-mail enabled us to begin doing business there very quickly and with very low start-up costs. We had just one person out there operating from a hotel room in the first instance, but he was able to provide a quality legal service."

The E-mail connection also enabled the lawyer, who was based in Malaysia, to use head office back-up facilities, Telfer explains. It was a low-risk way of putting a toe in the water without sacrificing any professionalism. "Now we have a lot of work there and have set up an office."

Masons uses the BT GNS service to ensure that an employee anywhere in the world can connect to the E-mail system, which is based on MS Mail and Banyan VINES, for the cost of a local call. The company can meet the legal business's "impossible deadlines" by working virtually round the clock, taking advantage of time differences between offices. It has also kept rates competitive by delegating work to regional offices where overheads are lower while allowing local offices to remain linked to the expertise at head office.

As E-mail establishes itself as a serious business tool, it is increasingly being realised that implementation of E-mail systems merits its careful planning.

Phil Bryant is a consultant with standards consultancy Level-7, which has helped the likes of the DSS and the Met Office with their E-mail systems. He feels a particular area for attention in E-mail implementations is the management of users' expectations.

"There is a perception that if you have E-mail on your PC and send a message to Joe Bloggs, the message reaches his desk within two seconds of your pressing the send key. Depending on what's going on behind the scenes, that may not be possible or economic," he explains.

Formalising service level agreements, even when the customer is an internal one, can help to clarify the users' minds and avoid disappointment. "You can agree that urgent messages will be delivered within a short timeframe, but they need to think about whether some can be sent overnight."

Another important aspect of planning is the prioritisation of mailbox allocation. Bryant advises, "If you're starting from scratch, don't just say 'Let's put it on when anyone gets a new PC.' You need to put on groups that have a real need to talk to one another. That way you can build up the momentum and get support from the top."

That doesn't mean you should delay E-mail implementation until there are vast squads of users raring to go. Martin Telfer again: "We've had E-mail for about five years, but if I were starting again I'd do it sooner. We waited until the penetration of PCs was reasonably high, but with hindsight if a group of five or six people had PCs it would be worth putting them on."

Day by day, more tools are coming along to facilitate the task of managing E-mail, both from the point of view of the system administrator and for the individual end-user.

Chris Earnshaw, business development manager with IMI Computing, says, "IT's productive for the sender to send a message

▶

with a couple of key-presses. but does the recipient experience the same benefits? Certainly it's not helpful if the overworked executive has to sift through a huge in-basket, just because it's easy to copy any number of recipients on each memo."

The key, he says, is not to get your secretary to deal with your E-mail, but to implement intelligent filters and agents. Pete Smith, operations manager at mobile satellite communications provider Inmarsat, agrees, "In any mature organisation the number of E-mails received increases and you need some process to filter out or re-route unwanted or low priority messages." He adds that this will become easier with the advent of communications servers allowing message-processing rules to be executed on servers rather than clients.

Once the board takes to E-mail, security takes on a new importance. Specialist company Boldon James works behind the scenes with companies including Bull and Siemens to solve problems such as trying to ensure that messages can not be tampered with en route. Senders and receivers need to feel confident about this and the latter also need to be sure that the message was sent by the person claimed, particularly if it says "give so-and-so a pay rise".

Boldon James X.400 specialist Tony Ennis says that standards are coming along for X.400 that will enable effective security features to be used even where the products running at the sender's end are different from those at the receiver's end.

E-mail is just one of a number of message facilities and it can be irksome to have to process all of them differently. Voice processing specialist Octel is working with Microsoft on a unified messaging system to enable E-mail, faxes and voice mail to be handled through a single system, in which there will be just one set of folders and mailboxes to be administered.

Octel's director of technology strategy, Henry Hyde-Thomson, says there are a number of technological challenges, not least the size of a voicemail message.

He points out, "Sixty seconds of voice with good compression is a quarter of a megabyte. That currently poses problems if you're talking about remote access to your mailbox, but it will be possible with next-generation client/server E-mail systems such as Microsoft Exchange.

Another problem Hyde-Thomson expects Microsoft Exchange to solve is that of unavailability due to database compaction. "With Microsoft Exchange, compaction is continuously happening in the background.

Other things are being done to make the system more robust. It needs to be able to act intelligently when problems arise, so that it can continue processing in the event of a network cabling failure, for instance."

Continuity of service is an issue for many users including Inmarsat, a round-the-clock. 365-day operation. Smith says, "People are used to having E-mail available and a lot of work stops if it goes down. We have three large message databases and they regularly have to be re-indexed which requires a shutdown for three hours or more even though we use

---

Guidelines for effective E-mail

- Implement E-mail workgroup by workgroup
- Prioritise mail and send less urgent messages off-peak
- Limit unessential E-mail. If social/company information is not time critical can it go in a news-letter?
- Consider conferencing systems or "discussion databases" as an alternative to sending multiple copies of memos
- Make employees aware of "netiquette". It is easy to be too blunt when using E-mail
- If using E-mail internally, lay down guidelines for E-mail contact with customers. Should all employees be able to send E-mail to customers?
- Implement filters to automate the prioritisation of mail
- Manage multiple post offices centrally if possible
- Be aware of security implications of external E-mail in particular
- Do not abandon all human contact. Two people sitting side-by-side shouldn't normally have to communicate via E-mail

▶

the fastest available machines. We currently achieve more than 99.9% availability but of course users want 100%."

From the administrator's point of view, software is emerging to reduce the headache of E-mail. Bryant says, "As the systems become more complex, companies often find they need to introduce management tools. For instance, central management stations that allow you to manage multiple message bases from a single point. Functions that you may need include the ability to set alarms when a queue builds up somewhere, and address book synchronisation, so that once an address is added to a post office on one server it is automatically propagated across the network."

In the next generation of software, not only are the administrative tools about to improve, but there will be another simplifying factor, predicts Hyde-Thomson. "Individual servers will get quite a lot bigger. Instead of hosting 50 to 100 users, a server will be able to accommodate 250 to 500. So there will be fewer servers to manage."

If E-mail administration sounds a headache, it is possible to outsource the whole thing, including the implementation. One company offering a specialised service is Paragon Software which provides anything from an E-mail connection for an individual user, to a mail-to-mail service for companies with internal E-mail wanting a Wan connection. Paragon will also build a complete company-wide system together with subscription-based X.400 services.

Facilities management of E-mail is one way to make users aware of costs. For those who implement and manage their own E-mail, there is the consideration of whether it is a good idea to charge, perhaps on a basis of per E-mail sent. Opinions differ on this one. Obviously there are problems in calculating the exact cost of each message, and most organisations are reluctant to discourage the use of what is likely to be the most efficient mode of communication.

Alan Beer, principal consultant at ICL's Solution Centre, which runs the company's internal 25,000-user mail network and implements E-mail for clients, says, "One option might be to fund the system centrally when first starting off, and then bring in localised charging to contain demand. But it is important the system doesn't cost more than the mail itself."

IMI's Earnshaw identifies a major problem with charging. "We have algorithms," he says, "but it's difficult to marry traditional, sender-pays charging with processing mail that comes in from another organisation. You can't charge the recipient because they might not have wanted the mail in the first place. You can share the cost among all internal senders, but as you get more external mail that becomes artificial. The whole charging issue is an area that's going to explode." ■

Reprinted with permission from *Computer Weekly*, 14th September 1995.

Summary continued

storage and output facilities required for preparing and viewing documents, which may employ several different media, were highlighted. Key non-technical factors that influence the deployment of true multi-media document preparation systems within companies were discussed.

Support for person-to-person information communication was the subject of Section 4.3. Two approaches to information communication were explained, the first involving the visible exchange of messages between sender and receiver(s) and the second involving the sharing of messages/information between users. Approaches to the implementation of these approaches were described. Electronic mail (e-mail), Tele-conferencing, and Chat facilities were described as systems with which computerised message exchange can be implemented. Joint Authoring Systems and Bulletin Boards are systems that can implement an information sharing approach to communication.

Although treatment of this subject is by no means exhaustive, the descriptions of MSS information handling functionality is sufficient for the reader to grasp the essential nature of this support. The next chapter of this book focuses on the MSS functionality available for passive decision making support. There are many ways of providing passive support for management decision making. However, all of the approaches are concerned with the request and retrieval of information reports from an MSS.

References

Bate J St J and Travell N (1994) *Groupware*. Alfred Waller Ltd.

Englebart D C, Watson R W and Norton J C (1973) The Augmented Knowledge Workshop. *Proceedings of the AFIPS National Computer Conference* Vol 42. AFIPS Press. pp. 9–21.

Gowan J A and Downs J M (1994) Videoconferencing human-machine interface: a field study. *Information & Management* Vol 27. Elsevier. pp. 341–356.

Frampton R (July 7th 1994) Just Do as I Say. *Computer Weekly*. pp. 32–33.

Kydd C T and Ferry D L (1994) Managerial Use of Videoconferencing. *Information & Management* Vol 27. Elsevier. pp. 369–375.

Long L (1989) *Management Information Systems*. Prentice-Hall.

Network Computing (1994) Mail messaging. *Network Computing* April 1994. pp. 52–57.

Walker J H (1981) The Document Editor: A Support Environment for preparing Technical Documents. *ACM SIGPLAN Notices* Vol 16 No 6. pp. 44–50.

Review questions

1 Discuss the factors that may influence a document creator's approach to document structure and presentation.

2 Describe and compare the Structure Editor and Template approaches to document preparation.

3 What is WYSIWYG?

4 What is a multi-media document preparation system? What are the issues that need to be addressed before these systems may become more widespread commercially?

5 Describe and compare the two general approaches to information communication.

6 Describe the features one may expect to find in an e-mail facility.

7 List, in order of decreasing richness of information communication, the following Tele-conferencing facilities: Videoconferencing, Audioconferencing, face-to-face meeting. Justify your order.

8 Describe and compare the Room-based approach and the Desktop approach to Video-conferencing.

9 When is Videoconferencing most effective for information communication?

10 What advantages does a Chat facility offer over conventional e-mail facility? What problem may be encountered whilst 'chatting'?

11 Describe two approaches to joint document authoring. To what organisational situation is each approach most appropriate?

12 What is a Bulletin Board?

Project idea

In pairs, visit a small company and perform an evaluation of their current MSS for information handling support. It may be best to start by interviewing the person in charge of in-house IS/IT (if such a person exists), who can give you an overall view of computerised systems within the company. With respect to each system identified, summarise its operation in terms of the functionality described within this chapter, who uses it and for what purpose(s).

Provide a description of your findings to be presented to your tutorial group. You may find that some of these systems are used by non-management personnel on behalf of a particular manager. By listening to the findings of your colleagues, trends in operation, purpose and use may be identified. Also, the omission of certain MSS functionality across several small organisations is also interesting. This can also form the basis of further tutorial discussions.

Note: If the above project is too large, then an alternative approach is to make the scope of the empirical study more narrow, by concentrating on only one or two aspects of MSS functionality (for example, Teleconferencing and/or e-mail).

CHAPTER 5

Passive Decision Making Support with MSS

5.1 INTRODUCTION

The functionality available within MSS for the support of information handling activities was described in Chapter 4. This chapter reviews the functionality currently provided by MSS for passive decision making support. Passive decision making support, as defined in Chapter 2, is concerned with the provision of information reports by an MSS, which can be used to support management decision making activities. Information may be provided to management on a periodic basis, for example on a weekly, monthly, quarterly or annual basis. Alternatively, the MSS may allow users to retrieve information for decision making as needed.

This chapter has the following structure. Section 5.2 focuses on the overall nature and scope of information reporting that MSS provide for passive decision making support within organisations. Section 5.3 then examines several possible methods by which users can interact with an MSS to request information reports. Section 5.4 examines several MSS implementations that provide passive decision making support. Finally, Section 5.5 provides a summary of the chapter.

As is the case in previous chapters, the emphasis of this chapter is on MSS functionality rather than on actual physical MSS implementations. In reality, physical MSS may provide passive decision making support in several different ways. Some may also provide active decision making support and information handling support.

At the end of this chapter the reader should understand:

- *The extent of support possible within MSS and the actual support provided by current MSS for passive decision making support.*

- *Two approaches of classifying MSS information reports, one based on the content of the report, and the other based on temporal issues concerning report definition and report availability to management.*

- *The basics of several methods which can be employed within MSS for requesting information reports.*

5.2 THE NATURE AND ROLE OF MSS PASSIVE DECISION MAKING SUPPORT

5.2.1 Role of information reporting in management decision making support

Passive decision making support is concerned with the provision of information reports to management on either a periodic basis or as needed. Internal and external data may need to be combined and processed in some way to provide a report containing information that is suitable for management use. A logical view of passive decision making support within MSS is depicted in Figure 5.1. Within the figure, management is depicted within an organisational context. The context determines what is, and what is not, considered to be information to each individual manager at any point in time. Thus, the organisational context influences the underlying data needs and the processing of that data by an MSS in order to provide management information (rather than reports of no value). MSS information requests, made either by management directly or by someone else on their behalf, invoke the required data processing operations on externally and/or internally sourced data. The resultant reports may be made available to management on either a periodic basis or as needed.

Information reporting for passive decision making support (hereafter shortened to *information reporting*) by an MSS is of potential benefit to all managerial levels (top, middle and lower), to all managerial functions (such as Finance, Marketing and Sales, and Production) and to all managerial activities (such as planning and control). In practice, the information reports provided by MSS implementations depend on the organisational need and the overall feasibility of providing such support. Economic, social, legal and technical factors all need to be taken into account during MSS feasibility evaluation. Figures 5.2 and 5.3 summarise the potential provision, and actual provision, of MSS information reporting in diagrammatic form respectively.

5.2.2 The content of MSS information reports

Typically, an MSS information report can be classified as being of one of the following three types:

- *An analysis report.*
- *An exception report.*
- *A plan of action report.*

An analysis report provides a view of a particular situation at a particular moment in time or over a particular timespan. A weekly total number of orders received or a monthly report of employee turnover are example analysis reports; they provide a summarised view of orders and personnel issues respectively within a specified timescale. An exception report provides details of situations where deviations, between what was considered acceptable and what has actually taken place, have occurred to the extent to which they are considered worthy of further management attention. A monthly report, showing the specific details of any orders received at least two weeks ago but still to be completed, is an example exception report. Exception reporting is employed frequently within organisations as it highlights clearly those aspects of company operations where improvements need to occur. If analysis reporting had been used in the order example above, then all orders would have been detailed. The report

Fig 5.1 A logical view of MSS information reporting

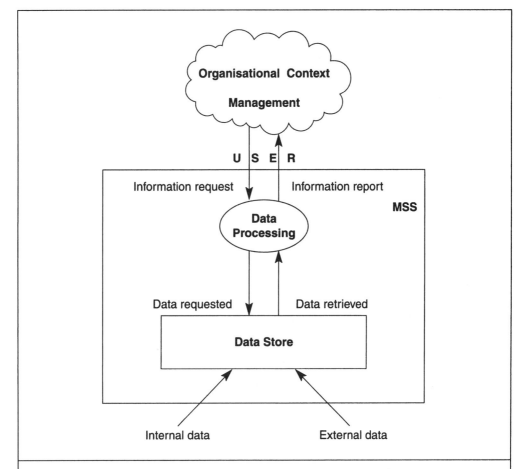

Within the figure, management is depicted within an organisational context. The organisational context and management within that organisational context determine what is considered to be information. The organisational context also influences the data required and the processing of that data in order to provide management information (rather than reports of no value). Information requests, either by management directly or on their behalf, invoke the required data processing operations on data that may be derived from both internal and external sources.

would then have to be checked manually to identify those orders that were incomplete and over two weeks old. Summary statistics concerning the number and percentage of these orders would need to be produced manually.

A plan of action is the third category of MSS information report. A weekly production schedule for a product is an example plan of action report. It provides a plan of production activity for the coming week. In order to result in a suitable plan of action, the MSS takes into account a variety of data, including:

- details of any unfulfilled orders for the product
- the current product's inventory details
- details concerning the available machinery

Fig 5.2 MSS information reporting and potential management decision making support

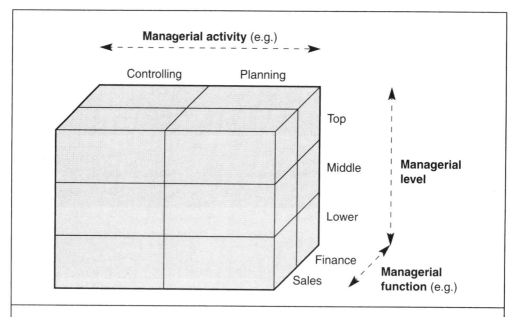

This diagram depicts the possibilities of MSS information reporting as a cube. Managerial levels (top, middle, lower) form the first dimension of the cube. Managerial activities (such as planning and controlling) form the second dimension of the cube and managerial functions (such as Production, Finance, and Marketing and Sales) form the third dimension of the cube. It is theoretically possible to provide MSS information reporting for all levels of management, for all functions of management, and for all activities of management. This is illustrated by the shading of the entire cube.

- the product's bill of materials (that is, the product's composition)
- details of the available parts' inventory.

A six-monthly personnel hiring plan, based on forecast increases in sales, is an another example of a plan of action report.

Although most reports can be classified as one of the above types, there may be situations where a report has the characteristics of more than one type of report. For example, reports which provide both analysis and exception details are becoming increasingly common as software offers more alternatives for highlighting exceptions (for example, by using colour).

All the above report types employ mathematical models within their report programmes (Chapter 6 describes mathematical models and the activity of modelling in detail). For example, totals or frequency counts are simple arithmetical formulae. When applied to a situation, they form very basic mathematical models. In the case of the six-month plan for personnel hiring, the MSS provides a forecasting mathematical model with historical sales data as input. Executing this mathematical model results in a month-by-month sales forecast for the six-month period. Each month's sales forecast, in turn, forms input to another mathematical model which predicts the total

Fig 5.3 MSS information reporting in practice

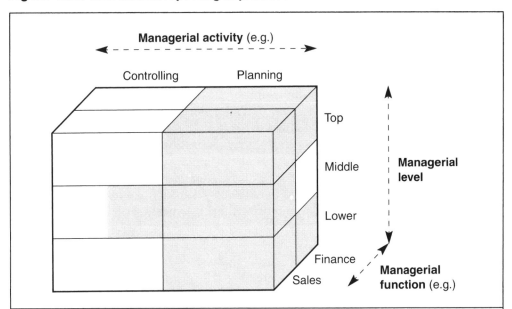

This diagram is identical to Figure 5.2, except that several portions of the cube are not shaded or are only partially shaded. This reflects the situation that, in practice, MSS information reporting covers, either partially or fully, only a subset of management activities and/or management levels and/or management functions. It is quite possible that one level of management is omitted from MSS support, whereas the other two are supported. Several physical MSS may provide information reporting for an organisation. For instance, each corporate section may possess one or more MSS implementations to satisfy departmental information reporting needs.

number of personnel needed to cater for expected sales within that month. Given the number of personnel already recruited and trained, the MSS reports the number that need hiring for that month.

Within passive decision making support, mathematical models are used solely to derive the required report. They are not used interactively in the support of decision making activity. For instance, there is no provision for storing model results for subsequent use in 'what if' and 'what's best' analysis. Interactive models, which are key to active decision making support, are discussed in Chapter 6.

5.2.3 MSS information reporting within planning and control

It is important to stress that plan of action reports are not the only reports that can aid the managerial activity of planning. Both status and exception reports can aid planning activities. For example, information regarding the percentage of orders not completed within an acceptable time frame (most likely to be presented as an exception report) may aid management selection between several alternative methods of tackling improvements in an organisation's current product manufacturing process and its relationship with order processing. A slightly higher percentage of unfulfilled orders than can be tolerated may lead to minor adjustments in current operational procedures only. Alternatively, a Business Process Re-engineering (BPR) exercise might be considered necessary if drastic improvements are warranted (BPR is the subject of Chapter 12).

The managerial activity of control can also be supported by more than one type of report. Even plans of action are important to the control functions, as they provide measurements (a set or range of values) against which information concerning actual events is compared. In order to appreciate how information reporting can aid organisational control in general, an overall generic view of control is required. General Systems Theory (GST, defined in Section 2.6.1) provides such a view. This is illustrated in Figure 5.4. Specifically, an organisational task is a process that has one or more input entities and produces one or more output entities. Entities can be either physical entities or information entities. Alongside a physical entity, there are usually one or more informational entities which provide details about that physical entity. It is through the information entities that organisational control is exercised. Some example organisational processes, and possible associated input and output physical and information entities, are presented in Table 5.1. Note that the physical and information entities are not always distinct physically (that is, being two separate artefacts), even though they can be considered logically distinct components.

An organisational process requires a control system to keep the process in step with organisational requirements. The control system monitors the state of the organisational process, comparing it to the expected state or to the range of states tolerated. If this comparison reveals under-performance of the organisational process then some form of remedial action needs to be taken. The control system decides on the remedial actions, communicating them, in the form of one or more information entities, to the point at which action can be taken. Effective action results in changes to one or more input entities to improve the process, which cause the requisite improvement within the output entity set. Monitoring the state of an organisational process can be approached in two ways: by monitoring the outputs (via the information entities) of the organisational process or by monitoring the inputs (via the information entities) to the organisational process. These approaches are known as *feedback* and *feedforward* respectively. Most organisational processes employ both approaches to control. Feedforward allows the inputs to be reviewed prior to the current processing cycle, so preventive measures can be brought to bear before wasteful processing takes place. However, looking at the inputs to a process in an attempt to anticipate potential problems carries a level of risk in the event of the problems not actually occurring. In contrast, reviewing the outputs of a process means that the problem has already occurred before being detected. There is less risk in predicting future processing outcomes, although this depends on the rapidity by which the information is communicated to the point at which actions are taken (see Lucey 1991 for a description of the reasons why information may be delayed and the problems delays may cause). However, feedback control means that remedial action is only effected in time for future processing cycles.

Within an organisation, control activities are management concerns. The potential support roles for MSS information reporting within organisational control can now be formalised based on the GST view of organisational control. Both the input and output

Fig 5.4 A general view of organisational control

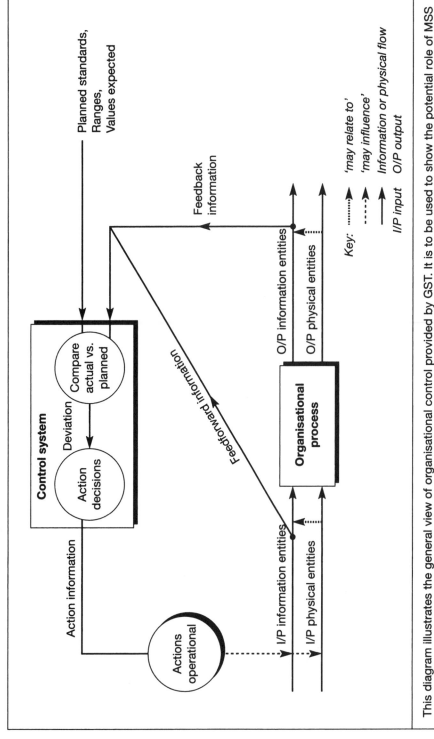

This diagram illustrates the general view of organisational control provided by GST. It is to be used to show the potential role of MSS information reporting within organisational control.

Table 5.1 Example organisational processes, and associated input and output entities

Organisational Process	Example Input Physical Entities	Example Input Information Entities	Example Output Physical Entities	Example Output Information Entities
Hiring an employee	Candidate employees	Candidate employee details	Hired employee Rejected candidates	Details of hired employee Reasons for acceptance or rejection
Processing orders	Orders received Labour	Order details Shifts and personnel details	Orders fulfilled Orders in progress	Quantity of orders fulfilled Percentage of orders fulfilled
Product manufacturing	Raw materials Machinery Labour	Quality and quantity of raw materials available Machine capacity Shifts and personnel details Bill of materials	Finished products Rejects Work in progress	Quality and quantity of finished products Reject rate Percentage of products finished

The table provides example organisational processes, and, for each process, some example input and output entities. Some input entities are physical (for example raw materials in the case of product manufacturing). These have associated information entities (for example information concerning the quality and quantity of the raw materials is a possible information entity associated with the raw material physical entity). It is through the information entities that control within organisations is exercised.

information entities may be provided using an MSS. These may then be compared against the planned standards and ranges agreed for the same time frame of reference. Indeed, the results of a comparison may be provided by an MSS, most suitably in the form of an exception report. As already mentioned, the planning of the expected standards and ranges can also be aided by MSS information reports. Finally, any decisions concerning the appropriate actions to take regarding an identified problem may also be aided by suitable information reports from an MSS. Figure 5.5 annotates the organisational control diagram presented in Figure 5.4 to highlight the potential roles of MSS to provide information reporting in support of organisational control activities.

Fig 5.5 The role of MSS information reporting in supporting organisational control activities

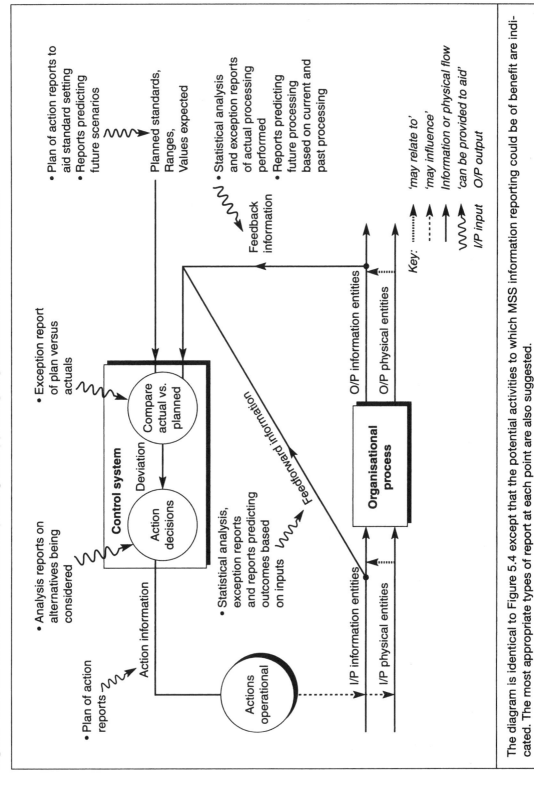

The diagram is identical to Figure 5.4 except that the potential activities to which MSS information reporting could be of benefit are indicated. The most appropriate types of report at each point are also suggested.

5.3 TEMPORAL ISSUES AND MSS INFORMATION REPORTING PROVISION

5.3.1 A four-way classification of MSS information reports

Section 5.2 established the general role of MSS information reporting within management work and identified a method by which MSS reports could be classified according to their content. In this section, a different and orthogonal classification of MSS information reports is derived from two important temporal issues:

- The time at which MSS information reports are first defined.
- The time or times at which MSS information reports are made available to management.

The first of the above issues allows us to distinguish between *pre-defined* and *customised* MSS information reports. Pre-defined MSS information reports are those reports whose structure and time span are defined either during MSS development or during subsequent maintenance activities. Specifications of these reports are usually developed by IS professionals in response to identified and repetitive management information requirements. On the other hand, customised MSS information reports are specified by the user of the MSS. The report is defined at the time of initial request, but could conceivably be stored within the MSS for later re-use. The MSS must enable the user to specify information requests easily and rapidly.

The second of the temporal issues allows us to distinguish between *periodic* and *as-needed* MSS information reports. Periodic MSS information reports are those that are made available to management only at fixed times, for example at the end of a month or a quarter. On the other hand, as-needed MSS information reports are available to the management as and when required. Combining the two methods of distinguishing MSS information reports, a four-part classification of reports is derived as follows:

- as-needed, pre-defined MSS information reports
- as-needed, customised MSS information reports
- periodic, pre-defined MSS information reports
- periodic, customised MSS information reports.

The first commercially available MSS provided periodic, pre-defined information reports. This was due to the technical limitations of the available computer systems to operate only in batch mode, coupled with the inability, from a logistical viewpoint, to satisfy management requests for information on a more frequent basis. The current trend in MSS development software is towards providing the capabilities to support as-needed information reporting. A variety of reports may be requested directly from a department's terminal or PC. Reports may be pre-defined, essentially providing an on-line version of the aforementioned batch reports with the advantage of the reports being available as and when needed. More frequently, however, modern MSS provide users with greater freedom to request customised information reports. Figure 5.6 summarises this trend in MSS towards the provision of as-needed and customised information reporting and reports.

The storage of the data within a MSS will influence the degree of customisation possible within information reporting. For instance, storing weekly sales figures means that daily sales cannot be reported. MSS data should be stored at the finest level of

Fig 5.6 Trends in MSS provision of information reporting facilities

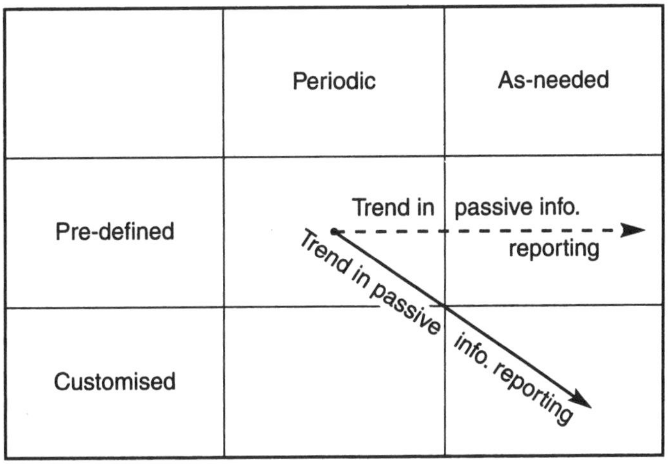

This diagram shows the four categories of information reports, derived from temporal factors associated with their definition and availability to management. The arrows superimposed on the diagram show the trend in MSS provision from supporting periodic pre-defined information reporting to supporting as-needed information reporting, predominantly of a customised nature.

granularity to satisfy all envisaged report requests. (This is easier said than done, as it involves predicting future, as well as knowing current, information needs.) Even when customised reporting is possible, the MSS data may only be updated periodically, for example once daily, once weekly or even once monthly. Daily data updates are, in most cases, more than adequate for management purposes. Providing data on a real-time currency basis, where changes in the underlying data sources are immediately available through the MSS, can lead to unacceptable system response rates to user requests. More complex and costly computer configurations are needed to support real-time data currency.

5.3.2 The importance of pre-defined MSS information reports

Customised MSS information reporting permits a user to specify the information required. Given the greater availability of software that supports the development of MSS with these facilities, why do organisations continue to develop systems that provide pre-defined information reports? In fact, pre-defined information reports often perform a critical organisational role. These reports, produced over the same time frame for disparate aspects of organisational activity (such as Manufacturing, R & D, Finance, or regarding operations associated with particular Strategic Business Units (SBUs)), provide management with a collective view of corporate health and performance. Co-ordinated action across all functions can then be taken when needed.

There are several other reasons why pre-defined information reporting capabilities are required in many organisations. Providing pre-defined reports to satisfy information needs that remain stable over time saves effort and resources in repeatedly specifying an identical report structure. Corporate annual reports are required by law from certain companies. Shareholders require reports at fixed time intervals regarding standard aspects of organisational performance. Many companies, particularly those within the public services sector, have obligations for providing standard information at fixed time intervals to one or more government offices, such as the Department of Education and Employment and the Department of Health in the UK, and the European Commission where European funding or laws are monitored. Millet and Mawhinney (1992) provide additional situations where pre-defined information reports can be advantageous to a company.

5.3.3 Interaction methods for requesting information reports from MSS

There are various ways of requesting information reports employed within current MSS. Figure 5.7 identifies several of the most common interaction methods, and to which category or categories of information report, described in Section 5.3.1, each method is appropriate. The remainder of this section discusses the appropriate interaction methods for requesting each type of information report in turn.

MSS Interaction methods for requesting as-needed, pre-defined information reports

Requesting a pre-defined information report on an as-needed basis may involve the selection of the appropriate report from a screen menu of report options. Within a GUI WIMPS environment, such as Windows, MSS applications may provide an iconic form of the menu. Each icon portrays a report pictorially. The user selects the required report by clicking on the associated icon. This type of interface is increasingly popular as it is very easy to use. A manager may be able to locate information directly rather

Fig 5.7 Interaction methods appropriate for each MSS information report category

	Periodic	As-needed
Pre-defined	• JCL or other system file • All approaches available to IS professional for providing information reports on an as-needed basis	• Screen menus of report options • Report icon selection • Drill down a hierarchical information report structure • Briefing Book
Customised	• *Use of customised approaches by IS professional on an as-needed basis in preparation of periodic information*	• Query language/Report generator • Forms-based interface • Dynamic use of pick-lists • Data-driven software deployment

The figure separates the variety of ways by which a user can request an MSS information report according to the type of report that is being adopted. The *italics* indicate the rarity of the situation, as in the case of periodic, customised information reports.

than having to delegate the task to a more computer-literate colleague. Software that supports the development of iconic interfaces continues to grow significantly.

Some more recent applications development packages allow MSS developers to set up a hierarchical structure of pre-defined information reports concerning aspects of organisational operations. Each level within the hierarchy provides more detailed information on an aspect of corporate operations presented in the level above. Indeed, the top level of the report hierarchy may provide little more than a menu for locating more detailed information reports further down the hierarchical structure. The user can then navigate through information, starting at the topmost level of the hierarchy and progressing, selectively, through successively lower levels of the hierarchy to uncover the increasingly detailed information of interest. This navigation capability, which enables access to information at increasing levels of detail, is called *drill down*.

Often, MSS development packages providing drill down also allow the creation of linkages, additional to those provided as part of the hierarchical structure, between reports at the same level or at differing levels of detail. They also enable developers to provide applications with high visual impact, by the creation of easy-to-use iconic menus and coloured, graphical representations of information. Thus, a web of inter-linked high impact information reports can be developed using these packages, creating a form of hyper-media system (see Section 3.3.6) for direct use by management. An example applications development package that provides all these capabilities is Lightship Professional from Pilot Software Inc. Working within the Windows environment, it allows a hierarchy of information regarding key aspects of corporate operations to be developed. Colour graphs, images, maps, text and tables can be combined to portray information in the most effective way. So-called hotspots are used to link levels of information. Hotspots are defined areas of the screen which, when selected with a mouse button, activate some underlying operation. A hotspot may be defined as an area on a map, or as an iconic 'button' to click on the screen, or even as a table's row or column label. Users drill down through the information presented by selecting appropriate hotspots. Traffic light colour coding (where red denotes under-performance, orange denotes borderline performance and green denotes satisfactory performance) is frequently employed as a standard indicator within applications, allowing users to identify easily the areas of poor performance and/or potential problem areas. Two example, inter-linked screens developed within Lightship Professional are presented and described in Figure 5.8. Additional information on the Lightship family of products can be found in Pinella (1991).

Rather than providing information in a hierarchical fashion, several applications development packages allow the definition of a computerised *Briefing Book*. Its purpose is to provide to top management, on an as-needed basis, a portfolio of highly summarised organisational performance information which spans a fixed time interval of organisational activity. Several sequentially ordered, high impact information reports comprise a Briefing Book. Colour and a highly graphical presentation of information are normally employed within reports. Management typically scan the reports directly. Both forward and backward progression through the reports is provided, typically by selecting a 'forward' or 'backward' icon with a mouse.

Powerplay, from Cognos Inc., provides a Briefing Book building module, called Portfolio. It allows both forward and backward progression through the reports. Drill down capabilities can be provided and linked to each report. (Powerplay is described further with regard to as-needed, customised information reporting. Supplementary information on Powerplay is provided in Cronk (1993) and Warren (1995).)

Fig 5.8 Drill down capabilities within Lightship Professional

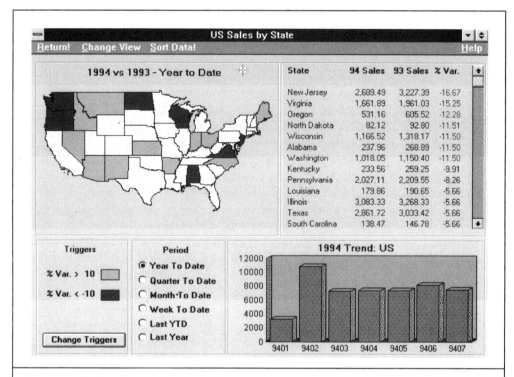

The screen in the diagram provides an overview of the company's sales performance, separated into regions. Each region is a hotspot, whose colour indicates its general performance according to the traffic-light colour coding scheme. Clicking on the red area for New Jersey would bring up a second screen that shows specific details on customer sales for the New Jersey region. Clicking on a customer name on this second screen would activate further drill down to greater detail concerning the selected customer.

Interaction methods for requesting as-needed, customised information reports

As-needed, customised information reports require the capabilities for specifying the information to be retrieved. The most common styles for providing this capability are via query languages/report generators. One very popular query language is SQL (Van Der Lans 1989). It allows the user to focus more on what information is required rather than how it is derived from the underlying database (invariably relational in nature). SQL allows portions of data to be extracted and combined with other data within the database to satisfy the information request.

In order to illustrate the basic information reporting capabilities of SQL, consider a relational database that contains the following sale and employee tables:

❑ *Viewpoint*

Manor Bakeries: taking the cake

Part of the RHM Group, Manor Bakeries is a manufacturer of well-known brand names such as Mr Kipling, Cadbury's Cakes and Lyons Cakes, and of retailer own-brands.

Keeping track of sales is not easy, however, with around 300 prime product lines plus many variants such as Christmas products. The direct customers, supermarket chains and some 14,000 smaller retail outlets, are supplemented by sales to agents and export orders. A fleet of 300 sales vans operating from 30 regional centres covers product distribution across the UK.

Manor Bakeries initially adopted IRI's DataServer as a management information system for marketing. As part of a broader move from bureau-based facilities, the company has more recently upgraded to DataServer Analyzer, a Windows-based market intelligence tool for providing commercial information.

This has enabled integration of detailed in-house data such as ex-factory and net sales, together with external market information provided via AGB SuperPanel. Indicative of the interest in this area, SuperPanel itself is supplied in native DataServer format, alleviating the previous overheads of conversion.

For Simon James, commercial information manager, the strength of this type of product is that it can be matched to the information needs and the technical capabilities of Manor Bakeries staff. Appropriate data views and ready-made reports can readily be set up for regional sales staff, national account managers, and market researchers alike.

"For the field sales force," says James, "this is an operationally based reporting tool which we've largely customised for them. For marketing, it allows people to look almost instantly, but in depth, at facets such as pack size performance, and how this has changed over time and under varying conditions." ∎

Reprinted with permission from *Computer Weekly*, 3rd August 1995.

Sale:

Item_ID	Date	Quantity	Emp_ID
P0101010	28-Sep-1995	2	1
P5550321	28-Sep-1995	45	2
P3434345	30-Sep-1995	3,000	4
P3434303	30-Sep-1995	3,000	4
P0101010	01-Oct-1995	4	2
P5550321	01-Oct-1995	35	2
P2223232	02-Oct-1995	104	3
P0234374	03-Oct-1995	1	1
P0435485	04-Oct-1995	40	2
P0101010	08-Oct-1995	3	3

Employee:

Emp_ID	Emp_Name	Sales_Division	Years_Employed
1	John Harris	North	6
2	Chris Blake	South	4
3	Reg Buckner	South	3
4	Tracey Fields	London	2
5	Lorna Boulder	North	1
6	Paul Eaton	North	1

The first table of data holds details of sales made by company employees. Each row of the table provides the quantity of sales of one product on one day by one employee. The data in the table covers the period of time from 28th September 1995 to 8th October 1995 inclusive. The second table of data relates an employee to the sales division that the employee works for, in addition to holding basic details about each employee regarding name and years of service with the company.

SQL allows information requests to be specified using the SELECT statement, which, in its basic form, takes the following structure:

SELECT the data items of interest
FROM one or more data tables
WHERE certain conditions are true

For example, to request details of all employees who work in the North sales division, an SQL SELECT statement could be specified as follows:

SELECT Emp_ID, Emp_Name, Years_Employed
FROM Employee
WHERE Sales_Division = 'North'

This would retrieve the following table of information:

Emp_ID	Emp_Name	Years_Employed
1	John Harris	6
5	Lorna Boulder	1
6	Paul Eaton	1

A more complex SQL SELECT statement is needed to obtain the names of the divisions that have sold at least one of product P0101010. Sales of P0101010 are in the sale table whereas divisions are named within the employee table. Thus, some combining or joining of the tables is needed to satisfy the information request. The way in which tables are joined together also needs to be specified within the SQL SELECT statement. A SQL SELECT statement satisfying this request can be specified as follows:

```
SELECT DISTINCT Sales_Division
FROM Sale, Employee
WHERE Sale.Emp_ID = Employee.Emp_ID
       AND Item_ID = 'P0101010'.
```

The first part of the WHERE clause of the above statement informs the computer system as to how to join the data within the two tables, in this case by matching the Emp_ID values in the sale table with the Emp_ID values in the employee table. The term DISTINCT in the first line of the query makes sure that no duplicate sales division names are reported. The result of this query is as follows:

Sales_Division
North
South

SQL is much more versatile than these basic examples suggest. For instance, it allows simple arithmetic functions to be performed over columns of data within tables, such as average values, total values and a count of the number of rows within a table. Boolean operators and other arithmetic operators such as 'less than', 'less than or equal' and 'greater than' can be used within the WHERE clause of an SQL statement. In addition SQL is not just a query language. It also provides a data structure definition language for defining new data tables. Indeed, the sales and employee data tables may well have been specified using SQL. Van Der Lans (1989) provides a clear in-depth description of the SQL language and its capabilities.

Other query languages/report generators are available. Some manipulate data in a two-dimensional form, as found within relational databases. Others manipulate data held in a multi-dimensional forms, allowing users to 'slice and dice' the underlying data according to their needs (the 'slice and dice' concept was introduced with regard to data warehouses in Section 3.3.9). Express*, from Oracle, provides a data structure definition and data manipulation language for multi-dimensional databases. The three-dimensional sales data illustrated in Figure 3.5 could be defined as part of a PC-Express database as follows:

DEFINE sales VARIABLE decimal <product store month>

This defines sales values as decimal values (there is no money data type in Express), and sales are dimensioned by product, by store and by month. Product, store and month are Express dimensions, whose values (such as 'Jan95' and 'Feb95' for the month dimension) need to be specified a priori.

* © Oracle Corporation 1996. All rights reserved. Telephone 0990-332200.

Supposing the sales of each product in January 1995, by each store, is requested by management. Express requires two commands to satisfy this request: the LIMIT command, which restricts sales details to the month of January 1995 only, and then the REPORT command to retrieve the required January details. The commands can be specified as follows:

LIMIT month TO Jan95
REPORT sales

Supposing the total sales for each product is now required for January 1995. This is also satisfied by the same two commands, but a total function is now included in the REPORT command:

LIMIT month TO Jan95
REPORT total(sales, product)

As specified, the total function provides totals for each product rather than totalling across all products.

Like SQL, the data manipulation language of Express offers much more than that suggested by these very basic examples. The REPORT command has many optional elements which can be included to customise the structure, content and presentation of the information retrieved. A library of mathematical techniques, including Forecasting, is available in the Express language. Programs combining Express commands can be developed and stored for later re-use.

For the technically able user, languages such as SQL and that provided within Express may be suitable for use. However, easier approaches to requesting as-needed, customised information reports are available. A Forms-based applications interface allows users to request information by filling in details on one or more screen forms. For example, supposing the same underlying sales data tables, as used in the SQL examples, have been created. In order to request information on employees within the North division using a forms-based approach, the user would fill in the division name 'North' within the division data entry slot appearing on the form relating to employee data. The user would also indicate the other data items of interest with respect to North division employees. For this request, the user indicates the data items by placing a * within the slots regarding employee's identification number, name and years of service. Running the request would then generate a query statement, possibly in SQL, based upon the user's input to retrieve the information. Figure 5.9 provides an illustration of the forms-based approach to requesting information reports from MSS.

Another relatively easy method of retrieving as-needed, customised information reports is by using a series of interrelated pick-lists to generate the required query. For instance, the first list provides the names of all the data tables (assuming an underlying relational database) that can be accessed. The user selects those that are of current interest. Further pick lists allow the user to select the data items of interest, how the tables of interest are to be combined, and what conditions are imposed over the data (such as only those employees from the North region). Once complete, a query, possibly in SQL, can be derived from the user's selections.

The final method of requesting as-needed, customised information reports to be discussed in the subsection is by the use of data-driven software. This software provides a vast set of general data manipulation operators for information manipulation

Fig 5.9 A forms-based method of requesting customised information reports

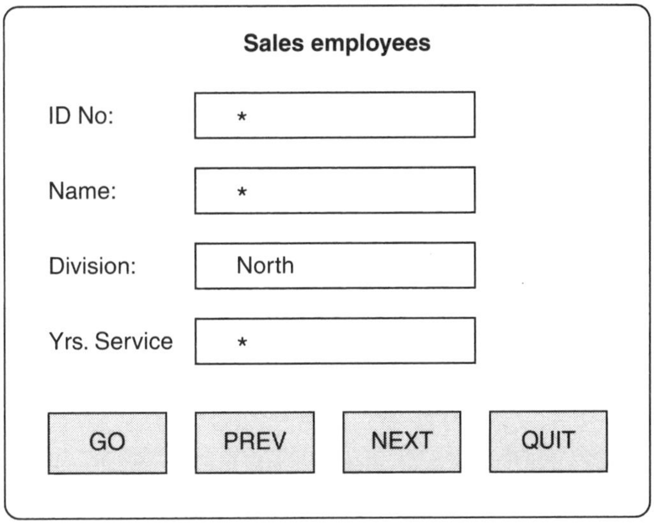

A user selects the items of interest by placing a * in the required data entry slots on the screen form provided. Any conditions are also placed against the data attribute to which they refer. Thus, the diagram shows the forms-based query that is requesting information on the identification numbers, the names and years of service of those employees that work in the North division. This forms-based query, when run, generates a command-based query, possibly in SQL.

and reporting. However, the structure of the data determines which of the operators can be employed at any point in time. Typically, the data is represented in a multi-dimensional format and the operators allow for 'slicing and dicing' the data, drill down, basic arithmetical operations on data, the development and storage of customised reports, and the presentation of information in a variety of formats.

Powerplay, from Cognos Inc., is an excellent example of software that provides data-driven customised information reporting. Claimed to be the first software of its kind, Powerplay incorporates a Transformer module which takes two-dimensional data from other spreadsheet, database and text-based environments, and produces a corresponding multi-dimensional data set (this facility is called *Information Packaging*). Wherever possible, Transformer works out the relationships between various data attributes automatically, for example the hierarchical relationship between year values (such as 1995), month values (such as May 1995 and June 1995), and day values (such as 15th May 1995 and 18th June 1995). As shown in Figure 5.10, these relationships can be viewed in a visual tree-like representation, and are used as the basis for defining the drill down possibilities upon data sets. The generic data manipulation tools are provided in Powerplay's Viewer and Reporter modules. These allow the data to be 'sliced and diced', combined and aggregated, and presented in many different presentation formats. Drill down of the data based on the identified relationships is also provided. Customised reports of key information can be developed and stored for later printing or used as part of the aforementioned Portfolio Briefing Book facility.

Express Analyser, from Oracle, also provides a graphical 'point and click' interface allowing easy analysis of the multi-dimensional data. The Selector tool is used to limit the view to a particular slice of the data or to perform more advanced analysis, such as finding the top five products for all the sales regions where the profit this year is greater than last year's profit. Since it is a graphical environment, the user can directly manipulate the layout or format of reports produced.

Powerplay, Express Analyser, and the data-driven approach, have a lot to offer organisations wanting to support as-needed, customised information reporting and reports. No programs, as such, need to be written, and changes to data structures or the addition of new data is easily and rapidly incorporated. Although the user of Powerplay needs to be fully conversant with its manipulative capabilities, it is expected that this type of software will become even more popular within organisations over the next few years.

Fig 5.10 Visual representation of data structure relationships within Powerplay

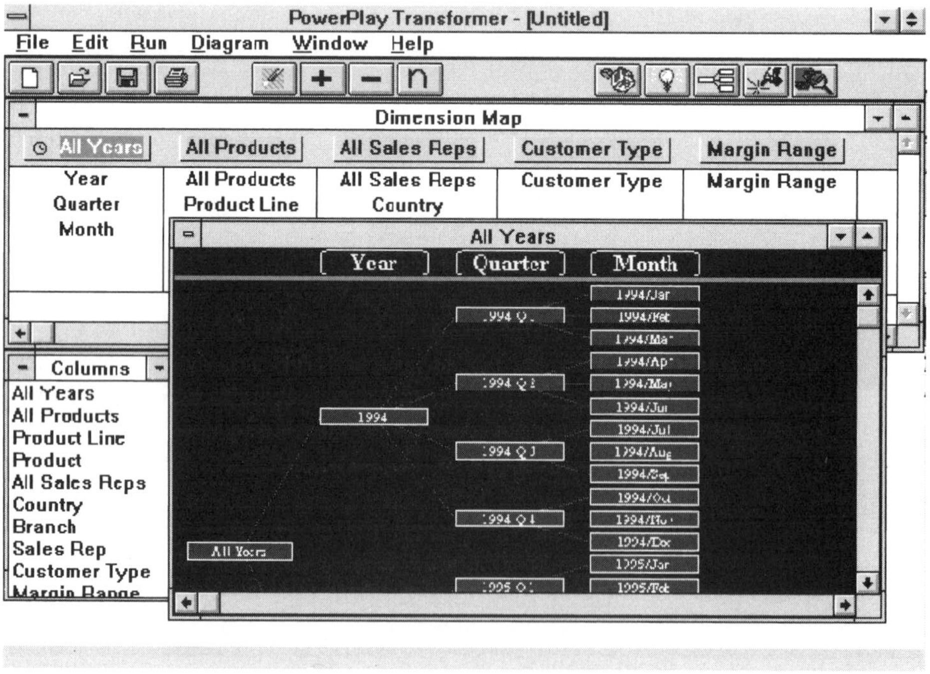

The diagram shows the visual tree-like representation of the relationships between year, quarter and month values as identified by the Transformer module of Powerplay. This structure will be used as the basis for drill-down (from years to quarters to months) within other modules of the Powerplay family of products.

Reproduced with permission from Cognos UK Ltd

Interaction methods for providing periodic, pre-defined information reports

Periodic reporting of pre-defined information reports may require the submission of a JCL or other form of system program by an IS professional. The system program activates the reporting programs and prints out the results. However, this is only one approach to requesting information. The MSS may provide the IS professional with one or more of the other aforementioned methods of requesting pre-defined information reports, although from a management perspective the reports are still only available at specified times of the year.

Interaction methods for providing periodic, customised information reports

It is difficult to consider an organisational situation where this type of reporting occurs as customised information reporting is invariably performed on an as-needed basis (even if a few days elapse between report request and receipt). An organisational situation might exist where managers submit customised information requirements to the IS

❑ *Viewpoint*

Touchline Insurance: minimising cost of sales

Touchline Insurance, part of the GAN Group of companies, was launched in 1993 to provide low-cost motor insurance, and now has 100,000 customers.

Managing director Sandy Dunn decided the company needed a sales and marketing system and opted for Brock Activity manager – supplied in the UK by Hampton, Middlesex-based Co-Cam – which went live in January 1993.

Touchline markets its services through a planned programme of newspaper, magazine and television advertising and a growing number of affinity group schemes with organisations such as Rolls-Royce and the Royal Mail.

Most calls come in on Touchline's 0800 freephone number and are distributed by an Aspect automatic call distributor, although a second priority number is used for prospects to call back when they make a decision following quotation.

Telesales staff are prompted through a screen-based script, which enables them to capture all the information necessary for a quotation to be made while maintaining conversation with the caller.

As well as providing the infrastructure for the direct sales operation, Dunn believes Brock's other strengths lie in its ability to produce detailed marketing campaign analysis.

Dunn says, "Like any other insurance company we are interested in calculating costs against enquires, quotes and sales, The system provides us with daily reports so we can make quick but informed decisions on how to apply our marketing budgets."

Touchline has worked with Brann Direct marketing to develop an MIS Workbench which allows demographic comparison between Touchline's customers and prospects and the population as a whole, providing better comparisons between television regions and newspaper catchment areas.

Dunn adds, "We compare our base data against external sources which enables us to look for new opportunities: where conversions are lower. It is a very powerful tool."

The MIS Workbench is linked to the customer and prospect database held in Brock which is also linked to a Digital Equipment system handling administration, claims, renewals and accounts.

Within the sales office, supervisors receive hourly reports on the number of responses and sales made as well as detailed analyses of individual performance in terms of sales or quotes made, with the additional facility for ad hoc reports as required.

In the future, Dunn believes Touchline will integrate its telephony and data management functions so that much more detailed analyses are available on telephone activity.

He adds, "Most insurance business comes down to people and how they interact. But in the direct sector, the computer system must underpin and facilitate those customer relationships."

"By freeing up our sales people to concentrate on customer service and because we can use our marketing intelligence more sensibly, Brock minimises our cost of sales and lets us be very competitive. It is a vital part of our business." ∎

Reprinted with permission from *Computer Weekly*, 29th September 1994.

Department when recognised, but then wait until all such requests are satisfied *en masse* at a certain time of the month or week. This could be considered an example of periodic customised information reporting. In this case, the IS Department may possess an MSS that provides one or more of the methods for requesting customised information reports that have been described below.

5.4   MSS INFORMATION REPORTING IN ACTION

Most medium-sized and large-sized companies will have at least one MSS that provides information reporting facilities to support management decision making. This subsection presents some real-life MSS that provide information reporting facilities to organisations. Most are presented in summary form in Figure 5.11. Three MSS have

Fig 5.11 Summary of example MSS information reporting facilities within organisations

● Many universities have MSS that provide information reports concerning students and courses. For example, reports that provide the total numbers of students on each year of a course and the total numbers of part time and full time students studying at the university are important not only to those involved in course management but also to senior management for financial control.

● An MSS employed within a Staffing Department of a large postal company enables management to review employee details and their postal duties, and any overtime and holiday entitlements planned. Overtime and attendance reports are two types of pre-defined reports provided by this system. The MSS also supports management decision making as to who is the most appropriate employee to cover for another employee's holiday period.

● Boots, a large UK-based pharmaceutical company, employs an MSS which provides reports on sales. Electronic Point of Sale (EPOS) terminals feed sales data to a central data store. Many reports can be produced, including sales by individual stores and by particular product line. This enables management to stay aware of the performance of individual stores and individual product lines.

● London Underground employs an MSS to monitor and control the organisation's Key Performance Indicators (KPIs). Information concerning passenger miles covered, lift and escalator utilisation, rolling stock availability, profit and loss, and crime statistics are provided through this system to senior management (predominantly).

The above examples, some more specific than others, together with the three more detailed examples in Section 5.4, highlight the variety of organisations that value information reporting by MSS. Most have a financial orientation, but many include other aspects of organisational importance, such as customer service and employee management issues.

been selected for greater attention and are described in the remaining paragraphs of this subsection. These MSS differ in terms of the organisational background, the scope and type of information reporting, and the interaction methods for requesting information reports. However, all are oriented, to some degree, towards financial control support. Although not all MSS information reporting is concerned with financial issues, surveys (see, for example, Fidler et al. 1993) indicate that financial applications predominate.

Example 1: CASE MIX

CASE MIX is a large-scale MSS employed within many UK healthcare providers (i.e. the hospitals that provide patient healthcare). It was identified as the answer to a widely perceived problem within large hospitals; data was available in many disparate locations spread throughout the hospital with no way of collating this data from which to derive useful management information. Government laid down the requirements specification for CASE MIX, with the development of actual CASE MIX implementations being farmed out to several consultancy companies. Thus, several different implementations of the same system were produced to run on different platforms and in different programming environments. Government funding was made available to hospitals for the purchase of a suitable CASE MIX implementation. A CASE MIX system extracts key clinical data from other databases within the hospital (Figure 5.12 provides an overview of the possible clinical data sources for a CASE MIX system). Combining this data with financial cost data, CASE MIX provides both periodic (weekly and monthly) information reports as well as information reporting on an as-needed basis. Reports are provided to both professional clinicians and hospital management. Amongst other aspects, the CASE MIX reports help management to identify areas of waste and inefficiency within a hospital, and to highlight areas which could most benefit from more resources. For example, a monthly analysis report, which provides the total healthcare costs related to a particular hospital department or related to a particular activity type (for example, blood tests), can be compared to the previously agreed financial budget to highlight where actions may need to be taken to control costs. Ward capacity and labour cost reports can also be provided to aid financial control and to help decisions as to where to target additional future resources.

The reports discussed so far support managerial control via feedback. Other reports provide some level of support for feedforward control. For instance, a report summarising patient record histories regarding a certain type of illness could be used to predict the expected treatment costs and expected length of stay of any new patient diagnosed with the same illness. Resources can be planned for this patient, and with respect to this illness in general, on this basis.

Example 2: A Timesheet MSS

A small-scale MSS is used to aid management of a large UK-based engineering contracting company in controlling their employees' activities and costs regarding current contract work. Each week, employees complete timesheets detailing the contracts that they worked on and the activities that they performed with respect to a particular contract. The time spent on each activity is also recorded. Standard contract and activity codes are used to classify the time spent in a given week. In addition a set of standard

Fig 5.12 Possible data sources for CASE MIX

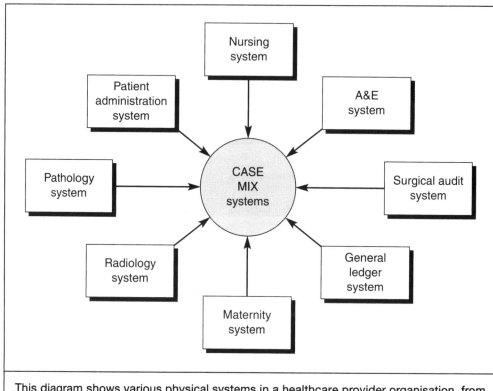

This diagram shows various physical systems in a healthcare provider organisation, from which the underlying data for CASE MIX may be sourced.

costs per unit of time for each activity is maintained by the MSS. At the end of each month, statistical pre-defined information reports are produced, detailing:

- the time spent on each activity within the given month on a particular contract and the overall labour cost
- the overall labour costs with respect to a given contract
- the profile of each employee's activities during the month.

These reports support feedback control. For example, a comparison of the actual labour cost figures against the expected labour cost budget for the current month highlights any deviations from the original monthly budget. This leads to financial control decisions being taken and associated actions being put into effect.

Example 3: An MSS to monitor retail performance

During a period of substantial organisational change, a large distributor and holding company for a large number of UK shoe retail companies decided to implement an MSS for pre-defined information reporting of retail company and individual shoe performances as and when needed. Prior to this system, most information reporting was performed on a functional basis, within little opportunity to view the corporate situation as a whole. The system required information from different functions to be consolidated and integrated to form a corporate multi-dimensional data set from which the MSS could derive useful management information. The system, originally available to 14 senior executives, provided financial information on sales and company performances at various levels of detail. This was principally a Briefing Book facility, but with drill down from any of the reports, via screen hotspots. This allowed management attention to focus on more specific details concerning a particular company or a particular product when needed. A customised information reporting facility was also provided to these users, in a similar manner to the data-driven approach mentioned in Section 5.3.3, but was not used often. At the outset, all retail data was collected on a periodic basis from each company's high street retail outlets. Later, EPOS data automatically captured data in most of the retail outlets, with hand-held data readers in those outlets without EPOS. The data was used to update the multi-dimensional underlying data sets each night.

The current system has 60 users, at all tiers of management. The emphasis of new development is on providing many more users throughout the company with as-needed, customised information reporting facilities, whilst ensuring that the senior management have access to the correct information reports via the Briefing Book facility with associated drill down. The provision of external information about competitors and market share is also a priority development task.

5.5   SUMMARY

This chapter has introduced the many ways that MSS provide passive decision making support to management by information reporting. The potential for, and reality of, MSS information reporting within management work were described in Section 5.2. Two categorisations of MSS information reports have been described within this chapter. The first categorisation, described in Section 5.2, is based on the content of information reports. Typically, an MSS information report can be categorised by whether it is an analysis report, exception report or a plan of action report. The second categorisation, described in Section 5.3, was based on two temporal issues associated with MSS information report definition and report availability to management respectively. This led to the following four-part classification of MSS information reports:

- as-needed, pre-defined MSS information reports
- as-needed, customised MSS information reports
- periodic, pre-defined MSS information reports
- periodic, pre-defined MSS information reports.

Section 5.3 described several potential methods by which each category of MSS information report could be requested. Within this section, some key concepts were introduced, such as drill down, hotspots, traffic light colour coding and Briefing Book facilities. Section 5.4 provided some examples of MSS implementations that provide information reporting facilities to management. This section illustrates the variety of

(Summary continued on p. 125)

CASE STUDY 1: ESSEX FIRE SERVICE

Hot stuff

by Alison Classe

Fire-fighting by computer might sound futuristic, but computers already have their part to play in organising operations, if not in wielding the hoses.

The Essex County Fire and Rescue Service (ECFRS) believes it is the first to have built a fully-computerised mobile command and control unit. The vehicle has already proved its worth at six major fires since its deployment in February this year.

Divisional officer Steve Blackwell says, "As well as recording everything for us, this unit is saving us a lot of time."

One of the most remarkable aspects of the system from the IT point of view is that it was built using standard technology – ordinary PCs plus a development environment more usually associated with office systems.

Together with consultancy Sophtlogic, the service has developed software for monitoring and logging every aspect of an incident. This system runs on a small local area network (Lan) on board the specially built vehicle.

There is a surprising amount of administrative work associated with fire-fighting: the on-board system logged 2,500 transactions in 20 hours at a recent major fire. This work is not bureaucracy, but the capture of vital information.

When fighting a fire, obviously you must know where all your resources are at a given moment – most of all the people. After the event, too, officers need to be able to analyse exactly what happened, both for debriefing and training purposes and to be able to account for their actions in the event of an inquiry.

As well as keeping records, there are also a large number of administrative tasks to be carried out during a fire, such as reporting progress to headquarters and ensuring that firefighters are relieved. All of these things used to be controlled manually but are now addressed by the system.

Fire brigades, generally, have got incident control down to a fine art with the help of mobile control. But ECFRS's computerised version of this control unit has Tardis-like capabilities. On the road, it is two metres wide, but, depending on the space available on arrival at an incident, sections of one or both sides can be hydraulically expanded to create an incident control area measuring up to four metres by three metres internally. This area can accommodate two control staff and two officers with reasonable comfort, and, says Blackwell, "it can fit in practically anywhere."

In the rear of the unit is a conference-room-cum-office for use by the fire commander. There is a generator in case mains power is not available, for instance when there is a barn fire and the unit has to park in a field.

The software for the unit was built by Sophtlogic working closely with Blackwell. Blackwell says, "I had two ground rules: everything has to be very easy to use, and we don't want people to be able to break it."

Blackwell sat down with Sophtlogic's consultant and explained the command and control procedures in great detail. Then the system was built, with extensive use of prototyping. The objective was a system which, in essence, reproduced the (already finely-honed) manual procedures.

Significant efficiencies were introduced, however. For example a unit has to maintain a "nominal roll" recording the names and ranks of those attending the fire, together with details of the vehicles. Now people and machines can be checked in seconds by reading bar codes into one of the PCs.

The system consists of a network of five PCs: four workstations plus a server. The software, developed using Blyth Software's Omnis 7, has a Windows front-end.

▶

Control staff log just about everything on the computer, including every radio or tetephone message exchanged with firefighters or headquarters. IT manager Chris Maas says, "When the price of mobile communications comes down enough, we may consider transmitting messages to headquarters in digital form, as well as, or instead of, voice."

End-users can pull up a site plan on screen – or sketch one for themselves using Paintbrush – and plot the positions of each appliance and individual, as well as the fire itself. Duties can be assigned by pointing and clicking on the diagram. The plans can be printed out and handed to drivers, instead of verbally explaining where to go. "It all saves valuable time," says Blackwell.

The system also enables staff to monitor the "inner cordon" – the area which during a major incident is cordoned off by the police. ECFRS has to monitor not only its own people but also police and ambulance workers who are inside the cordon, as well as any firefighters brought in from other brigades.

Each PC screen displays a panel of reminder buttons which turn from green to red when a particular area requires attention – for instance, when a watch needs to be retrieved, or one of the regular informative messages is due to be sent to headquarters.

A major function of the mobile system is to provide up-to-date reference data on the "fireground". It carries information extracted each morning from the HQ's main MIS system, also built with Omnis and incorporating an Oracle database. While garaged the vehicle is connected into the main HQ network.

That information includes digitised plans of all major sites in the area, which ECFRS inspects annually. There are also details of appliances, and (carefully secured) personnel information including medical records for use in the event of an injury.

This last feature Blackwell considers to be one of the most important benefits of the system. He explains that some of the reference data is quite volatile: for example, the MIS

keeps track of what hydrants are out of order, and having that information to hand on arrival at a fire can save precious moments.

The main advantage of using PCs to build the system, rather than special rack-mounted equipment, is that the kit can easily be replaced.

As for Omnis, Sophtlogic had already used it to build a number of systems for ECFRS, and the services senior administrative officer Paul Rudd says, "We saw no reason to bring in a new and specialised technology if a proven one could do the job."

A further reason for choosing Omnis 7 was the commonality of data with the existing MIS system.

While Omnis proved equal to the task, the circumstances in which the system runs provided some interesting design challenges.

Sophtlogic says that technically the most difficult thing was to design a system that combined performance with resilience. The system had to be able to continue processing in the event of a failure of any component. The PCs cooperate closely but are not dependent on one another.

Every item that is keyed in is written to an incident log, and this is used to update the system data. That data is held in a number of separate Omnis databases, a feature which adds an extra dimension of resilience. Once a transaction is on the incident log, any of the PCs can complete the work of updating the database.

Each PC maintains a "memory map" of the incident. A "watchdog" PC continually copies snapshots of all these memory maps to disc, so that if the system fails the latest map can be used for recovery. The system prints out each transaction as it is logged so the printout can be used to switch to manual procedures as a last resort.

Testing is more than an optional extra in a system like this and this one was given a hammering, both by Sophtlogic and its future end-users.

As well as validating the software, the team built a mockup of the incident control area to ensure that the ergonomics were right. All the

▶

potential operators went through a training programme that included a simulated incident. The system proved easy to learn, and Blackwell, a dab hand with a mouse, says the combination of Omnis and Windows is "brilliant" for the purpose.

The system has yielded unexpected benefits in addition to the planned ones. For instance, Blackwell says, "There is a display of appliances in attendance. That information had to be in the system, and originally I didn't think it would be very useful, but we've found that it's a good way to work out reliefs, since you can sort the display by time of arrival."

ECFRS is enthusiastic about the unit and system and has ideas for enhancements.

A current project is to create an online version of a manual officers carry to remind them how to deal with particular eventualities, such as the presence of various inflammable chemicals.

Future possibilities include integrating the plans with a geographical information system, to create a facility for zooming in from a street to a site to an individual building, which could help in directing drivers.

But as Maas says, "You have to be very careful about rolling out enhancements to a system like this, and plan your training. It's essential that the end-users understand what they're doing."

It is easy to see why user-friendliness, together with a good response, is ultra important. This is one system that is always used, figuratively and literally, in the heat of the moment. ■

Reprinted with permission from *Computer Weekly*, 6th October 1995.

CASE STUDY 2: KRAFT JACOBS SUCHARD

Kraft Jacobs Suchard: up-to-date

by Emma Mansell-Lewis

Kraft Jacobs Suchard is part of the world's largest consumer goods company, the Phillip Morris Group. Selling both to retail outlets and cash and carry warehouse, the company needs to provide sales staff with up-to-date customer information.

According to Peter Bowes, system devlopment manager at Kraft Jacobs Suchard, the existing system was unable to provide data in a user-friendly format. He says, "We had an in-house system based on Cics but it was limited in terms of flexibility. It just did not supply people with easy and ready access to information. Within the IT department we recognised that people were seeing reports and information feeds and re-keying them into their own PCs for analysis."

The company invested in the Empress sales and marketing system from IRI Software.

Based on client-server technology, it has created a single corporate DB2 data warehouse that can be accessed by a series of Express applications across a whole range of sales, marketing, finance, planning and executive support functions.

The first application to go live was the customer account management system, focusing on basic sales information viewed by major customer or trade sector for all products.

The benefits to date include ease-of-use and the ability to analyse customer and product sale information. Bowes adds that the system aids the efficiency of forecasts and make for better assessment of the impact of different pricing and promotional strategies, through a better understanding of customer and market dynamics.

▶

Says Bowes, "Access to data is important: we want to know what the customer has bought. Now we know very quickly who has bought a certain product and what volume of business is centred on a customer or product. We can now rank our customers via unique product codes and compare customers over time by products etc. Our sales department is now information-rich."

Kraft Jacobs Suchard has also developed applications for customer account profitability analyses and is using pre-packaged express applications for financial planning and budgeting and multisource sales and maketing analysis.

Bowes concludes, "What sales people want is easy access to product/customer information over time with lots of variables - right down to lowest volume product per week." ∎

Reprinted with permission from *Computer Weekly*, 29th September 1995.

Summary continued

organisational situations to which these MSS have been applied, although financial performance appears to be a key support area within the majority of these systems.

The next chapter of this book focuses on the third aspect of management support provision, that of active decision making support. As will be become clear, there are as many ways of supporting decision making actively as there are to support decision making passively. However, all active approaches require the formulation and interactive use of models.

References

Cronk R D (1993) EISs Mine your Data. *BYTE*. Vol 18 No 7. pp. 121–128.

Fidler C S and Rogerson S (1993) Current IS Practices within UK Based Organisations. *Information Management & Computer Security*. Vol 1 No 2. pp. 13–20.

Lucey T (1991) *Management Information Systems* Sixth Edition. DP Publications.

Millet I and Mawhinney C H (1992) Executive Information Systems: a Critical Appraisal. *Information & Management*. Vol 23. pp. 83–92.

Pinella P (1991) An EIS for the Desktop. *Datamation*. May 1st Edition. pp. 26–30.

Van Der Lans R F (1989) *The SQL Standard: a Complete Reference*. Prentice-Hall.

Warren L (1995) A Slice of Life. *Computer Weekly* February 23rd Edition. p. 35.

Review questions

1 What is meant by passive decision making support in the context of MSS design?

2 Give reasons why, in reality, one physical MSS does not at present provide organisations with full passive decision making support in all managerial activities, at all managerial levels and in all managerial functions. To what extent do you think this situation will change in the future (bearing in mind what has been described in Chapter 3)?

3 Describe the three types of MSS information report that can be provided, if we categorise MSS information reports in terms of their content.

4 Describe the feedforward and feedback approaches to control within organisations.

5 For each type of MSS information reports described in **3** in turn, describe how reports of this type may be of benefit within organisational planning and control activities.

6 Define the four classifications of MSS information reports that are based on temporal issues regarding report specification and report availability to management.

7 Contrast the approaches to information reporting provided by SQL and Express.

8 What is drill down? To what category of information report identified in **6** is this facility appropriate?

9 What is a Briefing Book facility?

10 What is traffic light colour coding used for?

11 What are hotspots?

12 To what organisational application area are most real-life MSS that provide information reporting capabilities currently applied?

Project idea

Find an organisation and conduct an initial review of current MSS that provide passive decision making support. This review may identify several physical MSS, so select one for further analysis. Interview, if possible, the MSS developer or a member of the IS development team, to ascertain:

- What its primary purpose is within the organisation.
- Who uses the output and for what purposes.
- What types of information reports are provided, both in terms of content (analysis, exception and/or plan of action reports) and in terms of their specification and availability to management (as-needed pre-defined vs. as-needed customised vs. periodic pre-defined vs. periodic customised).
- What types of interaction methods are supported by the MSS for requesting information, and whether they are the most appropriate ones for the type of MSS information reports being delivered.

You may find that an interaction method that you identify is not described in this book. In this case, make an educated guess as to whether you consider the method to be suitable to the type of information reports being produced.

Your review could then be presented as part of a tutorial discussion session on passive decision making support with MSS. That way, you learn from experiences of other members of your group, not just from your own study.

CHAPTER 6

Active Decision Making Support with MSS

6.1 INTRODUCTION

As highlighted in Chapter 2, MSS provide both active and passive support for decision making. MSS capabilities for passive decision making support have been described in Chapter 5. This chapter focuses on MSS functionality for active decision making support.

Active decision making support is provided by MSS through the interactive use of models. These models are often of a mathematical nature. A large proportion of this chapter is therefore devoted to several mathematical techniques, each of which prescribes a particular approach to the formulation and solution of mathematical models. The level of mathematical knowledge required to understand technique descriptions is deliberately kept as low as possible. The intention is to provide the reader with an overall appreciation of mathematical models and several of the techniques available for their formulation and solution. The reader should be able to identify when mathematical solutions to decision making situations are needed and seek specialist Operations Research (OR) or Management Science (MS) advice as a consequence.

Section 6.2 examines models in general and identifies several reasons why models, particularly of a mathematical nature, are important to organisations. Section 6.3 focuses on several mathematical techniques that are used in both the formulation and solution of decision situation models. Section 6.4 concentrates on techniques, each of which prescribes a particular group decision making approach. Section 6.5 examines MSS provision for active support of management decision making, starting with an overall view of MSS provision and then focusing on three aspects of MSS provision that need further explanation. The scope and wide-ranging nature of MSS provision for active decision making support is highlighted in this chapter. Finally, Section 6.6 provides a summary of the chapter.

At the end of this chapter the reader should understand:

- *What models are and how to categorise them.*
- *Why models in general, and mathematical models in particular, are important to an organisation facing many decisions.*
- *Several key mathematical techniques and how they are used to formulate and solve mathematical models.*
- *Several key techniques for structuring group decision making processes.*

- *The overall scope and nature of MSS providing active decision making support.*
- *The differences between MSS that actively support individual decision making and MSS that actively support group decision making.*

6.2 WHAT IS A MODEL?

6.2.1 Models and modelling

There are many definitions of the term 'model'. The definition adopted within this book is that a model is:

A representation and simplification of some abstract or concrete entity.

This definition is preferred to other model definitions because it recognises explicitly the modelling of both abstract entities (that is, entities that do not yet exist in the real world) and concrete entities (that is, entities that do exist in the real world). This is in line with the view expressed by Finlay (1989). Thus, a map of a new road scheme is a model, according to the model definition above, as it represents by pencil lines and arrows what may occur in reality at some point in the future. Other model definitions do not allow explicitly for this 'model of the future', referring solely to concrete entities.

A model is a *representation* and a *simplification* of something that either exists now or may exist in the future. If it was neither a representation nor a simplification, it would be the same as the thing being modelled, either intended or actual; hence it would not be a model. There are many ways that models represent something else, and some of these ways are discussed in Sections 6.3 and 6.4. Models do not take on all the intricate features of that which they are representing. Rather, they take on only those features that are important to their users. So, the aforementioned new road scheme model may not consider the actual positioning and style of traffic light signals (for example, whether the traffic lights are double tiered or whether one signal is to be positioned above the road): only their location along a particular street is important for those engaged in using the model for road scheme evaluation purposes. Traffic light locations may be represented by pencilled crosses on the map.

Modelling can be described as the activity of constructing models. It involves sub-activities such as:

- Finding out about the situation requiring the construction of a model, and establishing the objectives of the model to be developed
- Developing the model
- Testing and evaluating the model
- Monitoring the use of the model, and amending and/or enhancing it when circumstances change.

Modelling is a continuous process, ending when the model becomes obsolete and/or withdrawn from use. Models need to evolve in response to changing circumstances that have a direct bearing on the relevance of the model. As a result, most MSS that provide decision-specific models need frequent monitoring and adaptation to ensure currency of application.

6.2.2 Model classification

A model should take on the features considered necessary for it to function appropriately within the situation to which it is being applied. Since situations differ greatly, it is therefore no surprise that models differ widely in functionality and scope. Efforts have been made to classify models. For example, Caine and Robson (1993) separate models into those that are prescriptive and those that are descriptive. A prescriptive model is one that is used to find the 'best' alternative to a given decision situation specification. On the other hand, a descriptive model is one that describes the current or proposed situation and allows users to experiment with alternative scenarios. In addition to the prescriptive versus descriptive classification, Caine and Robson categorise models as:

- *Iconic* – where the model is a physical representation of that which exists or may exist in the future, but is smaller in scale and portrays only the features of importance. A small-scale model of a new housing estate, which is used to provide information to prospective buyers on how the estate will be arranged, is an example of an iconic model. The houses and landscaped gardens may closely resemble what is to be provided, but only the exteriors of the houses are modelled and the entire estate model sits on a table.
- *Analog* – where the salient properties of that being modelled are represented in a different way to that which either exists or may exist in the future. An example analog model is a graph. A bar graph of monthly sales, for instance, represents a particular month's sales by the height of a bar on the graph.
- *Mathematical* – where the salient properties of the thing being modelled are represented by mathematical formulae, symbols and relationships. For example, the following very simple statements provide a mathematical formula for the calculation of profit before tax:

    Profit = Sales – Costs

    Profit-after-tax = Profit – (Profit $*$ Tax-rate)

These types of models are also called symbolic models.

- *Conceptual* – where a diagrammatic approach is used as an intermediate representation between a situation being modelled and a mathematical model formulation. An example conceptual model is a flow chart diagram of a decision situation.

Caine and Robson's categorisations are not mutually exclusive. Mathematical models and conceptual models are subtypes of the analog model category, in that mathematical models are actually representing something via mathematical symbols and conceptual models are representing something using diagrammatic approaches. Iconic and analog are, however, mutually exclusive model categories.

6.2.3 Why are models important to organisations?

Many organisations develop models, at the cost of substantial human, material and financial resources. The question is, therefore, why are models important enough to merit development and continual evolution?

A model can provide insight into something that does not yet exist. This can yield substantial monetary and non-monetary benefits. Imagine trying to build a new housing estate without some idea of what it will look like, and how the amenities required by each house are to be provided. At the very least, buyers will not know what they are buying and may not want to invest their money into such an unknown quantity. Worse still, imagine constructing a house only to find that the foundations have been built on the land that was earmarked originally for the laying of the main drainage and sewer services to the estate. Even worse, imagine major design faults being identified in a house that has already been erected, for example the weight of the roof being inadequately supported by joists. If these issues are not evaluated in advance, then expensive re-building may need to take place.

The use of models can therefore lead to substantial cost avoidance, by improving understanding of an existing or potential situation, and in helping to minimise risk of failure. They can aid communication between individuals and organisations, providing a concrete view of something that may exist, presently, only in the minds of the few. Models also allow experimentation, by permitting the effects of alternative scenarios to be examined. In the case of the housing estate model, it may be possible to arrange houses and other features in different ways, allowing evaluation of each possible configuration by all parties concerned with its development. Predicting possible problems is also facilitated using appropriate models. For example, a model of a current production process may be used to examine the effects of a predicted increase in customer requirements. Contingency plans can be developed in plenty of time to cope with the new demands on resources caused by the expected increases.

6.2.4 The special properties of mathematical models

Models that are specified in a mathematical form have special properties. Firstly, mathematical models can be formulated in ways that enable them to be solved mathematically. There are techniques that prescribe particular approaches for both formulating and solving mathematical models (Section 6.3 looks at several of these techniques). Secondly, mathematical models are amenable to computerisation. Mathematics is a formal language which can be readily converted to a programming language format. In modern organisations, it is usually the case that mathematical models, beyond the most simple, are developed and solved using appropriate computerised systems.

Computerised mathematical model development and use have additional benefits to those suggested in the previous subsection. The calculatory performance of computers far outstrips human calculatory capabilities. This means that a greater number of alternatives to a decision situation can be considered within a computerised setting than within a non-computerised one over an identical time frame. This can lead to better quality decisions. Also, the solution of some models requires an immense number of calculations to be performed. It could take a person without computer assistance months to work out the results, if indeed they even tried, whereas a computerised version of the model could provide the results in a matter of seconds. Indeed, some techniques for formulating and solving mathematical models are not feasible to use in non-computerised settings, as model resolution is considered beyond human capabilities.

The development and use of mathematical models is a principal focus of attention in the next section of this chapter, and key techniques for active support of group decision making form the subject of Section 6.4. However, these are not the only models/techniques of importance to MSS. For instance, several techniques allow the development of conceptual models which are extremely beneficial to MSS development (see Chapter 7 for further information on MSS development) and analog models, such as graphs, are important MSS output presentation formats.

6.3 MATHEMATICAL MODELS AND ASSOCIATED TECHNIQUES

Mathematical models can be developed for, and used in, a wide variety of decision situations, although their application must always be in accordance with organisational requirements. Types of decision situations to which mathematical models have been applied include the following:

- *Allocation decisions* – when resources need to be allocated between several activities or products, and there are insufficient resources to cater for all activity or product requirements.
- *Distribution decisions* – where there are many possible ways of distributing goods between two or more locations, and the best routes need to be chosen. Issues that may need to be considered during route selection include the cost of a route, the bandwidth or maximum quantity possible down a route, the reliability of a route, and the time taken to use a route.
- *Activity scheduling decisions* – where (sub)activities need to be scheduled, as part of a larger activity, and the critical path established (i.e. the sequence of (sub)activities from the start to the finish of the activity, where a delay in any one of the (sub)activities causes a delay in the overall activity).
- *Risk/consequence analysis decisions* – where alternatives lead to consequences that possess elements of risk and uncertainty, and these need to be evaluated as part of the decision making process.
- *Futures' planning decisions* – where aspects of current operations, resources or products need to be projected into the future for examination.

Several mathematical techniques that can be applied within the formulation and solution of decision situation-specific mathematical models are listed in Figure 6.1. Each mathematical technique has its own flavour of modelling decision situations, and therefore is not always applicable to a given decision situation. Some mathematical techniques are oriented towards one of the types of decision situations listed above, whereas others are more general in nature and may be applied to several of the above types of decision situations.

The remainder of this section reviews the mathematical techniques listed in Figure 6.1 in turn. The objective is to provide the reader with an overall appreciation of each technique's purpose and application. It is not the intention to explore all the mathematical intricacies of the techniques. This is particularly the case with respect to Linear Programming, where the solution of a Linear Programming model requires a

Fig 6.1 Several techniques for the formulation and solution of mathematical models

• Weighted Score	• Simulation
• Mathematical Programming (Linear Programming)	• Forecasting
• Decision Trees	• Rule-based

The list comprises several of the mathematical techniques that prescribe a method for the formulation and solution of mathematical models. However, in every modelling situation, techniques need to be assessed against the requirements of the particular decision situation in hand.

higher degree of mathematical knowledge than in the case of any of the other mathematical techniques listed in Figure 6.1. For this reason, Linear Programming is covered to the level of model formulation only. For details on the methods by which Linear Programming models are solved, readers should consult Operations Research (OR) and Management Science (MS) texts (such as Strayer 1989 and Brickman 1989).

6.3.1 Weighted score technique

The Weighted Score technique is a simple mathematical technique that is applicable to decision situations where decision alternatives need to be evaluated against a set of criteria. In its simplest form, the procedure for formulating a model using Weighted Score technique is as follows:

1. The criteria of interest and the available alternatives are first established.
2. Each criterion is weighted by giving it a value on an integer scale, say between 1 and 10. The larger the value, the more important the criterion.
3. Each alternative is also given a score on an integer scale, say between 1 and 10, for each criterion. For example, if there are four criteria then each alternative should have four scores between 1 and 10, one per criterion. The larger the score, the better the alternative is with respect to that criterion.

The procedure for solving the model is as follows:

1. The value of a particular alternative can then be found by multiplying the score of that alternative for a particular criterion by the criterion's weight, for each criterion in turn, and then summing the resultant values obtained over all criteria.
2. This is done for each alternative in turn. The alternative with the highest final value is the preferred alternative and should be adopted.

Consider, for example, a decision to hire a new employee for an Analyst/Programmer post within an in-house IT department. In line with advocated methods of promoting objectivity in the personnel employment process, a set of criteria for the post was established at the outset of the hiring process. Several criteria relate to those factors or skills that must be possessed by any potential employee (that is, these form the set of mandatory criteria). The remaining criteria relate to those aspects that are desirable within a potential employee (these form the set of desirable criteria). A national press advertisement highlighted clearly the mandatory and desirable criteria, and these criteria were used to provide a shortlist of three suitable candidates, all of whom satisfied the mandatory criteria on paper. Interviewing the three candidates was considered an important next stage in the hiring process to authenticate application form contents (and, hence, each candidate's position with respect to the mandatory criteria) and to evaluate each candidate more fully with respect to the desirable criteria. Prior to interviewing, the interviewer listed the desirable criteria on a Criteria Reference Form and gave each a weight value between 1 and 10 to indicate the relative importance of each criterion to the job on offer. Table 6.1 shows the Criteria Reference Form that has been filled in thus far.

At the end of an interview with a candidate, the interviewer scored the candidate on each criterion on a scale, again between 1 and 10. At the end of the three candidate interviews, the Criteria Reference Form was completed by calculating the total value for each candidate, worked out in the manner described above. The completed form is shown in Table 6.2. From this evaluation, Candidate 1 had the highest overall score, and was therefore selected. In addition, the completed Criteria Reference Form served as a reference document for the decision, providing the basis for feedback to unsuccessful candidates and for the justification of selection when needed.

The Weighted Score technique can also be applied to group decision making situations. For example, personnel hiring decisions are frequently group decisions, involving two or more interviewers. A possible way of applying the Weighted Score technique in this group decision making setting is to fix the weight values of the criteria but to allow each interviewer to score a candidate separately based on the interview conducted with the candidate. The overall value for each candidate is calculated for each interviewer, deriving a separate rank of the candidates for each interviewer. Inter-

Table 6.1 The Criteria Reference Form for personnel hiring showing criteria and weight values

Criterion	Weight	Candidate 1	Candidate 2	Candidate 3
Previous Analyst/ Programmer experience	4			
Interpersonal skills	8			
Previous client base ---> new work	2			
Self-management skills and motivation	6			
Overall Value:				

Each criterion is listed on the left-hand side of the form, and a weight value between 1 and 10 is attached to each criterion which indicates its importance to the personnel hiring decision. So, for example, interpersonal skills are seen to be four times as important as the presence of a previous client base, and twice as important as previous Analyst/Programmer experience. The weights reflect the nature of the work involved in this post.

Table 6.2 The completed criteria reference form for the personnel hiring decision

Criterion	Weight	Candidate 1	Candidate 2	Candidate 3
Previous Analyst/ Programmer experience	4	6	3	6
Interpersonal skills	8	8	4	6
Previous client base ---> new work	2	1	3	4
Self-management skills and motivation	6	5	6	5
Overall Value:		120	86	110

The candidates have been scored on each criterion. A candidate's overall value can be found by summing each criterion's overall value, which is the criterion's score for that candidate multiplied by the weight value of that criterion. So, in the case of Candidate 1, the value is calculated as follows:

$$\text{Overall value of Candidate 1} = (6 * 4) + (8 * 8) + (1 * 2) + (5 * 6) = 120$$

The values for Candidates 2 and 3 are also calculated in the same way, leading to the overall values at the bottom of the Criteria Reference Form. The highest overall value indicates the candidate to be selected: in this case, it is Candidate 1. The ranking of the candidates is 1,3,2.

viewer's ranks may differ, as each interviewer may score a candidate differently based on the individual view gained of the candidate within the interview. The ranks provide guidance to subsequent group discussions. For example, supposing the ranks for three interviewers of the three candidates were as follows:

Interviewer 1 Ranking	*Interviewer 2 Ranking*	*Interviewer 3 Ranking*
Candidate 1	Candidate 1	Candidate 1
Candidate 3	Candidate 2	Candidate 3
Candidate 2	Candidate 3	Candidate 2

In this case, the ranks show Candidate 1 as the clear winner. On the other hand, supposing the ranks for the three interviewers were as follows.

Interviewer 1 Ranking	*Interviewer 2 Ranking*	*Interviewer 3 Ranking*
Candidate 2	Candidate 1	Candidate 3
Candidate 1	Candidate 2	Candidate 1
Candidate 3	Candidate 3	Candidate 2

There is no outright winner and subsequent discussion time may be needed in order to arrive at some overall consensus. Sometimes, the rankings may help to identify candidates that are not worthy of further consideration rather than indicating an outright winner.

The above method of applying the Weighted Score technique to a group decision making setting is only one of several possible 'variations on a theme'. Another variation is to allow group participants the additional capability to assign different weight values to each criterion. A further variation is to only allow weight values to vary between group participants (with the score for each alternative on each criterion being the result of group consensus). Another variation is where the individual participants' weight values of each criterion, and the individual participants' scores of each alternative on each criterion, are averaged across the group, prior to overall candidate score evaluation. This variation results in one overall ranking, and the winner can be identified easily. However, extreme variations between the individual participants' views of the importance of a criterion and of candidate score values are lost through averaging.

To summarise, the Weighted Score technique can be applied to both group and individual decision making situations, but must always be used with caution. Extreme views of individual participants, regarding the importance of a criterion or the scores of candidates, can be lost when averaging across group participants. Psychological make-up can also influence the effectiveness of this technique. Some people refrain from using the highest and lowest level score and weight values. Furthermore, the meanings attached to the weight and score values that lie between the highest and lowest values are unlikely to be wholly consistent across group members.

6.3.2 Mathematical programming techniques (linear programming)

Mathematical Programming techniques permit the formulation and solution of a mathematical model which results in the best solution to a given decision situation specification. Although often referred to as optimisation techniques, whether they do indeed result in the optimum solution for a decision situation is quite a different matter. This depends greatly on accuracy of the model formulation and how many qualitative issues need to be taken into account in decision making. However, within the limits of model specification, the solving of the model involves seeking the best alternative. Mathematical Programming techniques do not require the alternatives to be identified at the model formulation stage, only the ranges within which alternatives are required. Model solution involves the identification and evaluation of all pertinent alternatives.

Linear Programming is one of the simplest forms of Mathematical Programming techniques and is the focus of this overview. Moreover, the formulation of a model using the Linear Programming technique is covered only. This is sufficient to gain an appreciation of the merits of Mathematical Programming, in general, and Linear Programming in particular, without having to engage in overly complex mathematical issues. The reader will be in a position to at least identify situations where Mathematical/Linear Programming techniques may be of benefit, although any activities further than the formulation of a Linear Programming model will require specialist OR or MS expertise.

A Linear Programming model formulation comprises three interrelated specifications: a specification of the *variables* whose values are to be set during model solution, a specification of the so-termed *objective function* which identifies that which is being optimised, and a specification of the *constraints* to which the values of the variables must adhere.

The best way to explain how to formulate a Linear Programming model is through the use of an example. Consider a shoe manufacturing company. At the end of each week, a decision needs to be made concerning the quantity of shoes of a particular style to manufacture in the next week, so that the best possible expected profit is achieved. The company manufactures four basic styles of shoes; numbers 21, 31, 56, and 86. Each dozen pairs of shoes of a certain style has a standard expected contribution value to profit when sold, which is as follows:

Style	Profit contribution per dozen pairs in £s
21	120
31	90
56	150
86	170

In order to provide sufficient client choice, each style has a minimum number of dozen pairs that must be produced: 20 of style 21, 30 of style 31, 45 of style 56 and 20 of style 86. Each style requires leather and/or suede in its manufacture, and there are maximum weekly supplies of both materials (700 units of suede and 1300 units of leather). The requirements of both leather and suede units for each style per dozen pairs of shoes are shown in Table 6.3.

All shoes undergo both machining and finishing during the manufacturing process. Different styles of shoes have different requirements in terms of machining and finishing times, and these are also given in Table 6.3 per dozen pair. Due to labour availability restrictions, there is a weekly maximum of 1000 staff hours available for machining activities and a weekly maximum of 600 staff hours available for finishing activities.

This decision situation appears appropriate to be formulated as a Linear Programming model, as something is to be optimised (i.e. expected profit is to be maximised). There is also a set of variables (i.e. how many dozen pairs of each style to manufacture in the week) whose values need to be set to achieve the optimal solution. Finally, there is

Table 6.3 Manufacturing of shoe styles; material and human resource requirements

Style	Suede Requirements (in units per dozen pair)	Leather Requirements (in units per dozen pair)	Machining Time Required (in hours per dozen pair)	Finishing Time Required (in hours per dozen pair)
21	10	10	1	1
31	5	16	2	1
56	0	15	0.5	0.5
86	15	0	4	3

The table provides the individual material and human resource requirements of a dozen pairs of each style of shoe. For example, three hours of staff time are needed to finish a dozen pairs of style 86, whereas only one hour is needed to finish a dozen pairs of style 21.

a set of constraints with respect to the scarcity of both material and human resources, and the provision of client choice.

When formulating a Linear Programming model, the first issue to address is the identification and specification of the variables. In the case of the shoe manufacturing mix decision, four variables are needed, each one to hold the number of dozen pairs of a particular style to manufacture in a week. The variables are specified in the following manner:

Let $prod_{21}$ be the quantity of Style 21 to be produced per dozen pairs in a week.
Let $prod_{31}$ be the quantity of Style 31 to be produced per dozen pairs in a week.
Let $prod_{56}$ be the quantity of Style 56 to be produced per dozen pairs in a week.
Let $prod_{86}$ be the quantity of Style 86 to be produced per dozen pairs in a week.

The name given to each variable is arbitrary and is chosen by the model developer.

The second issue to address is the specification of the objective function for the Linear Programming model. A Linear Programming technique permits each decision situation to have one objective to which a solution is sought; for example, to maximise profit or to minimise cost. The objective function can be either to maximise something or to minimise something, but not both at the same time (such as seeking to maximise profit and minimise cost simultaneously). Furthermore, that which it is maximising or minimising must be capable of being specified in the form of a linear equation, that is a mathematical equation which has variables expressed to the power of one only, for example $prod_{21}$ and $prod_{31}$ but not $prod_{21}^2$ or $prod_{31}^2$. Each variable may have a multiplying factor, and the addition of variables (when combined with their multiplying factor) is commonplace.

In the case of the shoe manufacturing mix example, the objective is to maximise profit. Profit is the sum of the individual profits of each style. Each individual profit of a style is determined by how many dozen pairs of shoes of the style in question are manufactured multiplied by the expected profit for a dozen pairs of that style. An assumption is made here: that every pair of shoes of a particular style that is manufactured is sold to clients within the same week, and that there are no reject shoes or shoes returned by a client. This allows the number of dozen pairs of shoes of a particular style that are manufactured to be equated to sales. Assumptions are frequent within any model formulation and must be made explicit to any user of the model.

The formula for the shoe manufacturing mix objective function is therefore as follows:

$$\text{MAXIMISE } 120prod_{21} + 90prod_{31} + 150prod_{56} + 170prod_{86}$$

If the Linear Programming model for the shoe manufacturing mix decision was considered complete at this point, then the solution would give each variable the value of infinity, as an increase in the manufacture of each style, and hence sold, would result in a corresponding increase in profit. However, there are typically many constraints impacting on any situation. These may include financial limitations, the scarcity of human and material resources, restriction on available time, and limited capacities of machines and labour. The third aspect of a Linear Programming model formulation is the identification and specification of the constraints, to which any optimal solution must adhere. Several constraint equations may need to be specified, each of which represents some constraint that restricts the optimal solution. Like the objective function specification, each constraint equation needs to be expressed in the form of a linear equation. Each constraint equation refers to one or more of the specified variables.

There are several constraints that need to be specified for the shoe manufacturing mix decision. Firstly, there are constraints concerning material restrictions. Each style requires varied amounts of leather and/or suede, and the quantities of each material available is restricted. Looking at suede first, the sum of the individual suede requirements of each style per dozen pairs must not exceed a total maximum weekly supply of 700 units. The individual suede requirements of each style per dozen pairs is equal to the number of dozen pairs made of that style when multiplied by the quantity of suede used in that style per dozen pairs. Thus, a constraint equation, which specifies the restrictions on manufacture due to suede limitations, can be formulated as follows:

$$10\text{prod}_{21} + 5\text{prod}_{31} + 15\text{prod}_{86} <= 700$$

Note the absence of variable prod56 in this equation, as style 56 does not use suede in its manufacture.

A constraint equation concerning the use of leather can be specified in a similar way as follows:

$$10\text{prod}_{21} + 16\text{prod}_{31} + 15\text{prod}_{56} <= 1300$$

Note that style 56 uses leather (hence its presence in this equation) but style 86 does not.

In addition to material constraints, the shoe manufacturing mix decision needs to account for staff time limitations. The staff time constraint equations are specified in an identical manner to the material constraints, where the sum of the time requirements of each style per dozen pairs (time required for a particular style is the time for one dozen pairs of the style multiplied by the number of dozen pairs of that style being produced) must not exceed the total time available. Two staff time constraints, one for machining and one for finishing, are required. These are specified as follows:

Machining constraint:

$$\text{prod}_{21} + 2\text{prod}_{31} + 0.5\text{prod}_{56} + 4\text{prod}_{86} <= 1000$$

Finishing constraint:

$$\text{prod}_{21} + \text{prod}_{31} + 0.5\text{prod}_{56} + 3\text{prod}_{86} <= 600$$

Finally, each style has a minimum amount of dozen pairs that must be fabricated to provide sufficient client choice. Four constraints are needed to specify these restrictions, one for each style of shoe.

Minimum levels of production:

$$\text{prod}_{21} >= 20$$
$$\text{prod}_{31} >= 30$$
$$\text{prod}_{56} >= 45$$
$$\text{prod}_{86} >= 20$$

The Linear Programming model for the shoe manufacturing mix decision is now complete. The model is summarised in Figure 6.2.

The Linear Programming model for the shoe manufacturing mix decision is in the correct form (although probably not in the exact syntax) to be input to a computer-

Fig 6.2 The linear programming formulation for the shoe manufacturing mix decision

Variable Definitions:

Let $prod_{21}$ be the quantity of Style 21 to be produced per dozen pairs in a week.
Let $prod_{31}$ be the quantity of Style 31 to be produced per dozen pairs in a week.
Let $prod_{56}$ be the quantity of Style 56 to be produced per dozen pairs in a week.
Let $prod_{86}$ be the quantity of Style 86 to be produced per dozen pairs in a week

Objective Function:

MAXIMISE $120 prod_{21} + 90 prod_{31} + 150 prod_{56} + 170 prod_{86}$

Constraints:

$10 prod_{21} + 5 prod_{31} + 15 prod_{86} <= 700$ (Suede constraint)

$10 prod_{21} + 16 prod_{31} + 15 prod_{56} <= 1300$ (Leather constraint)

$prod_{21} + 2 prod_{31} + 0.5 prod_{56} + 4 prod_{86} <= 1000$ (Machining constraint)

$prod_{21} + prod_{31} + 0.5 prod_{56} + 3 prod_{86} <= 600$ (Finishing constraint)

$prod_{21} >= 20$ (Customer Choice constraints)
$prod_{31} >= 30$
$prod_{56} >= 45$
$prod_{86} >= 20$

To summarise, the formulation of a Linear Programming model takes the following structure. Firstly, identify the variables. Secondly, specify the objective function, which maximises or minimises some linear combination of the specified variables. Thirdly, specify the constraints as linear equations, each of which refers to one or more of the specified variables. It is worth noting that the model presented above is a particular type of Linear Programming, in that the values of the variables must always be integers (that is, one never produces a half or a quarter of a dozen, etc.). When selecting the method with which to solve this Linear Programming model, one which results in integer values for the variables is needed.

based Linear Programming package. This package, when requested, solves the model. This typically results in the best possible values of $prod_{21}$, $prod_{31}$, $prod_{56}$ and $prod_{86}$ so that the best possible value of the objective function is achieved whilst adhering to all of the constraints. The exception to this is when no solution that satisfies all of the constraint equations simultaneously can be found. In this case, a message is usually displayed, stating that there is no feasible solution to the model. As aforementioned, the methods used to solve Linear Programming models are beyond the scope of this introduction to the Linear Programming technique.

Computerised Mathematical Programming packages are readily available in the marketplace. It is computers that make Linear Programming and other forms of Mathematical Programming techniques viable for decision making support commercially; manual calculations were either resource intensive, taking days to work out, or, in some cases, impossible to perform.

6.3.3 Decision tree technique

The overall aim of the Decision Tree technique is similar to that of the Weighted Score technique: to find the best solution to a given decision situation from a set of pre-specified alternatives. However, the techniques are very different in their approach. The Decision Tree technique is illustrated through its application to the following decision making situation.

The MD of a large electrical appliance manufacturing company has an important investment decision to make. An independent inventor has just presented her new invention to the company with the possibility of including it within the company's product portfolio. The decision to be made by the MD is whether or not the company should invest in this new invention. At least £500,000 will be required to initiate production, and the MD estimates that the probability of success in the marketplace is fifty-fifty. If it is a success, however, an average annual income of £1,000,000 is predicted over the next five years (which is the length of time over which new inventions are initially supported and therefore evaluated, financially, within the corporation). The MD is fairly sure (about 90% chance) that competitors will, if the product is successful in the marketplace, undertake the development of a competing product. If a competing product is developed, then income to the company for the product's sales is expected to decrease to approximately £400,000 per annum from the second year of sales onwards.

If the MD decides not to invest in the invention, then there is an estimated 60% chance of a competitor investing in the product. If the competitor was successful in the marketplace (again, estimated at fifty-fifty), then the MD would have to decide whether the company should compete. The development of a competing product would cost £500,000 more for initial production set up than if the original invention had been invested in (as high-cost experts would need to be commissioned to develop a competing product). The revenue expected over the 5 years of competing product sales, given that the company is not a leader but a follower with respect to this product, is estimated at only £200,000 per annum.

Furthermore, deciding not to invest, with the competitors then investing and being successful, is also estimated to cost the company around £150,000 in lost sales and new customers for other product lines. However, having invested yet being unsuccessful is expected to cost little damage to the company's reputation (and considered to be negligible for the purposes of modelling the decision). The same is expected to be true if neither the company nor the competition invests.

A diagrammatic view of the Decision Tree model for this decision situation is provided in Figure 6.3. Re-reading the scenario provided in the previous paragraph whilst looking at this figure should provide initial insight as to the Decision Tree model's formulation. Note that those nodes on the tree where the MD has to make a decision are denoted by squares (so-called *decision nodes*) and those nodes on the tree where some consequence of a particular decision alternative, which is outside the control of the MD, occurs are denoted by circles (so-called *consequence nodes*).

When formulating a Decision Tree model in diagrammatic form, it is best to work from the left-hand side to the right-hand side of a page, with the overall decision being the root of the tree on the left-hand side. Probabilities (values between 0 and 1) are

Fig 6.3 The decision tree model for the product investment decision

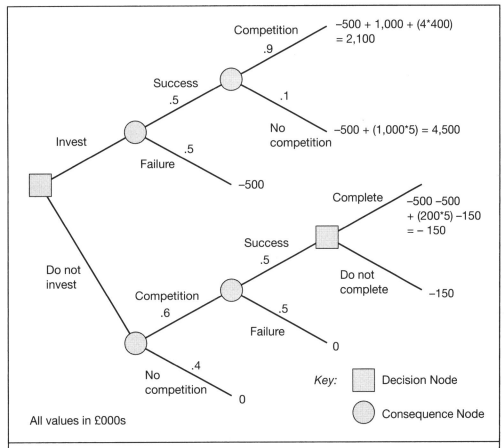

This diagram shows the Decision Tree model of the MD's investment decision. The overall decision is on the left-hand side of the diagram, and the values of particular options in the light of certain consequences occurring are given on the branches on right-hand side of the diagram. The probabilities of occurrence are also provided on the appropriate branches of a consequence node. Probabilities on branches from the same consequence node must always sum to 1. Assumptions made during the formulation of this model are: all investments are made over five years, and no gain is felt by this company if the competitor invests and the product fails.

attached to branches of the tree stemming from a consequence node. The sum of the probabilities on the branches stemming from the same consequence node must add up to 1. So, if there is 40% chance of something occurring then the probability on that branch should be 0.4, and the probabilities on all the other branches stemming from the same consequence node must sum to 0.6. Values are attached to the ends of the rightmost branches, indicating the worth of following the path from the root of the tree to that particular end point. When establishing the worth of a particular end-point, all values (both positive and negative in value), that are a consequence of that path being the actual one undertaken, are included. For example, the value of paths which represent the 'invest' decision being made, with no competing product in the second year of successful investment, is the income from the product over the five years (£1 million * 5 = £5 million) minus the set-up costs (£500,000) which is an overall total of £4.5 million. On the other hand, successful investment with a competing product being produced, would result in £1 million profit in the first year followed by £400,000 * 4 = £1.6 million over the next four years minus the £500,000 set-up costs. This results in a value of £2.1 million for this particular path.

When solving a Decision Tree model presented in diagrammatic form, it is best to work from the right-hand side to the left-hand side of the Decision Tree model. Taking each of the right-most nodes in turn, if the node is a consequence node then the value to be attached to that node is the expected value of the branches that stem from it. The expected value of each branch is found by multiplying the value at the end of each branch by its probability, and the expected value of the node is the sum of the expected values of each branch. Alternatively, if the node is a decision node then the *maximum value* of the branches is taken (it makes no sense to select a branch of lesser value to another). Having completed the process for all the right-most nodes, the process is repeated for the nodes adjacent to them. This continues until the values for all the nodes nearest the root are obtained. The branch with the node of highest value is the alternative that should be selected.

The Decision Tree model for the investment decision, given in Figure 6.3, can now be solved. Taking the right-most nodes, first. On the 'invest' path, the right-most node is a consequence node, so the expected value of that particular node is evaluated as follows:

$$(0.9 * £2.1 \text{ million}) + (0.1 * £4.5 \text{ million}) = £2.34 \text{ million}$$

The right-most node on the 'do not invest' path is a decision node. Both options are worth a loss of £150,000 so either is as bad as each other and is selected. The value of the decision node is therefore –£150,000.

The adjacent node on the 'invest' path is a consequence node, so its expected value is evaluated as follows:

$$(0.5 * £2.34 \text{ million}) + (0.5 * -£500,000) = £920,000$$

The adjacent node on the 'do not invest' path is also a consequence node, so its expected value is evaluated as follows:

$$(0.5 * -£150,000) + (0.5 * 0) = -£75,000$$

The adjacent node on the 'invest' path is the actual investment decision. This cannot be made until the value of the 'do not invest' path is completely determined. Turning to the 'do not invest' path, the adjacent node is a consequence node, whose value is:

$$(0.6 * -£75,000) + (0.4 * 0) = -£45,000$$

Now that the values of both nodes nearest the overall decision are available, the decision can be made. The branch with the greatest value is the chosen alternative. The preferred alternative is therefore to 'invest', as this has an expected value of £920,000, whereas there is an expected loss of £45,000 with the 'do not invest' alternative.

The Decision Tree technique can be used to answer 'what-if' type questions. Within the investment scenario, some of the probabilities and even some of the values (for example, the set-up costs and the expected annual income without competition) may be 'guestimates' on the part of the MD. By changing one or more probabilities, or one or more values, the amended Decision Tree model can be evaluated to see if the change(s) affect the overall decision. Using the Decision Tree technique in this way allows the sensitivity of a decision on key values and probability estimates to be determined. A properly designed computer-based Decision Tree model has advantages in that model modification and subsequent evaluation requires minimal effort.

Cooke and Slack (1991) provide additional applications and further discussion of the Decision Tree technique.

6.3.4 Simulation

Weighted Score, Linear Programming and Decision Tree techniques provide methods for formulating and solving mathematical models. They all seek to find the best solution, either from a set of pre-specified alternatives or across all possible alternatives that adhere to certain constraints. Simulation is different. A model is formulated that simulates something (in terms of its components and interrelationships) using a set of mathematical equations. Input and output variables are specified as part of the model. The model is then used to examine the effects of values of the input variables on the values of the output variables. Simulation can be used to identify potential problems (which may require several decisions to be made in their solution) or in the exploration for an acceptable alternative (but not necessarily the best) to a given decision situation. Simulation models are usually applicable to several decisions, not just one particular decision, within a particular area of operations.

An example situation where Simulation might be applied is that of inventory management. A possible Simulation model to aid an organisation's inventory decisions concerning a particular item of stock is given in Figure 6.4.

The model presented in Figure 6.4 represents, in mathematical form, the following organisational situation.

> The quantity in stock of some item at some time period t is equal to the quantity in stock in the previous time period, minus the customer demand in the current time period but with the addition of the quantity of any orders received in the current time period. The orders received are those orders made lead time periods of time ago (where lead time is the number of time periods between the placing of an order and the receipt of goods ordered). If the quantity in stock of the item in the current time period is either equal to or under the re-order level, then an order for a standard quantity of the stock item is placed in this time period. If the stock in the current time period of the item exceeds the re-order level, then no order is placed in this current time period.

The objective of this particular Simulation model is to explore the effects of input variables, such as customer demand, re-order level, quantity ordered, and lead time, on an item of stock's stock-out rate. The stock-out rate is the percentage of times that there is no items in stock, when the model is solved for several time periods. Some of the input variables remain at the same value across all time periods, whereas others may vary. The model given in Figure 6.4 specifies that the re-order level, standard quantity ordered, and lead time values remain constant throughout the time periods. The model specifies a varying customer demand input value for each time period.

Fig 6.4 An inventory management simulation model

$stock_t = stock_{t-1} -$ customer_demand$_t +$ quantity_ordered$_{t-leadtime}$

IF stock$_t$ <= reorder_level THEN
        quantity_ordered$_t =$ order_quantity
ELSE quantity_ordered$_t = 0$

The model encompasses some time-dependent variables, namely stock, customer_demand, and quantity_ordered. The notation stock$_t$ is a variable representing the stock value at time period t. Stock$_{t-1}$ is a variable whose value represents the stock in the time period before t. So if the time period selected is a day, then stock$_{t-1}$ is a variable whose value represents yesterday's stock.

For example, supposing this model is to be solved for ten time periods, starting from t = 1 to t = 10 where the time between any orders being placed and the same orders being received (that is, the lead time) is fixed at 2 time periods. The quantity of stock ordered at any time is also fixed at 20 items, and the re-order level is fixed at 10 items. At the outset, there are 25 items already in stock and nothing has been ordered: these values would also have to be set at the beginning of model use. The customer demand is to be modelled by a random number generator, which provides, for each time period, a number for the customer demand. Past sales indicate that no more than twenty of this stock item is ever required in any one time period. Hence, the random number generator is programmed to provide random, integer numbers between 0 and 20 only.

Running the model over ten time periods results in the values for stock$_t$ and quantity_ordered$_t$ as shown in Table 6.5, when the random number values for customer_demand$_t$ are generated as shown in Table 6.4.

An analysis of Table 6.5 shows that the stock-out rate (that is, where stock is either less than or equal to 0) is 40%, which, for most companies, would be excessively high! The values of the input variables can be varied and the model solved for the same number of time periods to examine the impact of the changes on the stock-out rate. Performing a series of these 'what-if' analyses may lead to a set of values for the input variables that provide an acceptable stock-out rate.

It is worth noting that both the Simulation model and the description of its use is very simplistic. Assumptions have been made in the development of the model. For example, lead time is taken to be always constant over time periods, and customers are not expected to purchase their goods elsewhere when stock-outs occur. These assumptions

Table 6.4 Generated values for customer_demand$_t$

t =	1	2	3	4	5	6	7	8	9	10
customer_demand$_t$	10	15	2	4	20	19	5	6	16	0

This table provides the values for customer demand generated in each time period.

are clearly simplifications, of which any model user should be aware. Furthermore, solving the model for ten time periods only is insufficient to get a statistically valid picture of the situation and its dynamics. A model needs to be solved over possibly thousands of time periods in order to create a realistic picture for a particular set of input variables.

There are many applications of the Simulation technique. Supermarkets may evaluate average queuing times at checkouts to ensure good customer service using a Simulation model. The number of customers arriving at the checkouts in any one time period may be modelled in a similar way to the customer demand in the inventory management model described above. Changes in the values of the input variables, for example the reduced time taken for a customer to progress through a checkout (which may reflect the possible introduction of tills with bar code readers) or the increased number of checkouts open, could be made and their respective effect on average customer queuing time explored.

Table 6.5 Stock$_t$ and quantity_ordered$_t$ values from solving the inventory management simulation model

t	customer_demand$_t$	stock$_t$	quantity_ordered$_t$
1	10	15	0
2	15	0	20
3	2 ·	−2	20
4	4	14	0
5	20	14	0
6	19	−5	20
7	5	−10	20
8	6	4	20
9	16	8	20
10	0	28	0

For example, the value for stock$_1$ is worked out using the model in Figure 6.4 by substituting t = 1 into the equations, thus:

$$stock_1 = stock_0 - customer\_demand_1 + quantity\_ordered_{-1}$$
$$= 25 \text{ (initial stock level)} - 10 + 0 \text{ (no orders made before running the model)}$$
$$= 15$$

stock$_1$ > reorder_level (set at 10), so quantity_ordered$_1$ = 0

For stock at t = 2:

$$stock_2 = stock_1 - customer\_demand_2 + quantity\_ordered_0$$
$$= 15 - 15 + 0$$
$$= 0$$

stock$_2$ <= reorder_level, so quantity_ordered$_2$ = 20 (the number always ordered).

The values in the remaining rows in Table 6.5 are worked out in an identical way.

6.3.5 Forecasting techniques

Forecasting is concerned with predicting what may occur sometime in the future. There are several approaches to forecasting, but all of these seem to fall into one of two categories: either using the past and present to predict the future or rejecting the continuous view of the world and using other factors as the basis of predictions.

One such family of techniques that lies in the former category of forecasting approaches is Time Series. These techniques require that what is being forecasted, for example a company sales forecast from previous sales, has a cyclical pattern of demand. Time Series Forecasting techniques formulate a mathematical model of the cyclical pattern. Some Time Series techniques also take into account other trends within the model, for example whether there is an overall upward trend. The mathematical model is then used to project a possible forecast for one or more future cycles.

A mathematical model, comprising several mathematical equations, can be developed to relate the key factors (which form the input variables to the model) to the prediction of the value of some variable. A forecast results from setting the values of the input variables and seeing the resultant prediction. For example, the next year's profit of a company is linked to its expected sales. Expected sales is influenced by issues such as expected customer demand and the competition in the marketplace, where expected customer demand is itself influenced by the general economic climate. As no use is made of historical trends or patterns, techniques that allow the formulation of these models fall into the second category of forecasting approaches.

6.3.6 Rule-based techniques

Although not normally considered to be a mathematical technique, the Rule-based technique has firm foundations in mathematics (logic) and is therefore included in this section.

A Rule-based technique supports the development of a model that comprises a set of rules. Rules are normally presented in the form of several IF..THEN statements (commonly referred to as *production rules*). For example, consider a UK-based textile manufacturing company which needs to decide whether, or not, to export garments to a country outside the UK. This type of decision is expected to occur many times over the next few months, each decision situation involving a different country. There are several factors that influence the decision whether or not to export. For instance, transportation costs must be sufficiently low, export tax laws need to be favourable, customer demand for the product must exist, and retailers need to be available and willing to adopt the garments as part of their product lines, before exporting of a particular garment to a particular country becomes feasible. Tax laws and customer demand themselves have factors of influence.

It is possible to specify the relationships between factors and their respective influence on the garment export decision in the form of a Rule-based model, part of which is presented in Figure 6.5.

To solve this model for a given decision situation, the user provides values for some of the input variables. Potentially, all the variables that are referenced in a rule's IF clause, but not in any other rule's THEN clause, require user input. However, actual user input depends greatly on the method by which the model is solved. *Forward chain-*

Fig 6.5 Part of a rule-based model for evaluating garment export decisions

IF demand_for_the_product = sufficient AND
   export_tax_laws = favourable AND
   retailers = available_and_willing AND
   transportation_costs = low
THEN decision = export

IF competitors = no_threat AND
   country_climate = suitable
THEN demand_for_the_product = sufficient

IF country = EFTA_member OR
   country = EC_member OR
   trade_agreement = yes OR
   import_duty_less_10 = yes
THEN export_tax_laws = favourable

This partially completed model states that four conditions need to be satisfied in order to consider exporting garments to the country in question: sufficient demand for the product must exist, the export tax laws must be favourable, retailers must be available and willing to take on the garments, and transportation costs must be sufficiently low. Sufficient demand for the product will exist if and only if competitors do not pose a serious threat to garment sales in the country in question, and that the garments are suitable for the climate of that country (it makes little sense to export heavy wool coats to certain Middle Eastern countries, for example). Tax laws are favourable if and only if the country is either in EFTA or the EC, or if there is a reciprocal trade agreement with the country, or if the import duty is less than 10% of garment sales. The rules presented in this figure are fairly simple in content and structure. Rules are often specified with an additional ELSE clause, and sometimes a measure of confidence in the conclusion of a rule can be given. The measure of confidence can be used to provide a rank of the decision alternatives in decreasing order of confidence. The variables (on the left-hand side of the = sign) can take both textual and numeric values.

ing and *backward chaining* are two key methods for rule-based model solution. The principal difference between forward chaining and backward chaining is that the former solves the model by working from the IF clause of a rule to the THEN clause of a rule (i.e. it works forwards through a rule), whereas backward chaining works from the THEN clause of a rule towards the IF clause of a rule (i.e. it works backwards through a rule). For instance, consider the garment export decision and assume that the model provided in Figure 6.5 is complete. If forward chaining was be used in its solution, processing would typically start within the selection of a rule that required the user to provide one or more values for input variables. In this example, the second rule may be selected with the user providing one of the possible values for both the 'competitors' and the 'country_climate' variables. Forward chaining would then use the rule to determine the value of the 'demand_for_the_product' variable. Forward chaining may then focus on the third rule in order to determine the value of 'export_tax_laws' via the user's provision of values for the four input variables specified in the rule's IF clause. Then attention may focus on the first rule, to establish whether or not to export. This would involve the user providing a value for the 'transportation_costs' input variable and a value for the 'retailers' variable.

Backward chaining, on the other hand, starts with a rule that establishes a value for the overall decision variable and works from this. In the garment export decision model, the first rule determines the overall decision. Backward chaining would then seek a rule that has any of the IF clause variables in the overall decision rule as a variable in its THEN clause. The second rule has 'demand_for_the_product' in its THEN clause, so processing control is transferred temporarily to this rule. Backward chaining then looks for a rule that has any of the second rule's IF clause variables in its THEN clause. There are none. The values for the second rule's IF clause variables must therefore be provided by the user. Once provided, the second rule can determine the value for 'demand_for_the_product' variable. The second rule has now served its purpose, and control transfers back to the first rule. Another rule may now be sought to establish the other variables in the first rule, in an identical manner above. The third rule will be selected and control passed to this rule temporarily. Values related to the third rule's IF clause variables will need to be provided by the user. When the user has supplied the required values, the value for the 'export_tax_laws' variable can be established using the third rule. Control then returns to the first rule again. Another rule to establish either the value of 'retailers' and 'transportation_costs' may be sought. There are none so the user provides these values. Once supplied, the first rule can now determine the overall value for 'decision', and a solution is found.

The above descriptions of forward chaining and backward chaining are very simplistic. The description has provided little explanation regarding the selection of rules beyond that specified by the method itself. Nothing has been said about what happens when a value for a variable is not that required by a rule. However, despite its simplicity, the description highlights the major features of each method. Forward chaining is the preferred method in situations where there are few variables, for which the user provides values, but where there are a large number of options for the overall decision. Backward chaining is the preferred method in situations that are the exact opposite of those conducive to forward chaining.

6.4   TECHNIQUES FOR GROUP DECISION MAKING SUPPORT

The Weighted Score technique was described with respect to both individual and group decision making situations. This section focuses on other techniques that can be employed within group decision making situations. Most of these techniques have a mathematical element. However, their overriding concern is with the structuring and control of a group decision making process. The following subsections focus on four key group decision making support techniques in turn.

6.4.1   The Nominal Group Technique (NGT)

This technique, described by Delbecq and Van der Ven (1971), requires all participants to be working concurrently on the group decision, and is usually employed within a

Fig 6.6 The Nominal Group Technique (NGT): an illustration

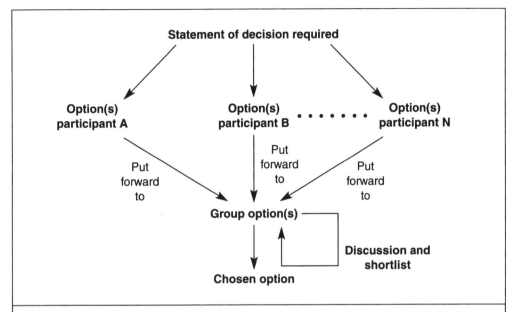

A statement of the decision to be made is first stated, leading to each participant composing a personal list of possible options. Once lists are completed by all participants, each participant selects those options to be put forward to the rest of the group. These options are then pooled to form a group list of options, which are then discussed collectively by the group. Participants may then be asked to rank the group options in order of preference. The sum of all the participant's ranks for a particular option is then calculated for each option in turn, leading to an overall group ranking of the options. From this, a subset of the highest ranking options are selected for further discussion and subsequent shortlisting, and so on until one option remains. This final option is the one that should be chosen for implementation.

face-to-face meeting situation. A possible implementation of NGT to decision making is as follows. The decision situation is first communicated to all participants. Each participant draws up a personal list of ideas with respect to the decision and recommends one or more alternatives for group consideration. The recommendations are pooled and discussed collectively by the whole group. A shortlist of the recommendations is then drawn up. This may be achieved by allowing each participant to rank each option, and then selecting the most highly ranked options when the ranks for each option are summed across the whole group. This 'discussion – shortlisting' cycle continues until an eventual winning option is established. Figure 6.6 summarises NGT in pictorial form.

6.4.2 The Delphi technique

Like NGT, this technique supports group selection of the best alternative to a given decision situation, but prescribes a different approach. Delphi is applicable to decision making situations when participants are involved in decision making at different times and are remote from one another, although it can be used in other situations.

Specifically, the Delphi technique attempts to migrate each participant's perspective of a certain decision making situation towards a common view, and hence to select the alternative that best fits the common view. A chairperson describes the decision situation in hand and disseminates the description, together with a questionnaire, to each participant. The questionnaire allows a participant to propose one or more alternatives, together with the reasons why each is appropriate. The completed questionnaire is returned to the chairperson, who summarises the alternatives and respective justifications. The resulting summary is sent to each participant together with another questionnaire to gain further feedback from the participants on alternatives they prefer or dislike. This 'summary and questionnaire' feedback cycle continues in the expectation that participants will alter their views when they are aware of the additional factors and alternatives brought to bear on the decision by other group participants. The cycle terminates when consensus has been reached. Figure 6.7 summarises the Delphi technique in pictorial form.

A substantial period of time may elapse between dissemination and receiving of questionnaires, which can be a disadvantage of this technique. IT speeds up this process greatly, however, via the provision of information communication tools, such as e-mail and facsimile. Also, participants need to be aware of the importance of the decision situation, and give it appropriate priority otherwise non-completion or late completion of questionnaires may result.

6.4.3   The brainstorming technique

This technique is employed typically within a small face-to-face meeting situation. The objective of a brainstorming session is to generate many ideas regarding the current decision situation. A motto of 'anything goes' is central to this technique, inviting creativity on the part of the group participants with 'no bounds'. Participants are encouraged to put forward any suggestions, however implausible they may seem at the outset. The time available for proposing suggestions may be limited to, say, twenty minutes. In some cases, a suggestion's implausibility may be due to some constraint relating to current practice and/or policy. Subsequent discussion may recommend the removal of the constraint, thereby making the suggestion plausible to implement.

Brainstorming can be used both to establish the nature of a particular decision situation and to identify alternatives and/or criteria for alternative evaluation.

6.4.4   Voting

Most of us, at least within a democratic society, have experienced some form of formal voting system in action (for example, during elections, opinion surveys). Types of voting systems include 'unanimity' (all must be in agreement) and 'majority rule' (where the opinion of the majority dictates the decision made).

6.5   MSS PROVISION OF ACTIVE DECISION MAKING SUPPORT

Section 6.2 introduced the concept of models and modelling, and Sections 6.3 and 6.4 have examined key mathematical and group decision making techniques. It has been

Fig 6.7 The Delphi technique: an illustration

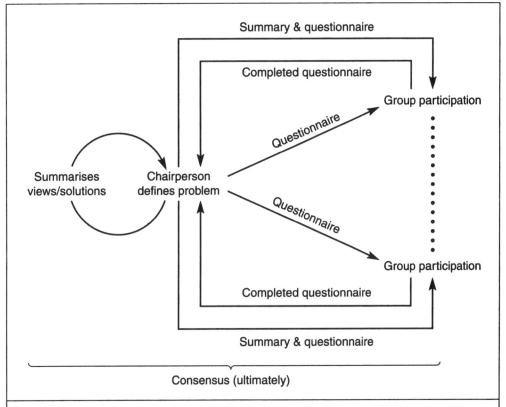

Summary & questionnaire

Completed questionnaire

Group participation

Questionnaire

Summarises
views/solutions

Chairperson
defines problem

Questionnaire

Group participation

Completed questionnaire

Summary & questionnaire

Consensus (ultimately)

Delphi involves the preparation, dissemination and summarising of a questionnaire. The summaries are used to provide consolidated information about the views of the group members as a whole, and may serve to alter the view of the participant reading it. This can lead to convergence of views and eventually to one preferred alternative. Typically, no more than three cycles of questionnaire preparation, dissemination and summarising take place within a particular Delphi technique application.

mentioned that computer-based models can be of benefit to organisations. Benefits already identified include the provision of more efficient and effective calculations of model solutions, the ability to perform analyses which previously could not be undertaken due to their sheer complexity or their time-consuming nature, and the ability to perform sensitivity analysis quickly, easily and more consistently. These benefits are only a subset of those that may occur with the introduction of computer-based models. Organisations have gained qualitative benefits from using computerised models, including making work more rewarding, improved understanding of the decision situation, improved understanding of business in general, and more flexibility in reporting methods. Furthermore, IS departments have found that the success of one computerised model within the organisation has made the path to further computerised model provision more smooth. In his book, Alter (1980) provides information on how Connoisseur Foods introduced and used an MSS for the active support of brand plan decisions. Eventually, its application yielded several of the aforementioned qualitative and/or quantitative benefits to the company and led to a more favourable view of further envisaged computerised model provision.

This section looks at the ways in which MSS provides active decision making support, starting with an overall view of MSS functionality available for active decision making support and then focusing in more detail on a few specific types of MSS functionality.

6.5.1 An overall view of active decision making support provision in MSS

A diagram of the logical architecture of any MSS that provides active decision making support is presented in Figure 6.8. The diagram reflects the diversity of support that can be provided by current MSS. It also reflects the bi-directional influences between management and their organisational context, on the one hand, and MSS provision for active decision support, on the other. Three principal and highly interrelated components of an MSS are distinguished. The first component focuses on data aspects, the second component on model and technique aspects, and the third component on interface aspects. All components perform vital functions which, together with their interconnections via links, provide the active decision making support required by the organisation.

The capabilities provided within an MSS implementation for active decision making support vary according to management requirements and the organisational context in hand. For instance, an MSS might need to be developed that provides one or more pre-specified models (for example, a Rule-based model and/or a Simulation model) to users. Alternatively, it may provide only a set of techniques that enable users to develop their own models. A further alternative is that the MSS simply provides the capabilities for developing either techniques or models. It is for this reason that some of the labels in Figure 6.8 are in brackets, highlighting their optional provision at the outset of MSS use. As the MSS is used, techniques and/or models may be created, stored and maintained for use in subsequent decision situations. Variation in data provision can also occur within MSS implementations. An MSS may be developed which has fixed data structures and even fixed data sets. Alternatively, only the capabilities for creating data storage structures, and for storing and maintaining data, may be provided at the outset of MSS use. Finally, variations in the interface provision may occur between MSS implementations. The MSS may provide a fixed interface to its users, in terms of both input and output presentation formats. Alternatively, only the capabilities for developing, storing and maintaining interfaces may be available at the outset of MSS use.

The essential aspects of the three MSS components are the Data Management System (DMS), the Model/Technique Management System (MTMS) and the Interface Management System (IMS). These provide the capabilities for creating and maintaining data, models and/or techniques, and interfaces respectively. Although in practice, MSS users may never use the functions provided by these three management systems directly, together they provide the fundamental support operations needed by any MSS that provides active decision making support. For instance, the MTMS provides the fundamental operations to permit the creation of models/techniques, the creation of models from techniques, the retrieval and storage of model/techniques, the solving of models, and the updating and deleting of models/techniques. The DMS provides the fundamental operations to permit the creation of data structures, the storage, retrieval, amendment and deletion of data, and the ability to extract data from other external and/or internal data sources. The IMS provides the fundamental operations to permit the creation, amendment, deletion, retrieval and use of interfaces.

Fig 6.8 The logical architecture of an MSS providing active decision making support

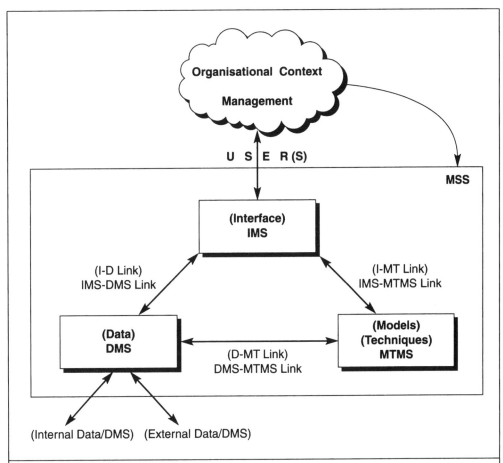

This diagram builds on the previous logical MSS architecture model provided by Sprague (1980). Management within an organisational context influences MSS design, and vice versa. Any MSS for active decision making support has three basic components: one that is concerned with data provision, one that is concerned with models/technique provision, and one that is concerned with interface provision. The Data Management System (DMS), Model/Technique Management System (MTMS) and Interface Management System (IMS) are always present, although possibly hidden from user view, as are the capabilities for creating and maintaining links between the components. The DMS may have capabilities to import data from other systems, both internal and external to the company. The components and their interrelationships together provide the active support operations needed by management within their organisational context, via the user(s) of the MSS.

The links between components are also vital elements of an MSS providing active decision making support. Depending on organisational requirements, an MSS may already have links specified between particular interface(s), data and models/techniques. The links allow users, for example, to request subsets of the data to view (via the I-D link), or to request a model to solve or a technique to be used to develop a model (via the I-MT link). A model or technique may need input either from the user (via the I-MT link) or from the MSS's data store (transferred using the D-MT link). The output of a model may be stored (transferred to DBMS using the D-MT link) for subsequent input to another model. On the other hand, the output might form the information that a user wishes to receive (via the I-MT link). At a minimum, an MSS needs to provide the underlying capabilities that enable the specification and management of the I-D links, I-MT links and D-MT links. These facilities are provided by the IMS-DMS link, the IMS-MTMS link and the DMS-MTMS link respectively. As in the case of the DMS, IMS and the MTMS elements, these essential link elements may not be seen by MSS users directly. Rather, their functionality may be reflected within the operation of the I-D, I-MT and D-MT links that they serve to create and maintain.

The architecture presents a very wide view of MSS functionality for active decision making support. In reality, a particular MSS implementation is more restrictive in its provision. It may provide only a set of models to support a particular type of decision, for example to support one organisation's production scheduling decisions. Apart from the restrictions that may be deliberately built into the MSS implementation by an MSS developer, the essential elements of each of the components may also restrict what it is possible to provide to MSS users. For instance, an MSS may be capable of supporting interfaces of a certain type only due to the restrictiveness of its underlying IMS. The data structuring and data facilities of an MSS may also be restricted due to the limitations of its DMS, and its MTMS may restrict the models and techniques that can be supported. For example, a spreadsheet package can be considered an MSS implementation. It can be used to develop simple mathematical models, but would not be suitable for the development of more complex ones such as Linear Programming models. A set of formulae beneath spreadsheet cells comprise a model. The interface possibilities are constrained by the facilities available within the spreadsheet package. Indeed, the interface through which a user interacts with a model may always be the standard spreadsheet interface provided by the package. The data structures are very simple, as data values are stored in user-specified cells and the data types available are those provided by the spreadsheet package. A decision situation requiring a rich data storage structure and set of data manipulation operations would find a spreadsheet package lacking.

The DMS element of an MSS data component may be provided by a DBMS, as it provides a rich set of facilities to support data structuring and data management. The same level of capabilities has yet to be provided for model/technique development and management. Several MSS researchers in the early to mid 80s proposed approaches to provide equivalent functionality within an MTMS as is available within a DBMS for supporting data structuring and management (see, for example, the papers by Elam et. al. 1980, Dolk and Konsynski 1984, Blanning 1986, and Applegate 1986). However, this research does not appear to have matured sufficiently to have significant commercial impact.

The functionality provided by the essential elements of the MSS components varies between MSS implementations. It is crucial to provide MSS that match organisational management's requirements, which embrace not only functional aspects but also user characteristics. Particular interface styles are more suited to certain types of user. Regarding user input to an MSS, a novice user or an infrequent user might find a command-based interface for the input of instructions to the MSS very difficult to use. A menu-based, forms-based and/or iconic-based interface may be preferred. Regarding

MSS output to a user, a tabular output format may be preferred to a graphical one. This may be due to the background of the individual where tabular representations of information predominate. In addition, certain output presentation formats have been found to facilitate certain types of operations more easily than others. For example, graphical representations facilitate trend spotting more than tabular representations (see, for example, the paper by Dickson et al. 1986 on graphical versus tabular information presentations).

The logical architecture in Figure 6.8 allows the term 'MSS' to designate either a computerised system that is completely configured for use within a particular decision situation, or a computerised system that can be configured to several decision situations of either the same type or of different types. Any computerised system from which an MSS implementation is developed is referred to as an MSS development package. It is possible that the same computerised system can be called an MSS in one organisational context and an MSS development package within another organisational context, as it is management and the organisational context that determine what is, and what is not, an MSS. Using a spreadsheet package as the example once more, this software may be viewed by management within one organisational context as an MSS providing active decision making support. In this case, the users configure the MSS, via template definitions, for particular decision situations as and when required. In another organisational context, the spreadsheet package may be considered to be the MSS development package. The MSS developer provides the templates required by management to support a specific decision situation. The templates, supported by the spreadsheet package, comprise the MSS for these managers.

Implicit in the above discussion is the justification that at least some MSS development packages can also be described as having the same logical architecture as that presented for MSS in Figure 6.8. Indeed, the logical architecture is sufficiently general to embrace not only MSS but also MSS development packages. However, an MSS and its associated MSS development package can be distinguished by comparing the breadth and depth of functionality available for supporting decision situations. This comparison is illustrated in Figure 6.9. An MSS development package is less specific but provides more basic functionality to each possible decision situation. On the other hand, an MSS implementation is more limited in its range of supporting decision situations, but will support them better due to the additional functionality that has been implemented using the MSS development package.

6.5.2 MSS employing interactive mathematical models: an overview

Several examples of MSS employing interactive mathematical models are provided in Figure 6.10. One particular type of MSS employing mathematical models, currently considered to be one of the fastest growing business applications, is that of Geographical Information Systems (GIS) (Beam 1994). Indeed, the European Market for GIS has an estimated annual growth rate of about 12% (Classe 1995). GIS are computer systems that capture, store, display and enable the analysis of spatial data (that is, data which is always associated with a spatial location). Data sets, each providing details of some spatially located property, are collated. Depending on the user requirements one or more of these data sets are superimposed onto a map-based interface, allowing the user to see the relationships between the data sets.

Fig 6.9 A comparison of an MSS and its development package in terms of functionality

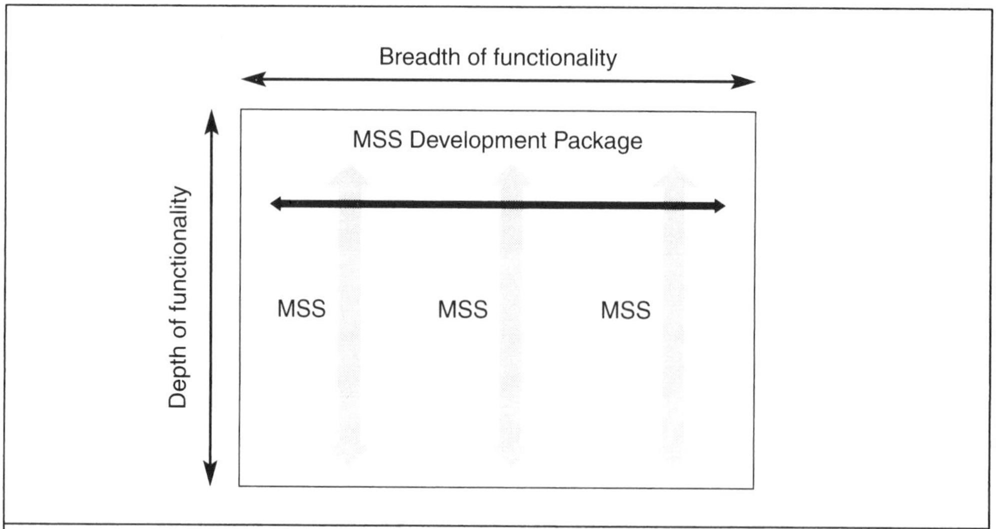

An MSS development package will be more broad in its support of decisions but provide less depth of functionality to each possible decision situation. On the other hand, an MSS implementation will be less broad in the range of decision situations it can support, but will have greater depth in functionality available to support the focal decisions. Many MSS implementations may be developed using the same MSS development package, each of which may have a different breadth of focus within the constraints on breadth due to MSS development package limitations.

Most GIS provide the following capabilities.

- The ability to show geographical features on a map, to zoom in and out of various areas of the map and to look at areas in varying degrees of detail (i.e. with only a subset of associated data shown), and to produce hard copy formats of map detail.
- Methods of querying the underlying data sets, of re-organising the data, and of comparing the data sets in various ways.
- Methods for analysing various data sets using simple mathematical models, with the output in both map-based format and also in more traditional tabular and/or textual summary forms.

Insurance companies have been quick to recognise the potential of this type of MSS to aid the development of more appropriate insurance policy estimates. GIS have been used to spot fraudulent behaviour in some insurers, where insurance premiums were currently too low because of false information being provided.

The water industry is also taking GIS seriously, with Northumbrian Water stating that their GIS data forms the core data of its business (Bicknell 1995). Currently, GIS in this area typically provide information concerning the physical aspects of water management such as pipe locations. In the future, these aspects will be linked to other

Fig 6.10 Example MSS employing interactive mathematical models

- An MSS aids the scheduling of midwives within a particular region of the UK. A model calculates the best schedule, given issues such as work limitations and policies on shifts and holidays. Ad hoc adjustment to the schedule is possible after it has been compiled automatically.

- An MSS helps management of a transportation company to decide whether or not random drug testing of drivers should be introduced. A Decision Tree model is used in this system, and what-if analysis is possible to examine the sensitivity of the preferred alternative.

- Pharos, developed by National Westminster Bank, is an MSS that allows any company to determine the European laws of importance to its operations and market.

- Marks & Spencer's Graduate Screening System allows applicants' application forms to be evaluated consistently and rapidly on the basis of a standard set of criteria. M & S have found that the system reduces the number of interviewees rejected at later stages of the interview process (DTI 1990a). A Radio 4 programme stated that currently 6% of all Curriculum Vitae are read in this way in the UK, whereas 20% of all Curriculum Vitae are read in this way in the USA.

- Curry and Moutinho (1994) mention MSS employing Rule-based models to support site location decisions and strategic competitive positioning, the former of which has been used within the Tesco retail chain.

- Mrs. Fields Inc., a purveyor of chocolate chip cookies in the United States, sells a variety of MSS employing Rule-based models concerned with product retailing and general management. The modules capture the retail expertise of Mrs. Fields Inc. (Newquist 1990).

- Interactive Financial Planning System (IFPS) provides financial techniques and database capabilities to support financial analysis applications (Turban 1993). It can be considered as either an MSS or an MSS development package.

- Even DBMS packages, such as Ingres (from Computer Associates), can be MSS, although they will more frequently be MSS development packages. They provide the capabilities to develop models operating on data held within a database.

Above are some examples of MSS employing interactive mathematical models. Each MSS adheres to the logical architecture of an MSS for active decision making support, as shown in Figure 6.8, as it has interrelated data, model/technique and interface components.

business data through the GIS, such as customer locations and attributes. This more integrated system will provide greater potential for customer service enhancement and business decision making support.

MSS that provide Rule-based models, or the facilities to create and maintain Rule-based models, are often capable of supporting a user's request for explanation as to how a particular decision was reached. The path of rules that has been followed within the model solution needs to be tracked, stored and subsequently presented to the user in an easy-to-read format. During the use of a particular Rule-based model, data is accumulated. This data comprises the values of the variables either provided by the

❑ *Viewpoint*

The town of St. Albans is scheduled as an ancient monument, so when residents wish to do any work that involves digging up the ground, they first have to fund exploratory excavation work. The district council is using Sysdeco UK's geographical information system (GIS) to assemble the first unified record of the town's history. The Berrymans, who were building a new drive, found their cottage was opposite a Roman basilica. An archaeological dig took place and uncovered traces of a second century Roman underfloor heating system. ■

Reprinted with permission from *Computer Weekly*, 14th September 1995.

user of the MSS or determined by rules within the model. After model solution and explanation, the data is typically deleted unless sensitivity analysis is to be performed. Sensitivity analysis allows a user to change the values of one or more input variables, and to solve the model with the new set of data values. For instance, supposing that the complete Rule-based model for the garment export decision (part of which was presented in Figure 6.5) has been implemented within an MSS, using the Rule-based technique provided within its associated development package. Having solved the model with one set of input variables, a user wants to examine the effects on the overall decision if the value of the 'competitors' variable changed from 'yes' to 'no'? The value of the 'competitors' variable, currently held within the data component of the MSS, is changed temporarily, but all other input data values remain the same as originally set. The model would then be solved using this temporary set of data values.

❑ *Viewpoint*

Gateway makes easy meat of grocery links

GATEWAY stores will later this month become the first European supermarket chain to download sales data automatically to some of its grocery suppliers. giving them joint control over replacing goods.

In a deal with GE Information Systems (GEIS), Gateway, Somerfield and Food Giant stores will trial an Electronic Data Interchange (EDI)-based system with 10 food firms including Bass, Cadbury and Nestlé.

The stores will send point-of-sale information in EDI format into a specially developed application running on GEIS's Tradenet electronic commerce network during a six-month pilot project.

The application uses a forecasting model to give suppliers a view of shopping trends. Suppliers will have an on-line connection to the application and will be able to modify the forecast in order to take account of occasional factors such as their own promotions.

But Karen Myers, supply chain director, insisted that the system did not give wholesale suppliers power over Somerfield's business, nor would it give some suppliers a competitive advantage. "They will absolutely not have a say in what goes on our shelves," she said.

"This represents a significant step towards the management of the supply chain as a seamless end-to-end process. By sharing better quality information with our suppliers, we will enable them to deliver better services, which in turn means we will be able to be more responsive to our customers," said Miles Clark, Somerfield's supply chain controller. ■

Reprinted with permission from *Computer Weekly*, 1st June 1995.

MSS employing interactive Rule-based models have, on occasions, made decisions that have been judged to be better than those made by a human expert working alone on the same decision situation. More common is the development of MSS employing interactive Rule-based models for routine decision making where the rules are easily established but success lies in the competent, consistent and quick assessment of possibly thousands of rules. Rules regarding complex tax returns and the provision of accurate pension forecasts to those nearing retirement are example situations where rules can be easily identified but are difficult to apply consistently in practice. In the case of pension forecasts, before the RPFA system was developed to support pension forecasting decisions at the Department of Social Security, one in 10 pension forecasts were inaccurate (DTI 1990b).

6.5.3   MSS providing active decision making support for groups

Most of the MSS implementations described in Section 6.5.2 are used by one individual to provide active support of management decision making, although several copies of the same system may be used within a company. In this section, we are concerned with a particular MSS implementation that supports group decision making.

The provision of MSS to actively support group decision making has been a popular area of research interest since the mid-80s, particularly in the United States. Several physical arrangements for these MSS have been proposed to reflect the variability found in group decision making situations. For instance, groups can be large or small (the threshold point between large and small group classifications is usually around sixteen participants), groups can be located within the same room or dispersed, and group participants may be involved in simultaneous decision making or perform their decision making activities at different times. De Sanctis and Gallupe (1985) provide an overview of MSS physical configurations that are applicable to support:

- groups whose members are face-to-face and where decision making is of limited duration
- groups whose members are dispersed and where decision making is of limited duration
- groups whose members are face-to-face and where decision making is prolonged
- groups whose members are dispersed and where decision making is prolonged.

Zwass (1992) provides pictorial examples of MSS physical configurations, one to support large groups and one to support small groups.

Although physical configurations differ to reflect the differing characteristics of group decision making situations, the capabilities provided by these MSS can be viewed in terms of the logical MSS architecture presented in Figure 6.8. These systems need to provide interface, data and model/technique support, just like MSS for individual decision making support. The differences are typically in the range of models/techniques supported and in the requirements for data support. In a group situation, group decision making techniques also need to be provided. Data may be collected from individuals, and pooled to form group data. The data component of the MSS must therefore be capable of supporting both individual data and group data requirements.

The remainder of this subsection focuses attention on the description and use of one particular type of MSS configuration. Often referred to as a *Decision Room* or

Electronic Meeting Room, this MSS is applicable for groups that are involved in simultaneous, face-to-face decision making. A Decision Room can be provided to cope with large group meetings, although the configuration described here is for use by small groups.

Figure 6.11 provides a diagram of a possible Decision Room layout. Here, a horse-shoe-shaped table arrangement is set out in the centre of the main room area. Terminals, which can be recessed into the table, are positioned around the table. These are the terminals at which group participants interact with the MSS. Around the Decision Room are small break-out areas where subsets of the group participants can sit and discuss issues privately, should this be necessary, or can take a break and relax. A public screen is positioned on the wall in front of the horseshoe-shaped table, on which any group results may be projected. Whiteboards are also provided. In addition, a separate terminal is located in front of the horseshoe-shaped table for use by the

Fig 6.11 A possible decision room layout

Key: WB = Whiteboard   FC = Facilitator's console   BOR = Breakout room

Seat   Terminal

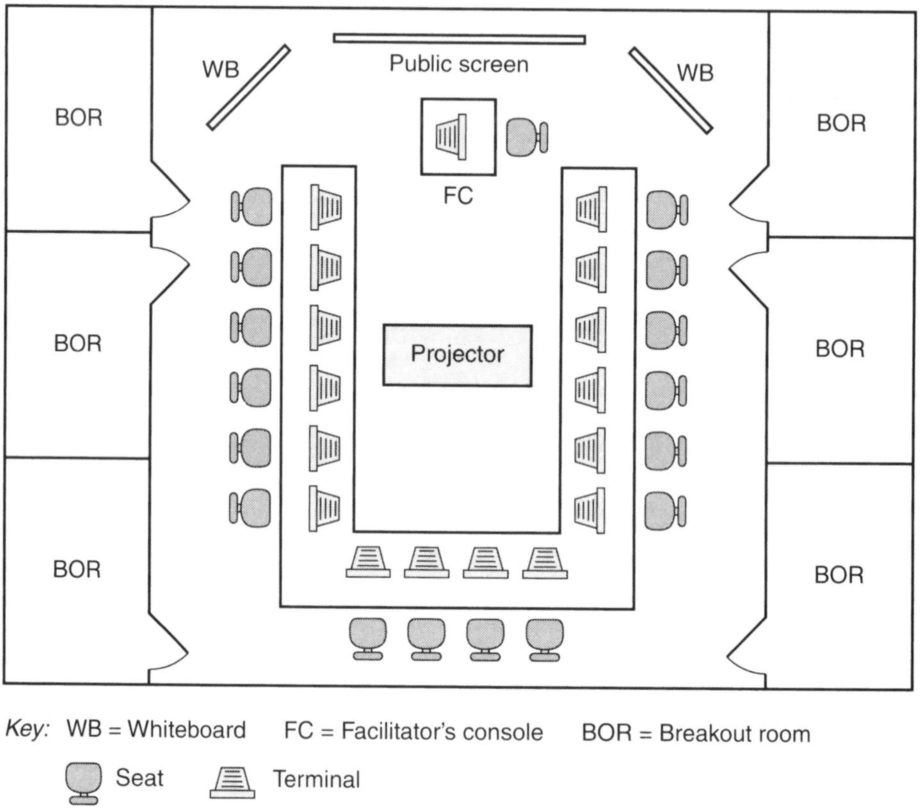

The decision room shown in this figure is for small group meetings (maximum capacity of sixteen managers in this case). A tiered meeting room may be needed for larger management meetings.

so-called facilitator. The facilitator is actually a role which may be played by more than one person. The facilitator steers the overall decision making process, and must be adequately briefed about a particular decision making situation so that the most appropriate techniques are applied. Any technical problems need to be dealt with quickly by the facilitator, so that they do not negatively influence the decision making process. In practice, two people may perform the role of the facilitator; one focusing on the business decision making aspects and the other focusing on the technical aspects of the role. The success of a group decision making activity using a Decision Room depends greatly on the effective performance of the facilitator role.

Each terminal may include access to mathematical models or techniques that a particular participant may wish to apply at appropriate times during group decision making. In addition, each terminal allows users to input the data required by a group decision making technique and to view outputs resulting from the use of the technique. Group techniques, such as NGT, Delphi, Weighted Score and Brainstorming, may be supported. For example, a Decision Room may support NGT in the following way. Firstly, the facilitator selects NGT from the menu of available group techniques displayed on the facilitator's terminal. This brings up an input screen on each of the participant's terminals, asking for a list of ideas on the current decision situation. Each participant is given a few minutes to input individual ideas concerning the decision situation. Afterwards, the facilitator asks each participant to identify the ideas to be put forward for consideration by the group. When all have identified their offerings, the facilitator instructs the MSS to aggregate the individual lists into a consolidated group list and to present the results on the public screen and at each individual member's terminal. The facilitator, in discussion with the participants, may amend the group list. Amendment may be needed when duplicate ideas exist in the list or when two or more ideas are better consolidated into one. Any changes to the list are relayed to the public screen and to each individual participant's terminal. When the list is finalised, the terminals are recessed, and face-to-face discussion of the ideas takes place. The terminals are then brought back into view, and the facilitator instructs participants to rank the ideas individually at terminals (rank of 1 for the most favoured, 2 for the second best, and so forth). After individual ranking is completed, the facilitator instructs the MSS to aggregate the values of individual members for each idea and to present the top 10 ideas (i.e., the ten lowest aggregate scores) to the public screen and to each individual participant's terminal. When achieved, the terminals are recessed once more and face-to-face discussion of the top 10 ideas commences. The same procedure for ranking, this time for the 10 ideas only, then takes pace, leading to the selection of the top 3 ideas for further discussion and ranking. This procedure continues until one idea remains.

Decision Rooms have been used to aid many decision making situations, for example to aid corporate strategic decision making (see Jessup and Kukalis 1990, for example). Cited benefits for group decision making include:

- better focus on the relevant issues than in a non-supported meeting
- an accurate record of decisions made being produced at the end of the meeting
- simultaneity of participant input, which speeds up the decision making process
- anonymity of participant's input, enabling greater and more equal participation by all involved.

However, Finlay and Marples (1992) highlight certain situations where Decision Rooms, particularly those involving high levels of IT support, could have negative effects on a decision making process and they claim that in some cases Decision Rooms offer little additional benefit over well-structured non-computerised decision making settings.

Several Decision Rooms are located in research establishments, which can be hired out to companies on a daily basis. This makes Decision Room capabilities available to smaller companies, where the provision of personal facilities is not financially viable. GroupSystems, from Ventana Corporation, and SAMM, developed at the University of Minnesota, are two examples of MSS for group decision making support which are available for commercial purchase (see Roth et. al. 1993 for a review of these MSS). GroupSystems has been installed in over 100 locations world-wide (Koenders and Robbins-Jones 1994).

6.6   SUMMARY

This chapter has described the functionality provided within MSS for active support of decision making. This provision requires the interactive use of models/techniques, or the capabilities for developing and using models/techniques. An overall description of models, their classification and benefits was first provided. Mathematical models have special features and are often employed within MSS. Several techniques to aid the formulation and solution of mathematical models were described at differing levels of detail, namely:

- Weighted Score (both for individual and group use)
- Linear Programming
- Decision Tree
- Simulation
- Forecasting
- Rule-based

Key techniques for structuring group decision making situations were also described.

The remainder of the chapter provided a view of MSS functionality for the active support of decision making. A logical view of overall functionality was first presented via the description of a logical architecture for MSS providing active decision making support. The architecture reflects the varied scope and nature of possible MSS provision. It also highlights the essential fact that it is management within their organisational context that determine what is, and what is not, an MSS. The distinction between an MSS and its associated development package was also discussed, as were the differences between MSS providing active support for individual decision making and MSS providing active support of group decision making. Examples of MSS in practice were presented, and attention was focused on particular MSS provisions, such as GIS and Decision Rooms.

This chapter completes the description of MSS functionality within this book. Chapter 7 focuses on development issues associated with an organisation's provision of MSS implementations.

References

Alter S (1980) *Decision Support Systems*. Addison-Wesley.

Applegate L M, Konsynski B R and Nunamaker J E (1986) Model Management Systems: Design for Decision Support. *Decision Support Systems* Vol 2 No 1. pp. 81–91.

Beam K (1994) Geographic Information Systems: A new way to look at business data. *I/S Analyzer* Vol 32 No 1. pp. 1–20.

Bicknell D (1995) Northumbrian Water taps into map system. *Computer Weekly* May 18th Edition. p. 12.

Blanning R (1986) An Entity-Relationship Approach to Model Management. *Decision Support Systems* Vol 2 No 1. pp. 65–72.

Brickman L (1989) *Mathematical Introduction to Linear Programming and Game Theory*. Springer-Verlag.

Caine and Robson (1993) Models for Decision Making. *Management Services* Vol 37 No 1. pp. 28–30.

Classe A (1995) Putting Britain on the Map. *Computer Weekly* May 18th Edition. pp. 36–37.

Cooke S and Slack N (1991) *Making Management Decisions* Second Edition. Prentice-Hall.

Curry B and Moutinho L (1994) Intelligent Computer Models for Marketing Decisions. *Management Decision* Vol 32 No 4. pp. 30–35.

Delbecq A L and Van Der Ven A H (1971) A Group Process Model for Problem Identification and Program Planning. *Journal of Applied Behavioural Science* Vol 7. pp. 466–492.

DTI (1990a) *Personnel Selection Screening: Graduates for Management*. HMSO, London, UK.

DTI (1990b) *Personal Forecasts and Advice: Retirement Pensions*. HMSO, London, UK.

De Sanctis G and Gallupe B (1985) Group Decision Support Systems: a New Frontier. *Database*. Winter Edition. pp. 3–10.

Dickson G W, De Sanctis G. and McBride D J (1986) Understanding the Effects of Computer Graphics for Decision Support: a Cumulative Experimental Approach. *Communications of the ACM* Vol 29 No 1. pp. 40–47.

Dolk D R and Konsynski B R (1984) Knowledge Representation for Model Management Systems. *IEEE Transactions on Software Engineering* Vol 10 No 6. pp. 619–628.

Elam J, Henderson J C and Miller L W (1980) Model Management Systems: An Approach to Decision Support in Complex Organisations. *Proceedings of the 1st International Conference on Information Systems*, Philadelphia, PA, USA. pp. 98–110.

Finlay P (1989) *Introducing Decision Support Systems*, NCC.

Finlay P and Marples P (1992) Strategic Group Decision Support Systems – A Guide for the Unwary. *Long Range Planning* Vol 25 No 3. pp. 98–107.

Jessup L M and Kukalis S (1990) Better Planning using Group Support Systems. *Long Range Planning* Vol 23 No 3. pp. 100–105.

Koenders L and Robbins-Jones T (1994) Electronic Meeting Systems: A Report on Current Research Findings. *Internal Research Report, University of South Australia, School of Information Systems*.

Newquist H P (1990) Experts at Retail. *Datamation* April 1st Edition. pp. 53–56.

Roth R M, Wood W C, Halm R and Power D J (1993) Building Group Decision Support Rooms using 'off-the-shelf' computing resources: prospects and issues. *Database* May Edition. pp. 21–31.

Turban E (1993) *Decision Support and Expert Systems* Third Edition. Macmillan.

Sprague R H (1980) A Framework for the Development of Decision Support Systems. *MIS Quarterly* Vol 4 No 4. pp. 1–26.

Strayer J K (1989) *Linear Programming & its Applications*. Springer-Verlag.

Zwass V (1992) *Management Information Systems*. Wm. C. Brown.

Review questions

1 What is a model? What is a mathematical model? What benefits can computerised models provide to organisations?

2 What other categories of models, apart from mathematical, are important to MSS design and development activities?

3 How can the Weighted Score technique be used in both individual and group decision making situations?

4 Compare and contrast the Linear Programming technique and the Decision Tree technique in terms of objectives and approach to model formulation.

5 What is the principal emphasis of the Simulation technique?

6 Describe the different approaches that can be taken to forecasting.

7 Compare NGT and the Delphi technique. How are they similar? How are they different?

8 What are the three logical components of an MSS that provide active decision making support?

9 What are the differences between an MSS and its associated development package?

10 Describe the purpose of GIS.

11 What is a Decision Room? What benefits may be obtained by using a Decision Room rather than performing decision making unaided?

Project ideas

Here are two project ideas.

Either: Perform an audit of a manager's current and potential use of MSS actively within his/her individual decision making. Your audit should include:

- A review of the manager's position and company.
- An assessment of the overall coverage of MSS for active decision making support employed by the manager.
- A review of the CBIS currently in use by this manager, and for what decision(s).

- Aspects of decision making that are not supported, and which MSS functionality may be of benefit to them.
- The reasons why those aspects of decision making are not currently supported.

Write a report of your findings, and present the results to your tutorial group. Discuss aspects of commonality and differences in the scope and nature of support provided across the managers that are studied by your tutorial group.

Or: Conduct a study of a group decision making situation, either within a company or within your university. During the group decision making, watch for characteristics of the group, such as:

- The techniques employed within group decision making.
- The presence of one or more key group members and their respective role.
- The relative participation levels and equality of participation of members.
- Whether any side-tracking occurs.

Based on your findings, assess whether a Decision Room would have been of benefit to the group decision making situation and why. Write a report of your findings to be used as the basis of a tutorial discussion.

CHAPTER 7

MSS Development: Approaches and Techniques

7.1 INTRODUCTION

Chapters 4 to 6 inclusive have explored MSS functionality, and Chapter 3 provides insight into several technological advances that are contributing, or may in the future contribute, additional MSS functionality. The focus of this chapter is MSS development approaches and techniques.

Many decisions need to be made during MSS development activities. For example, the most appropriate MSS projects for the organisation need to be identified. This involves establishing MSS projects which are in line with both corporate objectives and corporate mission, and determining whether a particular MSS project is feasible, from a variety of perspectives. Having identified an MSS project which is worthy of development, the overall development approach needs to be determined. Many techniques are advocated for use within MSS development, and a decision has to be made as to the most suitable technique or techniques for a particular MSS development. Indeed, a particular methodology may be chosen, which prescribes a set of MSS development techniques.

The structure of this chapter is as follows. Section 7.2 reviews the decisions and issues concerning the identification and selection of MSS projects that are in line with corporate objectives and mission, and the assessment of MSS feasibility. Techniques and methodologies to aid alignment and feasibility decisions are introduced. Section 7.3 discusses three overall approaches to MSS development, and under what circumstances each is most appropriate. Section 7.4 reviews several methodologies/techniques that have been developed specifically for guiding MSS development. This section also reviews the applicability of conventional IS development techniques to MSS developments. It is not the purpose of this chapter to provide a detailed account of conventional IS development techniques, as these are covered in mainstream Systems Analysis and Design texts. As stated in Chapter 1, it is assumed that readers of this book possess at least an introductory knowledge of conventional IS techniques and their application. Finally, Section 7.5 provides a summary of this chapter.

At the end of this chapter the reader should understand:

- *Some key techniques to aid the alignment of MSS development with corporate objectives and mission, and to aid MSS feasibility evaluation.*
- *The principal approaches to MSS development, and their relative strengths and weaknesses.*

- *Some key techniques, specific to MSS development, and when each is most effective.*
- *The extent to which conventional IS development techniques are of benefit to MSS development.*

7.2   MSS DEVELOPMENT: CORPORATE ALIGNMENT AND FEASIBILITY

IS developments must be identified, selected and managed effectively. Identifying and selecting IS developments which are in line with corporate objectives and mission ensure that IS resources (materials, labour and finances) are deployed to maximum effect. Evaluating the feasibility of any IS development project ensures that the IS can be delivered and employed within the organisational situation in hand. Social, economic, technical and legal issues need to be taken into account when addressing IS feasibility. Addressing alignment and feasibility issues at the outset of an IS project, whenever possible, reduces the chances of the resultant IS becoming yet another failure statistic.

The following two subsections focus in detail on MSS alignment and MSS feasibility. As an MSS is an IS, many of the issues mentioned in these subsections are applicable to IS in general. However, some aspects relate to MSS only or have particular importance to MSS, owing to an MSS's specialist role in decision making and information handling support. Some techniques embrace aspects of both alignment and feasibility. Where such a technique is described, attention is drawn to this overlap.

7.2.1   Alignment of MSS with organisational objectives and mission

An IS project should be considered only if it is in line with organisational strategy and mission. Even novel and risky IS projects that fall under the umbrella of R & D should reflect the organisation's R & D strategy, which in turn should be aligned with organisational objectives and mission.

R & D projects, if successful, can lead to changes in organisational objectives and mission. Whilst MSS can affect organisation and management work significantly, they do not normally result directly in changes to organisational objectives or mission. Rather, they serve to support existing organisational objectives and mission, to facilitate the identification of factors that may cause changes in the current organisational objectives and mission, and to facilitate the introduction of new organisational objectives and mission. For these reasons, it is uncommon nowadays to find MSS developments within the remit of R & D.

Identifying and selecting MSS projects which are aligned with organisational objectives and mission is the core emphasis of this book. Strategic Information Systems Planning (SISP), to be discussed in Part 3, results in the set of IS projects most needed by the organisation as a whole. A subset of these IS projects may be concerned with MSS development. In the absence of a SISP exercise, several researchers have derived useful methodologies for the identification of MSS projects that are in line with organisational objectives and mission. For instance, Boone's Information Success Factor (ISF) methodology (as described in Stein 1994) facilitates the identification of important MSS projects with respect to an individual manager's particular contributions to organisational goals (the term 'goal' is used in Boone's work in preference to 'objective'). The methodology consists of five sequential stages. It focuses principally on the identification of the leadership strategies adopted by an individual manager with respect to a business goal, and then on the identification of Information Success Factors (ISFs). Leadership strategies are defined as those personal tasks that the manager carries out in order to achieve the business goals. An ISF is an information entity that is considered to be critical to the success of an associated leadership strategy.

The five stages of the ISF methodology are as follows.

- *Stage 1: Business Goals* – identify the business goals, and prioritise them.
- *Stage 2: Business Strategy* – for the top ranked business goal, ascertain the business strategies of importance to the achievement of the business goal, and prioritise them.
- *Stage 3: Leadership Strategy* – for the top ranked business strategy, identify the leadership strategies that are to be implemented in order to achieve the business strategy.
- *Stage 4: ISFs* – determine one or more ISFs for each leadership strategy.
- *Stage 5: Identify Potential* – identify potential MSS projects, and select the most appropriate to implement. A proposed MSS may help achieve several ISFs. Alternatively, an ISF may be aided by several potential MSS projects in different ways.

These stages are repeated in sequence for each manager. Indeed, a subset of the stages may be repeated for the same manager to uncover, for example, the MSS projects that would help the second most important business strategy as well as the first. The methodology does have weaknesses. One weakness is the reliance of the methodology on the executive's views of business goals and strategies. These views may not exactly match the corporate view of goals and strategies. The person conducting the exercise should be aware of the corporate view and steer the manager's view towards consideration of the corporate view if at all possible. A second weakness is that the executive strategies need to be stable for a sufficiently long period of time so that the MSS, when implemented, is still of benefit. Highly dynamic strategies can make an MSS project redundant before it is implemented. The third weakness of the methodology is that it focuses on the requirements of individual managers rather than groups. Thus, group decision making support opportunities may be missed. Despite these weaknesses, Stein (1994) applied the ISF methodology to two real life situations, and found it to be effective in relating corporate issues to MSS requirements. Table 7.1 summarises the results obtained from an ISF methodology application.

7.2.2 MSS feasibility determination

MSS development must be feasible from a variety of perspectives: social, technical, economic and legal. Research has identified several social factors that influence the success or failure of MSS development. One vital factor is the presence of top management support throughout MSS development. Without top management support, the human, technological and financial resources required for MSS development are difficult to obtain. Top management support manifests itself in two ways. Firstly, a senior executive may act as an *executive sponsor* of the proposed MSS, actively supporting its development and representing its cause at senior management meetings. Indeed, the executive

Table 7.1 Results of an ISF methodology application

ISF Methodology Stage	Results of Stage for Metal Recycling Freight Company
Stage 1: Business Goals – identify the business goals, and prioritise them	• *Niche exporting* • Add value • Profitable business • Diversify
Stage 2: Business Strategy – for the top ranked business goal, ascertain the business strategies of importance to the achievement of the business goal, and prioritise them	• *Continuity in major contract* • Maintain skilled staff profile • Ensure accurate cash flows
Stage 3: Leadership Strategy – for the top ranked business strategy, identify the leadership strategies that are to be implemented in order to achieve the business strategy.	• *Foster relationships with supplier* • *Adhere to contract requirements* • *Provide prompt month end reporting* • *Monitor suppliers' industry position* • *Be proactive in contract negotiations*
Stage 4: ISFs – determine one or more ISFs for each leadership strategy.	• Assessment of relationship • *Collate textual information* • *Tap informal networks* • *Monitor supplier complaints* • *Monitor adherence reporting* • Be available to supplier • Explore direct link to supplier I/S
Stage 5: Identify Potential – identify potential MSS projects, and select the most appropriate to implement.	• External database • *PC-textual database* • Communications – fax, e-mail, voice-mail, teleconferencing • Financial modelling

The Freight company's core business is the importing and exporting of recycled metal. The ISF methodology was used with one senior executive of the company. The *italics* within the results column at each stage of the methodology show the issues that were selected as the focus of attention within the next stage of the methodology (except in the case of the last stage, where the project highlighted was the one selected for implementation). For instance, the preservation of current business was considered the most important business goal. This led to three strategies being considered at stage 2, the continuity with the major contracts being the most important. This business strategy had several associated leadership strategies. In total, several ISFs were identified for the leadership strategies. The ISFs led to the proposal of four potential MSS. The ISFs, that led to the PC-textual database project for the recording and analysis of supplier details, are highlighted.

Adapted from Stein 1994

sponsor may be an eventual beneficiary of the MSS. Secondly, a senior executive may act as an *operating sponsor* of the proposed MSS. This person oversees all MSS development work and ensures that the necessary resources are available to the development team. The person who acts as the executive sponsor may also act as the operating sponsor. The person(s) adopting the sponsor roles, together with representatives from other aspects of company operations, may form a champions' group. The MSS development staff can use the champions' group to test out ideas, and/or to collect information from, and to act as guinea-pigs for, prototypes, as required during MSS development. The group also promotes the MSS within the organisation. A champions' group has been found to aid MSS development significantly (Popovich 1992).

The MSS to be developed must be acceptable to those affected by it. There is a need for an appraisal of all the stakeholders in the MSS, including the intended user base (which may be a manager or a technical assistant working on a manager's behalf, or even several managers as in the case of group decision making activities), the manager(s) to be supported, and the personnel providing underlying MSS data. The following questions may be addressed within this appraisal:

1. What effects is the system expected to have on the power structure within the organisation? Who is likely to gain the most, and who is likely to lose the most?
2. What effects is the system expected to have on social groupings within the organisation? Will the system lead to new patterns of interaction between individuals and groups? Will the system lead to 'social isolation' of organisational members?
3. What effects is the system likely to have on the work and structure of management in general? For example, is it expected to reduce the demand for middle management work, leading to reduction of staff at that level? Could it make an individual's work more or less enjoyable?
4. Is the MSS development ethical?

Which questions are asked depends on the nature of the proposed MSS development. For instance, the second question may be more appropriate when either group decision making support or information communication support is the focus of MSS development. There may also be differences between the perceptions of the stakeholders and the technical team as to the social effect of an MSS and its magnitude. The perceived threat of a proposed MSS to the positions of stakeholders is often higher than the actual threat. However, it is the perceptions of stakeholders that are important as it is these that will determine whether a particular MSS is accepted once developed. The development team must consider ways of reducing the perceived threat of an MSS if this poses significant risk to the MSS's eventual success. Three possible ways, which could be used either individually or in combination, are as follows:

- *Stakeholder education as to the benefits of the system, and its expected effects.* Persuade stakeholders that the actual expected effects are less of a threat than that perceived, using sound logical arguments.
- *Attempt to create a felt need for the MSS within the organisation.* This may involve actually saying to selected stakeholders, when a problem or tricky decision situation arises, how the new system could help them if available. This has been found to persuade a stakeholder indirectly that the proposed system has value. The stakeholder can then act as an internal ambassador of the system. Changed perceptions of the proposed MSS are more likely when one or more internal ambassadors exist.

- *Compromise on issues within the technical design of the proposed MSS to lessen threats.* For example, one reason for eventual MSS failure is caused by neglect of social control issues by the MSS development team (Glover et. al 1992). An MSS may exert greater social control on individuals or groups than before. However, social control could have been reduced had the MSS been designed differently. For example, a proposed MSS may provide higher-level management with greater capabilities for viewing information concerning the performance of lower-level management. However, by designing the MSS to restrict access of higher management to only that information which is critical to their work, and where access permission has been granted by lower management, may lessen the fears of lower management (although this, in turn, can lead to problems in superior /subordinate relationships, and therefore needs to be approached sensitively and only within organisations with appropriate corporate cultures). This approach was adopted successfully within the Lockheed Georgia MSS described in Houndeshel (1992) and Turban (1993). (The general concept of social control is described in King and Iacono 1984.)

The intended MSS user base (that is, the person or persons who operate the MSS) is an important development issue. In some situations, one or more managers may comprise the MSS user base. In the case of active support for group decision making, such as Decision Rooms (described in Chapter 6), managers are invariably the MSS users, although both technical and business assistance is available via the facilitator role. One advantage of having a manager as the user of an MSS is that the manager is completely familiar with the decision situation, and knows what information and/or analyses need to be provided. However, the manager may not be sufficiently computer literate or adequately familiar with the operation of the MSS. The time needed to learn how to operate and use the MSS effectively may not be available. Furthermore, the manager may not want to use the system, happy to leave its operation to a technical assistant. The major disadvantage of having a technical assistant operate the MSS on a manager's behalf is the additional layer of communication that exists between the manager and the MSS. The manager may be unaware that incorrect analyses have been performed or that the information presented is erroneous. Despite this disadvantage, Hogue (1987) found that 95% of 18 MSS providing active decision making support had been used at some stage by technical assistants (often termed intermediaries) on behalf of management. Given management's generally increasing technical skills and knowledge, and the more user-friendly interfaces provided by modern MSS, it is doubtful whether Hogue's findings are representative of current MSS user bases.

Technical feasibility of a proposed MSS development is vital. The hardware, software and inter-connectivity (via LANS/WANS) needed for MSS development and use, and any relationships between the MSS and existing corporate computer systems, need to be assessed. Inadequacy of technology with regard to in-house MSS developments has been identified as the most common cause of systems failure (Glover et. al. 1992). Technical inadequacy can manifest itself in several ways:

- The response rate of the MSS may be unacceptably slow.
- The MSS may be unreliable or insecure.
- The method of interaction provided to the MSS user base may not be sufficiently user friendly.
- The MSS may not support the required business need (for example, the information provided may be either too summarised or too detailed).

- The underlying data sources may not be sufficiently mature to support the data requirements of the MSS effectively (Millet and Mawhinney 1992, Millet et al. 1992).

The existence of any of these problems can result in user frustration and/or non-use of an MSS.

In order to evaluate technical feasibility effectively, the development team needs to have some idea of the software with which the required MSS functionality can be provided (when a suitable 'off-the-shelf' MSS exists) or developed. Fidler and Rogerson (1995) provide a technique to aid selection of either an MSS or an MSS development package. The technique fits exactly with the functional view of MSS adopted within this book. In total, the technique requires two levels of functionality description. The first, so-called MSS *type description*, allows a set of candidate computerised systems to be identified whereas the second, so-called MSS instance description, facilitates the selection of the most appropriate candidate system. So far, only tentative proposals for the *MSS instance description* level have been suggested, and these are the subject of further research activities. The MSS type description involves the profiling of candidate systems and the functional requirements of the intended MSS or MSS development package, based on the following criteria:

- The *usage* patterns of the MSS – does the MSS support (in the case of candidate systems) or does it need to support (in the case of the functional requirements) as-needed and/or periodic usage?
- The *foundation* of the MSS – does the MSS support (in the case of candidate systems) or does it need to support (in the case of the functional requirements) applications that are data-oriented (passive support) or more interactive modelling-oriented (active support), or both?
- The *client* of the MSS – does the MSS support (in the case of candidate systems) or does it need to support (in the case of the functional requirements) one user, a set of individual users and/or a group working together on a task?
- The *communication* flow between MSS and client – does the MSS support (in the case of candidate systems) or does it need to support (in the case of the functional requirements) one-way communication from MSS to client or a bi-directional, interactive communication flow between client and MSS?
- The *management task* or tasks of the MSS – what task or tasks does the MSS support (in the case of candidate systems) or does it need to support (in the case of the functional requirements).

In addition, the *orientation* of each candidate system is highlighted. Orientation is concerned with the generality of the candidate system; whether it is appropriate to one specific application only or whether it is more widely applicable.

For some criteria, the developer can select more than one of the pre-specified values, whereas other criteria allow the selection of only one value. Profiling each candidate system and the functional requirements using the appropriate criteria allows a candidate system to be assessed against the functional requirements in a structured and consistent manner. The technique can help in producing a shortlist of the most suitable candidate systems from a functional perspective for more detailed, instance level description and selection. Figure 7.1 provides some example profiles of both candidate systems and MSS functional requirements.

Fig 7.1 MSS type description framework and examples

Candidate support system (CSS)	Orientation		Usage		Foundation		Client			Communication		Management task (MT)
	General/tool	App. specific	Periodic	As-needed	Data	Model	Indiv.	Set of indivs.	Group	Support to client	Both ways	
CSS perspective	✓	✓	✓	✓	✓	✓	✓	✓	✓	✓	✓	✓
Example profiles												
Company Briefing Book		✓		✓	✓			✓		✓		Strategic decision making
Spreadsheet package	✓			✓	✓	✓	✓	✓			✓	Financial analysis
			✓	✓	✓	✓	✓	✓	✓	✓	✓	MT perspective
												Example profiles
			✓		✓	✓	✓				✓	Consolidated divisional budgetting
			✓		✓	✓				✓		Company acquisitions

This diagram shows the profiling of two candidate computerised systems, using the orientation, usage, foundation, client, communication and management task criteria. The MSS functional requirements associated with two management tasks are also profiled against all criteria, bar orientation.

The economic feasibility of IS is often evaluated using the Cost Benefit Analysis (CBA) technique, where costs are evaluated against envisaged benefits. This technique relies on each cost and benefit being quantified in monetary terms, wherever possible. The costs and benefit values are then combined and analysed using a simple mathematical model, so that a payback period or a break-even point can be identified. CBA is unsuitable for evaluating the economics of most MSS developments. In other types of IS, such as DP systems, the majority of benefits are known and tangible (that is, they can be quantified in some way). On the other hand, the majority of MSS benefits are intangible and very uncertain. For instance, Keen (1989) provides the following list of benefits which have resulted from one or more MSS implementations:

- increase in the number of alternatives examined
- better understanding of the business
- fast response to unexpected situations
- ability to carry out situation analysis on an *ad hoc* basis
- enables new insights and learning
- improves communication
- better control

- cost savings
- better decisions made
- more effective teamwork
- time savings
- making better use of data resources

Only two of the above list, cost savings and time savings, can be transformed easily into monetary values. Several are difficult to measure in any way. Indeed, some benefits may not be identifiable at the outset of an MSS development: they emerge as the MSS is used over time.

Not only are benefits difficult to measure and quantify, but the costs of MSS development can also be difficult to ascertain accurately at the start of MSS development. MSS requirements, particularly those concerning active decision making support, may be unknown at the outset of an MSS project beyond an overall awareness that support is needed. Resources for development are therefore hard to estimate, although past experiences in MSS development can be useful in estimating requirements.

Given the above discussion, it comes as no surprise that many MSS developments are justified on the basis of management intuition rather than any formal evaluation process. Watson et. al. (1991) found that 45 out of the 50 companies that they surveyed initiated MSS development on the basis of management intuition alone. However, with the IS department being held increasingly accountable for investments made, a more informed approach is needed. Bird (1991) suggests constructing a portion of an MSS (at low cost) to help predict benefits more accurately. Indeed, Keen's Value Analysis technique for MSS development (Keen 1989), which is discussed further in Section 7.4, prescribes this approach. However, in certain development environments, as is typically the case where development work is contracted out to a third party, partial construction is not possible prior to contract acceptance. Furthermore, some MSS demonstrate value only after its user base has reached a critical mass. This is particularly the case with MSS that support information communication.

Information Economics (IE) (Parker et al. 1988) enables qualitative and quantitative IS benefits to be taken into account during economic feasibility evaluation. IE provides a framework for appraising, in addition to the cost avoidance and labour savings accounted for within CBA, the extra benefits of an IS in terms of its contributions to value-linking (the additional benefits due to increased linking between corporate operations, or between corporate operations and the environment), value-acceleration (the benefits that accrue from faster corporate operations, or from faster activity between corporate operations and the environment), and value-restructuring (the benefits that accrue from the changes expected in organisation structure and work practices). An IS is scored on each aspect of appraisal, using a 0–5 Likert scale for example. Two other scores on the same scale are also associated with an IS, the first of which reflects the match between the IS and the organisational objectives and mission, and the second of which reflects the level of competitive advantage expected of the IS.

IE allows selection between several IS projects to take place. The set of scores for each project is presented to management so that projects can be compared. An MSS project with a very bad CBA compared to other IS projects can be cast in a more favourable light with IE's additional value, alignment and strategy scores. Although more effective than using CBA, IE does have its weaknesses. Whilst embracing its importance, IE views strategic alignment as only one component of the appraisal process rather than as a fundamental prerequisite to the selection of any IS project. Secondly, transforming a set of disparate intangible and subjective benefits into a combined value between 0 to 5 is subjective to the individual performing the activity. People differ in terms of what is considered most significant. The process is also open to misuse as the numbers can be manipulated to promote a personal agenda.

An alternative approach to assessing the feasibility of IS investment has been proposed by McBride and Fidler (1994). Based on the so-called interpretivist approach, as described by Walsham (1993), IS investment is assessed in terms of a framework which covers:

1. The content and nature of the (proposed) IS and of the organisational problem which the IS addresses
2. The social context in which the IS is (to be) placed
3. The social process by which the IS influences (or will influence) the organisation
4. The linkage between the social context and the social process.

McBride and Fidler's framework takes into account the bi-directional influences between an IS and the social/organisational context in which it is placed. The framework distinguishes between the social context, which is a static view of the organisation's past and present, and the social process, which is a dynamic view of the organisation during IS development or procurement. The process of developing/procuring the IS, within the given organisation and social context, leads to changes to, or re-inforcement of, the organisation's norms, standards, power, and views and meanings attached to IS. These issues are considered explicitly in the fourth part of the framework.

The information to be gathered within each of the four enumerated areas of interest, forming the framework for IS investment evaluation, is described in Table 7.2. McBride and Fidler present two case studies to show how the framework can be applied in practice. Both examples refer to MSS developments, and focus on post-evaluation of investment decisions. Indeed, the framework is probably most easily applied within the post-implementation review stage of an IS project, although it can also be used for evaluating IS investment potential. For instance, a thorough evaluation of the historical social context within which the MSS is to be embedded, and of the content of the proposed MSS, may lead to predictions of how the MSS might influence the organisation (the social process aspects) and the potential social context/process linkage. Also, having a rich set of case histories of both unsuccessful and successful MSS implementations, which are evaluated against the framework, and comparing these to proposed MSS investments, which are also evaluated against the framework, may provide more insight into the organisational impact and value of the proposed IS investment than if assessment was based solely on intuition or on other formal evaluation methods.

In summary, an assessment of the feasibility of a proposed MSS leads to an informed view of the likelihood of that MSS being accepted by the organisation, together with an overall appraisal of the resources (technical, human and financial) needed to some degree of detail. Several development options for a particular MSS may be identified, each with differing resource requirements and potential impacts. Recommendations may be made regarding the option to adopt, although the final decision rests with management.

Table 7.2 An interpretive framework for IS benefits evaluation

Aspect of Evaluation	Information to be gathered
Content	• Problem to be addressed • Nature of products and processes the organisation is involved in • Nature of the information system to be procured or developed
Social Context	• History of previous approaches to the problem and the causes of the problem • History of IS usage • History of external forces applied to the organisation • Nature of social relations between participants: co-operation and or conflict • Barriers between social subgroups of interest • Nature of management structure which supports IS • Nature of the social infrastructure
Social Process	• Culture: nature of the subgroups • Response of different subgroups to the prospect of an IS • Extent of management support for the development or procurement process • Attitude of subgroups to organisational change expected from IS • Meanings attached to the IS by subgroups • Political effect of IS on autonomy/control balance within the organisation • Ethical issues associated with procurement/development of the system • Effect on quality of the work environment
Context/Process Linkage	• Extent to which IS appeals to organisational norms • Key meaning attached to the IS • Key themes highlighted by subgroups • Intended use of the IS for control or delegation • Power of subgroups to enforce IS acceptance

The left-hand side of this table highlights the four aspects that need to be addressed when either evaluating an implemented IS (during a post-implementation review) or justifying a possible new IS investment. The right-hand side of the table provides, for each aspect, a set of details concerning the organisation and the IS that need to be assessed.

7.3   MSS DEVELOPMENT

If an MSS project is worthy of organisational investment, a plan of ensuing development activities needs to be drawn up. Many (sub)activities will need to be embraced within the plan, including any software development activities required, any procure-

❑ *Viewpoint*

Reaping the benefits

Strangely enough, although many weary users may disagree, the purpose of most IT systems is to benefit the organisation, and contribute, eventually, to the bottom line.

Although this truth is glaringly obvious, a depressingly small number of organisations take steps to ensure that IT benefits are measured and monitored. Still fewer ensure that someone, somewhere, is named as responsible for ensuring that the benefits are actually achieved.

A survey of 60 IT managers in UK private companies, by John Ward of the Cranfield School of Management, found that very few (5%) had any kind of rigorous or formal practice of benefits management. But then, only just over half had formal methodologies for systems development, project management or investment appraisal (and only 20% had all three). Not surprisingly, a majority believed that they could significantly improve their current approach to managing IT benefits.

But what are the benefits that IT deliver? They are, of course, variable, but the most popular are those that most overtly affect the core of the business.

"The current benefits perceived to be provided by IT were heavily biased towards cost savings," points out Ward.

Improving management information is also seen as a major benefit, along with business processing re-engineering implications, such as improved process efficiency and the ability to support business change and growth, which rank highly.

There are other kinds of benefits, however, which are more difficult to measure because they are far less tangible. These can include improving morale and generating goodwill. Perhaps because, by their nature, such benefits are difficult to measure, 25% of respondents do not include intangible benefits in their IT project appraisal.

"Nearly three-quarters of respondents believed that their current project justification process fails to identify all available benefits," aid Ward.

Conversely, 86% of respondents believed that it is not possible to anticipate all potential benefits at the project approval stage, although only 19% have any process for trying to identify further benefits after implementation and then taking action to realise them.

But who determines the benefits, and then appraises whether they have been achieved by the new IT system?

More than 80% of respondents have business project managers, but the report found that their role is usually confined to managing the interface between IT and the user community, rather than actively managing a business project to deliver actual business benefits.

Allocating specific responsibility for realising business benefits to individual managers only happens in a third of companies. They usually give the task to a line or departmental manager. Clearly the situation overall is not satisfactory, otherwise so many IT systems would not be regarded as failed or flawed.

To reverse the situation, Ward says, the issue of benefits needs to be given greater priority, and not perpetually avoided. The realisation of benefits should be integrated thoroughly into the systems development process.

Until benefits management is given the prominence it deserves, IT systems will continue to be criticised. Those that cannot be proved to have succeeded will be deemed to have failed. ∎

Reprinted with permission from *Computer Weekly*, 3rd August 1995.

ment and installation activities regarding hardware, MSS ('off-the-shelf') and/or MSS development package(s), any activities concerning changeover from the existing system to the new system, and the post-implementation review activities. These activities are not unique to MSS projects: they occur in any IS project, and have been described in many IS Management texts (see, for example, Bell 1987, and Wysocki and Young 1990).

The focus of this section is principally on the three major approaches that are employed within MSS development: the traditional approach, the evolutionary approach and the hybrid approach. These form the topics of the following three subsections respectively. The fourth subsection focuses on the relevance of each approach to the development of particular MSS functionality.

7.3.1 The traditional approach to MSS development

The *traditional approach* to MSS development prescribes a series of ordered MSS development activities, which can be categorised as follows:

- *Requirements specification* – a thorough analysis of the current organisational situation, within which the eventual MSS is to be embedded, is undertaken. Specific needs of management are established. This leads to the specification of MSS requirements, both at an overall system level and with respect to individual managers. (Sometimes, feasibility assessment is viewed as an integral component of this activity rather than being viewed as a discrete task undertaken in advance.)
- *Design* – having specified the requirements, the MSS is designed. This may involve the conceptual design and physical design of programs (in terms of input, processing and output) and databases.
- *Implementation* – Programs and databases need to be developed from the designs. Both testing of individual programs and overall systems testing need to take place.

Each stage has defined deliverables, which are signed off at the end of the stage by management to confirm their completeness and accuracy. Once they are signed off, the next stage of development can proceed.

The motto of the traditional approach is 'to get things right first time'. Any backtracking to re-do or amend work performed within earlier stages of development is a sign of weakness in the previous work performed by the development team. The situations, to which this approach is most suited, are:

- where it is possible to define all MSS requirements clearly at the requirements specification stage, and
- where these requirements are sufficiently stable to persist from the time of MSS requirements specification to some time well after MSS implementation, so that the MSS is of benefit to the organisation in its initial form.

7.3.2 Prototyping within IS development and the evolutionary approach

According to Skidmore and Wroe (1988), a prototype is:

> *'.. a live working system and not just a paper-based design. Users can test its operations, and explore its facilities and so do not have to rely upon written descriptions' [p. 19].*

Within the context of MSS development, prototyping involves the building of a series of MSS prototypes, each of which is based on a statement of currently perceived requirements. When a prototype is ready, it is used to seek comments from users about its operation and/or scope. These comments, together with the current prototype, form the specification for the next prototype to be developed. Prototypes can be either horizontal, vertical or mixed. A horizontal prototype provides a breadth view of the intended MSS. It enables a user to assess the overall scope and presentation aspects of the intended system but does not address each individual processing requirement in detail. For example, a horizontal prototype may contain all the required input and output screens of the intended MSS but none of the underlying processing operations. The designer can provide a narrative description of the processing that is expected to occur between input and output screens to supplement the breadth view demonstrated by the prototype. A vertical prototype provides a depth view of some aspect of the intended MSS. An example of a vertical prototype could be the implementation of a possible mathematical model to provide active support for management decision making. The entire functionality of the mathematical model is embodied within the prototype, whereas other elements are omitted. Mixed prototypes incorporate aspects of both horizontal and vertical prototypes. A breadth view of most of the intended MSS functionality, but with some aspects being implemented in depth, could be provided by a mixed prototype.

The motto of prototyping is 'to expect that things are never right first time'. It is therefore suited to situations where user requirements are not clear at the outset of development. A trial and error approach is adopted to requirements determination by the development of successive prototypes. The motto implicitly presupposes that, although the requirements are unclear at the outset, eventually a final and sufficiently stable set of management requirements can be reached. However, in exceedingly dynamic environments, there may never be sufficient stability in user requirements and, in theory, prototyping never ends. This situation presents problems for IS management when attempting to distinguish between MSS development and MSS maintenance activities. A clear dividing line between development and maintenance activities may be needed for financial reasons or to enable the clear transfer of responsibilities from development to maintenance personnel. Alavi (1984) provides a general discussion of the strengths and weaknesses of prototyping for IS development.

Conceptually, prototyping can be viewed as a series of very rapid iterations of the activities found within the traditional approach where each iteration results in a prototype. This view is summarised in Figure 7.2. Ideally, less than two days elapsed time should pass between iterations.

Using prototyping within MSS development results in a prototype MSS. When a prototype has been developed, which matches the users' needs sufficiently, it may form the system to be delivered to the users. If this occurs, then so-termed *evolutionary prototyping* has taken place, as the final prototype becomes the eventual operative system. An evolutionary prototyping approach, or *evolutionary approach* for short, is said to have been adopted when evolutionary prototyping has taken place throughout MSS development. On the other hand, a prototype, when developed to match the users' needs sufficiently, may be discarded (although a specification of the user requirements that the prototype served to identify remains). In this case, so-termed *throwaway prototyping* has occurred. Throwaway prototyping provides partial MSS development coverage: it never forms an overall development approach.

7.3.3   The hybrid approach to MSS development

Both throwaway prototyping and evolutionary prototyping can be employed at appropriate stages of the traditional approach. For example, throwaway prototyping can be adopted to facilitate the requirements specification stage of the traditional approach. The final prototype is thrown away after the specification is agreed. Throwaway prototyping can also be used within the detailed design of a system, for example to aid interface development. Again, the final prototype is thrown away once the detailed interface specifications have been agreed. Evolutionary prototyping can be adopted within MSS design and implementation activities. In this case, the final prototype of

Fig 7.2 Prototyping as a series of iterations of traditional development activities

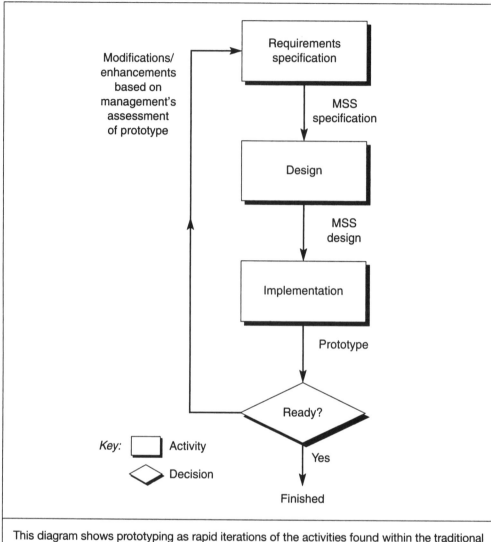

This diagram shows prototyping as rapid iterations of the activities found within the traditional approach. The difference between prototyping and the traditional approach lies not with the activities performed, but with the manner and timeframe in which they are performed.

the detailed design becomes the actual operational system delivered to the user base. In the context of the traditional approach, as described in Section 7.3.1, adopting evolutionary prototyping at this point in development forces iterations between the separate design and implementation activities. However, it must be remembered that the traditional development activities listed in Section 7.3.1 are separated arbitrarily. It would have been just as valid to have combined the 'design' and 'implementation' categories into one 'design and implementation' category, thereby maintaining a sequential, non-iterative ordering of activities even when evolutionary prototyping is adopted. The overall ethos of the traditional approach to MSS development is still predominant, even when evolutionary prototyping is used within MSS design and implementation.

A *hybrid approach* to MSS development is considered to have been adopted when either form of prototyping is used at some point within the overall context (and ethos) of the traditional approach.

7.3.4 Development approaches and MSS functionality

It is possible to develop MSS using either a traditional approach, an evolutionary approach or a hybrid approach. Which of the approaches is most suited to a particular MSS development depends on a variety of factors concerning the functionality and scope of the intended MSS, and the context in which development is taking place. This subsection examines the suitability of the three development approaches to the provision of MSS functionality for:

- information handling support
- passive support of decision making
- active support of decision making.

Information handling support

Most MSS implementations that provide information handling support are developed by software vendors and purchased 'off-the-shelf'. In some cases, however, customisation of an MSS development package may be needed. This is often performed by the vendor on behalf of the client, as part of the procurement agreement. Where responsibility for customisation rests with the client, it must be managed effectively. An evolutionary, traditional or hybrid approach can be used to effect the required customisation. Which is actually adopted depends greatly on issues such as the extent of customisation and whether the requirements for customisation are easy to identify. For example, an evolutionary approach to template development for an information preparation tool may be employed if template requirements are not completely known at the outset. If they are prescribed clearly, for example, within company policy statements, then it may be more appropriate to adopt either a traditional or a hybrid approach within customisation activities.

Passive support of decision making

MSS that provide pre-defined information reports are typically developed using either a traditional or a hybrid approach. Information reports are pre-defined when the requirements for information are known and relatively stable, which makes it possible to adopt a traditional development approach. However, evolutionary prototyping is often employed at the detailed design level to agree detailed information requirements and specific user interface issues. For example, the overall design of a Briefing Book facility may be ascertained at the outset of a project using, as a basis, the organisation's CSFs and KPIs. However, evolutionary prototyping may be adopted to establish the more detailed information content and user interface design of the Briefing Book. Indeed, even CSF/KPI specification may be adopted in an incremental manner (see Section 7.4.3) as part of evolutionary prototyping.

Development of an MSS that provides customised information reports requires the specification of the underlying data structures needed to support management's information needs, and the implementation of mechanisms by which data can be gathered. Interface development activities may also be required when implementing particular MSS interaction methods (e.g. forms-based). Hybrid or traditional development approaches are often applied to the development of MSS that provide customised information reports. For example, consider an as-needed, customised information reporting facility which is developed using a relational DBMS with SQL query facility. In this case, the development team needs to specify and develop the database, against which SQL queries will be formulated by users. The database requirements may be established at the beginning of the project by investigating the expected information requirements of each manager who is to use the information reporting facility. The information requirements form the basis for database design. Database implementation may be evolutionary in nature, allowing partial support to be provided as quickly as possible as well as providing an initial system for user training.

Active support of decision making

The evolutionary approach is very popular for the development of MSS that provide active support of individual decision making, although both hybrid and traditional approaches are plausible under certain circumstances. The main reason for the popularity of the evolutionary approach stems from the difficulty in ascertaining exactly what is required to support a manager's decision making activities actively at the outset of development. At best, a skilled MSS developer may be able to make some tentative proposals as to the required MSS functionality, which form the basis of an initial prototype.

Sometimes a hybrid approach to the development of these MSS is adopted. Typically in this case, prototyping is used to establish user requirements of the MSS, with the final prototype being thrown away. This approach occurs for one or both of the following reasons:

- To perform effective prototyping, development packages must enable prototypes to be developed quickly and easily. A downside of such packages, however, is the relatively slow handling of user requests. If an MSS must provide a very rapid response to satisfy regular management decision making needs, the prototype will have to be thrown away and a more responsive MSS designed. With the increases in processing power and more sophisticated methods of optimising the execution of user requests, the response rate of packages suitable for prototyping is increasingly acceptable for all but the most resource-intensive tasks.
- The development package used for prototyping may be restrictive in its provision of functionality. Whilst the package is suitable for prototyping purposes, the intended MSS needs to be developed with full functionality beyond the capabilities of the prototyping package.

Relatively simple MSS for active support of individual decision making may be developed by the eventual users of the MSS, rather than by separate IS professionals. The term *End User Computing (EUC)* is used to denote activities where users (non-IS professionals) develop their own support tools. For example, many current managers develop their own spreadsheet templates, allowing them to perform 'what-if' analysis with respect to a particular decision situation. These systems are usually developed using an evolutionary, trial and error, approach. EUC has both advantages and disadvantages. One potential problem is where the user has limited technical ability. This may lead to overly simple and inaccurate models being developed. A decision based on an unsound model may have serious consequences for an organisation (for more information on EUC, and its strengths and weaknesses, see Turban 1993).

An MSS that provides active support for group decision making is typically purchased from a vendor. It may provide several pre-defined modules, each of which supports a particular group decision making technique such as NGT or Brainstorming. Some individual decision making support modules may need to be developed for use by individual managers at appropriate points within the group decision making process. Like the provision of any other active support for individual decision making, an evolutionary approach or a hybrid approach is typically adopted within the development of these modules.

7.4 TECHNIQUES FOR USE IN MSS DEVELOPMENT

This section provides an overview of MSS development techniques, each of which provides a structured approach to performing one or more development activities. Emphasis is on those techniques that have been proposed specifically for MSS development. However, the role of conventional IS development techniques within MSS development is discussed at the end of this section.

7.4.1 Value analysis

Value Analysis (Keen 1989) could have been described in Section 7.1, as it is an alternative method of addressing the economic feasibility of an MSS. However, feasibility evaluation takes place within the context of actual development, rather than before development commences. Furthermore, prototyping is an essential part of this technique. For these reasons, it was considered more appropriate to review Value Analysis in this section.

The original objective of Value Analysis was to aid cost and benefit assessments of MSS that provide active support for individual decision making. However, the technique is general enough to be applicable to a wider range of MSS projects, essentially where costs and benefits are both hard to identify at project commencement and difficult to quantify. The technique does not require each benefit and cost to be quantified individually. Rather, attention is focused on the overall worth of an MSS to the organisation.

Value Analysis prescribes the following development steps. Firstly, a small subset of user requirements is identified. An assessment of the expected benefits of a prototype (referred to as Version 0 by Keen) that satisfies the subset of requirements is made (only a few benefits may be specified at this point). Then, the maximum amount that the company is willing to pay to achieve the stated benefits is ascertained. This amount must be low, so that the project is considered to be of low financial risk. The development of Version 0 only takes place when there is a high probability of Version 0 being developed within the stated financial maximum.

Version 0 provides a basis from which a more accurate specification of the full system (Keen calls this the Base System) can be derived. The costs of developing the Base System may be more accurately assessed now that Version 0 has been developed. In addition, a more accurate benefit assessment of the full system may be possible, due to management's experimentation with Version 0. For example, the use of Version 0 within the company may lead to an increase in management's overall understanding of corporate operations, a benefit not anticipated prior to Version 0. Management expect this benefit to extend across other aspects of corporate operations when they are supported by the Base System.

Costs and benefit assessments are reversed when considering the development of the Base System. The total cost to build the Base System is first estimated. Then management decide on the level and/or quantity of the envisaged benefits that need to be achieved in order to justify the costs of the full system. If there is a strong likelihood of attaining the chosen benefits to the required level then the project should proceed. If there is little likelihood of attainment, or Version 0 demonstrates little benefit, then the project should be abandoned before substantial sums of money are invested. The Base System can be developed using an evolutionary approach, and there is no reason why cost/benefit assessment cannot take place after the development of each Base System prototype.

7.4.2 ROMC

ROMC (Sprague and Carlson 1982) is a technique that supports the requirements elicitation of MSS that are to provide active support of individual decision making. ROMC is based on two fundamental principles:

- A manager finds it exceedingly difficult to articulate the way he or she makes decisions.
- An MSS should be highly process-independent, in that the MSS should not impose a particular method of decision making but allow a user to adopt whatever method is most appropriate for the current decision situation.

The second of the above principles has been debated. For example, Silver (1991) suggests several reasons why companies might wish to provide process-dependent MSS, forcing users to adopt a particular method of decision making. These include management's wish to instil more effective decision making practices within the organisation and to impose a uniform method of decision making that is fully documented and consistent.

ROMC is an acronym, standing for Representations, Operations, Memory aids, and Control mechanisms. Rather than asking 'how do you go about making this decision', an MSS developer focuses attention on:

- The visual representations that help the manager to conceptualise the decision situation and to communicate it to others
- The operations that the manager performs during decision making (where each operation can be categorised as to whether it is used within the Intelligence, Design and/or Choice phases of Simon's Decision Making model (described in Chapter 2))

- The memory aids available to assist the manager in performing operations and in forming the conceptualisations
- The control mechanisms which govern the ways in which decision making takes place or is communicated.

Anything that provides information during the decision making activity, but is not classed as a representation, is a memory aid. An operation relates to either a representation or a memory aid. The use of a verb by the manager, with respect to an activity concerning a representation or a memory aid, typically suggests that an operation is being performed. For example, the statement 'I extract customer details of interest' suggests that the manager in question performs an 'extraction' operation relating to a 'customer details' memory aid. Table 7.3 provides examples of representations, operations, memory aids and control mechanisms, which were identified during an MSS developer's fact-finding activities with the manager responsible for a charitable organisation's service location decisions.

The ROMC of the existing situation (although used here with respect to both the existing decision situation as well as a proposed MSS, Sprague and Carlson associate the ROMC acronym only with respect to the requirements specification of a proposed MSS) provides a basis from which a set of MSS requirements can be derived. The MSS requirements are also categorised in terms of ROMC. However, in this case, ROMC stands for:

- The representations of the decision situation that the MSS is to provide
- The operations the MSS is intended to support, each categorised as to whether it supports Intelligence, Design and/or Choice decision making phase(s)
- The automated memory aids, which will provide the required temporary and persistent storage
- The control mechanisms which will allow the user to interact with the MSS to perform the required MSS operations.

Each of the four components of ROMC for the existing decision situation do not always map directly onto the same component of ROMC at MSS requirements specification (for example, a representation used within existing decision making does not always map to an equivalent representation within MSS requirements specification). This may be due to one or more of the following reasons:

- The meaning of the term 'control mechanisms' is wider when used with respect to the existing decision situation than when used with respect to an MSS. Indeed, a control mechanism in the existing situation may be incorporated within an MSS operation. For instance, a company may have a standard policy, with respect to the annual decision of allocating bonuses to sales representatives, which states that bonuses can be awarded only to employees who have at least five years of service with the company. This control mechanism in current decision making may be reflected within the specification of an operation for a proposed MSS to support bonus allocation decisions. The operation extracts details of only those employees with at least five years service.
- An MSS supports, not replaces, a decision maker. Some of the ROMC components of the existing situation may therefore be omitted in the ROMC components for MSS requirements specification.

Table 7.3 Example ROMC for "Charity Services Location" decisions

	ROMC for Existing Situation	ROMC for possible MSS
Representations	• map of Britain • tables of capacity utilised at each centre for each disability type against maximum capacity allowed • tables of average mileage covered by clients to each centre	• computerised map interface • pie charts for analysis of total numbers of each disability type of each centre vs. maximum capacity (%s output) • bar charts for analysis of average mileage covered by clients of each centre vs. maximum average expected.
Operations	• draw current centres and associated catchment areas on map (I) • (re)-calculate average distance of clients within a particular catchment area (I, D, C) • (re)-calculate client numbers that use a particular centre per disability type (I, D, C) • compare maximum client numbers allowed per disability type at each centre with current/proposed client numbers (I, D,C) • re-draw catchment areas for existing centres (I, D, C) • draw on a new centre and associated catchment area, and re-draw existing catchment areas (D)	• show current charity centres and locations (I, D, C) • calculate average mileage for clients currently assigned to a particular charity centre, and compare to maximum expected (I, D, C) • calculate percentage capacity currently being assigned to each centre per disability type (I, D, C) • revise catchment areas (D) • add a new charity centre with a new catchment area (D) • save current configuration of centres and charity locations (D, C)

Memory Aids	• list of charity centres and their specific details (capacity per disability type, location, etc.)
	• temporary notepad and calculator for calculations
	• table of client details (including disability type(s) and location)
	• disability type code table
		• database holding data on:
		  • charity centres
		  • clients; their respective location and disability type(s)
		  • catchment areas
		  • disability types

Control Mechanisms	• no more than 90% capacity should be used in any centre for a particular disability type • average maximum distance between clients and centre should be 10 miles	• input via option buttons at the bottom of the screen • error messages • help messages on press of function key

This table shows an ROMC, both for the current decision making approach and for the proposed MSS, for a charitable organisation deciding where to locate charity centres and their associated catchment areas. Each operation, either used in current decision making or specified for the proposed MSS, is categorised as to whether it supports Intelligence (I), Design (D) and/or Choice (C) phases of Simon's Decision Making model.

- The ROMC based on the existing decision situation identifies what currently takes place. However, additional or alternative functionality may be provided by an MSS in order to improve decision making rather than just facilitate what happens at present.

ROMC has been applied effectively in practice (see Sprague and Carlson 1982 for examples of its application). It provides the MSS developer with a basic strategy for tackling the problem of requirements identification. It is most effective when applied to decision situations that have strong visual representations and relatively simple operations. When complexity lies within the operations, ROMC provides little more than a framework for establishing the operations of importance. In theory, ROMC can be adopted within any of the overall development approaches described in Section 7.3. However, it is probably most frequently used when development is evolutionary in nature, given that it is the most common approach for developing MSS for active support of individual decision making.

7.4.3 Critical success factor (CSF)/Key performance indicator (KPI) hierarchy

This technique is used to facilitate the identification and specification of requirements for an MSS providing passive decision making support. It prescribes a *top-down* approach to requirements identification and specification, where the focus of attention begins at the level of the entire organisation and finishes at the level of individual managers. As a consequence, the requirements of individual managers are aligned with organisational objectives. The opposite of a top-down approach, where attention is focused initially on the requirements of individual managers, is termed a bottom-up approach. A *bottom-up* approach does have some advantages. For instance, it encourages individual creativity rather than conformance.

Creating a CSF/KPI hierarchy involves the identification of CSFs at various levels of the organisation, starting from the organisational CSFs. Each organisational CSF may have one or more lower-level CSFs that contribute to its achievement. Each of the contributing lower-level CSFs may themselves have one or more contributing lower-level CSFs, and so the process of CSF specification continues until the lowest level of CSFs has been defined. A hierarchy of CSFs results from this process, as shown in Figure 7.3. Several KPIs, each identifying a measurable aspect of organisational performance, may be associated with a particular CSF. When this occurs, the achievement of a CSF can be gauged from the combined achievement levels of its associated KPIs. Not all CSFs will have associated KPIs: in this case, achievement of a CSF is gauged from the combined achievements of its respective lower-level contributing CSFs. CSFs that are at the lowest specification level must have at least one associated KPI. Finally, each CSF in the hierarchy may be associated with the particular management role that is responsible for its success.

The resultant CSF/KPI hierarchy provides the initial basis for MSS design. The successive levels of CSFs, together with their associated KPIs, can be used to define the overall structure for information reporting where drill down from one level of detail to the next is supported. In addition, the identification of the management role that is

Fig 7.3 An example partial CSF/KPI hierarchy for a goods manufacturing company

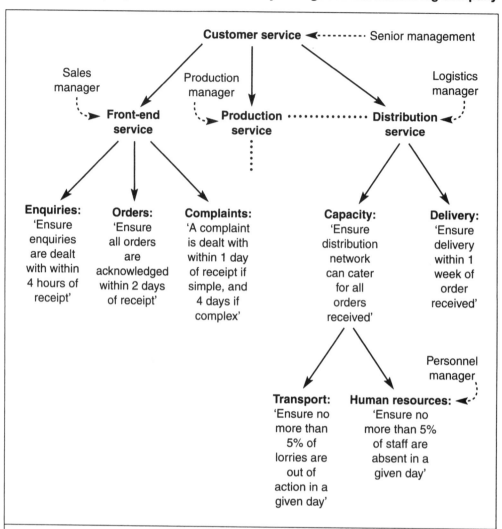

The partly completed CSF/KPI hierarchy above identifies several CSFs, KPIs and associated management roles. For instance, the 'customer service' organisational CSF has several contributing lower-level CSFs, including 'distribution service', 'front-end service' and 'production service'. 'Front-end service' has three associated CSFs, the KPIs of which provide, in combination, an indication of the achievement of 'front-end service.' Eventually, a range of values could be associated with each KPI, allowing the performance against the KPI to be categorised as either satisfactory, borderline or unsatisfactory. The 'front-end service' CSF comes under the responsibility of the Sales Manager role.

responsible for each CSF highlights both potential users and stakeholders of the MSS, and possible sources of underlying MSS data.

Although the CSF/KPI hierarchy technique has been applied effectively to MSS developments within several organisations, including London Underground (Callaghan

1992) and British Airways (Popovich 1992), its practical value has been debated. For instance, Bird (1991) considers that too much concentration on formal and comprehensive CSF/KPI specification can lead to 'over-intellectualising the process', resulting in an MSS staying too long on paper rather than delivering results. However, inadequate attention to information requirements specification at the outset can be equally disastrous for MSS development. There is no reason why the CSF/KPI hierarchy technique cannot be used within an evolutionary MSS development approach, where a partial CSF/KPI hierarchy is developed initially and prototyped. Later development iterations complete the hierarchy specification and its implementation. For example, an initial MSS prototype may be developed, which focuses on only the most important organisational CSF and the hierarchy stemming from this CSF. Later prototypes extend the number of organisational CSFs supported.

7.4.4 Structured situation analysis

Structured situation analysis (Mockler 1989) is actually a methodology which advocates several techniques for the development of MSS employing interactive Rule-based models. Having established that the target decision is suitable for MSS development, the methodology prescribes the following development activities, techniques and diagrammatic tools:

- Fact finding activities take place to investigate how the decision is made by the subject expert(s).
- Based on the fact finding investigations, a diagrammatic view of the decision situation is constructed as a set of *Decision Situation Diagrams*. Decision Situation Diagrams depict the overall decision to be made and the factors that influence the decision, either directly or indirectly. An example Decision Situation Diagram for the garment export decision (introduced in Chapter 6) is presented in Figure 7.4. The overall decision is depicted on the right-hand side of the diagram, and the factors found to directly influence the final decision are positioned adjacent and to the left of the final decision. Each of these factors may themselves have factors of direct influence. These are positioned on the Decision Situation Diagram to the left of the factor(s) that they directly influence. The process continues, until all the factors of influence on the final decision, either directly or indirectly, are shown on the diagram.

The garment export decision, as described in Chapter 6, is quite easily depicted in one Decision Situation Diagram as there are only a few factors of influence. Typical real-life situations possess many inter-related factors, which are difficult to manage on one diagram only. To cope with this, Mockler provides an abstraction mechanism for Decision Situation Diagrams, where a set of factors is represented as one combined factor on a higher-level Decision Situation Diagram. The individual factors that comprise this combined factor are depicted on a separate lower-level Decision Situation Diagram. Another way of enabling more than one diagram to be developed is to consider a factor as a (sub)decision in its own right, and to provide a separate Decision Situation Diagram for this (sub)decision. A reference to this factor will therefore appear on the leftmost side of one Decision Situation Diagram, and the rightmost of another Decision Situation Diagram.

Fig 7.4 A decision situation diagram for a garment export decision

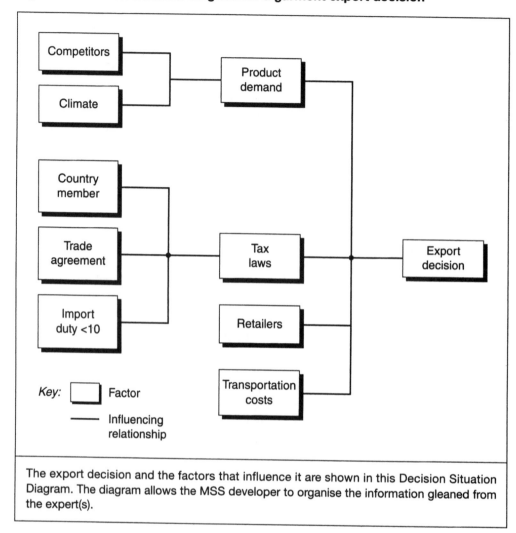

The export decision and the factors that influence it are shown in this Decision Situation Diagram. The diagram allows the MSS developer to organise the information gleaned from the expert(s).

- The set of draft Decision Situation Diagrams is refined and enhanced in the light of further discussions with the expert(s). For the aspects of the decision situation which are to be automated, a factor becomes a variable whose value may be found during the decision making process, either by user input or by rule invocation. The Decision Situation Diagram is annotated with the range of values which each variable can take.

- Attention is now focused on how the values of particular variables determine the value of another variable. Decision Tables are developed to specify the rules which relate influencing variables to those being influenced. One or more System Dependency Diagrams are also developed, typically one for each Decision Situation Diagram. Each of the System Dependency Diagrams may be very similar in overall structure to its associated Decision Situation Diagram, but references explicitly the relevant rules in the Decision Tables. Figure 7.5 provides the associated

System Dependency Diagram for the garment export Decision Situation Diagram in Figure 7.4. The abbreviations R_1 to R_{12} are used to link the relevant rules in the Decision Tables with the determination of the value of a particular factor shown on the System Dependency Diagram. Table 7.4 provides the Decision Table that specifies the rules for determining the overall value for the garment export decision variable. In total, three Decision Tables will be associated with the System Dependency Diagram in Figure 7.5, one for each variable whose value is directly influenced by the values of other variables.

- The Decision Tables provide the specification of a Rule-based model for the MSS. The rules are first converted into a pseudo-English format, and then translated into the syntax required by the target MSS development package. Once implementation is complete, the prototype MSS is available for user experimentation and testing.

Fig 7.5 A system dependency diagram for the garment export decision

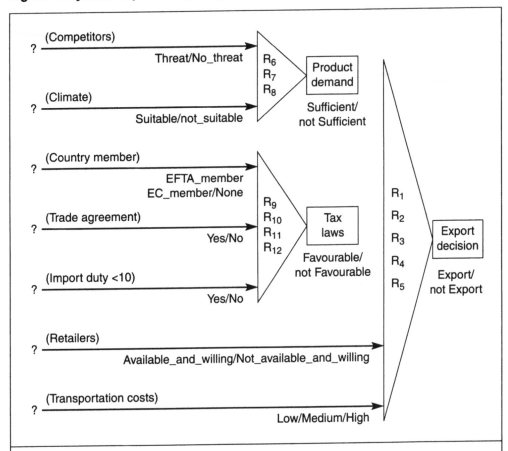

This diagram is very similar to the Decision Situation Diagram in Figure 7.4 in structure. The variables whose values are to be determined by user input are distinguished. Also, the diagram references one or more Decision Tables which hold the relationships between the values of the influencing variables and the value of the variable being influenced.

Table 7.4 A decision table for the overall garment export decision

| | | RULES | | | |
	R_1	R_2	R_3	R_4	R_5
Product-demand	Sufficient	Not _ sufficient			
Tax laws	Favourable		Unfavourable		
Retailers	A_and_W			Not A_and_W	
Transport-ation costs	Low				High/ medium
	Export	Not_export	Not_export	Not_export	Not_export

INFLUENCING VARIABLES (left vertical label)

VALUE OF INFLUENCED VARIABLE

The table defines Rules R_1 to R_4 inclusive (as they are referenced on the System Dependency Diagram in Figure 7.5).

- Any necessary modifications or enhancements, based on the assessment of the prototype, is made to the diagrams in sequence. This results in changes to the rule set and code for the next prototype MSS. This process continues until the expert(s) are satisfied with the functionality of the MSS prototype. The final diagrams, tables and pseudo-English version of the Rule-based model form part of the technical documentation for the MSS.

This methodology can be embraced within an evolutionary development approach, where different aspects of the highest-level Decision Situation Diagram are the focus of both more detailed specification and implementation over time. Lower-level diagrams are completed incrementally, covering only the functionality to be provided by the current prototype.

A possible problem with this methodology is the substantial time and effort required on the part of the development team to produce the diagrams required at different stages of the methodology, and to cope with the different diagrammatic notations employed. Computer-Aided Software Engineering (CASE) tools would certainly be of benefit to support this methodology.

7.4.5 Silver's MSS description language

The description language proposed by Silver (1991) focuses on the design of an MSS:

'..that affects or is intended to affect how people make decisions' [p19].

All MSS that support decision making affect the way in which decisions are made, albeit to varying degrees. Hence, Silver's description language appears to have wide applicability to MSS design.

MSS developers need to understand the underlying technologies available for MSS, MSS development and evolution, and the effects MSS may have on decision making. Silver's work focuses on the latter aspect. An MSS can have both positive and negative effects on a decision process. Both MSS design and the organisational context in which the MSS is embedded determine the effects of an MSS on decision making. In order to design MSS to maximise the positive effects and minimise the negative effects, the relationships between effects and MSS design need to be understood. A study of existing systems and their effects on decision making is a starting point from which to gain this understanding. A sufficiently powerful language needs to be provided in which the design of existing MSS and their respective effects on decision making can be described. The development of this language is the crux of Silver's research.

Silver proposes three levels of MSS description:

- Level 1: the *functional capabilities.*
- Level 2: the *user view.*
- Level 3: the *system attributes.*

The following paragraphs describe the three levels in turn.

Level 1: Functional Capabilities

The functions that an MSS provides to its user(s) are specified at this level. Functions may be described first at a fairly general level, and then at progressively more specific levels. For example, 'prediction' may be the most general description of one or more particular functions available within an MSS, with 'forecasting' being a more specific description of selected 'prediction' functions. At an appropriate level of description, actual models or techniques are specified. For instance, an MSS may provide two forecasting techniques: one based on Brown's Linear Expression and one providing forecasts using a simple exponential equation. Both of these techniques are linked to the 'forecasting' function description, which is in turn associated with the 'prediction' function description.

As shown in Figure 7.6, Silver provides a diagramming notation with which to describe interrelated MSS functions, and their associated techniques and models.

Level 2: The User View

This level describes how Level 1 functionality is presented to the user(s) of the MSS. The language proposed for this level is derived from other research work, including ROMC (described in Section 7.4.2). The description of each of the following four elements comprises the MSS description at Level 2.

- *Operators* – these are the individual operations that the system provides, as seen by the user(s) via the MSS interface. Operators vary in their generality and the descriptions at this level reflect these variations. For example, the 'graph' description may refer to a general graphing operator where users select the data to graph and the type of graph required. On the other hand, the 'graph sales' description may refer to

Fig 7.6 Example diagrammatic view of Silver's Level 1 description of an MSS

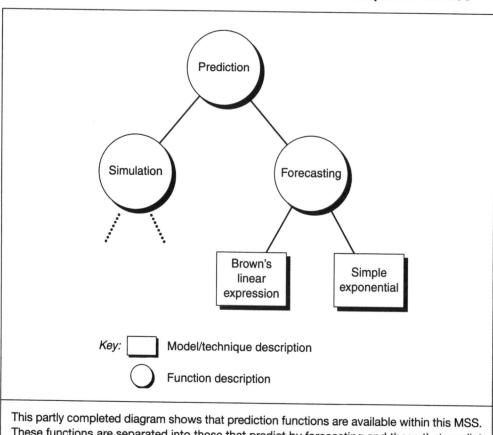

Key: ☐ Model/technique description

○ Function description

This partly completed diagram shows that prediction functions are available within this MSS. These functions are separated into those that predict by forecasting and those that predict by simulation techniques. This MSS provides two particular techniques for forecasting.

a more specific graphing operator where the data being graphed is pre-determined. Several operators may be described for each of the functional capabilities at Level 1.

Operators may have both inputs and outputs that are specified by the user(s) at operator invocation. Specifically, an operator can have one or more data inputs (unless the data is firmly embedded in the operator as in the 'graph sales' example above). Operators may have input techniques or models. For example, an 'optimal solution' operator may require the user to specify the model to be solved and/or the technique to use to solve the model. An operator may also have one or more input parameters, whose values are specified by the user during operation execution. For example, an input parameter may be required to determine the next stage of processing by a particular operator. An operator may also require one or more input representations (similar to the representations within ROMC), such as a map or graph. Output from an operator may be data retrieved by the operator, a technique or model (when the operator simply selects a technique for use by another operator or when the operator results in a domain-specific model), and/or one or more representation(s).

- *Navigational Aids* – these are the help and guidance system provided by the MSS to user(s).
- *Adaptors* – these are the MSS capabilities for creating and changing the navigational aids and operators. For example, a spreadsheet package's macro facility can be described as an adaptor, as it combines existing operators into a new aggregate operator.
- *Sequencing rules* – these describe the sequencing of operators enforced by the MSS. Sequencing may be mandatory between two or more operators or may occur only when certain conditions exist. Silver provides a diagramming notation, similar to that of network diagrams, to describe any sequencing of operators.

Level 3: The System Attributes

This level builds on the Level 2 descriptions to examine how the entire MSS affects decision making. An MSS may place greater or lesser restrictions on a decision making process to those existing prior to the MSS, owing to its functionality (when described at Level 2). Restrictiveness of the MSS due to its design (so-termed *system restrictiveness*) depends greatly on the quantity of operators provided (fewer operators may lead to more restrictive decision making), the sequencing rules enforced between operators (greater sequencing may lead to more restrictive decision making), the inputs to operators (more inputs of different types may lead to less restrictive decision making) and the presence of adaptors (adaptors may lead to less restrictive decision making as users can refine and enhance the operators available).

Apart from system restrictiveness, Silver discusses several factors that can lead to an MSS being perceived by a user to be more or less restrictive than it actually is (so-termed *perceived restrictiveness*). For instance, a user may stick to a few 'trusty' operators, rather than using others that are more appropriate because of a lack of time or training. The guidance provided by navigational aids also influences a user's perceived restrictiveness of an MSS. Guidance can be either informative or suggestive. Informative guidance simply highlights the possible ways to proceed regarding a particular decision making situation, whereas suggestive guidance actually suggests how to proceed. Guidance can also be either deliberate or inadvertent. Deliberate guidance is that which was designed as part of the MSS. Inadvertent guidance was not consciously designed and is unexpected. For example, the ordering of options on a help menu may inadvertently lead a user to select the first option. This may make the system feel more restrictive to the user than it actually is. It is possible to design guidance systems so as to minimise the potential of perceived restrictiveness. For example, the options on the aforementioned help menu may be presented in a different sequence during MSS use.

In summary, Silver has laid the foundations for a description language with which to study the effects of MSS design on decision making. Much research is still needed before the language is suitable for commercial application. Further studies of existing MSS are required to test and enhance the current description language. Despite its infancy, however, the work already has benefits for MSS development in that it highlights important design considerations of which MSS developers need to be aware. Eventually, it may be possible for an MSS developer to use the language within MSS design activities. Having established the restrictiveness required within an MSS (Level 3 issue), the organisational context in which the MSS is to be embedded (Level 3 issue), and the overall functionality to be provided (Level 1 issue), the developer could use the language, and the established relationships between the levels, to derive a Level 2 MSS description with the required restrictiveness and functionality.

7.4.6 Traditional IS development techniques and MSS development: a critical appraisal

The use of traditional IS methodologies and techniques, as described in many IS textbooks, is certainly more limited with respect to MSS than it is with respect to other IS (such as DP systems). Some methodologies and techniques are more applicable to MSS development than others. For example, Soft Systems Methodology (Checkland 1981, Checkland and Scholes 1990, Flood and Jackson 1991) has been used effectively within MSS development. Traditional fact finding techniques, such as interviewing, observing, researching the subject of current development interest, and questionnaire designing, disseminating and analysing (see Skidmore and Wroe 1988, for a brief description of these techniques) are as vital to MSS development as they are to any other IS development. Entity-Relationship (E-R) modelling (Howe 1989) can be applied to the detailed design of MSS databases. For instance, the ROMC of the proposed MSS for the charity service location decision (as given in Table 7.3) identifies the need for an underlying database. This database can be designed using E-R modelling. E-R modelling can also be used to design the database requirements stemming from the specification of a CSF/KPI diagram. The resultant two-dimensional tables can be converted into a multi-dimensional format for subsequent input to a multi-dimensional data storage facility, if required.

Flow Charts, Pseudo-English and Decision Tables can be applied to the detailed design of Silver's operators (see Section 7.4.5) and Sprague and Carlson's operations (see Section 7.4.2). Decision Tables and Pseudo-English have already been mentioned with respect to Mockler's methodology for developing an MSS employing interactive Rule-based models. Conventional hardware, software and communications configuration diagrams are useful to depict the logical and physical configuration of a proposed MSS, and to identify the locations of MSS data sources. As mentioned in Chapter 3, OO techniques have great potential for MSS development.

Data Flow Diagramming (Skidmore and Wroe 1988, Yourdon 1989) is one of the most popular IS techniques, and yet appears to have little benefit for MSS development. It is most suited to the analysis and design of DP systems, such as order processing systems, where a computerised system is to support organisational transactions and their respective data flows. An analyst may indicate some low-level management information reports on the Data Flow Diagrams (DFDs), which monitor the progress of transactions. Each report may be linked to an appropriate management role. However, with respect to active support of decision making and other types of information reporting systems, DFDs provide little support to MSS development. They may help to identify decision situations to which MSS can be applied, and the options available to, and the data requirements of, each decision situation. However, they offer little benefit to MSS design when complexity lies in the *collation and consolidation of data, interactive or non-interactive model design, the presentation of information, and user interaction methods.*

7.5 SUMMARY

This chapter has focused on MSS development issues. Specifically, Section 7.2 provided an overview of alignment and feasibility issues regarding a proposed MSS project, and highlighted some techniques to aid one or both of these activities. A SISP exercise is considered to be the most effective way of determining those MSS projects that are in line with corporate objectives. It is this approach to alignment between corporate objectives and MSS that forms the subject of Part 4 of this book.

Section 7.3 focused on MSS development approaches. Three major approaches to MSS development, namely the traditional approach, the evolutionary approach and the hybrid approach, were described, and reviewed in terms of their respective suitability for developing MSS providing (a) information handling support, (b) passive support of decision making and (c) active support of decision making. Several techniques and methodologies, which have been proposed specifically for use within MSS development, were described in Section 7.4. An overview of Silver's description language was included within this section, despite its relative immaturity, because of its potential for supporting MSS design activities. Finally, some comments were made with respect to the appropriateness of conventional IS techniques to MSS development.

To conclude, this chapter has provided an overview of the existing research and practice regarding MSS development. Although MSS development has already received a fair share of research attention (Silver 1991), this must be sustained to ensure that development approaches, techniques and methodologies embrace any additional MSS functionality that new technologies provide and cater more effectively for the development of integrated MSS with wide and disparate functionality.

References

Alavi M (1984) An Assessment of the Prototyping Approach to Information Systems Development. *Communications of the ACM* Vol 27 No 6. pp. 556–563.

Bell R (1987) *Management of Systems Development*. Hutchinson.

Bird J (1991) *Executive Information Systems: Management Handbook*. NCC Blackwell.

Callaghan M (1992) EIS and Total Quality in Holtham C (ed.) *Executive Information Systems and Decision Support*. Chapman & Hall. pp. 171–180.

Checkland P B (1981) *Systems Theory, Systems Practice*. Wiley.

Checkland P and Scholes J (1990) *Soft Systems Methodology in Action*. Wiley.

Fidler C S and Rogerson S (1995) The Term 'Management Support Systems' Comes of Age. *Systemist* Vol 17 No 4. pp. 219–232.

Flood R L and Jackson M C (1991) *Creative Problem Solving*. Wiley.

Glover H, Watson H J and Rainer R K (1992) 20 Ways to Waste an EIS Investment. *Information Strategy: The Executive's Journal* Winter 1992. pp. 11–17.

Hogue J T (1987) A Framework for the Examination of Management Involvement in Decision Support Systems. *Journal of Management Information Systems* Vol 4 No 1. pp. 96–110.

Houndeshel G (1992) Selecting Information for an EIS: Experiences at Lockheed-Georgia, in Watson H J, Rainer R K and Houndeshel G (eds.) *Executive Information Systems: Design, Development, Impact*. Wiley. pp. 177–189.

Howe D R (1989) *Data Analysis for Database Design* Second edition. Arnold.

Keen P G W (1989) Value Analysis: justifying Decision Support Systems, in Sprague R H and Watson H J (eds.) *Decision Support Systems: putting Theory into Practice*. Prentice-Hall. pp. 65–81.

King R and Iacono S (1984) Computing as an Occasion for Social Control. *Journal of Social Issues* Vol 40 No 3. pp. 77–96.

Long L (1989) *Management Information Systems*. Prentice-Hall.

McBride N and Fidler C S (1994) An Interpretive Approach to Justification of Investment in Executive Information Systems. *Paper presented to the UK Conference on the Measurement of Information Technology Benefits/the Evaluation of Information Technology Investment*. Henley College, UK.

Mockler R (1989) *Knowledge-based Systems for Management Decisions*. Prentice-Hall.

Parker M M, Benson R J and Trainor H E (1988) *Information Economics*. Prentice-Hall.

Popovich A (1992) EIS Evolution at British Airways, in Holtham C (ed.), *Executive Information Systems and Decision Support*. Chapman & Hall. 1992. pp. 181–191.

Silver M (1991) *Systems that support Decision Makers: Description and Analysis*. Wiley, Chichester.

Skidmore S and Wroe B (1988) *Introducing Systems Analysis*. NCC Publications.

Sprague R H and Carlson E D (1982) *Building Effective Decision Support Systems*. Prentice-Hall.

Stein A (1994) Information Success Factors: the Fourth Generation of EIS. *Proceedings of the 12th Annual Conference of the Association of Management: Bridging the Gap* Vol 12 No 1. pp. 54–64.

Turban E (1993) *Decision Support Systems and Expert Systems: Management Support Systems* Third Edition. Macmillan.

Walsham G (1993) *Interpreting Information Systems in Organisations*. Wiley.

Watson H J, Rainer R K and Koh C E (1991) Executive Information Systems: A Framework for Development and a Survey of Current Practices. *MIS Quarterly* March Edition. pp. 13–30.

Wysocki R J and Young J (1990) *Information Systems Management Principles in Action*. Wiley.

Yourdon E (1989) *Modern Structured Analysis*. Prentice-Hall.

Review questions

1 Why is the alignment of any IS project with organisational objectives and mission vital to modern organisations?

2 What are Information Success Factors (ISFs)? How are they used within Boone's ISF methodology to identify MSS projects?

3 Is the ISF methodology a top-down or a bottom-up approach to IS project identification? Justify your answer.

4 Describe two ways that top management support can be provided.

5 How might the IS development team try to reduce the perceived threat to stakeholders of a new IS?

6 What are the advantages and disadvantages of having manager(s) as the direct user(s) of an MSS?

7 How can technology influence the success of a proposed MSS development?

8 Describe Fidler and Rogerson's approach to MSS/MSS development package selection.

9 How does Information Economics (IE) aim to overcome the weaknesses of Cost Benefit Analysis (CBA)? In your opinion, do you think it does overcome the weaknesses of CBA? Justify your answer.

10 Describe the four components of the framework for MSS feasibility proposed by McBride and Fidler.

11 Distinguish between the traditional, evolutionary and hybrid approaches to MSS development. To what situations, in general, is each most suited?

12 When is evolutionary prototyping an approach?

13 What overall approach would you typically expect to find adopted within the development of an MSS for active support of individual decision making, and why?

14 What is EUC?

15 Describe the principal objectives of the Value Analysis technique.

16 What does ROMC stand for? For what is ROMC used?

17 What is a CSF/KPI Hierarchy? To the provision of what type of MSS functionality can a CSF/KPI Hierarchy specification be beneficial, and why?

18 Describe the role of each technique prescribed in Mockler's methodology for developing MSS that employ Rule-based models.

19 List the three levels of MSS description covered by Silver's language. How do these levels of MSS description interrelate?

20 What is system restrictiveness? What is perceived restrictiveness?

21 When can the following conventional IS techniques be applied to MSS development:
Entity-Relationship (E-R) Modelling?
Interviewing?
Decision Tables?
Data Flow Diagrams?
Flow Charts?

Project ideas

Here are two project ideas. The first project provides an excellent starting point for the second, although either can be performed separately.

1 In pairs, visit a manager within a local company and use the ISF methodology to identify MSS projects that are important to him/her. Write a report of your activities, which should include:

  ● a table of the results of applying the ISF methodology with the manager, which should be presented in a similar structure to that shown in Table 7.1

- a critical review of the ISF methodology given your experiences (what did you find easy, and what did you find difficult?)
- any tips you would give to a would-be user of the ISF methodology.

Present your findings to the rest of your tutorial group. A tutorial discussion should follow to discuss common issues and identify weaknesses in the ISF methodology, together with any suggestions of methodology improvement.

2 In pairs, interview a manager within a company about his/her work, to identify a particular decision that could be supported by MSS and its characteristics. Provide a small report as to how you might approach the development of this MSS, and the techniques which you might employ within that development, with appropriate justifications. If possible, conduct one or more further interviews to illustrate the use of each technique you have selected with examples based on your findings. The report should be presented to the rest of your tutorial group. This way, you can learn from each other about how the techniques may be employed in real-life situations.

CHAPTER 8

MSS Summary

8.1 SUMMARY OF PART 2

This part has introduced the reader to the topic of Management Support Systems (MSS).

Specifically, Chapter 2 laid the foundations for the study of MSS, by introducing several key concepts and terms such as:

- management, and management levels, activities and roles
- the pervasive nature of decision making and information handling (i.e. information preparation and communication) within management work
- individual and group decision making, and the decision making process
- the appropriateness of MSS to supporting semistructured decision situations
- the difference between data and information, the characteristics of information, and possible information/data sources.

The descriptions associated with the above concepts and terms provided the basis for the definition of an MSS as a *CBIS that supports management via its support of decision making and/or information handling activities*. A logical MSS framework, based on a functional view of MSS provision, was also proposed. Essentially, this framework separated MSS functionality into that provided for:

- the support of information handling
- the passive support of decision making
- the active support of decision making.

Viewing MSS provision from a functional perspective is a unique feature of this book. Part of the justification for this view was one of the two principal objectives of Chapter 3. Chapter 3 began with a brief review of the historical evolution of MSS. This was followed by a discussion of several recent technological advances and their respective implications for MSS provision. These discussions highlighted the general trend towards greater potential and actual provision of integrated computerised systems (in terms of hardware, software and communications facilities). As systems integration becomes easier, MSS developers can more effectively focus their attention on the real issue of concern: that of matching MSS functionality to organisational needs. Already, technological advances have enabled companies to achieve greater system integration, enabling the development of a physical MSS implementation with the functionality normally attributed to more than one traditional MSS type (for example, a Management Information Systems (MIS) or a Decision Support Systems (DSS)).

The classical approach to describing MSS (that is, by describing each traditional MSS type in turn) has always been problematic, as there is no standard definition of each system type and MSS functionality invariably overlaps between system types (although actual overlap depends on the system type definitions currently being adhered to). Nowadays, this approach offers little in the way of benefit, given the trend towards, and current capabilities for, greater systems integration. Corporate management are concerned with the functionality provided within MSS, not with how they are labelled.

The second principal objective of Chapter 3 was to introduce several key recent technological advances of significance to MSS provision. Advances, such as these, not only offer MSS developers new opportunities for increased systems integration, but also provide enhanced functionality of potential use within MSS implementations. MSS developers must keep abreast of new technological advances and assess their potential significance to MSS provision.

Chapter 4 focused attention on MSS functionality for the support of management's information handling activities. Both information (document) preparation and information (message) communication support were reviewed, whilst bearing in mind the fundamental underlying operations concerned with information storage and retrieval. Current document preparation systems, most commonly reflecting a Template approach, provide support for information preparation. Available facilities for the support of information communication include e-mail, Audioconferencing, Videoconferencing (both room-based and desktop) and Joint Authoring Systems.

Chapter 5 reviewed the many ways that MSS provide passive decision making support to management via information reporting. An information report can be classified in terms of its content (i.e. as an analysis report, exception report or plan of action report). The roles of each category of report was examined with respect to the planning and controlling activities of management. A second, orthogonal classification was defined for information reports, based on two temporal issues concerning information report definition and report availability to management respectively. Using this classification, an information report can be categorised as being one of the following four types:

- an as-needed, pre-defined information report
- an as-needed, customised information report
- a periodic, pre-defined information report
- a periodic, customised information report.

The methods by which a user can interact with an MSS to request an information report were reviewed for each category of information report in turn. During this review, popular concepts within modern MSS implementations, including drill down and Briefing Book, were explained. To illustrate the variety of organisational situations to which these MSS have been applied (although predominantly to situations where financial performance is monitored), some example MSS that provide information reporting facilities to management were described to varying levels of detail.

Chapter 6 reviewed MSS functionality for active decision making support. Active decision making support is provided by the interactive use of computer-based models and/or techniques, or the capabilities for developing and using models and/or techniques. Models and techniques therefore formed the focal topics of a substantial portion of this chapter. An overview of models, model categorisations, and the organisational benefits gained from the application of models, was provided. Attention was then focused principally on mathematical models and associated techniques, as these models are frequently employed within MSS that provide active decision making support. The following techniques for the formulation and solution of mathematical models were described individually:

- Weighted Score (both for individual and group use)
- Linear Programming
- Decision Tree
- Simulation
- Forecasting
- Rule-based

Several key techniques for structuring group decision making situations were also described.

The remainder of Chapter 6 focused on MSS functionality for active decision making support. A logical architecture for an MSS providing active decision making support was first presented. The logical architecture embraces the wide variety of physical MSS implementations that actively support management decision making activities. It also highlights the essential role of management in determining what is, and what is not, considered to be an MSS. The primary differences between an MSS and its associated development package, from a functionality perspective, were described in this chapter, as was the additional functionality required of an MSS providing active support for group decision making to that of an MSS providing active support of individual decision making. Particular MSS provisions, such as Geographical Information Systems (GIS) and Decision Rooms, were reviewed. As in the case of MSS providing passive decision making support, several examples of MSS providing active decision making support were used to illustrate key concepts.

Having reviewed MSS functionality in Chapters 4 to 6 inclusive, Chapter 7 focused on MSS development issues. Any MSS project should be aligned with corporate objectives and mission, and be feasible to develop within the given organisational context. Some techniques were outlined to facilitate MSS alignment and/or feasibility, although the most effective approach to MSS alignment, via SISP, is to be discussed in Parts 3 and 4 of this book. When development activities are needed to provide the MSS functionality to match organisational need (irrespective of whether the development involves the simple tailoring of a development package or a full scale programming activity), an overall development approach must be chosen. Three such approaches available to the MSS developer, namely the traditional approach, the evolutionary approach and the hybrid approach, were reviewed. Some observations were made concerning the relative popularity of the three approaches for the development of MSS functionality concerned with (a) information handling support, (b) passive decision making support and (c) active decision making support.

During MSS development, an MSS developer may employ many techniques and/or methodologies. Several techniques and methodologies, which have been developed, or are in the process of being developed, for use specifically within MSS development, were reviewed. Finally, comments were made as to the suitability of traditional IS techniques to MSS development. Whilst several traditional IS techniques are beneficial, one or two mainstream Systems Analysis and Design techniques, for example Data Flow Diagramming, are not as suited to MSS development as they are to other IS developments.

Throughout this review of MSS, emphasis has been placed on the importance of matching MSS functionality to the organisational context in hand. Furthermore, MSS development approaches, methodologies, techniques and associated diagrammatic tools, must match the organisational context and the functionality being provided for that organisational context.

Indeed, as shown in Figure 8.1, there are mutual relationships between the opportunities for MSS provision, MSS development support (in the form of structured approaches, methodologies, techniques and tools), and the organisational context in which an MSS is to be embedded. Although simple, this figure is a very useful. For MSS developers, the diagram highlights explicitly the interrelationships between MSS provision opportunities, MSS development support and organisational context. For researchers, it identifies areas of continued research activity. For instance, recent technological advances, such as Virtual Reality (VR) and Multi-media, provide opportunities for enhanced functionality within MSS. However, this technology will only be applied effectively when organisational situations are identified which really need this functionality and when MSS development support is available to facilitate the implementation of an MSS with this additional functionality. Appropriate development approaches, methodologies, techniques and tools to support enhanced and/or more integrated functionality, and the relationships between functionality and organisational context, will continue to form worthy topics of research.

As explained in Chapter 7, the alignment of MSS projects with corporate objectives and mission ensures that the right systems are targeted for development. Part 3 focuses

Fig 8.1 The mutual relationships between MSS provision opportunities, MSS development support and organisational context: towards effective MSS provision

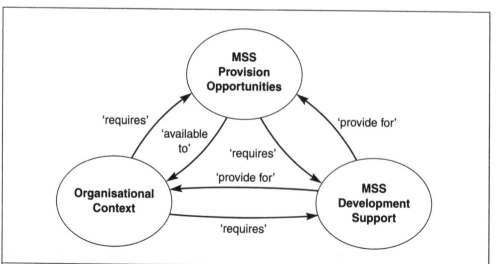

Mutual relationships exist between the three aspects shown in the above diagram. In order to be effective in the provision of MSS, MSS developers should always be aware of these aspects and their interrelationships. This diagram highlights these interrelationships explicitly. It also identifies research areas regarding MSS development and use.

on Strategic Information Systems Planning (SISP), considered to be the most effective method of ensuring the alignment of all IS developments, including MSS, with corporate objectives and mission. Part 4 explores the specific relationships between SISP and MSS in depth.

The remainder of this chapter provides case studies of MSS provision at Grace Dearborn and the Automobile Association. Many of the key concepts introduced within this part of the book are highlighted within these case studies.

CASE STUDY 1: GRACE DEARBORN LTD

As part of W R Grace, Grace Dearborn operates within the water treatment and paper industry with a multimillion pound turnover. The company operates to national and international quality standards. The company is in the process of globalisation with strategic projects being undertaken across countries and the service to important customers being co-ordinated across Europe. The UK operation employs 450 people of which half are involved in sales. The company headquarters is at Widnes and there are four services centres, at Warrington, Enfield, Glasgow and Dublin. There are similar operations in the Benelux countries, Germany, France, Italy, Scandinavia and the Iberian peninsular.

Transaction processing systems are run on a mainframe computer in France which has telecommunications links to offices in the UK (as well as other European offices) for the purpose of data transmission. There are systems to support sales order processing, manufacturing and purchasing. A front-end processing system has been developed called Eurosoft which extracts data from the mainframe computer daily and transmits this to a Wang computer located in Widnes. This is primarily data required by the sales force. Management reports are generated using this down-loaded data. Originally, these were hard copy reports but are now available on-line.

The computer at Widnes has e-mail, provides a front-end batch update from the mainframe computer and provides files for importing to the spreadsheet package run on the notebook computers. All of the sales force are provided with a notebook computer which has Symmetry, a spreadsheet, a word processor, a presentation graphics package and e-mail facilities.

Symmetry is a system used by Grace Dearborn to capture market intelligence. This is a distributed marketing database system operating across a network comprising a central database and notebook computers in the field. Currently, there are over 100 notebook computers in use. Symmetry provides support to the sales force in their daily interaction with customers and it is used to communicate data to the centre for decision making support on a corporate scale. Data required from the mainframe is transferred monthly. Figure 8.2 shows the information flows within Symmetry. The database holds client and prospect profiles. There are about seven thousand customers and five thousand prospects held within the system. Data is broadly divided into contacts history, product opportunities, customer narratives, action lists, events history. Action lists trigger letters and quotations to be produced, which in turn are logged on the events history. Letter creation is eased through the use of one of the many standard letters available. The sales representative enters a minimum amount of information which is transmitted to a service centre for completion and distribution. Customer narratives, held in the notepad section, provide an *aide-mémoire* and record details of customer quality plans. The latter is important as quality accreditation, for exam-

►

ple BS5750, has to be updated periodically, typically every 12 months.

On a daily basis, sales representatives record details of the contacts made with clients. Each contact is an event in the system. For each event the following data is input:

- the date
- the event duration
- the project number, if applicable
- the event code
- text description of the event

This data is transmitted each day to the central databases located on the computer at Widnes.

The event code is considered vital in building up intelligence about interaction with the customers and about changes in customer requirements. Codes are used to analyse overall patterns of behaviour and trends in the customer base.

The imported data from Eurosoft is varied, satisfying specific needs; it may comprise, for example, sales history or total monthly business or details of customers. The sales force manipulate this data to produce analysis often in graphical form. Standard macros have been developed for this but some of the sales force develop their own routines. Combining Eurosoft and Symmetry data provides an even richer resource which when manipulated in the spreadsheet can produce, for example, market effort versus sales analysis and service adjusted margins reports. There are opportunities to provide exception reporting, and drill down facilities.

The collation and filtration of field intelligence enables Market Development Specialists and District Managers to gain new insights regarding the company products and changes in the market place. For example, analysis of new product lines can be provided and a competitor intelligence report generated by product lines, by districts or for the whole country. This new knowledge informs corporate strategy decision making by the Business Line Managers and the European Marketing Manager.

Grace Dearborn have addressed the issue of ensuring that all those involved in the sales and marketing effort within the company are kept informed of current events relating to its products, customers, prospects and competitors. Decisions taken throughout the marketing and sales cycles are supported by relevant information. Computer technology has been used to facilitate communication between a geographically dispersed workforce. The company considers it is using enough technology and not too much in this endeavour. It has accomplished a workable relationship between its legacy systems and systems based on new technology in order to provide market intelligence systems that have enabled the company to gain competitive advantage and realise its goals. ∎

This case study is published in conjunction with Grace Dearborn Limited

Fig 8.2

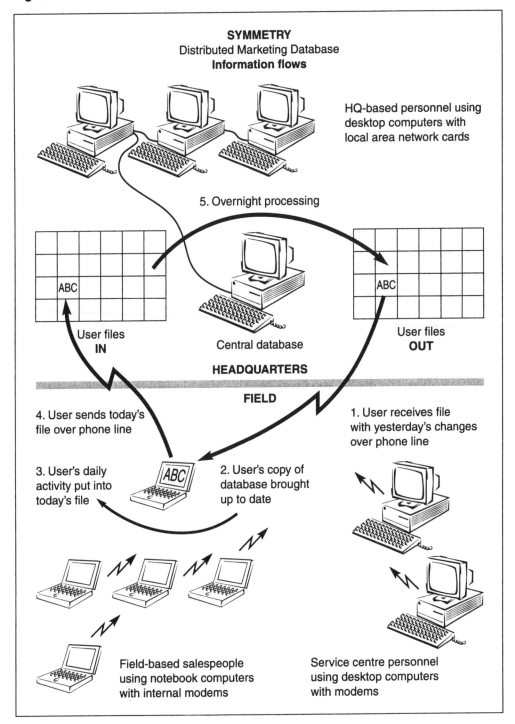

SYMMETRY
Distributed Marketing Database
Information flows

HQ-based personnel using desktop computers with local area network cards

5. Overnight processing

ABC

ABC

User files
IN

Central database

User files
OUT

HEADQUARTERS

FIELD

4. User sends today's file over phone line

3. User's daily activity put into today's file

2. User's copy of database brought up to date

1. User receives file with yesterday's changes over phone line

Field-based salespeople using notebook computers with internal modems

Service centre personnel using desktop computers with modems

CASE STUDY: AUTOMOBILE ASSOCIATION

A vehicle for change
by Julia Vowler

The AA is dependent on IT. The £750m organisation spends £1m a week on it, and employs 650 IT staff. It has two IT centres, seven operational centres, seven ICL Series 39 mainframes linked by X.25, 480 terminals and 15,000 workstations, including mobile terminals. It has the largest private data network in Europe, the largest number of mobile radios in Europe and 260 FM radio sites.

As well as the membership section, which is developing the AA Help system, there are two other major business divisions – AA Insurance and AA Commercial Services – as well as a corporate headquarters providing management services (including IT), finance and legal departments.

The AA Help command and control system is being delivered in a phased roll out. From spring 1996 it will be handling the AA's six million breakdown calls a year.

Phase one: call handling. Here the AA's 1,800 call staff deal with pleas for help from stranded motorists. Calls can be prioritised if the member is especially vulnerable, for example diabetic or with small children. A gazatteer database can be accessed to identify the member's location. The system went live in April 1994.

Phase two: customer service. This entails call handlers accessing customer records, held on an ICL mainframe, to check a caller's level of membership and the type of service they are entitled to. Handlers can then access a new Ingres service history database to show up previous breakdowns to see if there's a pattern. The system goes live this month.

Phase three: resource and rostering. A management information database which will allow the AA to predict what resources will be available over the following 12 months for servicing call out and patrol requirements. Due to be complete by the end of 1995.

Phase four: deployment. Identifies location and dispatches rescue patrols to breakdown sites on an optimum basis. Due to go live by spring 1996.

Phase five: extending service delivery into home assistance sector. Currently in development. ■

Reprinted with permission, *Computer Weekly* 17th August 1995

PART 3

Strategic Information Systems Planning (SISP)

'Annual income twenty pounds, annual expenditure nineteen nineteen six, result happiness. Annual income twenty pounds, annual expenditure twenty pounds ought and six, result misery.'

Charles Dickens

CHAPTER 9

What is Strategic Information Systems Planning (SISP)?

9.1 INTRODUCTION

The aim of this chapter is to introduce the concept of Strategic Information Systems Planning (SISP) within the context of the organisation and its corporate strategy.

Firstly, the evolution of Information Systems usage leading to a more strategic role for IS is discussed. The issue of maintaining a corporate focus is considered in Section 9.3. The concepts of strategic alignment and Strategic Information Systems (SIS) are highlighted in this section. This leads to the examination of SISP and the development of a more appropriate definition in Section 9.4.

The nature of and the participants in a SISP exercise are discussed in Section 9.5. A method for selecting participants is outlined together with the concept of nested phases planning and controlling the SISP exercise.

SISP methodology concepts are described in Section 9.6. The three-layered methodology model is explained as is a classification framework to aid effective selection of methodologies and techniques. An overview of some of the more common methodologies and techniques is given in preparation for the chapters which follow.

At the end of this chapter the reader should understand:

- *What a corporate mission is and how IS/IT should be properly aligned.*
- *What a SISP is and appreciate the fundamental elements of a SISP.*
- *What Strategic Culture Building (SCB) is.*
- *The need to involve appropriate people in a SISP exercise in order to develop an acceptable strategy which can be implemented.*
- *In outline, several methodologies and tools in the SISP area.*

9.2 THE EVOLUTION OF INFORMATION SYSTEMS USAGE

In its infancy, computing was concerned with automating functions at the operational level of organisations. Routine clerical activity was replaced with powerful transaction processing systems capable of significant efficiency savings. It was a time when there was only one technology and there were few stakeholders as applications were confined to a few departments and addressed low-level tasks. Computing was viewed as a cost. This data processing era was an era dominated by technology push in the strive to exploit such a powerful resource. The leading edge focus for technology application was transaction processing.

As the technology evolved and expanded so the emphasis changed. Additional tabular reporting was added to existing systems and the concept of management information systems was born. Passive decision making support (as described in Chapter 5) became commonplace. Tactical management activities were starting to be supported as was a greater range of functional activities within organisations. There were now more influential stakeholders including those at board level. Several technologies were emerging such as data communications and micro technology. The leading edge focus for technology application had switched to information reporting. (A more detailed discussion of these issues is included in Chapter 3.)

Today, the sophistication and complexity of the converging technologies are self-evident. There now exists a business push to invest in and exploit these technologies. Strategic management activities are being supported. Decision making support is more active. There is a much broader ownership of systems. The leading edge focus for technology application is now decision support and competitive advantage (see Chapter 6).

Overall, the technology is no longer restricted to automating back office functions. It is creating new manufacturing methodologies that outstrip the old, it is generating entirely new classes of products and services, it is bringing new levels of internal co-operation to nation-wide and world-wide organisations and it is opening up important new ways of buying and selling (Ernst & Young 1989). Thus the role of information systems and the information systems function in organisations has quickly evolved into a core feature of the modern organisation. The main factors driving this change are:

- The potential of information systems to deliver competitive advantage.
- The pervasiveness of information technology in organisations.
- The critical dependency of organisations on IS for daily operations.
- The growth of inter-organisation systems.
- The integration of telecommunications with IS functions.

9.2.1 Strategic Information Systems (SIS)

It is important to differentiate between Strategic Information Systems (SIS) and all other types of information systems which are developed to satisfy organisational needs. It is the role and impact of an information system which determines whether it is a SIS.

A typical definition of SIS is by Reponen (1993) who defined Strategic Information Systems as systems which are designed to bring competitive advantage or have resulted in a competitive edge. However, this perspective is too narrow. Cavaye and Cragg (1993) provide a more balanced view of SIS. They suggest that a SIS is used to support strategic decision making, or to support or shape an organisation's competitive strategy, or it might be used as a combination of both. For a system to be considered a SIS it must satisfy two essential criteria:

- The system is directly linked to the business strategy.
- The system significantly affects organisational performance.

Consider, for example, a stock control system within an organisation. This would be linked to the business strategy if product availability was a key issue or if cash tied up in finished goods was adversely affecting cash flow. The stock control system would only be considered a SIS if the satisfying of customers' orders or the improvement in cash flow provided the company with a competitive advantage or if it offset its competitors' advantage.

Linking to the business strategy is achieved either by creating new strategic options or by having a direct role in strategy implementation. Improvement in organisation performance can be achieved through providing competitive advantage or by reducing the advantage of competitors. Competitive advantage is reliant upon both inter-organisation systems which provide effective links between customers, suppliers and distributors, and internal systems which significantly improve productivity and performance. The strategic potential of IS/IT is enormous because it can be instrumental in:

- raising entry barriers
- increasing the negotiating power with suppliers
- creating new dependencies for customers
- offering new products and services or worthy alternatives
- changing the grounds for competition or the nature of the stakes.

It is important that this potential is utilised in line with the corporate mission and associated business strategy.

9.3 MAINTAINING A CORPORATE FOCUS

The mission statement is a powerful instrument which, if properly constructed and used, can significantly influence the actions of all areas within an organisation. Campbell and Tawadey (1990) put the mission statement into the context of a mission model, entitled 'The Ashridge Mission Model', which comprises four elements: purpose, strategy, values and behaviour standards. Purpose describes why the organisation exists whilst strategy focuses on how the purpose might be achieved. Values are what the organisation cherishes and believes in. Finally, behaviour standards are the policies and patterns existing within the organisation which guide and colour how it operates. Whilst the elements of the mission model might be well documented in some organisations, in others this is not the case. Nevertheless, the key issues are whether such elements have been addressed and whether the organisation's stance is clearly understood by all employees. Such a stance provides a clarity of direction and promotes commitment and loyalty in the employees. Strong links between the four elements will result in a strong mission. The Ford Motor Company is a good example of an organisation which has a strong mission backed by appropriate actions and initiatives throughout the organisation. The mission (organisational purpose), values and guiding principles (standards of behaviour) of the company are shown in Figure 9.1.

It is vital to link the strategies of the individual elements of an organisation to its overall purpose and strategy. To be effective the linkage must be two-way. This is because some overall goal might require an action within part of the organisation which is not feasible. This being the case, it is essential that this goal is modified or even abandoned. Such situations are common within the IS/IT area. For example, a bank's goal of responding to customer account queries within 10 seconds of the receipt of the request might involve the development and implementation of new information systems and supporting communication networks that are either not currently technologically feasible or resilient, or the cost may be inhibiting. The overall

Fig 9.1 The mission, values and guiding principles of the Ford Motor Company

Mission
Our mission is to improve continually our products and services to meet our customers' needs, allowing us to prosper as a business and to provide a reasonable return for our stockholders, the owners of our business.

Values
- People
- Products
- Profits

Guiding Principles
- Quality comes first
- Customers are the focus of everything we do
- Continuous improvement is essential to our success
- Employee involvement is our way of life
- Dealers and suppliers are our partners
- Integrity is never compromised

The mission statement is a powerful instrument which can significantly influence the actions of all areas within an organisation.

corporate direction will have to be modified on the basis of this information so that the overall organisational strategy and the strategy of the IS/IT area remain in line.

The concept of linkage is often referred to as strategic alignment where the strategies of the individual elements within an organisation are linked to achieve some overall goal. The linkage of business, information and human resources is crucial to the well being of an organisation. The strategic triangle model described by Ernst & Young (1990) illustrates the importance of this concept. The model is shown in Figure 9.2. There are three possible linkages:

- *Information Systems and Human Resource* – This alignment aids organisational effectiveness as well as the traditional efficiency gains associated with such an alliance.
- *Information Systems and Business* – This linkage can result in innovative solutions to business problems, for example the introduction of automatic teller machines (ATM) in the banking sector.
- *Business and Human Resource* – Hierarchical structures which are prevalent in larger organisations may not necessarily be the most appropriate way of operating. This linkage enables organisations to remain dynamic and helps them to respond to changes in their environment.

The concurrent existence of the three linkages is strategic alliance. Organisations which successfully combine the abilities to innovate, respond to change and streamline will produce enhanced corporate value. The Ernst and Young survey suggests that the achievement of these linkages is difficult. Of the organisations surveyed, 20% had an information systems and business link, 42% had an information systems and human

Fig 9.2 The strategic triangle model from Ernst & Young

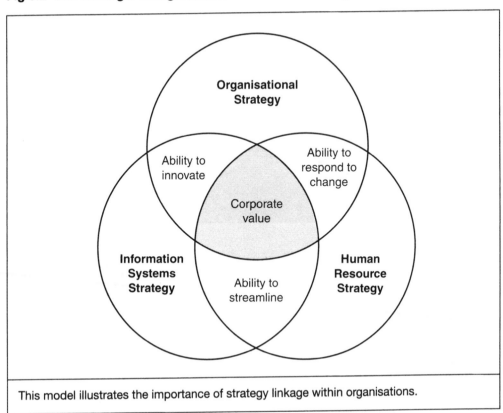

This model illustrates the importance of strategy linkage within organisations.

resource link, 42% had business and human resource link and only 7% were achieving enhanced corporate value. The overall conclusion was that the main driver, the business strategy, was not playing an active enough role in ensuring the best return on IS/IT investment nor was it creating a dynamic organisational structure to exploit IS/IT.

Organisations must ensure that there is a strong link between the mission statement, the organisational strategy, which includes both business and human resource strategy, and the information systems strategy. Such links must be dynamic and iterative. The information systems strategy will ensure that sufficient attention is devoted to system development, albeit internally or externally resourced, product and customer service enhancement, and research. The balance of activity will be dependent on the nature of the organisation and its environment. These relationships can be seen in the model shown in Figure 9.3. The Strategic Information Systems Planning (SISP) and the Strategic Culture Building (SCB) process attempt to derive an IS strategy which is aligned to the organisation as a whole. SCB encourages people within an organisation to be forward-looking and to consider their work and decisions in an organisational context rather than a parochial context. SISP is the way in which perceptions and conceived ideas, resulting from the strategic culture in an organisation, can be turned into effective actions. SISP and SCB will be considered in more detail in the sections that follow.

Fig 9.3 Developing an aligned IS strategy

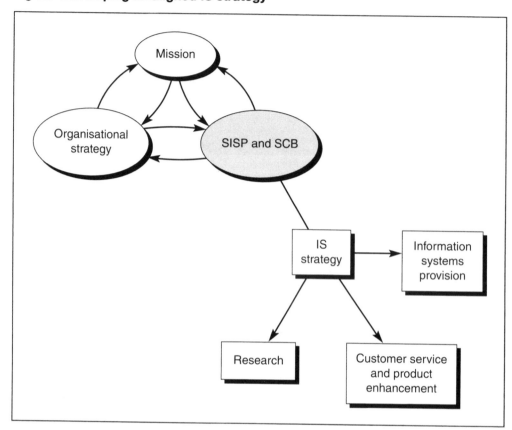

The combination of and interaction between SISP and SCB are very important in establishing a properly aligned IS strategy which is considered achievable by all concerned. This is illustrated in Figure 9.4. SISP deals with the more mechanistic aspects of strategy formulation through analysis, planning and alignment whilst SCB is concerned with the more behavioural aspects such as ownership, communication, vision and motivation.

9.4   DEFINING SISP

SISP has evolved over a number of years in line with evolution of the underpinning technologies and the change in the leading edge focus for technology application as previously described. The original objectives of SISP were:

- to improve communication with users
- to increase management support
- to improve resource requirements forecasting
- to determine more opportunities for improving information systems provision
- to identify new applications which provided a greater return on investment.

Whilst these objectives are still relevant, additional objectives have been added. These include:

Fig 9.4 The interaction between SISP and SCB

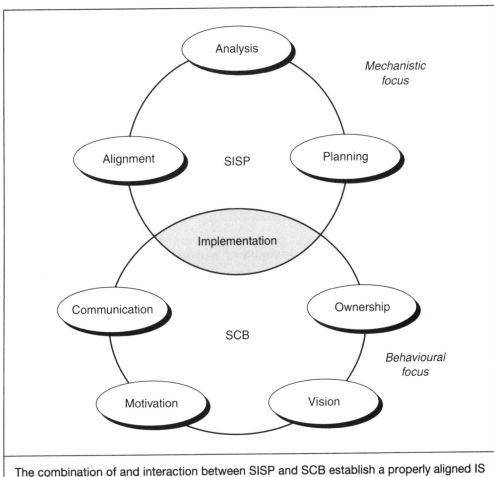

The combination of and interaction between SISP and SCB establish a properly aligned IS strategy.

- to develop an organisational IS architecture
- to identify strategic IS applications.

Organisations are increasingly looking towards value-for-money in their IS/IT systems. They can ill afford to engage in IS development without first ensuring that the investment of resources is being put to the best strategic use. It is therefore no surprise that an increasing number of organisations are engaging in formalised SISP activities. Indeed, in a recent empirical survey of 76 companies, by Fidler, Rogerson and Spiers (1993), only two of the 73 respondents indicated that they were unaware of any SISP being performed in their companies. Many aids have been developed to help those undertaking SISP activities but in practice the majority of SISP activists do not use formal approaches. One study, by King, Hufnagel and Grover (1988), found that 55% of respondents did not use formal approaches in their SISP activities. It may well be that there is an overabundance of aids coupled with the fact that little guidance is available for choosing an appropriate aid. Guidance is an issue which will be addressed in more detail at a later stage in Chapter 11.

A strategic focus is vital for effective management in the complex, turbulent and dynamic environment of the modern organisation. (This is discussed further in Chapter 11.) The size of the organisation and the number of people involved in the management process will influence how this focus manifests itself. In small organisations with few managers, SCB is likely to be predominant, whereas in larger organisations, with many more managers resulting in a more complex situation requiring greater control and co-ordination, it is likely that SISP will be predominant. Both SCB and SISP will exist in all organisations but the relative amounts will differ dependant on a range of factors such as the size and structure of the organisation, the nature of the people in the organisation and the business environment. The continuum of SCB and SISP combinations is shown in Figure 9.5. For example, a small organisation of simple structure, whose employees respond well to directives rather than using a lot of initiative and which is operating in quite a volatile market place, is likely to have a predominant SCB, positioned towards the left of the continuum. This is because the organisation, environment and structure factors indicating SCB predominance outweigh the people factors which indicate SISP predominance. The continuum is an indication of what might be the best combination for a given organisation. In all cases, the fundamental issue is that organisations must aim for durable competitive advantage which can be sustained and built upon so that it can flourish and progress over an extended period.

Fig 9.5 The continuum of SCB and SISP combinations

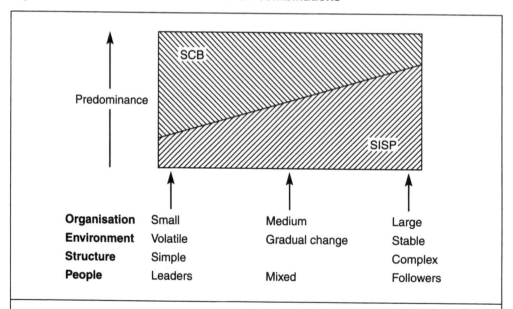

Both SCB and SISP will exist in all organisations but the relative amounts will differ dependant on a range of factors such as the size and structure of the organisation, the nature of the people in the organisation and the business environment.

9.4.1   Alternative definitions

The evolution of SISP has been accompanied by many definitions of SISP. It is useful to consider some of the more recent attempts in the context of strategic management support systems:

- Lederer and Sethi (1988) explained that SISP is a dichotomy. On one hand, it is the process of identifying a portfolio of computer-based applications that will help organisations realise their business objectives whilst, on the other, it is concerned with identifying high impact applications which are likely to achieve competitive advantage. They further explained (Lederer and Sethi 1992) that SISP comprises two distinct elements: to influence organisational strategies, and to align MSS objectives with organisational goals.
- Remenyi (1991) defined SISP as the process of establishing a programme for the implementation and use of IS in such a way that it will optimise the effectiveness of the firm's information resources and use them to support objectives of the whole enterprise as much as possible. He put great emphasis on how firms can identify strategic information systems or information systems that will give a competitive edge.
- Reponen (1993) suggests that strategic planning of information systems is an interactive learning process for the creation of a strategy for business process redesign (BPR) and development incorporating information technology. The strategy presents plans for information systems design, implementation and operation for this purpose.
- Earl (1993) gives the SISP exercise a broader perspective. He argues that the SISP exercise is more than a method or technique. Process and implementation issues are also important. Together these interdependent elements form an approach. The combination of SISP and SCB, described previously, is in line with this thinking.

These definitions have their own strengths as well as there being commonality in their overall themes. There tends to be an emphasis on competitive advantage which is inappropriate for non-profit-making organisations where the primary goal might simply be the best service regardless of cost. In other words, the focus is on value-added and not competitive advantage. In deriving a new definition four key issues need to be addressed:

1. SISP should be suitable for all types of organisations regardless of their mission, industry sector and financial status.
2. Strategic alignment incorporating the appropriate feedback from the information systems strategy should be encouraged by the SISP.
3. SISP should consider all types of systems.
4. SISP should promote a strategically-oriented culture.

Thus a more general, all-embracing definition is suggested:

> *SISP is the means of identifying application systems which support and enhance organisational strategy and provides the framework for the effective implementation of these systems.*

This definition addresses the four key issues in that 'organisational strategy' accommodates all types of organisation, 'support and enhance' encourage feedback and strategic alignment, and 'provide the framework' helps promote a strategic culture.

9.5 SISP PARTICIPANTS AND ACTIVITIES

The creation of a viable strategy and the successful implementation of that strategy are dependant upon who is involved and represented in the planning process and whether the activities undertaken by these participants form a comprehensive coverage of the issues related to the desired output from the exercise. Each organisation is different in the way it is structured, the way it operates and the outputs produced, whether they are products or services. For this reason, the participants and the nature of activity are likely to vary from organisation to organisation. However, a general description of both is useful in that it provides a starting point which can then be tailored to specific organisational situations.

9.5.1 Key players in the SISP process

A number of stakeholders are associated with any organisation. Stakeholders are individuals or groups who can affect, or be affected by, the actions undertaken within an organisation. There are different sets of stakeholder which include:

- Owners
- Employees – both managers and workers
- Unions
- Capital providers
- Government – at local, national and international levels
- Customers
- Suppliers
- Community groups
- Competitors

It is from this list that the SISP participants are drawn. Participation by owners and employees is obvious but other groups may well participate in particular situations. If a manufacturing company was wishing to improve its supplier to customer chain then it would make sense to involve representatives from both groups. Similarly, if an organisation wished to form a strategic alliance with a competitor in an attempt to increase market share through synergy then participation in the SISP activity by a competitor might be legitimate. The drive for efficiency gains through IS/IT exploitation by a large local employer might potentially mean a reduction in the work-force or employment from a different work-force group. In such circumstances the involvement of unions and relevant community groups might be beneficial. These issues are further discussed in Chapter 11.

In general, the most common group of participants is drawn from employees. This group can be further subdivided into executive management, middle management, knowledge workers and IS/IT professionals. Each represents a separate group being: clients and owners; general users; information artisans and specialist users; and developers and service providers respectively. The various combinations of these participants will result in different emphasis and different outputs. Table 9.1 shows the likely outputs from teams with different profiles. The outputs will either be focused on the local functional areas or exhibit a wider corporate perspective. The resulting output will be up to three strategies representing the information need, the informa-

Table 9.1 Participants in the SISP process

	Executive Management	Middle Managers	Knowledge Workers	IS/IT Professionals	*Strategy Focus*
Representing →	clients, owners	general users	information artisans, specialist users	developers, service providers	
SISP Team Combination →			✔	✔	local IT
		✔		✔	local IS
	✔			✔	corporate IT
		✔	✔		local I
	✔		✔		corporate I
	✔	✔			business
		✔	✔	✔	local I/IS/IT
	✔		✔	✔	corporate IS/I
	✔	✔		✔	corporate IS
	✔	✔	✔		corporate I
	✔	✔	✔	✔	corporate I/IS/IT

The creation of a viable strategy and the successful implementation of that strategy are dependant upon who is involved and represented in the planning process.

tion systems to satisfy the information need and the information technology required to deliver the information system portfolio.

When a team is brought together to develop a strategy it must be capable of and committed to achieving this goal. There is considerable evidence to show that organisations have difficulty in forming teams which successfully undertake the SISP activity. In their empirical study, Lederer and Sethi (1988) identified the key problems in using SISP methodologies and discovered several factors resulting in problematical SISP activity.

Of the top ten problems identified, five related to participation. These were:

- It is difficult to secure top management commitment for implementing the developed strategy (rated 1).
- The success of the methodology is greatly dependent on the team leader (rated 3).
- It is difficult to find a team leader who meets the criteria specified by the methodology (rated 4).

- It is difficult to convince top management to approve and use a methodology (rated 8).
- It is difficult to find team members who meet the criteria specified by the methodology (rated 10).

Of the contributory factors that Lederer and Sethi found, four are particularly interesting in the context of participation.

1. Organisations that have a tactical or financial focus to planning, which implies only lower management involvement, have more severe problems than those with a strategic focus where the IS manager has less trouble justifying resources for the SISP and its subsequent implementation.
2. Organisations with less participation by IS personnel in business planning have more severe problems than organisations with greater participation.
3. Organisations where the IS manager reports to a financial controller has more severe problems than organisations where the IS manager reports to the Chief Executive. The more senior the IS manager, the easier it is to instigate SISP exercises and to secure the involvement of relevant personnel.
4. Surprisingly, organisations where top management initiate the SISP process have more severe problems than organisations where SISP is IS-initiated. It is believed that initiation by top management is often a result of dissatisfaction with IS.

The relationship between senior management and IS is crucial in the successful undertaking of SISP. In particular the relationship between the Chief Executive and the IS manager will greatly influence the participation of others in the SISP process. A set of attributes leading to a productive relationship has been put forward by Feeny, Edwards and Simpson (1992) based upon in-depth investigations in 14 large organisations based in the UK. Attributes were sub-divided into three:

Chief Executive Attributes
- general management and or marketing background
- change-oriented leadership
- attended IS/IT awareness seminars
- experienced IS/IT project success
- perceives IS/IT as critical to the business
- positions IS/IT as agent of business transformation

Organisational Attributes
- personal and informal executive style
- executive workshops on strategic issues
- IS manager accepted into executive team

IS Manager Attributes
- analyst background and orientation
- promotes IS/IT as agent of business transformation
- contributes beyond the IS/IT function
- accurate perception of Chief Executive's views on business and IS/IT
- integrates IS/IT with business planning
- profile stresses consultative leadership and creativity

9.5.2 An overview of SISP activities

The precise nature of activity in a SISP exercise will be dependent on the approach adopted and the support offered by appropriate methodologies and techniques. However, it is possible to describe, in general terms, the main components of a SISP process and how these are related. The major components of SISP activity comprise:

- Define the scope of the SISP exercise – obtain authorisation, establish team, create timetable and allocate responsibilities
- Understand and interpret the business requirements – establish the corporate strategy and corporate CSFs, review existing IS/IT, identify potential IS/IT applications
- Define the organisational information needs and the underpinning systems architecture – establish the ideal solution
- Formulate the Information, Information Systems and Information Technology strategies – derive these in order though interactively
- Present the final output to the client – deliverables are predetermined in the exercise scope

Many of the descriptions of the basic SISP components are centred around the notion of *the phase* (for example, Ward, Griffiths and Whitmore 1990, Remenyi 1991 and Peppard 1993). The conventional approach to phases, as is the case in its use in SISP, is that progress is in sequence: a preceding phase closing before a succeeding phase commences and new phases drawing upon information from the earlier phases. This approach does not reflect reality accurately as there are many instances where phases run concurrently and where phases have to be revisited because of some change in requirements or in the operational environment. For example, interpreting the organisational need may require the initial definition of the ideal systems architecture as this can be fed back to the participating group to judge their reaction to the type and cost of support. A lukewarm response would suggest that the identified need was not high priority, assuming that the solution does in fact satisfy the specified need. An alternative approach, which is one taken here, is that of nested phases as shown in Figure 9.6. A phase opens with a specification of what has to be done. The work is then undertaken and finally the completed work is evaluated. Work comprises the work in the particular phase plus all the work in the nested phases below. For example, the task of defining organisational information need can only be truly finished once the final outcome of the exercise is presented and accepted by the client as this is confirmation that the problem or need has been understood and a realistic solution proposed. To reach this stage might require several iterations around the nested phases.

SISP is not a one-off exercise. Within a single exercise there are likely to be several iterations some of which might include a feedback into the organisational strategy resulting in a change in the overall organisational direction and therefore leading to a change in the scope of the SISP exercise in hand. As part of the strategic culture, SISP exercises will occur regularly to empower strategic thinking within the organisation. This ongoing process can be seen in Figure 9.7.

❑ *Viewpoint*

Why IT and business managers must talk by Bill Boyle

Technological change has always led to massive upheavals in the workforce, making old sets of skills redundant while creating whole new areas of expertise. Yet one group of workers is always left floundering by change: managers. Wholesale change among the workforce is only slowly followed by the necessary adaptation of middle and senior management.

This is what Computer Associates (CA) boss Charles Wang argued in his book *Techno Vision*, published last year. He said the rapid development of IT had in most firms produced a rift between business managers and their colleagues responsible for delivering IT solutions. He called this "disconnection".

Wang's book dealt mainly with the US. But CA wondered whether the issue was a significant problem in the UK too. The answer, delivered by a survey conducted by two consultants Spikes Cavell of 90 of the Times Top 1,000 companies, is an emphatic "yes".

The report, entitled *IT and Corporate Strategy – Towards a Common Goal*, reveals that 58% of business managers simply have no idea what goes on in their IT departments. This is despite the fact that most business managers say they view IT as the most important business function that supports their departments.

According to the report there is "a basic lack of understanding" and "a lack of participation and joint commitment to the company's goals and objectives" between business managers and their IT departments.

The rift is spelt out in comments recorded in the report from both sides of the divide. One business manager said IT managers were "wrapped up in their own little wired world". A typical comment from one IT manager was: "Business manager refuse to join the 20th century and get to grips with technology".

Some 70% of business managers complained that IT managers talk in technical terms, and 62% believe that IT managers get carried away with technology. More seriously, 34% of the business staff claimed that IT managers lose sight of the business issues, while 28% said that they follow their own agenda.

On the other side, 30% of IT managers thought business managers were insecure about asking technical questions and 24% said that business managers rarely, or never, share strategic objectives with them.

A high proportion of the business managers (84%) felt that IT managers were aware of company objectives, yet only 64% of IT managers were comfortable with the level of information they received.

Jay Huff, UK marketing director of CA, commissioned the survey. He said that with IT set to play an increasing role in business performance, firms could not afford to allow this divide to continue. "All the easy fixes to ensure your IT gives you business advantage have been done now," he said.

The report found that most firms recognise the problem exists, and have attempted to tackle it with structures such as IT strategy groups, which bring together IT and business managers. But while 79% of the companies surveyed have an IT strategy group, 31% of business managers and 15% of IT managers did not know who chaired the group.

A common complaint from IT managers is that their department does not get its share of attention at the highest levels, and the survey backs this up. Only 41% of executives responsible for IT report to the chief executive officer; 25% report to the finance director. According to the survey this is a traditional structure, based on the historical growth of companies, which perpetuates the "disconnect".

Even here there is a difference in perceptions. When asked who was responsible for IT overall, 66% of IT managers said it was the chief executive officer, finance director or operations director. The business managers, on the other hand, said it was the responsibility of the IT/MIS manager or a senior IT manager.

Whatever the truth, the report suggests that firms that do not have IT represented on the board pay a price. In those companies where the person with overall responsibility for IT sits on the board, the incidence of separate business units duplicating work by developing similar applications is very much reduced; only 29% as opposed to 46% in companies where the IT director does not sit on the board.

The report does have some good news. When business managers were asked if they felt their company was getting sufficient return from their IT department, 74% answered "yes". And when asked to rate the department on a scale from 1 to 5 the business managers gave an average of 3.7, with "usefulness", "quality of applications" and "business benefits" all scoring over 4. ■

Reprinted with permission from *Computer Weekly* 29th June 1995.

Fig 9.6 The nested phases of a SISP exercise

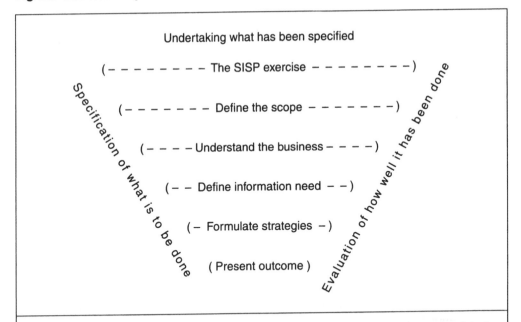

There are many instances where phases run concurrently and where phases have to be revisited because of some change in requirements or in the operational environment.

Fig 9.7 SISP iterations within an exercise and as an ongoing activity within SCB

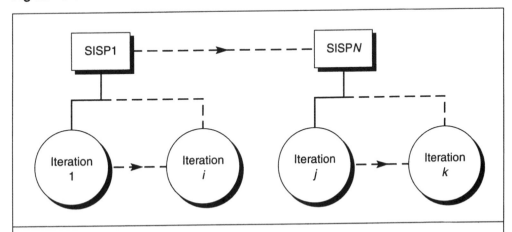

The first SISP exercise will comprise *i* iterations. At a later stage, this exercise will be followed by another which builds upon the outcomes of the previous exercise and so on. The Nth exercise in this ongoing activity comprises *j* to *k* iterations, the *j*th iteration building upon the last iteration of the previous exercise.

9.6   SISP METHODOLOGIES

Several methodologies to guide SISP have been developed, for example Business Systems Planning (BSP) from IBM. In the context of this book, a SISP methodology is considered to be a purpose-built set of SISP techniques that together provide support for part or all of the SISP process. A SISP technique provides a structured approach to performing an activity within SISP. These may draw upon the use of one or more SISP tools, which could, for example, allow the technique to be viewed diagrammatically. Indeed, many of the techniques are frameworks reliant upon grids for technique definition and usage, for example SWOT analysis (standing for Strengths, Weaknesses, Opportunities and Threats) can be considered a SISP technique, even though it has wider application in that it can be used in corporate strategic planning as well as SISP. SWOT analysis prescribes the activities of eliciting the strengths, weaknesses, opportunities and threats of the organisation and for analysing them to elicit areas requiring IS development. It uses a grid tool for categorising the four sets of attributes.

The three-layered view of a SISP methodology as shown in Figure 9.8, from a methodology to technique(s) to tool(s), coincides with the layers suggested by Lederer and Gardiner (1992).

A SISP technique can also, in certain circumstances, be considered a SISP methodology in its own right. In the SISP methodology definition, the set of SISP techniques may have only one member. This is useful as certain techniques are frequently described as methodologies in their own right. For example, Value-Chain Analysis has been considered a component activity of some SISP methodologies, such as Strategic Application Search, and yet is frequently considered as a SISP methodology in its own right even though its creator, Michael Porter (1985), conceived it from a business strategy perspective. In other words, what is considered a SISP technique and what is considered a SISP methodology depends, to a large degree, on context. The SISP methodology definition used here accommodates these different situations.

Fig 9.8 The three-layered SISP methodology

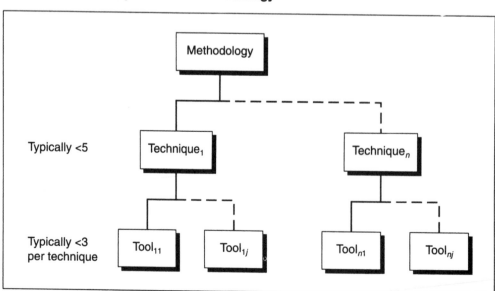

9.6.1 Methodologies in context

Simply applying a SISP methodology is insufficient to ensure successful outcomes. In the context of SISP, vision and creative thinking are vital. Vision and creative thinking are promoted through SCB. Mintzberg (1992) discusses this issue at length, highlighting that formulating strategy at whatever level, be it at a corporate or at an IS/IT level, requires creativity on the part of the management group involved and that SISP is doomed to failure if it becomes a ritualistic process using formalised procedures without visionary thought. This visionary thought needs to be coupled with extensive knowledge of aspects, both internal and external to the organisation, which are important to the development of a suitable strategic plan for IS/IT. These aspects include the strengths and weaknesses of the organisation's work-force and assets, as well as those of its competitors. Creativity in SISP needs to be tempered with objectivity, to ensure that the ramifications of any proposals are well thought out and the proposals are evaluated in a disciplined manner. The organisation must also be ready to accept SISP. Existing methodologies and techniques must be known and understood. New offerings must be evaluated as they become available. An appropriate subset of SISP methodologies and techniques must be selected which best fits the task in hand. This is becoming an increasingly difficult task. The number of commercially available SISP methodologies and techniques continues to rise. How can an organisation, faced with selecting between several SISP methodologies, ensure that the one chosen is appropriate? There is evidence that the initial selections of SISP methodologies by organisations are not always the most appropriate. For example, Earl (1993) found that an average of 2.3 methods have been employed over time in the 21 UK-based companies he surveyed, reflecting a trial and error approach. Some methodologies or techniques have been more difficult to employ than others in certain contexts. Mainelli and Millar (1988) reported that British Rail, for example, found Value Chain Analysis difficult to employ in their strategic planning activities.

9.6.2 Choosing a SISP methodology

A framework for classifying and comparing SISP methodologies is needed to provide guidance on which methodology is most appropriate for the organisation's requirements. Such a framework provides insight into why certain SISP methodologies are used more than others, and highlights aspects for improvements within current SISP methodologies which would render the methodology more useful in practice. The progression towards an approach to aid classification and comparison of SISP methodologies mirrors the progression within the IS development methodology domain, where classification approaches for IS methodologies have been proposed to aid evaluation of the many IS methodologies now in existence. The works of Episkopou and Wood-Harper (1986), Flood and Jackson (1992), and Jayaratna (1994) are prime examples.

Classifying a SISP methodology involves measuring the methodology from three perspectives: the ease of use of the methodology; the scope of the methodology; and the orientation of the methodology.

- *Ease of use* relates to the relative difficulty, or complexity, of applying the methodology to a given situation. A SISP methodology of low complexity is considered easy to use, whereas a SISP methodology of high complexity will be more difficult to use.

- *Scope* refers to classifying a SISP methodology on the extent to which it covers the SISP process. Some methodologies provide more techniques covering more aspects of SISP than others.
- *Orientation* refers to the SISP approach to identifying areas of IS investment. Approaches vary between a predominantly data-driven approach, such as BSP, and a predominantly business objective-focused approach, such as CSF. This perspective identifies the SISP orientation and maps this to an organisation's salient characteristics.

Classifying a SISP methodology for a particular context from these perspectives, as illustrated in Figure 9.9, is comprehensive. The ease of use, or complexity, perspective looks at micro aspects of a SISP methodology, examining its make-up and the characteristics of the strategic planning group that will be using the methodology. The scope perspective looks at the coverage of the SISP methodology over the entire SISP process. Together, these two perspectives provide a breadth and depth view of a SISP methodology, where breadth relates to scope and each activity within its scope is evaluated as part of the ease of use measurement. Finally, a SISP methodology can, as a whole, promote a certain orientation towards the SISP process. This holistic effect is examined in the third perspective, that of orientation, and provides a macro view of the SISP methodology within an organisation. The use of the classification framework for evaluating SISP methodologies will be considered in more detail in the next chapter.

Fig 9.9 The classification framework based on three perspectives

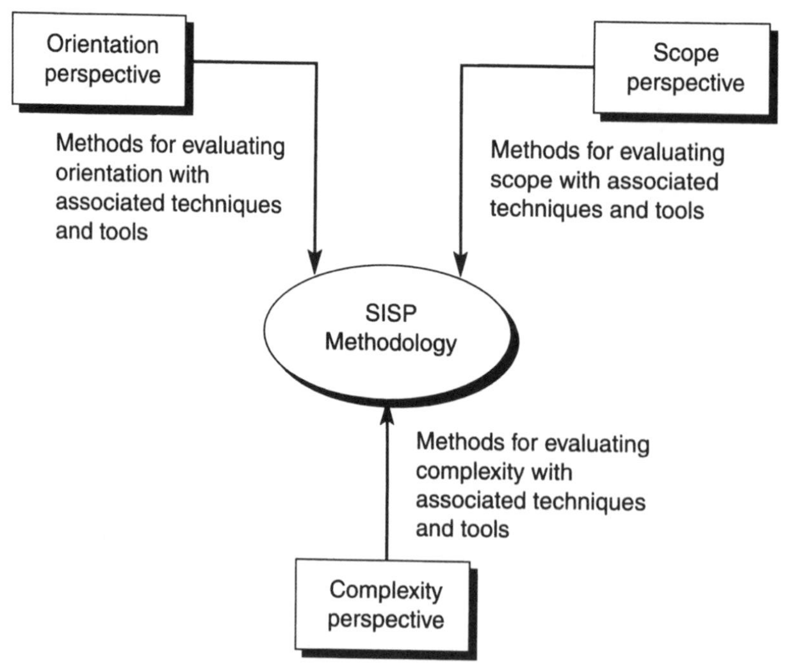

A framework for classifying and comparing SISP methodologies provides guidance on which methodology is most appropriate for the organisation's requirements.

9.6.3   An overview of SISP methodologies and techniques

There are numerous methodologies and techniques which can be used in the SISP process. A recent survey of over 20 textbooks and refereed articles, conducted by the authors, revealed 25 different techniques and 30 different methodologies. Some of the offerings described were related and some had derivatives described which had only minor modifications and so were not included in the total of 55. It is not the purpose of this book to describe in detail all offerings, other books (for example, Ward, Griffiths and Whitmore 1990 and Remenyi 1991) have addressed this issue effectively. A selection of the most commonly cited offerings, which represents typical methodologies and techniques currently available, has been chosen. These are briefly described here and then some are considered in more detail in the next chapter.

- *Five Forces Model* – This widely accepted model by Porter identifies five basic forces determining an organisation's competitive structure. These forces are: the bargaining power of the organisation's suppliers, the bargaining power of the organisation's customers, the threats of new entrants into the market, the threat of new or substitute products and organisational rivals.
- *Strategic Option Generator* – This enables a manager to analyse the relationship between IS/IT and the three strategic targets of the organisation's operating environment: suppliers, clients and competitors. Account is taken of the main orientation that an organisation can adopt in the search for competitive advantage; these being: differentiation, cost reduction, innovation, growth and alliance.
- *Strategic Relevance and Impact Grid* – As the name suggests, this often-cited matrix focuses on the strategic importance of IS. With dimensions of current systems and future or planned systems four quadrants are formed with each having a different implication for IS planning decisions.
- *Boston Consultancy Group Matrix* – This matrix categorises products according to their present market share and the future growth of the market. A product which survives a new market evolves clockwise through the quadrants to reach maturity.
- *SWOT Analysis* – The analysis identifies strengths, weaknesses, opportunities and threats of the current organisational situation. Strengths and weakness are mainly internal and are about present reality. Opportunities and threats are mainly external and are about future prospects.
- *Value Chain Analysis* – This is a technique for analysing the sources of competitive advantage. An organisation's strategically important activities are defined and subdivided into primary activities (comprising inbound logistics, operations, outbound logistics, sales and marketing, and service) and support activities (comprising corporate infrastructure, human resource management, technology management and procurement).
- *Critical Success Factors* – Rockart's much-used methodology attempts to define the few key areas that dictate organisational success. It has evolved into a special-purpose information planning approach to identify opportunities in a top-down manner.
- *Business Systems Planning* – BSP comprises top-down planning with bottom-up implementation. It documents the business objectives and defines the business process, the data necessary to support the business processes and the information architecture.
- *Customer Resource Life Cycle* – This helps in identifying new opportunities for the successful application of IS/IT. Opportunities are possible throughout the resources

life cycle and this structured approach provides a powerful framework within which to function.
- METHOD/1* – This is a top-down approach to SISP. It starts by identifying the organisation's mission and develops business objectives and strategies together with CSFs. It supports the development of long-range plans and helps formulate tactics to change the organisation as it implements the plan.

The most prominent management concept of the 1990s is Business Process Re-engineering (BPR). BPR is the analysis and design of work flows and processes within and between organisations. Many have taken the view that BPR will replace existing strategy planning approaches but there is little evidence to support this view. The relationship between BPR and SISP is discussed in further detail in Chapter 12.

9.6.4 SISP meta-models

The meta-model is a higher level of extraction which is useful within the SISP area as it enhances understanding and leading to more effective use.. Through the meta-model concepts, techniques and methodologies can be clarified, compared, categorised, evaluated and integrated. In some ways METHOD/1 exhibits some of the attributes of a meta-model but shall remain in the methodology category in the context of this book. Three meta-models have been developed for SISP:

- *Ward's Strategy Framework* – This provides a way of consolidating disparate techniques in order to identify an organisation's required applications, their priorities and to deploy resources successfully to implement these systems. The framework has three themes: assessing the need for immediate investment, appraisal of IS/IT as it relates to the organisation and identifying potential future investment
- *Earl's Multiple Methodology* – This is based on the premise that no single IS strategy formulation will work. The approach considers business plans and goals in a top-down manner, current systems in a bottom-up manner and IS/IT opportunities in an inside-out manner. Several of the well-tested techniques are drawn together in this approach which would be more appropriately named as Multiple Methodology Framework.
- *Earl's Five Approaches* – This is concerned with choosing the most suitable overall approach to SISP for an organisation. The five approaches identified through empirical research are Business-led, Method-driven, Administrative, Technological, Organisational.

9.7 SUMMARY

Both the size and range of the impact of IS/IT have increased as IS/IT has evolved. This all-embracing core organisational facet requires effective strategic management. The leading edge focus for technology application is now active decision support and competitive advantage. The associated SIS must link to the business strategy and significantly affect organisational performance. The mission is a powerful instrument

* METHOD/1 is a trademark of Andersen Consulting

☐ *Viewpoint*

Thinking strategically by John Henderson

Should IT strategy be aligned to business strategy? No points for guessing the right answer. But between the policy and the practice is, all too often, a yawning abyss. One of the main reasons is that IT planning is seen as less than enthralling by many businesses.

"When I did a technology planning exercise with senior executives they told me they would never participate in one again!" recalls John Henderson, professor of management information systems and director of the Systems Research Center at the Boston University School of Management. "They said they found it boring, rigid and frustrating, which is not motivating for busy people".

So unpopular was the task that one executive told Henderson that the usual practice was to draw straws – whoever drew the shortest straw had to be the IT champion.

So what does a senior line manager need to consider in order to leverage the company's IT investment?

"Firstly, strategic alignment is not a static concept. The IT perspective must change as the organisation and its market changes", says Henderson.

Those changes come from two sources. The first is external – the typical pressures on a business which determine its competitiveness. The second source of change is internal – the structure of the organisation and how that affects its ability to execute the corporate business strategy.

"For example, you can decide that one of your distinctive competencies is speed to market, but what is then tough is to change the business processes in order to deliver that".

This requires IT to change in order to support changed business processes.

"An IT strategy starts with positioning the company in its marketplace, because that affects the long-term capacity of business to acquire technology", says Henderson.

Henderson stresses the continual importance of referring IT to corporate positioning.

"An IT architecture is not a strategy", he warns. It is, of course, merely a means of delivering a strategy.

Henderson believes strategic perspectives divide into four broad types.

Companies that concentrate on the strategic execution of their core competence have a style of management that can be defined as executive leadership, and which sees the IT managers as a product manager and the function of IT to be responsive. Performance is judged in financial terms.

Companies with strategic perspectives that focus on their competitive potential have business visionaries at the top; the IT manager is part of the top management team, IT is there to add value, and performance is judged by the impact of the product or service on the market.

Companies that concentrate on service level have a prioritiser at the top, look for executive leadership in the IT manager, see IT as a business within a business, and measure performance by customer satisfaction.

Finally, companies that focus on their technological potential have a technological visionary at the top, a technological architect as the IT manager, use IT to enhance the company's technological competence, and measure performance in terms of flexibility and growth.

"Each of these models has strength and weaknesses, but they force you to think about the links, both vertical and horizontal, between business and IT", says Henderson. ■

Reprinted with permission from *Computer Weekly*, 9th February 1995.

which, if properly constructed and used, can significantly influence the actions of all areas within an organisation and, therefore, promotes strategic alignment.

SISP is the means of identifying application systems which support and enhance organisational strategy and provides the framework for the effective implementation of these systems. SISP, together with the fostering of a strategic culture, assists in the realisation of corporate objects. The right combination of Executive Management, Middle Managers, Knowledge Workers and IS/IT Professionals involved in SISP will ensure that a viable strategy and implementation plan are developed. In general, SISP involves

(Summary continued on p. 234)

CASE STUDY: BODY SHOP

Body building

by Candice Goodwin

The desktop systems manager has an ecology degree, and "priority concern for the environment" is a corporate differentiator, yet profit margins have never fallen below 12% for the past five years. It could only be the Body Shop, which continues to confound financial analysts with its bewildering mixture of political correctness and sharp business acumen.

The company's IT strategy is a similar mixture. Many of its IT decisions do not come down to pounds and pence. The desire to save trees was a major factor behind its investment in electronic mail (E-mail), and it has carefully calculated that, on the basis of current message traffic, E-mail saves four trees a month from the chop.

On the other hand, the company has often shown unusual hard-headedness about only investing in new technology when there is a clear business need. For example, it will only start to introduce integrated point of sale systems (Epos) next year.

Nick Eastwood, head of corporate services at the Body Shop, is unapologetic about the company's policy. "It wasn't until the late 1980s that the Body Shop started to develop anything resembling a coherent IT strategy," he says.

"But don't confuse lack of IT with lack of business expertise. That is a critical mistake a lot of organisations make, and one of the reasons why so many major systems implementations fail. Almost invariably you will find that when people have great systems, it is because they have been shaped by the business experience that has evolved in the company over a long time".

Eastwood says that Anita and Gordon Roddick, the Body Shop's managing director and chairman respectively, are "reasonably demanding and sceptical about some of our IT investment – they question the payback".

He agrees that there is room for scepticism. "The computer industry is second only to the fashion industry in terms of re-inventing itself," he says. "The number of times people have said that it is critical for business to participate in a particular technology, whether it is Unix or client-server. Yet client-server is an absolute minefield; it's completely unproven in terms of business benefits."

The company's robust financial performance suggests that it has not suffered from its downbeat approach to IT. As Eastwood points out, its modus operandi does not require advanced technology, "Because the Body Shop is a franchise operation, a lot of the basic infrastructure processing functions are not very complicated."

The Body Shop's customers are its franchisees, of which there are 180 in the UK. Elsewhere, the company deals with a single head franchisee in most markets, making a total of only 45 overseas customers. Similarly, although most Body Shop franchisees still manage their businesses with nothing more complex than an electronic till, the empty shelves and missing line items sometimes apparent at Marks & Spencer – which only recently started to integrate its point-of-sale terminals with its stock control – are not much in evidence at the Body Shop.

We don't suffer from stock-outs very much because the product line is fairly stable," explains Eastwood. "Our bestsellers (White Musk Eau de Toilette, Vitamin E Cream, Peppermint Foot Lotion, in case you were wondering) have remained roughly the same for years."

So why is Eastwood worried that his company's grasp of IT issues "is not as sophisticated as it needs to be?"

▶

One issue, of course, is that the company's market position, though strong, is not unassailable. And after years without a real UK competitor – unless you count product ranges such as Sainsbury's Nature's Compliments, and mail order operations such as the ill-fated Cosmetics To Go – it now faces a potential rival in Bath and Bodyworks, a Body Shop clone from the US which has now started to set up its first shops in the UK.

Though Bath and Bodyworks is not yet big enough to be a serious threat, Eastwood sees the integrated Epos due to be rolled out into stores during the first quarter of 1995 as one brick in a "defensive wall" against this and future competition.

"Integrated Epos would allow us to be much more focused – react faster to retail sales information," he says.

"We could improve space allocation – make it much more scientific. We'd like to be able to track the impact of promotions, or the way shops are laid out, but you can't do that unless you have day-to-day information. You have to learn how to use that information over quite a long period of time, But it should enable us, over two or three, years, to make product pricing, promotions and discontinuation decisions much faster".

Another factor is that the UK market now has practically all the Body Shop outlets it can reasonably hold, and in order to sustain growth the company has to find ways of generating more revenue from its existing shops.

As Eastwood explains, this has resulted in a shift in emphasis within the organisation. "Until two years ago, the Body Shop was very much product-led. The emphasis was on finding and making new products, then pushing them out into the sales network and seeing if they sold. Now, because we're reaching saturation point with our shops, we're looking more at short-term sales tracking and systems to help us manage that data. We've got 250 shops in the UK – what do you do with 250 paper reports each with 2,000 line items?"

Integrated Epos systems will be an important first step towards generating the information the Body Shop needs to fend off rivals and generate new growth. The company has invested around £4m in developing PC-based systems for its franchises, which will enable it to get detailed weekly retail sales information instead of the summaries it currently receives.

ICL has done the application development work, tailoring and integrating two existing packages to create the application software, and will also provide the PC hardware.

Although Body Shop franchisees are obliged to wear the green corporate livery, their choice of IT solution is up to them, and take-up of the new systems will, says Eastwood, be "entirely voluntary".

The 40 company-owned shops will be using the Epos, and will provide useful information. Eastwood is confident, however, that the majority of franchisees will take them on.

We've consulted them, of course, and the feedback is that they want an Epos but can't individually afford to hire someone to build one," he says.

The Epos is tailored to the Body Shop's specific requirements – which include a much heftier back-office component than you would expect in most retail products on the market – but the company has chosen to base it on existing products.

"Our philosophy is very much to be package-driven," Eastwood explains. "We go for mature, stable, well-programmed products: the focus is very much on making them work, rather than the whole best of breed stuff you read about, With a bloody great write-off at the end."

This pragmatic approach has been used to good effect at the Body Shop head office and warehouse. Rather than bespoke software, the Body Shop's HP 9000s run the Chameleon in Manufacturing software suite for integrated manufacturing, financials and sales order processing, and the Dispatcher package for warehouse control.

▶

Though the Body Shop avoids carrying out software development in-house, it has taken the opposite approach with its computer services.

The help desk, the IT training and the Macintosh engineering support are all run in-house: engineering because it is cheaper that way, and training and helpdesk services because the Body Shop wanted to provide added value that it believed it would not find externally.

"We didn't just want to teach people how to use the systems, we wanted them to learn how to use the environment we have." says Tony Adderley, the company's IT manager who has 36 staff.

"That might include the naming conventions we use, and our rules for what you should and shouldn't do over the E-mail system."

Because IT is seen as a way of enabling staff to do their jobs better, the Body Shop is keen that the training service is widely used, and has therefore bucked the industry trend towards charging out computer services. "What's important is the growth in the internal service

and meeting end-user expectations, so internal training is free." Adderley explains.

But if all this sounds disappointingly sensible, not all the company's IT decisions are geared towards the bottom line. When it comes to desktop computing, the Roddicks are apparently less questioning of the payback: Microsoft Office is now on all of the company's 500 Macs, representing an investment of well over £100,000 in desktop software alone.

Within the Body Shop this investment is also viewed in terms of more intangible benefits. The Microsoft Mail E-mail system has swiftly become a part of the corporate culture: in a recent campaign on behalf of the Ogoni tribe in Nigeria, the Body Shop used E-mail to get messages to the entire company in minutes, telling them where they could send letters and faxes in support of the campaign.

It is not the usual way of justifying an IT investment – but so far, the Body Shop's unusual approach to decision-making has served it well. ∎

Reprinted with permission from *Computer Weekly*, 1st December 1994.

Summary continued

understanding and interpreting business requirements, defining organisational needs and underpinning systems architectures, and formulating the information, information systems and information technology strategies. The precise nature of the SISP exercise will depend upon the approach adopted and the nature of the organisation. SISP is not a one-off exercise. Within a single exercise there are likely to be several iterations some of which might include a feedback into the organisational strategy resulting in a change in the overall organisational direction and therefore leading to a change in the scope of the SISP exercise in hand. As part of the strategic culture, SISP exercises will occur regularly to empower strategic thinking within the organisation.

A SISP methodology is a purpose-built set of SISP techniques that together provide support for part or all of the SISP process. A SISP technique provides a structured approach to performing an activity within SISP. There are many methodologies and techniques available for the SISP process. Choosing a SISP methodology involves considering ease of use, scope and orientation.

This chapter has provided an overview of the main issues within SISP. The chapters that follow address these issues in more detail. In particular, detailed discussion of the popular SISP methodologies and techniques will be covered in Chapter 10. This will be followed by an indication of how to undertake a SISP exercise in Chapter 11. With the advent of BPR, Chapter 12 considers the nature of this activity and how it relates to the SISP landscape.

References

Campbell A, Tawadey K (1990) *Mission and Business Philosophy*. Butterworth–Heinemann.

Cavaye A L M, Cragg P B (1993) Strategic information systems research: a review and research framework. *Journal of Strategic Information Systems* Vol 2, No 2, pp 125–137.

Earl M J (1993) Experiences in strategic information systems planning. *MIS Quarterly* Vol 17, No 1, pp 1–24.

Episkopou D M, Wood-Harper A T (1986) Towards a framework to choose appropriate IS approaches. *The Computer Journal* Vol 29, No 3, pp 222–228.

Ernst & Young (1989) *The landmark MIT study: management in the 1990s*.

Ernst & Young (1990) *Strategic alignment report: 1990 UK survey*.

Feeny D F, Edwards B R, Simpson K M (1992) Understanding the CEO/CIO relationship. *MIS Quarterly*. December, pp 435–448.

Fidler CS, Rogerson S, Spiers N (1993) Current IS practices within UK-based institutions: an empirical investigation. *Information Management and Computer Security* Vol 1, No 2, pp 13–20.

Flood R L, Jackson M C (1992) *Creative Problem Solving*. John Wiley, Chichester.

King W, Hufnagel E, Grover V (1988) Using information technology for competitive advantage. in Earl M J (ed) *Information Management: the Strategic Dimension*. Oxford University Press, pp 75–86.

Jayaratna N (1994) *Understanding and Evaluating Methodologies, NIMSAD: a systemic framework*. McGraw-Hill, Maidenhead.

Lederer A L, Gardiner V (1992) The process of strategic information planning. *Journal of Strategic Information Systems*. Vol 1, No 2, pp 76–83.

Lederer A L, Sethi V (1992) Meeting the challenges of information systems planning. *Long Range Planning* Vol 25, No 2, pp 69–80.

Lederer A L, Sethi V (1988), The implementation of strategic information systems planning methodologies. *MIS Quarterly* September, pp 445–461.

Lloyd B (1992) Mintzberg on the rise and fall of strategic planning. *Long Range Planning* Vol 25, No 4, pp 99–104.

Mainelli M, Miller D (1988) Strategic planning for information systems at British Rail. *Long Range Planning* Vol 21, No 4, pp 65–75.

Peppard J (editor) (1993) *IT Strategy for Business*. Pitman Publishing, London.

Porter M J (1985) *Competitive Strategy*. Free Press, New York.

Remenyi D S J (1991) *Introducing Strategic Information Systems Planning*. NCC Blackwell.

Reponen T (1993) Strategic information systems – a conceptual analysis. *Journal of Strategic Information Systems* Vol 2, No 2, pp 100–104.

Ward J, Griffiths P, Whitmore P (1990) *Strategic Planning for Information Systems*. John Wiley, Chichester.

Review questions

1 What is a strategic information system? Give some examples.

2 What is the significance of a mission statement on the introduction of information systems?

3 Describe the possible strategic alignment situations for an organisation.

4 What is the difference between SISP and SCB?

5 Define SISP.

6 Who are the key players in a SISP exercise? Explain the factors which influence the choice of players.

7 Why must SISP be iterative?

8 Explain the three-layered concept.

9 What are the key factors in choosing a SISP?

10 Name and describe five SISP tools.

Project ideas

You are the newly appointed Information Systems Director of a domestic appliances manufacture that is about to set up a new manufacturing plant in the Midlands. Apart from yourself, all other senior management is drawn from organisations within the international conglomerate. Your task, according to the CEO, is to get IT working and supporting other areas within the company. Your have been in the post 10 days and this morning the CEO contacted you to say the next board meeting was in seven days time and the first item on the agenda was IT strategy. He tells you that you will be expected to give a 20 minute presentation outlining corporate IT strategy for the next five years.

Tasks
You will need to make a lot of assumptions about the organisation.

- From the information given in this chapter devise an effective plan of action to undertake this strategic exercise
- Develop a strategy for the organisation (you will have to make a lot of assumptions)

CHAPTER 10

SISP Methodologies, Techniques and Tools

10.1   INTRODUCTION

This chapter considers a number of methodologies and techniques in more detail. Those chosen are commonly used in developing strategies for information systems and information technology utilisation or are the offerings from some of the leading international consultancy companies.

The three-layered view of a SISP methodology was discussed in Chapter 9. A SISP methodology was defined as a purpose-built set of SISP techniques that together provided support for part or all of the SISP process. A SISP technique was defined as a structured approach to performing an activity within SISP. It was explained that these techniques might draw upon one or more SISP tools, which could, for example, allow the technique to be viewed diagrammatically. For this reason, tools are not covered separately. They are indirectly covered through the discussion of specific techniques.

Some of the more popular techniques are described in Section 10.2. The purpose of this chapter is not to provide a comprehensive catalogue of the plethora of techniques available. It is rather to provide a subset of useful techniques which the reader could use in practice. Together they provide insight into the types of techniques available.

The much-used Critical Success Factors methodology is discussed in Section 10.3. This is followed by the contrasting approaches of three of the leading international consultancy companies. Each has developed its own methodology for deriving IS/IT strategies for its clients.

At the end of this chapter the reader should understand:

- *The concepts of some SISP techniques.*
- *How to use the Critical Success Factors methodology*
- *The approaches to SISP and SCB of some leading international consultancy firms*

10.2   TECHNIQUES

Techniques are the main elements of SISP methodologies but they can also be used independently to complement other approaches or to undertake a specific analytical task. Two of the classic techniques are described in this section. They have both been used extensively in practice in a variety of situations including the IS/IT domain.

10.2.1 Five forces model

The Five Forces Model, conceived by Porter (1979), has been widely used in the development of business strategies. Its popularity is due to its focus on competition. Indeed Porter (1979) states that 'the essence of strategy formulation is coping with competition', a sentiment held by the industrial and commercial communities at large. Competition can exist in forces that go beyond the established combatants of a particular industry. Customers, suppliers, potential entrants to the industry and substitute products or services are forces which act upon a business from beyond the boundaries of the industry in which it would normally perceive its competition to be. This is illustrated in Figure 10.1. To derive a strategy for dealing with these forces and to flourish despite them, an organisation must understand how these forces operate within its industry and identify ways of adjusting to them and, where possible, taking advantage of them.

The Five Forces model can be used to analyse the effect of IS/IT within an industry and how IS/IT can be exploited to gain competitive advantage. This was first considered by Porter and Millar (1985) and Cash and Konsynski (1985) and subsequently by several others, for example, Earl (1989), Peppard (1993) and Silk (1991). Given such

Fig 10.1 Porter's five forces model

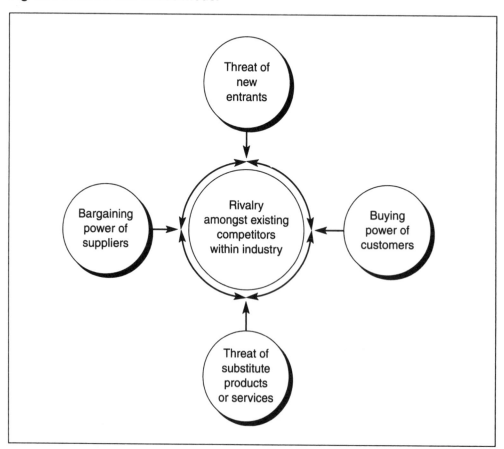

commentary, it is clear that this technique is valuable in deriving an IS strategy. Each of the five forces is now considered in the context of IS/IT strategy.

1 Competitor rivalry

Factors which create conditions of intense rivalry include:

- Competitors are numerous or are roughly equal in size and power.
- Industry growth is slow.
- The product or service lacks differentiation or switching costs.
- Fixed costs are high or the product is perishable.
- Capacity is normally augmented in large increments.
- Exit barriers are high.
- The rivals are diverse in strategies, origins and personalities

A company can improve matters through strategic shifts which essentially reduce the effects of these external forces on its profitability. For example, in recent years super-market chains have used IT to gain competitive advantage through having a more responsive stock control system based upon shelf stock levels and point of sale stock recording. This has meant popular lines can be replenished quickly to satisfy demand and unpopular products can be withdrawn as soon as possible, thus reducing the financial loss of holding unwanted goods. Long-term buying habits can also be fully investigated with the advent of this application.

2 Threat of entry

With a new entrant comes the threat of diminishing market share. Barriers to entry reduce this threat and include:

- Economies of scale.
- Product differentiation.
- Capital requirements.
- Cost disadvantages independent of size.
- Access to distribution channels.
- Government policy.

IT is now a central function for organisations operating within the finance sector. The capital cost for establishing an IS/IT infrastructure is considerable even for the smallest finance house. Furthermore, the banking telecommunications network is very tightly controlled and subject to government regulation making access by a potential entrant to the sector difficult. Consequently, significant barriers have been created which hamper potential entrants to the sector.

3 Supplier bargaining power

Factors that can make a supplier group powerful include:

- It is dominated by a few companies and is more concentrated than the industries it sells to.
- Its product is unique or at least differentiated, or it has built up switching costs.

- Its is not obliged to contend with other products for sale to the industry.
- It poses a credible threat of integrating forward into the industry's businesses.
- The industry is not an important customer of the supplier group.

Just-in-time (JIT) manufacturing and the supporting Electronic Data Interchange (EDI) are examples of how supplier power can be countered by reversing the roles where the supplier becomes electronically dependent on receiving regular orders for its components. With the advent of the global information superhighways it is possible to search the world for suppliers thus reducing the power of the local specialist supplier.

4 Customer buying power

Factors that can make the customer group powerful include:

- It is concentrated, or purchases in large volumes.
- The products it purchases from industry are standard or undifferentiated.
- It earns low profits, which create great incentive to lower its purchasing costs.
- The industry's product is unimportant to the quality of the buyer's products or services.
- The industry's product does not save the buyer money.
- The buyers pose a credible threat of integrating backward to make the industry's products.

Within the IT services industry there are examples of buyers integrating backwards. BOC created Datasolve and the Rover Group formed Istel, both of which were later sold off as going concerns. With the advent of the global economy many organisations are using the Internet to increase market size and visibility and in so doing are reducing individual customer power.

5 Threat of substitute products or services

There are two criteria for substitute products that can cause problems for industries competing against it:

- If the substitute products are subject to trends improving their price-performance trade-off with the industry's products.
- If the substitute products are produced by industries earning high profits.

There are numerous examples of IS/IT creating substitutes. Digital watches replaced analogue watches particularly at the lower end of the market. Electronic calculators caused the death of the slide rule and logarithmic tables. Books, magazines and newspapers have to face the challenges of alternative products using multimedia technology and the World-wide Web.

Mainelli and Miller (1988) explain that the Five Forces Model is an effective way of structuring many of the results of a strategic study. For example, it can be used to categorise each identified information need as helping the organisation to address the five forces, or it can be used to rank existing IS/IT investment based upon the perceived relative importance of the five forces.

10.2.2 Strategic relevance and impact grid and its adaptations

McFarlan and McKenney (1983) were among the first to understand the relationship between organisational strategy and the impact of information technology. They developed the Strategic Relevance and Impact Grid, as shown in Figure 10.2, for comparing the strategic impact of current operations to that expected through IS/IT application. The grid comprises four quadrants, each representing a different organisational environment for IS/IT.

Support Neither existing nor proposed systems that are located in this quadrant are expected to affect corporate strategy directly. However these systems will improve management and performance. For example, word processing and e-mail systems might be placed here.

Turnaround The systems in this quadrant are those which have high potential and are likely to be of future strategic importance. For example, the use of a multimedia system to replace instruction manuals on a production line might have the potential to increase product quality for a manufacturing company.

Factory Located in this quadrant are those systems which are critical to sustaining the existing business. Traditional data processing systems will reside here. This is the engine room of the organisation. Systems have high operational value but low strategic worth. For example, stock control and billing systems are likely to be placed here.

Strategic The systems in this quadrant are those which are critical to the future success of the organisation. Given the strategic emphasis, the planning of these systems must be very closely integrated with planning for new corporate activity. For example, computer-integrated manufacturing might be considered as an essential, large investment for a manufacturing organisation to compete in its marketplace and increase its market share.

An organisation's application portfolio will change as the organisation evolves. New systems will be introduced and old systems will be retired. New opportunities will occur as the technologies advance. The need to invest in IS/IT might become greater because of the activities of competitors. This means that systems will move from one quadrant to another. For example, some years ago the capability of information and communication technology resulted in potential being identified to dispense cash to customers of banks automatically. This application was located in the Turnaround quadrant. Once the technology had been proven, it was then possible to produce a system which would improve customer service whilst reducing staffing. The Automatic Teller Machine (ATM) systems thus became Strategic systems, vital to the long-term growth of banks. Today, all banks and most building societies operate ATMs. They have become an essential part of the daily operation of these companies. Thus, ATMs today are located in the Factory quadrant.

This is a powerful technique that can address a variety of issues. It can be used to review existing systems and so identify any lack of IS support for areas which are vital to the well being of the organisation. In a recent consultancy assignment for Business Link Leicestershire, the authors used this grid to compare perceived and real / potential corporate worth of existing systems resulting in remedial action being taken to

Fig 10.2 Strategic relevance and impact grid

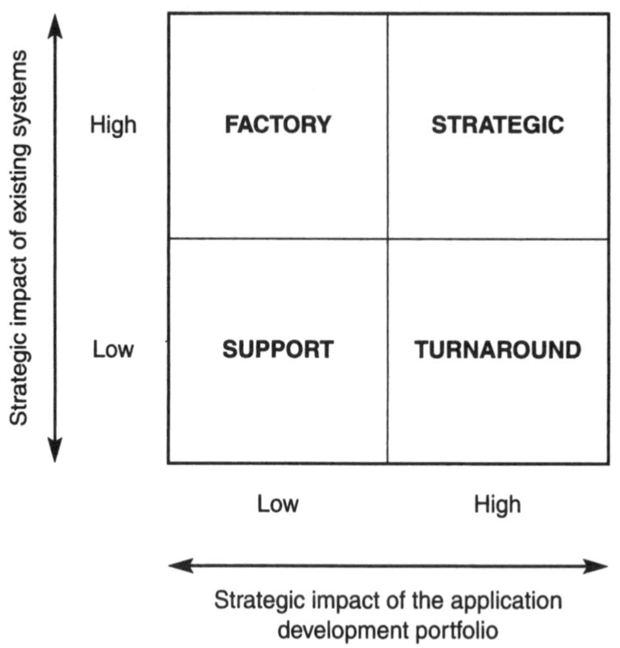

High	**FACTORY**	**STRATEGIC**
Low	**SUPPORT**	**TURNAROUND**
	Low	High

Strategic impact of existing systems (vertical axis)

Strategic impact of the application development portfolio (horizontal axis)

Existing and proposed systems are placed on the grid according to their perceived value. Gaps or over-emphasis can be quickly identified and corrective action instigated in the form of a modified strategy.

improve the effectiveness of systems in support of daily operations. This matrix analysis technique is very useful because, as Ward et al (1990) explain, it reduces 'an apparently infinite continuum of alternatives to a manageable, pertinent number of discrete options from which high level directions can be determined'.

There have been many adaptations and interpretations of McFarlan and McKenney's original grid. An interesting example is the Benefit-Beneficiary Matrix developed by Gibson and Hammer (1985) and illustrated in Figure 10.3. Through defining three domains the matrix identifies evolutionary development of IS in an organisation and provides a foundation on which to develop an IS strategy based on existing and new technologies. Domain 1 is concerned with systems which improve highly repetitive activities within organisational departments. A gain in efficiency and, subsequently, effectiveness is the focus of this domain. Domain 2 is concerned with improving the support of individuals in order to realise gains in efficiency through, for example, word processors, and in effectiveness through, for example, the use of spreadsheets for decision support. Finally, Domain 3 is concerned with the relationships between the organisation and both its customers and its suppliers. Examination of these relationships might result in the redefinition of individual and functional responsibilities as well as an overall change in organisation operation and a realignment of the services

Fig 10.3 Benefit-beneficiary matrix

Benefits \ Beneficiary	Individuals	Functional units	Whole organisation
Efficiency	**Domain 2** Task mechanisation	**Domain 1** Process automation	**Domain 3** Boundary extension
Effectiveness	Work improvement	Functional enhancement	Service enhancement
Transformation	Role expansion	Function redefinition	Product innovation

This extension of the original grid provides a more flexible tool to use in the analysis of IS usage and future demand.

and products offered. The matrix helps in problem and opportunity definition, and in identifying where the benefits lie in problem resolution and opportunity take-up, and what these benefits might be. This leads to focusing on the appropriate technological solutions and deciding which problems and opportunities take priority.

10.3 METHODOLOGIES

Methodologies provide a framework in which to analyse performance, identify problems and derive acceptable solutions. This section briefly describes a selection of SISP methodologies to provide the reader with a general appreciation of what is available and how it can be used.

10.3.1 Critical success factors methodology

Rockart (1979) developed the Critical Success Factors (CSF) approach as a way of investigating the information requirements of executives within organisations. Rockart explains that CSF are those small number of critical areas where things must go right for the organisation to prosper. The approach has gained widespread popularity within IS strategy development largely due to its intrinsic conceptual simplicity and to

❏ *Viewpoint*

Extract from "Under the knife" by Charles Walker

The never-ending drive for efficiency in the NHS has put IT in the front line of the battle against the effects of cutbacks and shortages ... Meanwhile, demand for better IT grows apace, driven by the need to make the health service ever more efficient and cost conscious. In July this year, an Audit Commission report concluded that £220m spent each year by hospitals in England and Wales on IT "often failed to benefit patient care".

The public spending watchdog found widespread disenchantment with IT systems among end users with more than half the nurses surveyed protesting their systems delivered little or no benefit. Training, support and data quality also came under fire.

The commission argued that trusts are held back by "a vicious circle of poor understanding of information issues, negative attitudes and inadequate representation right at the top of the organisation". ■

Reprinted with permission from *Computer Weekly*, 28th September 1995.

it requiring relatively few resources to utilise. The approach was later expanded by Bullen and Rockart (1981) into a SISP methodology. This early work has been modified and expanded upon. For example, Martin and Leben (1989) describe, in detail, a working version of the methodology and CSF analysis has become an integral part of many of the approaches of leading consulting firms as is the case of Andersen Consulting and METHOD/1.

CSFs are those key areas of activity in which favourable results are absolutely necessary for a particular manager's goals to be realised. The main focus is upon the executive's own experience and intuition in determining the factors that are critical to the success of the organisation. Rockart (1982) undertook a study of nine top information systems executives to ascertain the fundamental issues facing IS in servicing organisational needs. He identified a number of CSFs for each organisation, derived the generic CSFs for IS executives and used these as the foundation for defining the role of the IS executive. The CSF set comprised four CSFs:

- Service – the effective and efficient performance of necessary operations and the perception of service by clients
- Communication – the communication between business and technology
- IS human resources – the need to satisfy changing needs with technically literate and managerially competent human resources
- Repositioning the IS function – the evolution of the IS function into one which affects and supports all aspects of the business

CSFs are hierarchical. The CSFs at one level become the goals at the next level down. Goals are the ends and CSFs are the means to the ends. For example, the CSFs of a software house might be product innovation, quality of sales and user literature, scope of marketing and service, and ease of use of product. At the next level down, the goal of product innovation might be dependent upon three CSFs, use of CASE tools, object technology and the retention of top quality software engineers. Finally, the goal of object technology might be dependent upon three CSFs, robustness of approach, staff training, tool support. When using the CSF approach for SISP, managers from the different levels in the organisational hierarchy must be interviewed. The resulting CSFs are consolidated to form a collective set of CSFs for the whole organisation. Thus implicit individual CSFs are encapsulated in explicit organisational CSFs.

The working version of the CSF methodology described by Martin and Leben has two facets, namely process and product. The process facet, as illustrated in Figure 10.4 commences with the creation of the team and ensuring the team fully understand the scope of the exercise and the context in which it is being undertaken. Following this is a management workshop to ensure management fully understand and are committed to the exercises. The interview process is similar to any systems analysis fact finding interview activity. A consolidated list of CSFs is created together with the critical

Fig 10.4 Critical success factors methodology process

Brief the CSF team

↓

Conduct senior management
briefing workshop

↓

Undertake CSF interviews

↓

Integrate and refine CSFs

↓

Conduct senior management
strategy workshop

↓

Articulate strategy

This serial set of processes leads the organisation in a structured manner to derive a strategy founded upon those key areas of the organisation where success is mandatory if the organisation is to survive and flourish.

information set, the critical decision set and the critical assumption set (see the product facet discussion below). The strategy workshop provides the opportunity for senior management to fully discuss the findings of the exercise and arrive at a consensus view. Finally the IS strategy is articulated.

The set of products output from the CSF methodology are shown in Figure 10.5. The mission was discussed in Chapter 9. Overall management goals are the high-level pointers derived from the mission. As discussed earlier, the goals are achieved through addressing the CSFs at the next level of decomposition. Three lists follow from the CSF. The critical information set outlines the information required to track the CSFs. Underlying the mission, goals and CSFs are certain assumptions regarding the business and its environment. Such assumptions must be validated as necessary. Certain critical decisions need to be made in order to facilitate the CSFs. For example a decision might have to be taken to restructure MSS activities on the bases of advances in fuzzy logic and neural nets application. It is these three lists which form the major input for articulating the IS strategy. As Martin and Leben state,

> *'Critical success factors, and their associated information systems and [management] support systems ... become a vital part of the ongoing process of management.'*

10.3.2 The Andersen Consulting approach

Andersen Consulting is one of the leading international consultancy firms offering a range of services to all sectors of business and commerce as well as the public sector.

Fig 10.5 Critical success factors methodology products

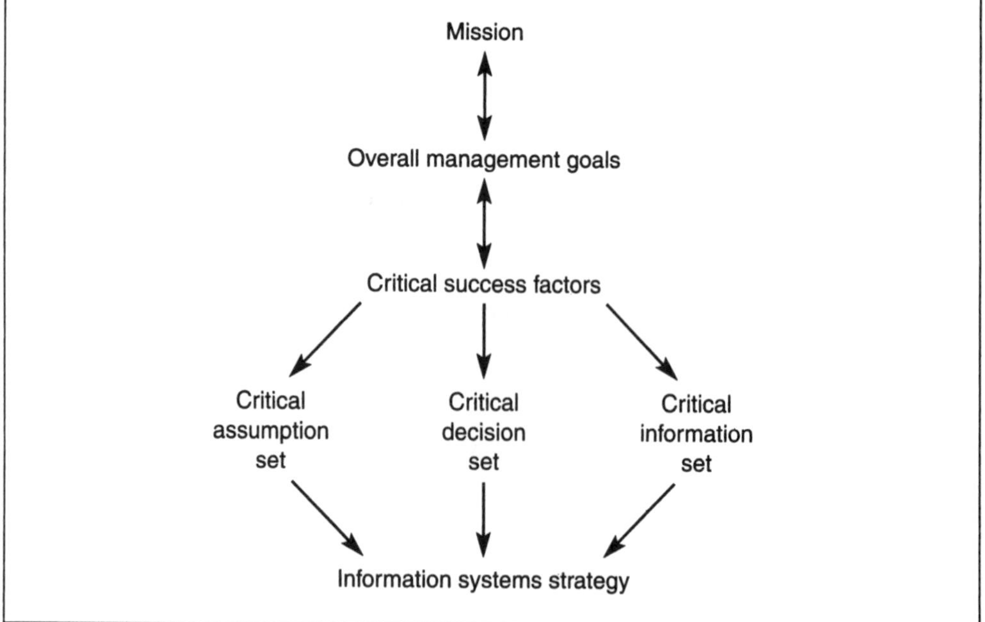

Each deliverable forms the input to the next process.

According to the Management Consultancy survey reported by Abbott (1995), it was the leading management consultant in 1995 (for the fourth consecutive year) and the third major IT consultant.

METHOD/1 from Andersen Consulting is one of the leading methodologies. It provides a development road map by describing a predictable and repeatable process for building information systems. This comprehensive methodology addresses information planning, design, implementation and maintenance. It has evolved into a methodology offering nine fully integrated development routes, as shown in Figure 10.6, which can be scaled and adapted to cater for all sizes of organisations and projects. In addition, it focuses on a number of development approaches, including client/server, host-based and package systems.

Only the Information Planning phase will be considered here. This comprises 10 sections or segments; the first five are used to formulate strategy, taking into account existing organisational status, whilst the remaining five are used to refine the strategy and provide action plans which can be used to drive later elements of the methodology. As can be seen in Figure 10.7, the 10 segments are interrelated with each being broken down into a number of work elements or tasks. A number of steps are defined for each task and, where appropriate, output objects are specified for steps. Deliverables are specified for phases, segments and tasks. The objectives of Information Planning are stated by Andersen Consulting (1995) as being:

- To define the information needs of the organisation's business functions.
- To identify new opportunities for using information to achieve competitive advantage.
- To define information technology requirements to satisfy an organisation's strategic objectives.
- To define the data, application, technology and organisational requirements for supporting the business objectives and functions.
- To define the activities required to implement the information strategy.

Fig 10.6 The nine development routes of METHOD/1

- Information Planning

- Large Client/Server Development

- Small Client/Server Development

- Rapid Client/Server Development

- Large Host-based Development

- Small Host-based Development

- Rapid Host-based Development

- Packaged Systems

- Production Support Systems

Fig 10.7 Information planning in METHOD/1

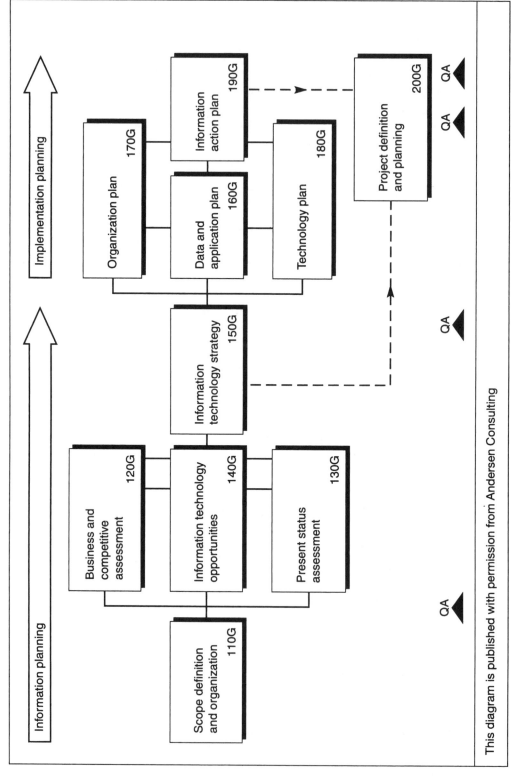

This diagram is published with permission from Andersen Consulting

These objectives are in line with the SISP definition given in Chapter 9. The major outputs from the Information Planning phase are:

- Information Action Plan which is a summary of the findings and recommendations of the information planning project.
- Information Technology Strategy Report which documents the recommended high-level strategies for the organisation's information technology environment.

Many techniques are used within Information Planning. Michael Porter's Five Forces Model and Value Chain Analysis are both used in the Business and Competitive Assessment segment. The value chain is a useful tool for analysing the organisation at a detailed level to determine exactly how a product or service is produced. The chain documents where and how value is added to the product or service.

A number of more generalised techniques are utilised in several of the segments:

- Information Modelling or Entity Relationship Modelling enables information requirements of an organisation to be identified and analysed independent of the technology.
- Decomposition Analysis is useful in progressively breaking down information into the required level of detail. For example, it can be used to investigate organisation structure and function relationships within a business.
- Matrix Analysis is a way of interrelating information gathered during the information project. For example, it can be used to compare key performance indicators against business objectives and to compare identified problems with perceived critical success factors. Many matrices are specified as output objects which are used as input to subsequent segments. For example, an Information Strategy Matrix which describes components that will meet the information systems requirements within the planning horizon and identify the strategies needed to achieve the desired information system is an output from the Information Technology Opportunities segment. Similarly, a Management Assessment Matrix which documents management's evaluations of the activities performed by the information systems department is an output from the Define Strategic Information Needs segment. Both matrices are used as major inputs to the Information Technology Strategy segment which develops high-level technology strategies that sustain organisational information requirements.

One of the striking features of METHOD/1 is its heavy emphasis on management support and management reporting. Indeed, there is a specific task, Obtain Management Commitment, in the Scope Definition and Organisation segment. The objectives of this task are to establish continued senior management involvement in the information planning project and to communicate project scope and objectives to key personnel. Andersen Consulting, quite rightly, argues that senior management provides leadership for the organisation and establishes its culture. Therefore, involvement of senior management is a prerequisite for success in the development of the information plan, as it ensures that the project's objectives and strategies are consistent with those of the organisation and, furthermore, it increases the project's visibility and verifies its importance to the whole organisation.

The methodology stresses the need for formal and informal management briefings during an information planning exercise. Five formal management briefings are recommended where key planning deliverables can be presented. In sequence, these are identified as:

- Review of Project Scope and Approach
- Review Results of Current Status Report
- Presentation of Information Technology Strategy
- Presentation of Organisation, Data and Application and Technology Plans
- Presentation of Information Action Plan

This SISP approach has been used by many organisations across the world. Mainelli and Miller (1988) reported how a team of three Andersen Consulting members and three corporate members developed an IS strategy for the reorganised British Rail. The study focused on the five sectors within British Rail, namely Freight, InterCity, Parcels, Provincial and Network Southeast. The use of a methodology was considered essential in order to ensure suitable procedures were used and that the work was completed as quickly as possible.

A tailored methodology was developed to meet the specific requirements of British Rail. This was based upon METHOD/1, as it was seen to provide the basic procedural structure, and a selection of business analysis tools focused on IT. Utilising the methodology's adaptability characteristic enabled a suitable customised methodology to be derived.

The methodology was successful in identifying opportunities in line with the perceived needs by British Rail management and provided a structure which carefully handled the breadth of management's demand. Mainelli and Miller listed a number of benefits of the approach and these are summarised in Figure 10.8.

METHOD/1 is a very powerful methodology of which SISP is only one element. Its structure enables it to be adapted to differing situations and it is possible to substitute new techniques for those specified in order to accommodate specific contextual requirements or to take advantage of a newly developed approach.

Fig 10.8 The key benefits of an adapted METHOD/1 approach

- Easily understood
- Promotes innovative use of IS/IT
- Equal consideration of all elements of an organisation
- Helps to eliminate information redundancy and omission
- Achieves management consensus through strategic alignment
- Allows for ongoing strategy updates
- Focuses quickly on high priority issues

Using the adaptability characteristic of METHOD/1 a customised methodology was developed for British Rail which had significant benefits. These can be generalised into a list of benefits of using METHOD/1.

10.3.3 The KPMG approach

KPMG Management Consulting is a major international consultancy firm operating throughout the world and incorporating several specialist operations. According to Abbott (1995) it was the seventh largest firm in management consultancy in the UK in 1995 and fourth in IT consultancy. For over ten years KPMG has been evolving its approach to strategic planning for its clients. As one of its companies, Nolan Norton & Co. has been at the forefront of this work.

The SISP methodology by KPMG, Dynamic Systems Planning, comprises eight distinct, though interrelated, stages as shown in Figure 10.9. The methodology and each stage are customised for each strategy exercise, drawing on a repertory of standard techniques. If a suitable technique is not available then a new one is created for the specific task and added to the pool for subsequent projects. So the methodology's pool of techniques is continuously maintained and updated. The aims of the methodology are to seek a broad view concerning the direction and aspirations of the organisation, to define in an objective way the organisational business drivers, to consider IS in the context of all ongoing and planned initiatives within the organisation and so to develop a realistic IS strategy typically for a three to five year period. However, in today's fast-moving business environment, an IS strategy cannot be cast in stone, and needs a degree of flexibility built into it, depending on the perceived likelihood and extent of business change. Dynamic Systems Planning specifically addresses this issue of flexibility which is vital to ensure the ongoing relevance and value of the resulting strategic plans. It would also recommend mechanisms to review the strategy on a regular basis, or whenever there is a major business change.

Initially issues are addressed at a high level, with further specific detail being added, if required, at a later stage. The needs of organisations vary considerably and can be accommodated within the methodology. For example, smaller organisations tend to

Fig 10.9 The KPMG approach to SISP

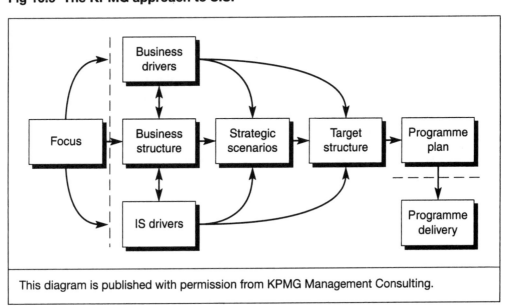

This diagram is published with permission from KPMG Management Consulting.

require more detailed guidance than larger layered organisations. IT staff tend to be less comfortable with looking at the business in a new light in organisations where IS/IT has been a key integral part of the business for many years, for example in the banking and insurance sectors. Considerable cultural differences exist within complex multi-national organisations which will impact upon any strategic programme and must be catered for.

Focus

This initial stage ensures that the work is focused on the key underlying issues and that there is a shared understanding of the work to be undertaken, the style and scope of the result, and the actual deliverables of the project. Sponsorship at board level is secured at this stage. It is here that the methodology is adapted to fit the specific requirements of the organisation and the strategic study. It is important that organisational measures of performance are clearly understood, whether related to the financial performance, customer perspective, processes or continuous improvement. These measures will be used to assess the effectiveness of the developed strategy. A vital element in the Focus stage is agreeing the involvement of key stakeholders and the style of working of the core team who will undertake the exercise and 'own' the strategy.

Business Drivers

The objective of this stage is to gain a thorough understanding of the business, its competitive pressures, its internal tensions and its market, product/service, economic and other goals, for these will significantly influence the IS strategy. Typically Porter's Five Forces Model is used to analyse the competitive environment. A second model is used to consider how the business plans respond to its competitive environment. The model focuses on the interactions between five elements, namely vision and goals, relationships and structure, values and culture, processes and systems, and people and resources. The outcome of this stage will be details of the business direction together with a list of possible strategic opportunities, for example building a learning organisation, or improving market share or providing a new service. The assumptions on which the IS strategy will be developed will be agreed with senior management.

Business Structure

The objective of this stage is to assess the opportunities for changes to business processes and the implications for IS support. This involves building a business model of the organisation and its external relationships. Various techniques are used to create applicable views, which might include a process view, a functional view, value chains, informal influence networks, a location map and data models. This composite view provides in-depth knowledge of how the organisation works and how capable it is of meeting the challenges of its environment. The outcome of this analysis is the identification of key processes that need improvement or redesign and a structure against which to map IS support.

IS Drivers

This stage investigates the potential impact of new technology, the use of technology by competitors and other industries, existing organisational information systems, the underpinning technology, and the organisation's ability to implement strategic change.

By looking externally, the organisation's relative position can be assessed and new ways of exploiting the technology can be identified. An internal investigation using various diagnostic techniques, such as the Strategic Relevance and Impact Grid described in Section 10.2.2, IS management process maturity and effectiveness review, and IS human and technical resources analysis, will uncover applications and service portfolio shortcomings, misalignments and excessive costs.

Some short-term recommendations for improvement may result but longer-term recommendations emerge from the Target Structure stage (see below) once the demands on IS are established. This stage also establishes the baseline for planning the implementation of the strategy.

Strategic Scenarios

The Business Drivers, Business Structures and IS Drivers stages all feed into the Strategic Scenarios stage where a number of strategic options are developed. For example, a company may wish to reduce the lead time from customer order to despatch but needs to consider the implications of simply reducing the cycle time or making the radical change from produce-to-plan to produce-to-order. Similarly, an organisation may wish to investigate the impact of radically different strategies, for example focusing upon creating outstanding products or focusing upon customer service. This is a creative process in which future business and IS scenarios are generated. These are then compared in order to create and agree a compelling, yet implementable vision of the organisation in the future. This scenario will cover a number of perspectives including business processes, effects on customers and suppliers, organisational roles and responsibilities, and the information systems portfolio. Links to the overall business direction are clearly identified as are outline costs and benefits.

Target Structure

The objective of this stage is to refine and expand the chosen scenario. This is done under a number of categories as shown in Table 10.1. The business structure categories provide a clear and detailed focus of how the organisation is to be changed and how the effectiveness of that change is to be judged. This in turn leads to demands for support from those involved in implementing this new business plan. Together these varying demands form the demand side architecture. IS resources need to be available to satisfy these demands. These are identified by considering the items in the supply side architecture. This information is then used to identify discrete business projects and their supporting IT infrastructure.

Programme Plan

The Programme Plan stage addresses the following issues:
- Implementation strategy
- Programme management and control
- Links to other change initiatives
- Change management approaches
- Communications
- Benefits management
- Strategy and plan maintenance

Table 10.1 The framework for expanded detail of the chosen scenario

Business structure	Demand side architecture	Supply side architecture
• Redesigned processes	• Application structure	• IS skills
• Organisation, roles and responsibilities	• IS proposals	• IS organisation
• Performance measures and targets	• Data models	• Technology use
• Management plans	• User roles	• Supply strategy
	• Education and training	• IS management practices
		• Standards and methods
The target business and IS structure provides more detail for the chosen scenario which enables specific projects to be identified, cost and benefits to be calculated and detailed implementation plans to be formulated.		

The plan needs to recognise that there will be different target dates for different elements and that the business and its environment are continually changing. Therefore, the programme plan not only provides direction for individual projects but also promotes a strategic culture and mechanisms which enable the organisation to respond to future change.

Programme Delivery

This is the culmination of the strategic exercise. Senior managers maintain involvement through monitoring the programme via the plan. The strategy provides a framework in which to make new decisions and modify actions in response to organisational and business environment changes.

10.3.4 The Boston Consulting Group approach

The Boston Consulting Group is a long-established international consultancy firm with over 30 offices located in the business centres of the world. It offers a comprehensive set of methodologies, techniques and tools which address the various aspects of business management and operation. Its integrative approach to consultancy promotes alignment of the different corporate resources, capabilities and actions of its clients. This approach involves undertaking specifically focused assignments whilst maintaining a holistic perspective of the client organisation.

This section considers just one methodology, Strategic Workforce Development (SWD) (The Boston Consulting Group, 1994) which promotes strategic culture in organisations. As explained in Chapter 9, the combination of and interaction between SISP and SCB are very important in establishing a properly aligned IS strategy which is considered achievable by all concerned. The overall aims of SWD are to ensure that organisational change is facilitated, that the workforce is regarded as a valuable corporate asset, that key skills are nurtured, that workforce morale is high and that work groups operate effectively. The realisation of these aims will result in a strategic culture being sustained.

SWD comprises six steps, as shown in Figure 10.10, which address four central issues:

1. Choosing the overall level of staffing, choosing the right mix of in-house and contracted-out activities, and ensuring that resources are efficiently used.
2. Identifying, developing and maintaining employee skills that are critical to the organisation's success.
3. Motivating successful behaviours among employees through reward systems, cultural norms or other means.
4. Enhancing group capabilities through the design of jobs, work processes and team structures.

Assess the Drivers of Change

The aim of this step is to develop an understanding of the organisation's workforce and the forces that are affecting it. These will include aspects of corporate policy, technology utilisation, the labour market and the business environment as a whole.

Segment into Job Families

The aim of this step is to split the workforce into groups comprising jobs of a similar nature. These groups are called job families. The step establishes which families are priority and warrant further review. This comprises identifying:

- Those involved with the business processes that are critical to the success of the organisation.
- Job families with current deficiencies, for example weak performance or under-staffing.
- Job families in need of change because of, for example, changing technology or work methods.

Define Job Family Needs

The objective of this step is to define current and future development needs of the part of workforce identified as being vital to organisational success. This involves analysing the impact of the drivers of change on job family activities. This leads to the identification of required changes in workforce capabilities. Staffing levels may need to be adjusted. Existing skills may need to be enhanced or replaced. Employee motivation may need to be lifted through, for example, alternative promotion paths and providing the necessary training to allow staff to compete for these new opportunities. Finally, changes in group structures and processes may be necessary to enable a strategic culture to flourish.

Evaluate Approaches to Meeting Job Family Needs

The Boston Consulting Group describe a set of management tools that may be used to resolve each type of job family need. This set is shown in Table 10.2. The choice of

Fig 10.10 The six steps of Strategic Workforce Development

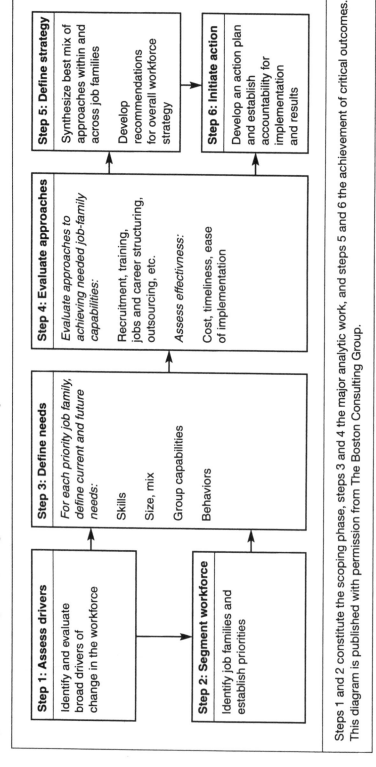

Step 1: Assess drivers

Identify and evaluate broad drivers of change in the workforce

Step 2: Segment workforce

Identify job families and establish priorities

Step 3: Define needs

For each priority job family, define current and future needs:

Skills

Size, mix

Group capabilities

Behaviors

Step 4: Evaluate approaches

Evaluate approaches to achieving needed job-family capabilities:

Recruitment, training, jobs and career structuring, outsourcing, etc.

Assess effectivness:

Cost, timeliness, ease of implementation

Step 5: Define strategy

Synthesize best mix of approaches within and across job families

Develop recommendations for overall workforce strategy

Step 6: Initiate action

Develop an action plan and establish accountability for implementation and results

Steps 1 and 2 constitute the scoping phase, steps 3 and 4 the major analytic work, and steps 5 and 6 the achievement of critical outcomes. This diagram is published with permission from The Boston Consulting Group.

Table 10.2 The management tools to address workforce needs

WORKFORCE NEEDS		MANAGEMENT TOOLS										
		Hiring/ Recruiting	Transfers	Retention	Outsourcing	Training	Career Progression	Job Structure	Work Processes	Reward Systems	Communication	Culture
	Workforce Size, Mix	✔	✔	✔	✔							
	Employee Skills	✔	✔		✔	✔	✔	✔				
	Group Capabilities					✔	✔	✔	✔	✔	✔	
	Employee Behavior					✔	✔	✔	✔	✔	✔	✔

✔ Primary Tools

In the context of this book, the management tools set is best considered as a set of techniques. Each specific approach to meeting a job family need has different characteristics and associated issues. For example using outsourcing to satisfy a deficiency in employee skills will be dependent upon availability, cost task interdependence and confidentiality. This diagram is published with permission from The Boston Consulting Group.

tools will depend on effectiveness, cost, ease of implementation and fit with existing organisational programmes.

Define Strategies Across Job Families

Having analysed the priority job families in detail, this step consolidates the necessary actions required to achieve the necessary changes that have been identified. Thus a strategic action plan is established for the organisation which will guide the effective development of a workforce that can contribute fully to the organisation's strategy, its development of competitively distinctive capabilities and the creation of a strategic culture with the workforce which sustains success.

Initiate Action

The task in this final step is to define and begin to implement detailed action plans. It is important to establish senior management attention and support in advance of this implementation and involve them through the programme.

10.4 SUMMARY

This chapter has considered a selection of popular SISP techniques and methodologies. Sufficient detail has been provided for the techniques together with the CSF methodology to enable the reader to use them in SISP activities. The examples of methodologies offered by major international consultancy firms were compared and contrasted.

With so many different techniques and methodologies being available it is vital that careful consideration is taken in the selection of an approach. This is discussed further in the next chapter. Methodologies, techniques and tools are no substitute for clear thinking and insight. However, they do help is to organise and present ideas and they can be extremely powerful if applied in a flexible and pragmatic manner. This will be considered further in the next chapter.

CASE STUDY: EUROPEAN PAPER GROUP

IS Strategy for a European Paper Group

Background

Whilst some markets operate around long-term bulk orders for regular delivery, certain other markets require a highly responsive service (typically next day delivery) and such is the nature of the paper industry. The industry is also very cost competitive and requires a high level of investment in plant. These factors have driven paper companies to have local merchant operations to meet the required customer service levels, given that manufacturing is ideally located near the source of the main raw material – wood pulp – which in turn is usually situated near softwood forests, well away from the markets. The big paper manufacturers therefore generally face a supply chain problem.

The need for an IS strategy

PaperCo is part of a group which sells other wood and paper products. It has a number of major mills in Northern Europe, and has recently acquired several new sales organisations and merchants in countries where it did not operate previously. During the last decade, it had developed a leading edge computer system which allowed its merchants to input orders on-line into its mills' order processing system, track progress to delivery at the sales organisation and produce invoices. At that time the mills were the most powerful parts of the organisation and the system was designed primarily around their need to collect orders quickly and schedule production efficiently.

More recently the support for this core application had been reduced and little in the way of enhancement had been carried out. The business had also changed by altering the relationship of the merchants to the mills. Previously the merchants had received a percentage of the selling price whereas now they are profit centres (some not even wholly owned), and may even sell competitive products. They now buy at a transfer price from the mills and set their own sales prices. The group culture has moved from a focus on production volumes and cost to a focus on the customer and profitability. There was also an increasing demand for the merchants (and their customers) to know with some accuracy, if they had no local stock available, when their supplier orders would be received, or whether they needed to be made specially to order. These factors led the organisation to question

▶

whether this core sales system was viable for the future, and in general what systems should be common and how much local merchants should be allowed to 'do their own thing'.

The business drivers and processes

An examination of the business direction with the senior management led to a recognition that in order to decide which systems should be common and which local, a model of the business processes needed to be established. This was duly done and as a result a business opportunity was uncovered to redesign the total supply chain to optimise stock levels, production capacity and customer service needs. This together with changes in performance measurement and accountabilities in the organisation was the main driver for the development of a new IS strategy.

IS review

An IS review was carried out for the central systems group (which managed the core sales system), the relatively small IS groups (in some cases one person) in each merchant, and the manufacturing systems at each mill. This review was focused on the functional quality (user view) and the technical quality (IS view) of the old core sales system together with the capabilities of the IS people in the merchants. The review revealed that the most recent users of the core sales system regarded it quite well whereas users with longer experience had a lower satisfaction. A number of areas for enhancement were identified. Technically the application was quite sound but it was based on an 'old' environment (COBOL and an IBM mainframe).

There was a large variety of manufacturing systems and platforms at each mill and some mills were considering replacement.

Strategic scenarios

The business decided to press ahead with the redesign of the supply chain from sales to mill production scheduling and distribution, and this work was carried on in parallel with the IS stream but coordinated with it. This redesign required a number of factors to be considered, such as the rules for trading between the mills and the local sales organisations, and the allocation of orders. It also led to the creation of a new central group in the organisation to coordinate logistics world wide.

Target structure

The mapping of the current core sales system on to the business process model indicated that the sales system's scope was far beyond that required for the redesigned supply chain – for example it carried out some financial functions. The scope of the future core sales system was defined and agreed and this led to a policy for which systems needed to be common and what could be local with defined interfaces to the common systems. The next question was whether the existing platform for the new system should remain the same. A number of alternatives were examined:

1. Continue to upgrade system on the IBM mainframe,
2. Upgrade only the core parts of the system dealing with the supply chain, and migrate non-core parts to local systems,
3. As above but replace the core with a standard package,
4. Distribute the application to local platforms using a standard common package.

The strengths, weaknesses, costs and risks of these options were evaluated and option 2 was chosen. The old system worked predominantly with dumb terminals whereas the upgrade was planned to work using a PC front end to improve user-friendliness and local analysis capabilities. This meant that standards for local platforms (particularly PCs) needed to be established and an overhaul of the communications architecture was needed. The new network was outsourced together with voice telecommunications to save money.

There were considerable non-financial benefits in having a common manufacturing system for the mills, run on local platforms, including the simplification of interfacing to the new core sales system. The strategy was therefore to get the mills to agree on a preferred (i.e. not mandatory) manufacturing system which would then guide the choice of hardware platform. When a mill wanted to change its systems it had to make a clear business case for not migrating onto the preferred common system.

Option 4 was rejected as a result of recognising that business flexibility would come from a very high degree of information sharing across PaperCo: a distributed computing solution would be extremely complex and difficult to manage.

Programme plan

The projects identified included :

- Communicate IS strategy, changes in business direction and agree on business unit consequences.
- Redesign common sales/supply chain business process.
- Enhance core sales system.
- Agree on a preferred common manufacturing system and install in two mills.

- Redesign mill to sales organisation transport system.
- Establish a central supply chain co-ordination function.
- Establish improved price rules and new pricing systems.
- Review financial systems.
- Introduce a new Management Information System.
- Personal productivity (introduction of PCs with common software).

These projects were all planned out over a two-year time frame with strong co-ordination between projects and change management considerations.

Learning point

The key learning for the client was the need to rethink certain fundamental business processes and rules as a prerequisite for improving IS, and the need to invest in the existing systems rather than adopting a distributed solution which at first appeared attractive and low cost, but would actually have been very complex to manage. ∎

Reprinted with permission from *KPMG Management Consulting* 1995.

References

Abbott P (1995) Survey. *Management Consultancy*, July/August, pp 16–29.

Andersen Consulting (1995) *METHOD/1 Information Planning Version 9.5*, Arthur Andersen & Co.

The Boston Consulting Group (1994) *Strategic Workforce Development*. The Boston Consulting Group Inc. Boston MA

Boynton A C, Zmud R W (1984) An assessment of critical success factors. *Sloan Management Review*. Summer, Vol 25, No 4.

Bullen C V, Rockart J F (1981) *A primer on critical success factors*. CISR Working Paper Number 69. Sloan School of Management, MIT, June.

Cash J I, Konsynski B R (1985) IS redraws competitive boundaries. *Harvard Business Review*, March–April.

Earl M J (1989) *Management Strategies for Information Technology*. Prentice Hall, Hemel Hempstead.

Lee M C S, Adams D A (1990) A manager's guide to strategic potential of information systems. *Information and Management*. Vol 19, pp. 169–182.

Madnick S E (editor) (1987) *The Strategic Use of Information Technology*. Oxford University Press.

Mainelli M R, Miller D R (1988) Strategic planning for information systems at British Rail. *Long Range Planning*, Vol 21, No 4, pp. 65–75.

Martin J, Leben J (1989) *Strategic Information Planning Methodologies*. Prentice Hall.

McFarlan F W, McKenny J L, Pyburn P (1983) The information archipelago – plotting a course. *Harvard Business Review*, January–February, pp. 145–156.

Peppard J (editor) (1993) *IT Strategy for Business*. Pitman Publishing London.

Porter M E (1979) How competitive forces shape strategy. *Harvard Business Review*, March–April, pp. 137–145.

Porter M E, Millar V E (1985) How information gives you competitive advantage. *Harvard Business Review*, July–August, pp. 149–160.

Remenyi D S J (1991) *Introducing Strategic Information Systems Planning*. NCC Blackwell.

Rockart J F (1979) The changing role of the information systems executive: a critical success factors perspective. *Harvard Business Review*, March–April, pp. 81–93.

Rockart J F (1982) The changing role of the information systems executive: a critical success factors perspective. *Sloan Management Review*. Fall, Vol 28, No 1.

Silk D J (1991) *Planning IT: Creating an Information Management Strategy*. Butterworth Heinemann Oxford.

Ward J, Griffiths P, Whitmore P (1990) *Strategic Planning for Information Systems*. John Wiley Chichester.

Review questions

1 What are the five competitive elements? Give examples of each.

2 What roles can the five forces model play in a SISP exercise?

3 Explain the strategic relevance and impact grid.

4 What are the objectives of information planning in METHOD/1?

5 Explain the three domains in the benefits-beneficiary matrix.

6 What is the Critical Decision Set. Illustrate your answer with suitable examples.

7 What are the major differences and similarities in the SISP approach between KPMG Management Consulting and Andersen Consulting?

8 Explain the role of Strategic Strategies in the KPMG approach.

9 Is Strategic Workforce Development relevant to SISP? Justify your response.

Project idea

The aim of this project is to investigate the usefulness of a SISP tool. Undertake the following tasks:

- Identify six common information systems used within manufacturing organisations.
- Using the Strategic Relevance and Impact grid decide upon the value and role of each system. Justify your decision.
- Contact two disparate manufacturing companies who utilise IS/IT and identify where each company would allocate the six systems on the grid. Try to get more than one view from each company.
- Analyse the collected data to ascertain differences and similarities between your original ideas and the perceptions of both organisations
- What conclusions can be drawn from this outcome?

CHAPTER 11

How to Perform a SISP Exercise

11.1 INTRODUCTION

Having considered what SISP is in Chapter 9 and looked at typical techniques and methodologies in Chapter 10 it is now time to consider the practical implementation of a SISP exercise. The SISP exercise is a short, intensive period of gathering and filtering information and drawing conclusions. Many senior members of staff and management will have to devote much time in interviews and feedback and this represents a commitment to the subsequent implementation. It is an investment for the future. Given the short timescales and the need to involve many people within the organisation it is essential that the right approaches are adopted.

Section 11.2 considers the factors which influence the successful outcome of a SISP exercise. One of the most important factors is the composition of the SISP team and this is discussed in detail in Section 11.3. Account must be taken of the profile of an organisation. This is the subject of Section 11.4. Given the numerous methodologies and techniques available it is important to choose an appropriate one. A way in which this can be done is covered in Section 11.5. Section 11.6 gives a checklist of how to undertake an effective SISP exercise. Finally, Section 11.7 provides a summary of the chapter.

At the end of this chapter the reader should understand:

- *The factors that influence the success of a SISP exercise*
- *The composition of a SISP team*
- *How to select appropriate methodologies and techniques.*

11.2 SUCCESSFUL SISP

There are many factors which affect the outcome of a SISP exercise. For example, KPMG (1994) suggest that the success of a SISP exercise depends on a number of factors that have coloured the approach adopted by KPMG as described in Chapter 10. These factors are summarised as:

- Ensuring that the IS strategy supports the organisation's mission and helps to achieve business goals.
- Producing a strategy which can be adapted when circumstances change.

- Identifying improvements to business processes and structures in conjunction with better IS support rather than assuming existing processes and structures.
- Taking into account new technology and competitors' use of IS.
- Recognising business projects, rather than IS projects, which could involve changes to technology, processes, organisational arrangements, people, culture and performance measures.
- Understanding the capabilities of the organisation to manage change and its existing information systems function.
- Promoting strategy ownership by the organisation's management.
- Taking strategy forward to implementation.

Due to the relatively short timescale of a SISP exercise, Barker (1988) explains that it is vital to use every means possible to gain an understanding of the business. These include:

- Active participation of key executives, opinion leaders, representative workers and others who collectively understand what is needed.
- Early correction of opinions, ideas and the business model.
- An effective and thorough feedback session to resolve misconceptions.
- Taking due account of previous work and existing systems since duplication of effort damages credibility.

Strategy formulation has evolved alongside information technology evolution. One of the main reasons for this is that as the technology has advanced so its impact has been greater and wider within organisations. How a SISP exercise is undertaken has changed through experience. According to Miles (1985), four major lessons have been learnt from these experiences.

1. *Strategy formulation relies upon realistic challenge.* This involves ensuring that corporate goals are reconciled with the realistic achievement potential of the organisation.
2. *Strategy is not operational planning.* A strategy is a blend of creativity, analysis and operational knowledge, whilst an operational plan is a numerical representation of this strategy.
3. *Each organisation is different.* A SISP exercise should be carefully tailored to the organisation and issues in question. The processes and concepts in strategy formulation must reflect differences in organisational characteristics and potential.
4. *Strategy must be integrated.* SISP exercises must involve management at all levels. The overall organisational aims must be clearly understood by all. Organisational components must be transparent, mutually appreciated and operating in harmony. Working together creates a common understanding and real commitment within management teams.

To facilitate improvement a feedback mechanism should exist that monitors and controls the SISP process. This will ensure that it is functioning effectively and provides the basis for corrective action if it is not. Baker (1995) argues that such feedback mechanisms rarely exist and this could be the main reason why SISP is often perceived to be problematic. Thus experiential learning by SISP participants is not being used to refine the SISP approach within organisations and so the lessons learnt, as described by Miles, go unheeded.

11.3 TEAM MEMBERS

Regardless of the approach adopted to achieve strategic advancement in the use of IS/IT, the one thing that remains constant is the need to establish an effective working relationship between IS personnel and staff within the rest of the organisation. Whilst it appears obvious that good teamwork will improve the chances of success, it is another thing to achieve this in practice. The creation and sustaining of an effective partnership was the subject of empirical research undertaken by Henderson (1990) in which he interviewed a number of executives within organisations to ascertain the IS-client relationship within organisations and how these were sustained. Henderson identified six areas that need to be addressed:

- *Education* – Shared knowledge is a critical element in the ability to participate in and influence decisions. Training in activities where there is a high interdependency between IS and other staff is essential. Team members must understand and appreciate the value of each others contributions. It is important that team members have experience of the organisation's social and cultural ethos.
- *Joint planning* – SISP must be a joint activity in which agreement on perceived benefits is achieved through negotiation and a common goal is identified and articulated. The activity must be ongoing and iterative.
- *Measurement and control* – The team must have the ability to identify and create appropriate measures to monitor activities and judge performance.
- *Effective use of teams* – Teams must comprise all relevant organisational functions as this is the means of securing wide commitment and accessing diverse knowledge and experience.
- *Multi-level team strategy* – It is important to establish rapport across all levels of the organisation so that a strategic culture is promoted through the organisation. Different aspects of strategy formulation will require input from not only different areas of the organisation but also staff operating at different levels.
- *Technology* – This is used to facilitate communication amongst the team using, for example, e-mail, video conferencing, and the use of group decision making support facilities.

11.3.1 The role of consultants

There is frequently a role within a SISP exercise for an outside consultant. A consultant can introduce a degree of objectivity which might be difficult for those within the organisation who are too close to the problems and who have vested interests. A consultant will be able to suggest courses of action which might be effective though unpopular and therefore employees might be reluctant to put them forward themselves. Finally, consultants can bring expertise to the exercise which is not available within the organisation and will be able to direct and encourage staff in undertaking the SISP exercise in an effective manner. This was the case at Business Link Leicestershire (this case study is described in detail in Chapter 15), where the authors acting as consultants used various SISP techniques to derive an IS strategy. The staff at BLL were guided through the exercise and were spared the task of having to learn how to apply the techniques. This enabled them to focus upon the findings and consider what the resulting action should be taking into account the consultants' observations and recommendations.

11.3.2 Team structure

The team undertaking the SISP exercise must represent all interested parties. The composition of the team will vary between organisations and will depend upon the scope of the exercise. This was discussed in detail in Section 9.5.1, where it was explained that the strategic focus of the exercise was dependent upon who was involved in the planning activity. For example, an exercise which is being undertaken within a small autonomous division of a large conglomerate is likely to have a small localised team to produce a detailed divisional strategy. Only a brief outline will be passed upwards to the centre. In contrast, an exercise which is to develop an IS strategy for the whole of a large multi-national organisation will involve several layers of management throughout the organisation, including significant effort from the senior executive. Consultants are likely to be involved in this major exercise.

The team structure shown in Figure 11.1 comprises representatives from all relevant functional areas within the organisation, representatives from the IS department and staff representatives. The latter are included because due consideration should be given to the impact on social groupings, staff establishments, changes in work profiles. Senior executives must provide input to the exercise as well as being the recipients of the output. It is important that there is real support and commitment at the highest levels and hence the inclusion of an executive sponsor. Within the team there must exist sufficient SISP expertise to ensure the appropriate choice and use of methodologies and techniques. The team leader will greatly influence the success of the exercise. The team leader must by objective, equally comfortable with business and IS/IT matters, and politically astute.

Fig 11.1 SISP team structure

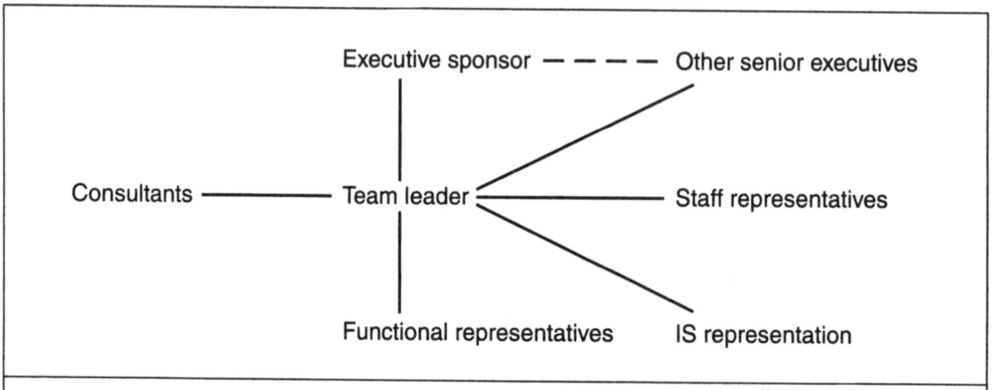

The diagram shows the different groups likely to be involved in a SISP exercise. The team composition will vary for each organisation as will the role, responsibility and authority of each individual.

11.4 ORGANISATIONAL DIFFERENCES

Each organisation, even within the same operating sector, is different. An organisation will have its own operating style which is influenced by the operating environment, the organisation's decision makers and its work force. There are two main characteristics of organisational difference that will influence the utilisation and effectiveness of SISP. These are size and stability. It is common for organisations to be categorised as small / medium (often termed SMEs) or large. SMEs typically have a workforce of less than 400, a turnover of less than £10m and a small number of operating locations. Large organisations are characterised by large workforces, several operational locations, large turnovers, divisional organisation structures and several lines of business. Stability is concerned with the influence of the operating environment. A volatile environment caused by, for example, new competitor products, or a shrinking or expanding market, or radical new legislation, will cause an organisation to be dynamic. A stable operational environment where a status quo might exist between competitors and the size of the market is stable will make an organisation more static in its business approach.

SISP methodologies tend to address the needs of large organisations and need to be adapted for smaller organisations if they are to be effective. The reason for this is examined by Bergeron and Raymond (1992). They explain that SMEs have advantages related to their size and flexibility in that they can rapidly change orientation, implement major decisions and relocate to new markets. However, they lack financial, human and information resources to undertake thorough analyses of their operations and environments and so planning and decision making tends to be intuitive. This, coupled with the dependency on a few key individuals, leads to significant challenges for the development and implementation of IS. In these situations, the main thrust of the adapted methodology is to derive an IS portfolio focused on competitive advantage. The activities within the methodology are simplified and reliance on a mentor, probably a consultant, to guide the owners and managers through the SISP process is stressed.

An evaluation of 56 organisations, by Burn (1993), focused on the relationship between organisational types and alternative patterns of IS development. Burn found that the planning approach changed as organisations become more mature in their use of IS/IT and as IS/IT permeates the organisation. There is a tendency to change from a bottom-up or functional-based orientation to a top-down orientation and, finally, to the use of a multiple approach in a mature environment. Burn also found that different types of organisations preferred different approaches. Simple organisations preferred bottom-up approaches, professional and manufacturing organisations preferred top-down approaches. Where divisions existed within organisations, a multiple approach was prevalent.

Organisations which have goals other than profit (for the shareholders) will be influenced by different factors when undertaking SISP. Local government organisations are a good example. Flynn and Hepburn (1994) present a case study of a UK metropolitan council which examines over an 11 year period the approach the council has evolved to develop an IS strategy. It was found that the approach had remained basically non-strategic and IT-led primarily because of three main forces which were determining the nature of planning. These were the views of the departments, the views of the central IT unit and the views of the centre comprising the executive group and pressure groups including councillors. Departments sought autonomy to develop their business activities which in turn led to applying IT to activities and problems independent of other departments. The central IT unit was able to provide shareable data and economies of scale in hardware and software division but did not understand either departmental business activities or information needs. The executive and pressure groups were not convinced about the electoral benefits of IT and government legislation had created a climate in which council services needed to be efficient and competitive. This case study illustrates the tensions that can develop within an organisation when different factions have different agendas. Such situations become organisationally political rather than strategically focused.

11.4.1 Matching organisations and SISP approaches

An indication of the appropriate strategic approach for an organisation can be identified using the two organisational characteristics of size and stability. This is done using the organisation structure grid shown in Figure 11.2. Within each quadrant are specified four major attributes of the strategic approach. These are: frequency, team, approach and dominant philosophy. The frequency of undertaking a strategy exercise is important. This will either be periodically, say every 12 months, or on an *ad hoc* basis to respond quickly to changing circumstances. The team size will vary dependent upon the size of the organisation and the likely impact of the derived strategy. The approach adopted will range from being informal to being very structured or formalised. The

Fig 11.2 Organisation structure grid

	SIZE	
	Small/medium organisations	Large organisations
Static	• Periodic frequency • Small team • Informal approach • Planning domination	• Periodic frequency • Medium/large team • Formal approach • Planning domination
Dynamic	• *Ad hoc* frequency • Small/medium team • Informal approach • Culture domination	• *Ad hoc* frequency • Medium/large team • Formal approach • Planning and culture balanced

STABILITY

The grid indicates the overriding principles to adopt in different organisations in order to improve the chances of a successful IS strategic approach.

dominant philosophy is concerned with whether a planning process is more prevalent or whether a strategic culture pervades. This idea was discussed in Chapter 9.

Thus, identification of the quadrant in which a particular organisation is located results in some guiding principles being identified for addressing strategy effectively. For example, a small manufacturing company operating in a growing marketplace with a small number of similar sized competitors needs to approach IS strategy in a dynamic way (frequency) so that it can respond quickly to market forces and have the opportunity to become the market leader. The small group (team) involved in strategic formulation must interact in a flexible way (approach) and encourage a proactive workforce (strategic culture). In general, organisations will be placed in either the small/medium-dynamic quadrant or the large-static quadrant.

11.5 CHOOSING METHODOLOGIES AND TECHNIQUES

Connor (1993) points out that the selection of an appropriate methodology or technique is often difficult because of the number available and because they are not directly equivalent. Different approaches are applicable to different situations. In a survey of 73 organisations, Fidler, Rogerson and Spiers (1993) found that organisations using SISP tend to use more than one approach. There is a greater tendency to use methods in organisations with more IS staff which is related to the size of the organisation. This proliferation of methods could indicate a need for tighter control as different departments are adopting different approaches to their planning needs. Alternatively, it may indicate the inappropriateness of a single approach when faced with disparate problems within organisations. It is clear that guidance is needed to identify what is an appropriate technique or methodology for a given situation.

11.5.1 A classification framework for SISP

A classification framework for providing such guidance has been developed by Fidler and Rogerson (1994a and 1994b). The framework involves the evaluation of methodologies on two dimensions: structural complexity and application complexity. Structural complexity is the complexity that exists within the methodology itself. It is concerned with the composition of the methodology and the rules governing its application. Application complexity is concerned with the participants and their background, aims and experiences, with organisational and societal influences on SISP, and with SISP evolution. Structural complexity is independent of the context in which the SISP methodology is being applied, whereas application complexity encompasses the contextual aspects.

The criteria for evaluating structural complexity are:

1. The ability of the methodology to adapt to requirements
2. The number of possible ways techniques can interrelate
3. The rule prescriptiveness within the methodology
4. The number of techniques within the methodology
5. The constituency of the methodology
6. The potential for ambiguity in terminology.

Criterion 5, constituency, relates to the decomposition of the methodology into its constituent elements based upon the three-level decomposition model of a methodology techniques to tools which has been explained in Chapter 9. Criteria are interdependent. For example, if the methodology rule prescriptiveness (criterion 3) is high, complexity will be reduced and it is likely to constrain the possible interactions between techniques (criterion 2) which again will reduce complexity. This structural complexity model can be applied to techniques themselves by simply considering a technique as a one-technique methodology.

The criteria for evaluating application complexity are:

1. The evolution rate of the methodology – does it change frequently or remain static?
2. The objectives of the participants – are they unitary (all of one mind), pluralistic (not all of one mind but wishing to achieve consensus) or coercive (not of one mind and not intending to be)?
3. The planning policies of the organisation – how prescriptive are they?
4. The number of participants involved
5. The participants' experience of SISP – are they new to the process or have they encountered similar situations before?
6. The participants' comprehension of the terminology used – are there possibilities of misrepresentation and ambiguity amongst individuals and the group as a whole?

Criterion 1 is concerned with difficulty of use. If a methodology evolves rapidly then it is more difficult to maintain currency in the use of that methodology. Again there is criteria interdependency. For example, where the number of participants is small (criterion 4), it may be less likely that they operate coercively (criterion 2).

By allocating values to these criteria comparisons can be made of different methodologies and techniques. The way in which values are allocated is shown in Figure 11.3.

Having derived the values for structural and application complexity these can now be used to consider who should be involved in the SISP excise. This is important because the exercise is reliant upon effective use of the methodology being evaluated. A complexity grid, as shown in Figure 11.4, is used in this evaluation. The four quadrants on the grid represent the need for different expertise in undertaking the SISP exercise. Information systems expertise is required to cope with high structural complexity as a working knowledge of the methodology, experience of several practical applications of the methodology and, possibly, some formal training is required. Senior IS professionals are more likely to possess such skills than any other group. Hybrid expertise is needed to cope with high application complexity. This expertise embraces an adequate competence in using the technology and an adequate competence in the application area being investigated. Where both structural complexity and application complexity are high, a person (or persons) with in-depth knowledge of the tool and the business situation is required, almost a 'super hybrid'. This will enable a better fit between SISP methodology utilisation and organisational need to be achieved. Minimal help is required with a methodology of low structural and application complexity.

The complexity grid can be used in a variety of ways. For example, by keeping structural complexity constant, it can be used to investigate the merit of using a particular methodology over a wide range of application situations. This would be a useful analysis for management consultants offering SISP services. Positioning different methodologies on the same complexity grid over similar application contexts

Fig 11.3 Structural and application complexity values

Value Criteria	1	2	3	4	5
STRUCTURAL					
S1 Ability to adapt	none	change parameters	change operation	change rules	change concepts
S2 No. of ways to interrelate	only one way	a few	several	many	free hand
S3 Rule prescriptiveness	very stringent	stringent	some freedom	loose	very loose
S4 No. of techniques	< 2	< 4	< 6	< 8	>= 8
S5 Constituency of methodology	see Note 1				
Constituency of each technique	see Note 2				
Constituency of each tool in a technique	simple	relatively simple	average	relatively intricate	very intricate
S6 Ambiguity of terminology	very clear	clear	average	unclear	very unclear
APPLICATION					
A1 Evolution rate	static	slow	gradual	fast	volatile
A2 Objectives of participants	unitary		pluralistic		coercive
A3 Planning policy	very formalised	formalised	some structure	unstructured	non-existent
A4 No. of participants	< 5	< 10	< 15	< 20	>= 20
A5 Experience of SISP	considerable	significant	some	scant	none
A6 Comprehension of participants	full	in outline	some	unclear	little

Each criterion is given a value on a five-point Likert scale where 1 represents the least complex and 5 represents the most complex. The table provides guidance as to what each value represents.
Note 1 This is the summation of individual technique constituency values divided by the number of techniques
Note 2 This is the summation of the individual tool constituency values divided by the number of tools.

Fig 11.4 The complexity grid

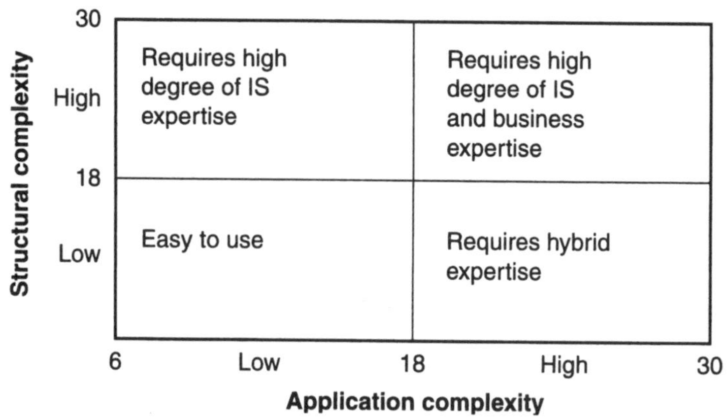

The vertical axis represents structural complexity and the horizontal axis represents application complexity. The values are the summations of the six respective criterion values.

provides a way of comparing methodologies, as well as giving advice as to how to support the methodology in use. This approach was used in an empirical research project undertaken by Partridge, Fidler and Rogerson (1994) to compare a number of SISP techniques. The majority of techniques were found to be just below the mid-point line of structural complexity indicating some IS input in all situations.

Another method for evaluation and comparison is the spatial profile shown in Figure 11.5. A visual profile of a methodology is produced by plotting its 12 criteria values onto the chart and joining up these 12 points. Shapes will differ between methodologies when in the same context and by viewing charts of different methodologies it can be seen where complexity lies, with application complexity, where the shape is oriented to the bottom, or with structural complexity, where the shape is oriented towards the top. The size and shape indicates the relative overall complexity of the methodology.

To illustrate how the complexity framework might be used, the complexity grid and spatial profile chart are now produced for the Business Link Leicestershire case study. For the SISP exercise, the consultants chose a set of appropriate techniques with the results of one feeding into another. By using different tools it was possible to analyse the organisation from different perspectives. The techniques used were SWOT analysis, Critical Success Factors, Information Needs Analysis and Matrix, Strategic Relevance and Impact Grid, and Value Chain Analysis. Together they formed a customised methodology. It is the analysis of this customised methodology that is shown in Figure 11.6. The spatial profile chart illustrates how the adopted approach is quite complex mainly due to the inherent flexibility of a 'bespoke' methodology such as this. The complexity grid highlights the need for a considerable amount of IS and business expertise to ensure that this is an effective approach. Given that this is a typical business link, the analysis provides an indication of the resources that are required to undertake a SISP exercise in any business link and highlights the particular aspects of the approach that require careful management.

Fig 11.5 Spatial profile

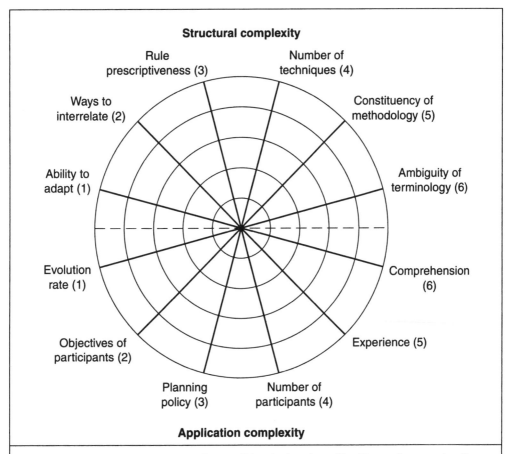

The five concentric circles represent the possible criteria values. The 12 equally spaced radii represent the 12 SISP complexity criteria, the six on the top representing structural complexity and the six on the bottom representing application complexity. The criteria are ordered to convey which criteria are central to each dimension and which criteria lie on the boundary between the two dimensions. Values are mapped onto this chart to produce a methodology profile.

In choosing a particular approach the emphasis must be on selecting an approach that is going to be effective and not selecting the simplest approach. Organisational situations are often very complex and require sophisticated analysis. It is likely that sophisticated analysis will result in higher SISP complexity. The key is to choose an effective approach which is a complex as it has to be.

11.6 AN OUTLINE APPROACH

Regardless of the organisation and its associated operational environment, there are some general pointers that can be followed in undertaking a SISP exercise:

Fig 11.6 An evaluation of the SISP approach used for Business Link Leicestershire

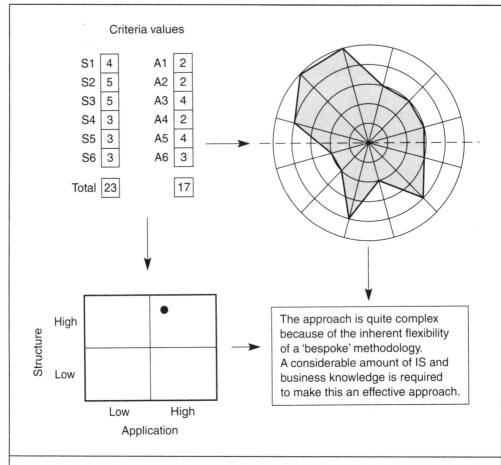

Criteria values

S1	4	A1	2
S2	5	A2	2
S3	5	A3	4
S4	3	A4	2
S5	3	A5	4
S6	3	A6	3

Total 23   17

Structure — High / Low

Application — Low / High

The approach is quite complex because of the inherent flexibility of a 'bespoke' methodology. A considerable amount of IS and business knowledge is required to make this an effective approach.

The complexity criteria values were derived by analysing the way in which the SISP exercise was undertaken, focusing on how effective techniques had been and how participants had performed during the exercise. The value for methodology constituency was derived by summing the values allocated to each of the five techniques used. Each technique utilised one tool and so tool value and technique value were the same.

- *Identification/realisation of need.* There must be an intelligence within the organisation which ensures IS strategy formulation takes places at the right time.
- *Decide upon scope.* The scope of the exercise must be clearly defined so that sufficient resources are allocated and all interested parties are aware of what is expected and what is going to be delivered at the end of the exercise.
- *Securing commitment.* Senior management must be committed to the exercise and visibly demonstrate this commitment
- *Team membership.* A team, including the team leader, must be established which has the necessary skills and experiences and represents all interested parties.
- *Decide upon approach.* The team must decide upon the approach based upon the organisational characteristics and the scope of the exercise.

❑ *Viewpoint*

How to write an IT strategy in six pages
Peter Sole

Page 1. State why this brief is important
A single paragraph to grip the reader with the importance of the document.

Page 2. Define the goals
Between three and five really important things for the business. Set them out as one-line headings with two or three bullet points, in English. For instance: reduce stock losses by 50% over three years by: installing systems for telling branch managers what stock they have; installing bar coding to track stock movements; installing new burglar alarms. It is written in business language with no discussion of technology.

Page 3. Identify the gaps
Put the five goal headings across the top of a grid. Down the left side identify the processes in the business. For each goal, identify the levels of systems support available in the processes. Where there are none, that is a gap that will have to be filled to implement the strategy. Rank the gaps by priority.

Page 4. Summarise the plan
Over a spread representing no more than three years, diagram the time scales for projects and IT work in three sections. This is a sort of Gantt chart, but it is meant to give top management a general idea of when the various projects should be started and finished.

At the bottom of the chart are bars indicating activities for "staying alive" or continuing the IT work that keeps the current business going. This is between 30% and 50% of the IT resource. Above that is a small amount of IT resource in a team devoted to quick projects. This is the commando team of quick-response specialists who can be deployed for tactical, "quick-win" projects. At the top are bars showing the major projects needed to fill the gaps identified on the previous page. Give a broad picture of when the big things are going to occur.

Page 5. Spell out the IT details
Optional reading for the business people. What the staffing, training, or technology implications are. This is the traditional focus of most IT strategy and planning documents and it has to be worked through. But it is not something senior management will be particularly interested in and it should be summarised as a simple statement of what the IT operation needs to do in order to deliver the plan.

Page 6. Call to action
This final page summarises the strategy and spells out the business benefits that will follow successful implementation. By answering the "So What?" questions it is a call for action. ■

Reprinted with permission from *Computer Weekly* 18 May 1995.

- *Undertake study*. This can only happen after the scope is defined, the team established and the approach confirmed.
- *Report findings*. The findings and recommendations of the study should be reported to the key decisions makers.
- *Implement results*. Recommendations should be acted upon once authorised and possibly modified.
- *Review approach*. The way the exercise was undertaken should be reviewed and account should be taken in future studies of the lessons learnt.

11.7 SUMMARY

This chapter has considered the practical aspects of undertaking a SISP exercise. There are many factors which influence how successful SISP is. These were discussed in Section 11.2 and led to discussions on team composition in Section 11.3, organisational differences in Section 11.4 and choosing a SISP approach in Section 11.5. Team composition and management commitment are vital ingredients to successful SISP. This is often an area where an organisation can benefit from independent input from, for example, a consultant. Without doubt, the philosophy and members of the organisation will have a significant impact on the way the organisation operates and plans for the future. Therefore this must be taken into account when contemplating a SISP exercise. As has been seen in previous chapters, there are many different methodologies and techniques in the SISP area. Which approach to adopt needs careful consideration and should be done in a systematic way. Section 11.5 explained a way in which to decide upon an approach.

There is often reference, particularly in the trade press, to the demise of SISP and how it has been superseded by Business Process Re-engineering. In the next chapter the relationship between SISP and BPR will be explored. In practice, the undertaking of a strategy exercise under the BPR flag will be subject to many of the issues discussed in this current chapter.

CASE STUDY: DEVELOPING AN IT STRATEGY

Putty in your hands
by Claire Hunt

Until now, the process of design through to implementation of an IT strategy often took up to four years or so, leaving many companies swamped by endless strategic reviews. Everyone agreed that decisions about how to use which IT products for the next five years required on-going decisions to be made about business strategy.

However, according to some senior IT personnel, the latest perceived wisdom is that long-term business strategy is not as important to IT decisions as many think.

Brendan Murray, IT director of Volvo UK, says, "Companies should not try to predict what will happen in two years' time. Technology moves so fast that the most effective solutions are those flexible enough to grow and change with the business. If you have that, long-term planning is not so crucial."

John Lawson, head of service delivery at National Power, agrees, "Of course IT should support what the company wants to do now and in the future. However, IT can actually challenge the business strategy because it finds better ways of doing things. New technology can make obsolete the business systems and methods which were appropriate before that technology arrived."

He adds, "In my opinion, business and IT strategy go hand in hand. I would prefer not to use the term 'IT strategy' at all." The traditional approach to formulating an IT strategy has been to spend roughly three months analysing company objectives, critical success factors and key performance indicators and, finally, obtaining board level commitment. Six months is then spent defining the necessary applications and selecting the appropriate architecture, a further year spent selecting or developing the applications, and yet another year implementing the system.

One problem with this long, drawn-out approach, while undoubtedly rigorous, is that a high proportion of organisations experience changes in their business needs so often that the applications are obsolete almost immediately upon completion, if not before.

▶

For example, three years ago IBM, ICL and Digital Equipment were all positioning themselves as hardware vendors and their internal systems would have supported that. In the light of a changing market, these companies are now focusing on services and they will need to ensure their internal systems now reflect that change.

Another problem is that systems designed in this way will provide information for managing and controlling business but do not drive increased efficiency and effectiveness into the underlying processes. The IT solutions developed in the traditional way are not challenging the existing business processes, merely supporting them.

Consultancies are now using a new approach to developing IT strategies. According to David Parton, strategy consultant with ACT Business Systems, "From the outset of a strategy development there should be a decision to deliver benefits back to the business within three months. Before those benefits can be delivered, corporate objectives must be defined. Based on current business processes, an analysis of the process required to meet those objectives must be made and the process redesigned. Applications to operate these new processes must be built or bought."

Parton adds. "A major difference between this and a traditional approach is that this is ongoing with new deliverables being seen every three months."

Few companies, and even fewer large organisations, will be able to start from scratch with IT. Once re-engineered processes have been developed, the implementation strategy is very dependent on existing investments, particularly with recent recessive market forces.

At Volvo's UK headquarters in Buckinghamshire, the current computer system is centred on IBM midrange equipment. This was dictated by systems designed for that environment which were made avaiiable to Volvo free of charge by the company's worldwide headquarters in Sweden.

"What we could control," comments Brendan Murray, IT director of Volvo UK, "was devolvement of the system to the end-user. We have now centralised computer operations with support and development of systems located close to the end-user. The first point of contact regarding a problem with the system is the development team."

The company currently has five midrange machines. Many PCs are connected to AS/400s and, although they are not properly networked,

---

ABBEY NATIONAL: ADAPTING OVER TIME

Abbey National Direct at one time relied on a Data General MV proprietary system to process all its work for its 70 staff, but later purchased Aviion, Data General's open systems offering.

Johann Edward, IT manager, says, "Owing to speed problems we were experiencing with the proprietary system, we went out to tender and decided to move to Unix reduced instruction set computing (Risc) boxes which will provide us with scaleability for any future plans."

In making this decision, Edward looked at what the company wanted to achieve and how it wanted to achieve it. Coming from a PC background, Edward also considered the high quality of software available for that platform at low prices, the reliability of PCs, and the fact it would be possible to swap between hardware and software vendors.

"The beauty of an open system is that I can swap any component – hardware, software or database – and keep the impact of that change to a minimum."

The key pointer of success for the company is that it solves the needs of the business and, according to Edward, "IT strategy comes second to that, although these days you don't have to compromise. Things to remember when developing an IT strategy are, firstly, that no system is ever right from the first implementation and provision must be made for changes to be made inexpensively and easily.

"Spending too much time, effort and money on trying to achieve instant perfection is a waste of resources," he continues. "Open systems allows for this and helps you to avoid the second trap, which is to depend too heavily on one supplier."

But he warns against switching suppliers too readily. "Develop a good working relationship with your supplier. A great deal of support and understanding is required when developing a system together and it is better to switch only when absolutely necessary. Our aim is to cultivate good relationships with suppliers, but the choice is always there for us."

▶

end-users can use financial and pipeline information in this way. The AS/400s act as gateways into the electronic mail system.

Six months ago Volvo undertook a study into networks and decided to standardise on Novell. However, following Volvo's and Renault's planned, but now aborted, partnership, by the end of 1993 it had been expected that between 30 and 40 PCs would be connected to a local area network (Lan) server.

Renault had already adopted a Lan server and, to avoid any problems with interconnectivity, Volvo changed its strategy. Both had independently chosen OS/2 as the network operating system. Some of the IT decisions were clearly out of the control of the local office. However, Volvo UK's financial director has been involved in the development of the system and changes to IT, and the current system is designed to support the business strategy.

To ensure IT fits into the overall business strategy, the board of directors will discuss and approve major decisions in this area. Whether or not financial sign-off is required, any decision of a strategic nature that may affect the company significantly is always presented to the board.

In the early 1980s Volvo in the UK had a centralised ICL mainframe operation. Murray says, "The major business factors that instigated a move away from this was: the desire to develop systems more quickly than was possible in the mainframe environment; a firm commitment to business systems which were more responsive to the business user; and a system in which the latter would be involved in the design and would therefore be happy to own it."

To achieve this, Volvo originally placed its first three AS/400s in the end-user departments for staff to work on. This gave them the sense of ownership the company aimed for but it did result in unnecessary duplication. For reasons of efficiency, the answer it seemed was to centralise the hardware and decentralise the software.

Murray says, "The most dynamic area of the business in computing terms is dealer communications. Previously these dealers have been equipped with Videotext systems but they now have their own systems endorsed by Volvo. The interface to dealers' computers is the most likely area to change."

To address this possibility, Volvo has looked for vendors which can supply functionality but it has not become obsessed with how they provide it. "The dealers' systems are based on Unix where the hardware can be mixed and matched," says Murray, "but functionality is not a problem. Whatever motor manufacturers want to do, the technology is there to do it, including virtual reality for the design of cars, from which we benefit in Sweden."

Stuart Walters who until recently was responsible for the IT strategy at AMD UK, and moved to STA Travel as group systems manager, advises, "Always use the right tools for the job. In many cases whether they are proprietary or open is irrelevant because if the system performs well for three years, it has paid for itself."

Although this is dependent on the corporate policy with regard to capital write-off, he says, "if proprietary works for three years, it may be relevant to switch to open systems after that."

Apart from paying close attention to business strategy and identifying the systems available, what else must be taken into account when developing an IT strategy?

Lawson from National Power believes that relationships within your own company are very important because a company is nothing without its people. "Sponsorship of ideas is necessary right from the very top of the company down to the end-users. I recommend board approval of any major IT decision because IT traverses all business areas," he says.

▶

"In some cases the good of the company must be weighed up against requests from individual departments. Line managers who will be affected by any change or decision must agree to support it, and end-users, who have to wait some time before seeing the results of any new move, will need to know what is going to happen and why."

In addition, people take time to adopt new ideas. "Don't end up with stragglers down the mountain," advises Lawson. "Ensure people have time to assimilate new ideas and catch up with new technology and systems before rushing off to the next post. Agree stages at which this time will be allowed."

So, argues Lawson, do a little PR, spread the mission statement and, later, remind people of the benefits they are seeing. The focus of the IT strategy is more people-oriented than ever before.

NATIONAL POWER: DRIVEN BY BUSINESS

When the Central Electricity Generating Board (CEGB) was privatised and National Power was born, the job of change management was vast. Here was an organisation that was expected to change both culturally and functionally into a company whose business objectives had moved almost overnight from "keeping the lights on" to "making a return on investment".

The finance director at that time had overall responsibility for the company's IT and he devised a plan as to how IT could be used for business advantage as well as a means of cultural change. The IT director's mission statement was "Business advantage through Information Technology."

The IT strategy was broken down further to include: to be business driven; to use packaged solutions wherever possible; to build small core teams of National Power staff who understood the business; to buy in expertise when made necessary by lack of internal knowledge or fluctuating requirements; and not to recruit vast numbers of IT staff.

The aim was to build an enterprise-wide infrastructure on which to place applications that would provide for integrated voice and data and allow common access to all services, preferably with a single log-on.

According to John Lawson, head of service delivery section for National Power, "We could have cobbled together islands of automation, but we had a special opportunity to start from scratch and we wanted to build a layered architecture which would tackle the most complex situation. "We wanted to ensure we could identify between technologies which were emerging and those which were proven," continues Lawson. "This was key for us when we selected PC local area network operating systems Pathworks and Decnet."

Once electronic mail, spreadsheets and graphics were up and running successfully, National Power integrated TCP/IP and Unix. The system currently consists of two IBM-compatible mainframes (Amdahl), a large number of distributed Digital Vax systems, and IBM-compatible PCs.

The next step was to understand the computer maturity of the people in-house and to discover whether they were prepared to take responsibility for IT in areas which are most relevant to them.

According to Lawson there are three different categories of system which are appropriate for different tasks. "Many people do not make a clear distinction between: a legacy system, which could be on any platform; the infrastructure system, which handles payroll and other automated tasks which do not give strategic advantage; and systems which will exploit the company's position in the marketplace."

He argues, "Each of these should be afforded different strategies and solutions and sometimes the best solution is to let the end-user have more control and to have more ownership."

Lawson looks at the adoption of IT as a tactical matter. "If you look at the way open systems is developing, it is obvious that no long-term strategy is appropriate because no one knows where it will lead," he says. "To align IT closely to the business forces tactical thinking because next year your competitor might take advantage of a product you had no way of knowing would be on the market. Suddenly you have to integrate that into your own plans."

So what key pointers to a successful system does Lawson look for? "I know our system is working because end-users are taking it for granted and integrating it into their daily work. Senior managers are using it themselves instead of relying on other people to use it for them."

▶

DEVELOPING AN IT STRATEGY: THE KEY POINTS

Key points to consider when developing an IT strategy:

1. Define your corporate objectives.
2. Align your IT strategy with your business strategy.
3. Allow your IT strategy to challenge existing business processes and re-engineer these where necessary.
4. Do not choose your system based on what is happening currently. Think about what might happen in the future.
5. Do not disregard an option because it is not in vogue. It might be the best option in the short-term.
6. Think about the pay-back period and the company's financial policies.
7. Look for packaged software solutions before committing to bespoke software.
8. Consider whether your requirements be served best by different types of solutions. For example; could you use your existing mainframe to do certain tasks while implementing new solutions for others?
9. Ensure sponsorship from the highest level in the company, any relevant managers and, where feasible, affected staff.
10. Make time for internal and external PR.
11. Understand the change curve in your company. How long will it take for staff to learn to use this? How many stable periods do we need, to allow stragglers to catch up? Build these into the strategy.
12. Do not underestimate resources required to do the job.
13. Be cautious about employing too many people who will not be needed.
14. Do not believe promises to deliver the earth. Distinguish between a tool to achieve an end and a solution to a problem.
15. Do not be obsessed with projects. Keep your eye on the total picture.
16. Do not accept development plans which are longer than nine months because end-user requirements will change. ∎

Reprinted with permission from *Computer Weekly* 9th December 1993.

References

Baker B, (1995) The role of feedback in assessing information systems planning effectiveness. *Journal of Strategic Information Systems* Vol 4 No 1, pp. 61-80.

Barker R (1988) *Case Method Tasks and Deliverables*, Version 1.0, Oracle Corporation UK Limited.

Bergeron F, Raymond L (1992) Planning of information systems to gain a competitive edge. *Journal of Small Business Management* Vol 30 No 1, pp. 21-26.

Burn J M (1993) Information systems strategies and the management of organisational change – a strategic alignment model. *Journal of Information Technology* Vol 8, pp. 205-216.

Connor A D (1993) Successful strategic information systems planning. *Journal of Information Systems* Vol 3, pp. 71-83.

Fidler C S, Rogerson S (1994a) Strategic information systems planning: its adoption and use. *Information Management and Computer Security* Vol 2 No 1, pp. 12-17.

Fidler C S, Rogerson S (1994b) *Choosing the right tools for the job; classifying SISP methodologies*. Association of Management's 12th Annual Conference, Dallas, USA

Fidler C S, Rogerson S, Spiers N (1993) Current IS practices within UK-based organisations. *Information Management and Computer Security* Vol 1 No 2, pp. 13-20.

Flynn D J, Hepburn P A (1994) Strategic planning for information systems – a case study of a metropolitan council. *European Journal of Information Systems*, Vol 3 No 3, pp. 207-217.

Henderson J C (1990) Plugging into strategic partnerships: the critical IS connection. *Sloan Management Review* Vol 31 No 3, pp. 7-18.

KPMG Management Consulting (1994) *KPMG's approach to IS strategic planning*, Version 3.

Miles A W (1985) Reintegrating strategy, in: *The Strategy Development Process*, Boston Consulting Group, pp. 1-6.

Partidge C, Fidler C S, Rogerson S (1994) *Empirical research into the classification of SISP techniques*, Internal working paper, De Montfort University.

Review questions

1 What major factors affect the success of a SISP exercise?

2 Why should a Chief Executive be involved in a SISP?

3 What are the essential qualities of an effective team leader?

4 Explain structural and application complexity.

5 List four advantages and four disadvantages of using a consultant for an information strategy exercise.

6 What ar e the four key attributes of a SISP approach?

7 Explain why and when multi-disciplinary skills are required for a SISP exercise.

8 List the key activities in a SISP exercise

Project idea

Find an organisation which has recently undertaken a SISP exercise. Conduct an analysis of the way in which the exercise was undertaken. Focus on the following aspects:

- How did the exercise come to fruition?
- Who was involved in the exercise and for how long?
- What methodolgies/techniques were used?
- What was the opinion of team members about the effectiveness of the approach?

Use the various analytical tools described in this chapter to undertake this project and to present your results.

Your review could be presented as a report to the organisation in which you identify the strengths and weakness of its approach.

CHAPTER 12

Business Process Re-engineering

12.1 INTRODUCTION

Business Process Re-engineering (BPR) is a very popular approach taken by organisations in an attempt to improve organisational effectiveness and efficiency. According to Harvey (1995), there has been an explosive growth of BPR activity over the past few years. A survey of 128 UK companies undertaken by Business Intelligence found that 87 had undertaken BPR projects. Of these, 15% focused on a single process, 47% on several processes and 31% on corporate-wide activity.

As has been explained in Chapter 9, the pervasive nature of IS/IT leads to the necessary alignment of IS/IT focus with the overall corporate focus. Therefore, this book would be incomplete without a discussion of BPR and its impact on IS/IT. Consequently, the purpose of this chapter is to provide a brief overview of BPR and the key associated issues, and to consider the roles BPR might play in IS strategy formulation. There are numerous sources that provide detailed descriptions of BPR, some of which are used as references in this chapter. This chapter does not duplicate that material but draws upon it to consider BPR in the context of IS/IT. Section 12.2 considers various definitions of BPR and the fundamental steps within the approach suggested by the leaders in the field. Sections 12.3 and 12.4 discuss the key issues surrounding the use of BPR whilst Section 12.5 looks at the relationship of BPR to SISP and SCB.

At the end of this chapter the reader should understand:

- *The concepts of BPR*
- *The relationships between BPR and SISP*

12.2 WHAT IS BPR?

Davenport (1993) indicated that in the early days of systems development evolution, it was anticipated that systems analysts would redesign processes before applying information technology. He argued that this did not happen and manual systems were simply automated, achieving incremental change rather than breakthroughs or innovation. This appears to be the fundamental plank on which BPR has been built. It is argued that BPR considers systems in a broader perspective and frees organisations from preconceptions and mindsets bounded by an infrastructure that already exists.

12.2.1 Definitions

There have been many definitions of BPR. It is useful to consider some of these.

- Davenport and Short (1990) – 'The analysis and design of work flows and processes within and between organisations.'
- Hammer and Champy (1993) – 'The fundamental rethinking and radical design of business processes to achieve dramatic improvements in critical, contemporary measures of performance, such as cost, quality, service and speed.'
- Gallaire (1994) – 'A vision-led structured methodology for the fundamental rebuilding of business processes through the balanced interaction of work tasks, people, information and technology.'
- Wastell, White and Kawalek (1994) – 'The endeavour to augment organisational performance by improving efficiency, effectiveness and adaptability of key processes.'

Each of these definitions focuses on the corporate whole and how that might be improved. This focus is elaborated upon by Norman (1993) who points out that successful **BPR** demands holistic vision, a coherent strategy process, shared understanding, excellent communications, challenging goals and an unremitting support for customer value.

12.2.2 BPR steps

Hammer (1990) proposed seven principles to adopt when undertaking BPR initiatives. These are outlined in Table 12.1. Davenport and Short (1990) identified five steps in BPR, shown in Table 12.2, that organisations successful in BPR undertook. Identifying objectives, setting challenging targets, identifying critical and bottleneck processes, problem identification, innovative use of IS/IT and implementation that embraced organisational and technical aspects are considered vital in BPR projects.

Current practical approaches have been greatly influenced by this earlier work. The Boston Consulting Group (1993) divide BPR into three stages: preparation, transformation, and consolidation of strength and position. As well as the actual redesigning

Table 12.1 Hammer's seven principles of re-engineering

1 Organise around outcomes, not tasks – one person performs all the steps in a process and the customer has just one point of contact
2 People who use the output should perform the process – those who need the result should do the process themselves – why have intermediaries?
3 People who produce the information should also process it
4 Treat geographically dispersed resources as if they were centralised
5 Link parallel activities instead of integrating their results – co-ordinate the same type of work in the process, not after it.
6 Put the decision point where the work is performed – build in control to let the process workers be self-managing
7 Capture information once and at its source
Hammer's original principles include many implicit and explicit references to IS/IT.

Table 12.2 Davenport and Short's five steps in re-engineering

- Develop business vision and process objectives
- Identify processes to be re-engineered
- Understand and measure existing processes
- Identify IT levers
- Design and build a prototype of the process

Here the dependence on IT is very explicit.

of organisational processes, careful preparation and consistent follow-up must take place. Preparation includes defining purposes, goals and the rationale for change together with the building of commitment and establishing the BPR team. Transformation involves the redesign of key processes, integrating and validating these processes and building the infrastructures to support these redesigned processes. It must also include mechanisms to communicate objectives, generate commitment and achieve early results. Consolidation is concerned with creating a learning organisation in which superior processes are transformed into recognised capabilities, and the culture promotes customer-focused process excellence.

12.3 CULTURE ISSUES

BPR is concerned with the significant and often radical change in the way goals are achieved. This entails a strategic shift in culture to one where the learning organisation and continuous change are the norm. This entails moving from hierarchies and boundaries to teams and networks, from directing and controlling to empowering and facilitating, and from analysis and risk aversion to action and calculated risk taking. The success of the BPR approach will be greatly influenced by the acceptance of the approach by all those involved in it and affected by it. Whilst there are micro or organisational issues that affect the degree of acceptance there are also macro issues at national or societal levels that need to be recognised.

12.3.1 Macro cultural issues

It is not clear that BPR is effective in all industrialised countries. Bowles (1995) reported that 88% of organisations in the USA use BPR. Of these only 30% considered the approach to be wholly successful. Bowles reported that only 12% of organisations in Europe used BPR. He suggested that cultural differences have a significant impact on the acceptance of the BPR approach. He argued that the USA is more focused on the short term, a high risk taker, more willing to spend money and more willing to accept change compared to Japan which takes a very long-term focus, promotes a group culture, follows consensus opinion and accepts the status-quo. European countries lie somewhere between these two extremes. This marked contrast in cultural outlook will have a significant impact on the strategic outlook. This is illustrated in Figure 12.1.

Fig 12.1 The impact of culture on attitude to change

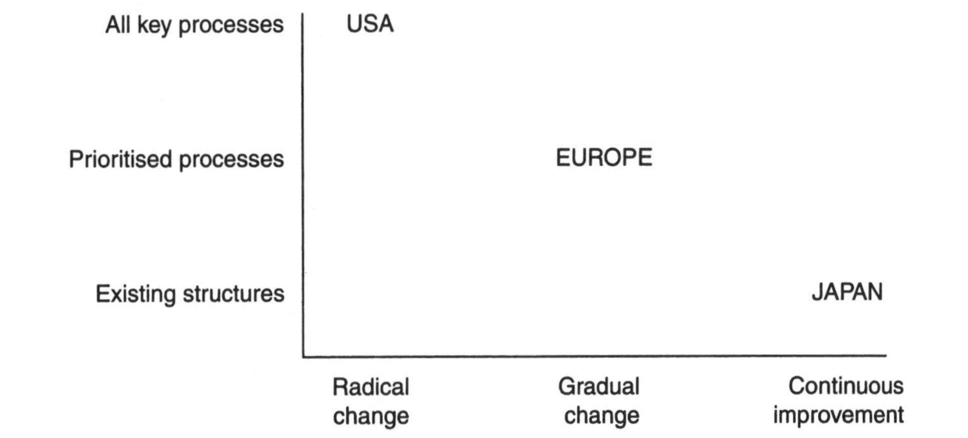

Organisations in the USA are willing to accept radical wholesale change covering all processes. European organisations are more likely to consider the critical processes and gradually change them to become more effective. Japanese organisations adopt a philosophy of continuous improvement within existing structures. Hammer's original obliteration concept might have gained acceptance in the USA but was always likely to fail in other countries because of the cultural differences.

12.3.2 Micro cultural issues

Respondents to the survey undertaken by Harvey (1995) were concerned about the shortcomings of consultants hired to undertake BPR projects. Prevalent concerns included the lack of understanding of organisation culture and political issues together with a lack of recognition of people aspects. Respondents felt that these issues must be addressed if BPR is to be successful. It is these issues which Norman (1993) sees as the underbelly of the process iceberg. He explains that most organisations are simply unaware of the scale and difficulty of realigning the culture and reforming corporate thinking and action.

12.4 OBSTACLES

A survey of 400 senior IS managers, undertaken by Deloitte and Toche in 1993, pointed to a number of obstacles that prevent BPR success. These are shown in Table 12.3 and comprise a wide range of issues requiring attention from both top-down and bottom-up perspectives. The Boston Consulting Group (1993) suggests there are a number of principles that guide BPR success and overcome these obstacles. These principles centre upon creating value for the customer and ensuring that senior management provide effective leadership throughout the organisation that ensures a culture is established in which the way work is undertaken is constantly challenged.

❑ *Viewpoint*

A lesson to be learnt from Indian culture
by Alan Howard

The Naskapi indians in Western Canada are successful hunters. Before venturing out they ask the question "Where should we hunt today?" To answer this question they take the shoulder bone of a caribou and hold it over a fire until it cracks. They hunt in whichever direction the crack points.

An interesting story but what does this teach us about IT strategy? There are a number of lessons. The Naskapi strategy is successful for four reasons. First, they have a clear objective. Second, they believe in the strategy. Third, strategy formulation is so quick and simple that they spend little time on it and thus spend more time hunting. Fourth, if they don't find game that day no one person is to blame.

Compare that to IT strategy formulation in many organisations. A clear business plan does not exist. It is very rare to win total support for a strategy. Strategy is agonised over for months on end. If the strategy fails the consultants and/or IT manager are sacked and the process begins again under the auspices of a new leader.

Perhaps there are two aspects of western culture which mitigate against successful strategy formulation – individualism and formal rational thinking. Excessive individualism makes it difficult for people to work in teams and to be philosophical about so-called "failure". Failure is taken personally and heads roll or careers are stunted.

Western training and culture focuses on rational views of the world. Eastern cultures view life as a continuous cyclic process rather than a series of sequential and discrete events. Change is evolutionary rather than revolutionary.

For Western managers there is nothing quite as satisfying as doing a rigorous and wide-ranging diagnosis of a situation. The problem is that the diagnosis quickly gets out of phase with changing realities. The longer the diagnosis lasts the greater the chances that the goalposts have moved.

Lengthy analysis also raises expectations about outcomes. In strategic planning for IT and information systems, managers must accept that the business, technological and organisational environments are changing so rapidly that strategy must be as much about awareness, intuition, learning common-sense and sophisticated loss cutting actions as about long-term planning. No plan by itself guarantees success.

An enterprise must instill confidence in its staff, get them moving in some general direction and make sure they learn from events. Just in-time strategies will suffice. Trying to anticipate everything that will happen and all the resources needed is a futile task. Invest in general knowledge, wide-ranging skills and competent people.

Given the diversity of information technology and uncertainty about the future, many different strategies are possible. What we can learn from the Naskapi is that whatever the strategy people must have a clear mission. The strategy must not be too complex.

A critical mass of people, ideally everyone, must believe in the strategy. Finally, if the strategy doesn't work, maybe it isn't just the leaders fault! ■

Reprinted with permission from *Computer Weekly*, 31st March 1994.

12.5 BPR, SISP AND SCB

Given the major impact that BPR has on an organisation and that this impact involves the generation, dissemination and use of information to sustain the redesigned processes it is inevitable that IS/IT has a central role in this activity. Earl (1994) explains that much of the BPR output is dependent on IS/IT. For example, telecommunications often figures in reducing co-ordination costs or increasing the scope of co-ordination, and shared databases are commonplace in the provision of information across and during processes.

Speaking at the European IT Conference, Zuccaro (1994) explained that the Benetton Group was a global business which had a global product portfolio, a common market approach, a world-wide standardised shop image and global financial management. In this situation, for the business processes to succeed globally it is essential to

Table 12.3 Obstacles to business re-engineering success

Resistance to change	60%
Limitations of existing systems	40%
Lack of executive consensus	38%
Lack of a senior executive champion	36%
Unrealistic expectations	28%
Lack of cross-functional project teams	25%
Inadequate skills	22%
IS staff involved too late	16%
Project charter too narrow	12%

have effective IS/IT. He suggested that it was not the sophistication of the technologies used that mattered, but the innovation of practices and technologies generally available together with deep knowledge of the business structure and processes.

Gallaire (1994) explained that at Rank Xerox the role played by IS/IT in BPR is critical where it applies but it is not ubiquitous. For example, a paradigm shift in document processing from print and distribute to distribute and print was only possible through the use of telecommunication networking and new IT devices. This is in stark contrast to Hammer's opinion who said at a London seminar (1995) that IT is an absolute enabler for BPR and without it BPR cannot be undertaken.

The central role of IS/IT is undisputed but the nature of the role is a matter of conjecture as illustrated by the Benetton and Rank Xerox examples. There are two schools of thought on the role of IS/IT in BPR. The first proposes that BPR is enabled by IS/IT. Earl (1994) reported one company would only approve IS projects if they were conceived as part of a BPR programme. In these situations, BPR acts as an IS screening mechanism through identifying possible applications, considering the likelihood of IS/IT support and deciding which systems to invoke. The second school suggests that BPR should be driven by IS/IT. Earl (1994) suggests that in this situation BPR is an approach to SISP forcing IS initiatives to be business oriented and aligned to other organisational initiatives.

The relationship of BPR to SISP and SCB needs to be considered in the context of these two schools. The first issue to consider is where the points of interaction occur. This is illustrated in Figure 12.2. SISP will interact with BPR primarily in the preparation and transformation stages; the nature of the interaction is dependent upon the school. SCB will interact with BPR primarily in the preparation and consolidation stages. This interaction is less dependent upon the school because the outcome of SCB and the equivalent facet of BPR is more about establishing a learning organisation and an empowered workforce rather than the enhancement of some process, possibly through the use of IS/IT.

The nature of interaction between BPR and SISP is dependent upon the school. In the IS/IT enabled school SISP and BPR are more likely to be undertaken as separate though related activities. BPR provides the overriding focus for SISP ensuring that the IS and the underpinning IT sustain the organisational regeneration programme developed through BPR itself. In the IS/IT driven school there is likely to be a greater

Fig 12.2 The points of interaction of BPR with SISP and SCB

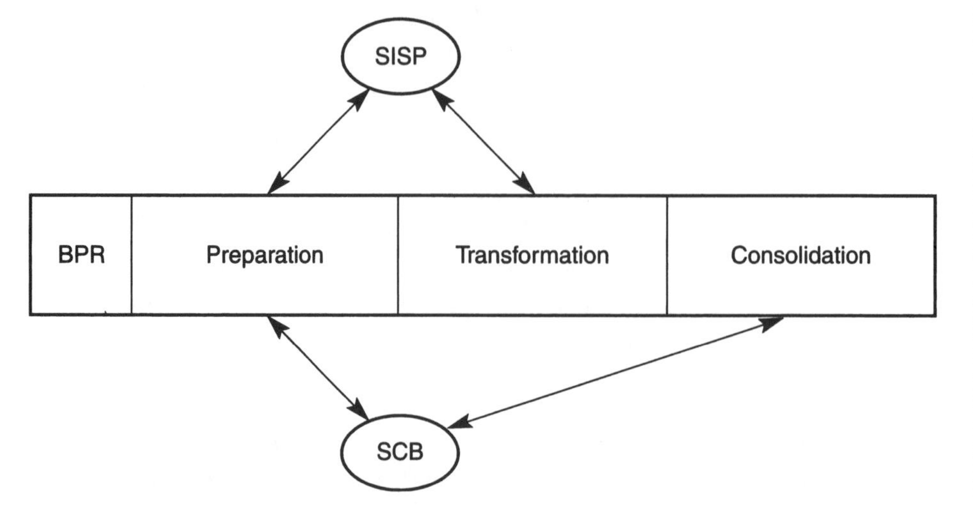

The points of primary interaction are shown in this figure. The nature of the interaction between BPR and SISP will depend upon whether an IS/IT enabled or IS/IT driven philosophy is adopted. The BPR/SCBP interaction is more universal.

overlap in SISP and BPR activity. SISP will provide strong pointers as to how and where IS/IT can be effectively applied. This will colour the BPR output and drive it towards more technology-dependent regeneration programmes. These relationships are illustrated by the diagrams in Figure 12.3.

12.6 SUMMARY

This chapter has considered, in outline, the facets of BPR and how it relates to SISP and SCB. BPR is a popular strategic approach used by many organisations to provide a new perspective on the current business position and the future potential.

There is a consensus among the leading advocates of BPR as to how the activity should be undertaken in broad terms although fine detail does differ. This was briefly discussed in Section 12.2. and followed by a longer discussion, in Sections 12.3 and 12.4, about the organisational and cultural obstacles that influence the successful uptake and outcome of BPR.

These sections provided the necessary background in order to consider the main issue of this chapter which was the relationship of BPR to SISP and SCB. It is universally accepted that IS/IT has a central role to play in BPR but there is much conjecture as to what this role should be. This issue was discussed in Section 12.5. It was explained that the differing roles were dependent upon whether an IS/IT enabled philosophy or and IS/IT driven philosophy was adopted.

It seems that BPR is concerned with evolving organisations so they are equipped to cope with changes in the operational environment and to extend the strategic horizon

Fig 12.3 The interrelationship of BPR with SISP and SCB

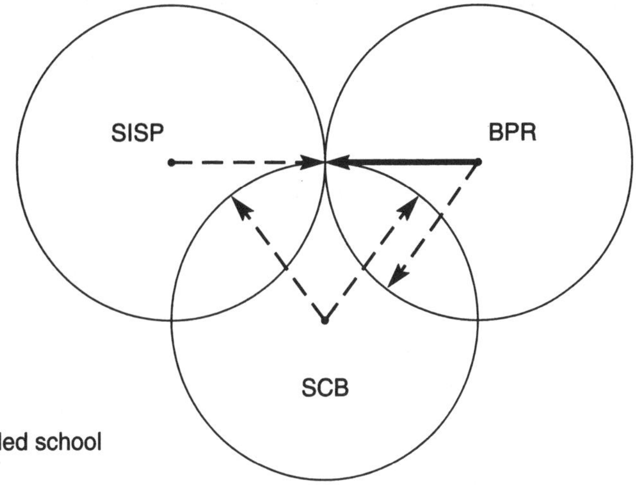

(a) IS/IT Enabled school

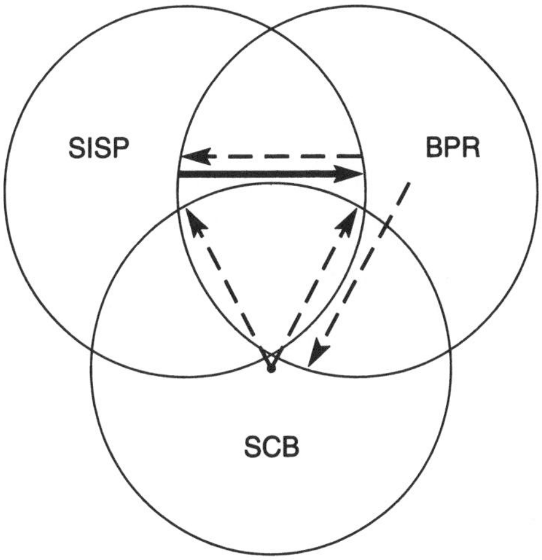

(b) IS/IT Driven school

BPR to SISP is the dominant relationship in the IS/IT enabled school whereas it is SISP to BPR in the IS/IT driven school. The broad arrow in the diagrams depicts the dominant relationship but it can be seen that there still exists a relationship in the other direction. SCB influences SISP and BPR in a way which tends to be independent of the school.

through the adoption of new approaches to work. IS/IT must have a role to play in this activity. The activity itself is a fine balance between empowerment and chaos. This is cleverly paraphrased by the title of a painting by Lindsey Marcan:

> *'The art of progress is to preserve order amid change and to preserve change amid order'*

❑ *Viewpoint*

Is there life after BPR for the IT department?
by John Kavanagh

IT directors are split over their role in business process re-engineering (BPR) and their own future beyond it – but all agree that they must get closer to their business end-users.

This emerged during a major debate last week on a motion that successful BPR will see the end of the corporate IT structure as we know it. Around 50 senior IT people turned out for the event last week, organised by the British Computer Society's IT directors forum, Elite (Effective Leadership in IT).

One risk to the future of IT departments is that few live up to the ideal, according to John Stratton, managing director of the insurance industry's Polaris electronic trading initiative. He proposed the motion.

Stratton says the ideal is a department which is responsible for corporate IT, a centre of excellence for rare skills, and a strategic unit with a clear view of the business goals and the vision to apply IT for competitive edge.

But reality is very different, Stratton believes.

"Having a central function providing programs which are shared by a range of business units raises questions of who owns the systems," he argued.

"If this isn't decided, the IT department decides, when the systems should really be in the hands of the business. This leads to business goals not being met. Shared programs may be stifling the business."

Too many IT departments have a "not invented here" philosophy, develop systems using unique technology and do not report through the business, Stratton believes.

"This must change – and the corporate IT structure must change with it. BPR will bring that change. The IT function will have a role, but not as we know it now it must get closer to the business."

There is little dissent on this last point.

Les Macintosh from insurance company General Accident has been through BPR "because the IT structure couldn't enact the essential change needed to keep us in business".

"There was no business ownership," he told the debate audience. "Systems were shared across each area but when something had to change it couldn't be done, because IT didn't know who was directing the change. So everything was controlled by IT."

Even Colin Palmer, who opposed the motion, agrees.

But Palmer. a consultant and former IT director at Thomson Tour Operations, says economic, market and technology trends mean that IT departments have already been changing since the late 1980s.

Even so, their traditional role will continue: big companies ranging from airlines to banks need big corporate systems to control accounts, inventory and other critical data.

"It is inconceivable to such organisations that they should not have very strong computer-based management of this data," Palmer said, "IT will continue at the heart of such organisations for the foreseeable future."

Company growth also demands a central function, Palmer believes. It provides common systems across organisations and borders and cuts overall systems costs.

Central IT could even bring benefit if a remote office develops its own little application: "Other users see it and want it, and corporate IT has the capability to handle this demand and the infrastructure to support it."

Stuart Ward from Nuclear Electric goes further: he says IT should lead BPR.

"BPR is all about changing processes, and that cuts right across the organisation.

"The IT function is uniquely placed to have the vision of how information systems can support the business. IT is uniquely placed to be the guardian of the information asset. And it is uniquely placed to be the guardian of the organisation's process model, because it is independent: senior managers often have vested interests and are the biggest blockers of chance."

John Aris, former head of consultancy KPMG's Impact research programme, highlighted three choices for the IT director here.

He could keep his traditional delivery role – but that could lead to IT being contracted out.

He could take a "governance" role: taking part in corporate policy-making and interpreting it into systems.

Or he could be an agent of change, responsible for a BPR programme supported by the chief executive.

The debate revealed mixed views here.

"The drive for BPR must come from senior executives, not from IT," said Geoff Robinson from Iceland Frozen Foods. "There's no BPR Holy Grail that belongs to IT."

Marion Carney from Costain said change was inevitable: "Unless the IT structure changes, you can't get BPR anyway."

With the proviso that they need to get closer to the business, the IT managers ended by voting that today's IT structure would continue. The motion was defeated by 24 – 14 – but with an audience of 50 that leaves a considerable number unsure about the future. ■

CASE STUDY: UNION CARBIDE

The link between business process re-engineering (BPR) and IT is so close that whenever a BPR project begins one of the first questions facing the project manager is 'where does IT fit into the project?'

Why is this link so strong? Simply because IT is used in almost every business process from paying an invoice, to loading a truck for dispatch, to turning a valve in a petrochemical plant. Each of these steps is either initiated, controlled or recorded by an IT function, so if you change the steps, you have to change the IT function.

This formula also works the other way, however, since every IT project has an element of BPR – and if it doesn't, maybe some questions should be asked! Today, senior managers are acutely aware of the high cost of IT projects, and will only undertake them if big benefits result. They know that the only way to get substantial benefits is to change the way people work because there are not enough savings in just doing the same things with a better computer system.

Global System Integrators

When Union Carbide started a worldwide campaign two years ago designed to re-engineer the company, the senior management recognised this link from the start. To help them with such a massive project, they engaged KPMG to be the Global System Integrators. The objective was clearly defined: '... provide the IT infrastructure needed to support a re-engineered company'. "It doesn't matter which end of the telescope you use to look at the problem." says Nick Beaton, the KPMG manager of Union Carbide's European project, "BPR and IT are locked together. "

Focus on distribution

In Europe the project had a very strong focus on distribution logistics, its goal being to improve the 'product to customer' supply chain. Though there are some production facilities in Europe. Union Carbide Europe imports the vast majority of all the products it sells, and the existing software supporting the distribution process was near the end of its useful life. The level of integration and flexibility in the system were no longer adequate for the changing market conditions and customer demands.

A key factor in the success of a project involving IT and BPR lies in managing the balance between the two. The reason for this is partly that most BPR exercises require workshop participants to recognise bottlenecks and come up with new ways to eliminate them. This is very important, but it must be carefully monitored for practicality. If there is no technology available at a reasonable price for implementing the ideas, the exercise can be a waste of time.

Complex relationship

"The traditional model of the users sitting down and listing all of their requirements in a blue sky environment, with the IT department writing the software to meet these needs, is dead," says Nick Beaton.

"The relationship is much more complex than that. There must be balance, and a practical approach to getting the results. Break the problems up into high level issues which must be solved regardless of the system, and low level issues which must be solved by the system."

Review bottlenecks

The first practical tip is to determine which high level business areas can be analysed for savings before the final software package has been selected. The bottlenecks at the high levels must be reviewed for re-engineering opportunities, but when the subject matter starts to go into detailed areas, analysing it may be a waste of time if the eventual software has not been selected yet.

For Union Carbide it was clear that some business processes could be re-engineered without knowing which final software would be used, while in other areas it was necessary to

▶

wait until the package was selected. One decision which was taken very early in the project was to stop 'double invoicing' whereby the European HQ invoice the country sales offices, and they in turn invoiced the customers. It was clear that this giant bottleneck could be solved very simply, with only minor (if any) changes to any software system, even the existing one. This is a good example of a business process which should be changed regardless of the software, because it is fundamental to the business.

Explore functionality

The second practical tip is to make sure that the users explore the functionality of the selected software system so that they can change work processes in the low level issues. Too often there is a tendency to want to change the system rather than to try and exploit the functionality which exists.

This was particularly relevant at Union Carbide, because a decision had been made at a worldwide level that Union Carbide would implement standard software packages without modification – a strategy which became known as 'Vanilla Flavoured Software'. This decision was taken after reviewing options which included developing a bespoke system and using one package installed on one computer in the US with lease lines to every office in the world. The selected package was BPCS from Systems Software Associates (SSA), and the implementation strategy was to use this software without modification in all of the international affiliates, with each responsible for its own implementation.

The 'Vanilla strategy'

The 'Vanilla strategy' meant that users had to learn how to use the software in detail so that they could get the best out of it. "Do not underestimate this part of the process," says Nick Beaton. "A successful implementation can only come through knowing the software thoroughly." At Union Carbide KPMG played a major role in training senior management in some of the more important points of the software so that informed decisions could

be made about its use.

The third tip is to let the functionality of a standard package ask some of the re-engineering questions. If a package is being used at thousands of sites, but does not seem right for yours, look carefully at your current process.

Sometimes this challenges accepted practices and starts people thinking about the value of those practices.

Complex formula

In Union Carbide's case it was interesting that there was a complex 'post sale' formula for calculating the transfer price of the stock shipped from the US. When it became obvious that BPCS would not perform this calculation in 'vanilla form' the users responded well by abandoning this years' old practice. "When we looked hard at this process we found it caused a lot of administrative work for virtually no benefit," says Allan Nielsen, Union Carbide's European finance director. "The value of using this method had diminished over the years, but we still kept it. We were right to get rid of it."

This method of challenging does not always result in a change to the work practice, however. Even if the outcome is that the work practice stays, at least it has been questioned and tested.

For example, two areas which were of special concern to Union Carbide resulted in minor modifications being made to BPCS. The first of these was the integration of quality and safety data for each product into the order entry system. Union Carbide decided it needed more functionality than was provided by the standard software, and they decided to integrate the large database of the customer specifications with product analysis results, so that the customer service representative could always be sure that the right product batch is sent to the customer.

Integration

The second area was the integration of the logistics system into the order entry system. The

►

customer service representative who takes the order is also responsible for arranging the correct transport for the shipment, including customs documentation. This was integrated very closely into the order entry system so that the customer is offered the best service level possible.

The fourth practical tip is to use the implementation as a vehicle to change things - even in areas which are not touched directly by the software package. At Union Carbide this happened in a number of areas. For example, a worldwide initiative was started to harmonise product codes, chart of accounts codes, warehouse numbers, etc in the future, but it is something which theoretically could have been done with the old system. It was the catalytic effect of the whole process of re-engineenng and software implementation which made it politically achievable.

Management commitment

The fifth tip is to get the senior management deeply involved in the process. BPR and systems implementation by their very nature cause change and disruption. Staff only 'buy into' this process if they see the senior management committed to that change as well. "We achieved this with the Union Carbide project by getting some of the most senior people in the organisation to go to the European states offices and conduct short training courses in BPCS," says Nick Beaton.

They had been prepared following a special course put together by KPMG which allowed them to show the sales staff how to enter an order and prepare it for shipment. "You can imagine the impact this had on anyone who had doubts about the software or the company's commitment to implementation," says Francis Szczech one of the Union Carbide senior managers who led the course.

And the sixth tip is to invest heavily in training in a project of this magnitude. People have a fear of the unknown, with many believing that they will not be able to do their jobs if everything changes. Everyone responds positively to training which is carefully prepared and delivered in a professional way. Union Carbide made a substantial investment in training to ensure that all staff were ready to perform when the new system went live. The course participants were all brought to Antwerp to a central training centre which was established for the project. Each of them received a training manual with details of all the examples in the course, and they had to take two examinations which were marked by the tutors and handed back for review.

It cannot be emphasised too forcefully that IT plays an important role in BPR projects. Sometimes IT is influenced by the business and sometimes the business is influenced by IT, but in all cases it is necessary to keep these

References

Boston Consulting Group (1993) *Re-engineering and Beyond*. Boston Consulting Group.

Bowles G (1995) Software AG's approach to BPR, *The Butler Group Business Process Re-engineering Seminar*.

Davenport T H (1993) *Process innovation: reengineering work through information technology*, Harvard Business School Press.

Davenport T H, Short J E (1990) The new industrial engineering: information technology and business process redesign. *Sloan Management Review*, Summer, pp. 11–27.

Earl M J (1994) The new and old of business process redesign. *Journal of Strategic Information Systems*, Vol 3 No 1, pp. 5–22.

Gallaire H (1994) Re-engineering a corporation: a pathway to new productivity. *European IT Conference Proceedings*, Commission of the European Community.

Hammer M (1990) Re-engineering work: don't automate, obliterate. *Harvard Business Review*, July–August, pp. 104–112.

Hammer M, Champy J (1993) *Re-engineering the Corporation*. Harper Collins.

Harvey D (1995) BPR – facing up to the truth. *Management Consultancy*, Sept, pp. 25–30.

Norman D (1993) Getting reengineering right. *Management Advantage Briefing Paper*, No 2.

Wastell DG, White P, Kawalek (1994) A methodology for business process redesign: experiences and issues. *Journal of Strategic Information Systems*, Vol 3 No 1, pp. 23–40.

Zuccaro B (1994) Business process at Benetton: the crucial role of IT. *European IT Conference Proceedings*, Commission of the European Community.

Review questions

1 Give a definition for BPR.

2 Outline the major activities to be undertaken in a BPR initiative.

3 Explain why European-based organisations might balk at using BPR in its original form.

4 State three major obstacles in achieving a successful BPR outcome and suggest ways in which these obstacles might be overcome.

5 Explain the difference between IS/IT enabled BPR and IS/IT driven BPR.

6 Is SISP the same as BPR? Explain you answer.

7 Is SCB the same as BPR? Explain you answer.

Project idea

Periodically, popular computer magazines, such as Computer Weekly, Computing and Datamation, publish articles on how organisations have utilised IS/IT in achieving organisational goals. Some examples have been included within various chapters of this book. Review current editions of these magazines and choose two articles relating to organisations operating in contrasting business environments.

For each of these organisations:
● Identify the business goals
● Identify the key information systems used to realise these goals
● Decide whether it is an IS/IT enabled or IS/IT driven organisation
● List the potential obstacles and advantages in undertaking a BPR initiative

Now consider the differences and similarities between your responses for each organisation and explain why this is so.

Give a short presentation of your findings to your tutorial group and lead a discussion of the major issues raised by your investigation.

CHAPTER 13

SISP Summary

13.1 SUMMARY OF PART 3

This part has introduced the reader to the subject of information systems strategy formulation. The main focus has been on Strategic Information Systems Planning (SISP) but consideration has also been given to Strategic Culture Building (SCB) process and Business Process Re-engineering (BPR).

Chapter 9 introduced the concept of SISP within the context of the organisation and its corporate strategy. A discussion about the evolution of information systems within organisations demonstrated the necessity of alignment with the organisational mission. Indeed, it was explained that it is vital to establish a two-way link between the strategies of the individual elements of an organisation, including IS/IT, to the overall organisational purpose and strategy.

Much has been written about using IS for competitive advantage. This narrow perspective was broadened to the concept of IS adding value to organisational activities so catering for all types of organisation. It is the concept of adding value to organisational activity that is the foundation of an IS/IT strategy.

It was suggested that the approach to SISP is based upon the principles that:

- SISP should be suitable for all types of organisations regardless of their mission, industry sector and financial status.
- Strategic alignment incorporating the appropriate feedback from the information systems strategy should be encouraged by the SISP.
- SISP should consider all types of systems.
- SISP should promote a strategically-oriented culture.

A new definition of SISP was proposed as being *the means of identifying application systems which support and enhance organisational strategy and provides the framework for the effective implementation of these systems.* Similarly SCB was defined *as the means of encouraging people within an organisation to be forward-looking and to consider their work and decisions in an organisational context rather than a parochial context.* The combining of SISP and SCB to provide effective strategic focus for IS was discussed.

The three-layered view of a SISP methodology was introduced which comprised a methodology level, a techniques level and a tools level. A SISP methodology was defined as a purpose-built set of SISP techniques that together provide support for part or all of the SISP process. It was explained that a SISP technique provides a structured approach to performing an activity within SISP. There are many methodologies and techniques available for the SISP process. Choosing a SISP methodology involves considering ease of use, scope and orientation. Equally important is the issue of establishing an effective group of people to undertake the SISP activities. Both issues were discussed in this chapter.

Having placed SISP in context and considered several important interrelated issues, Chapter 10 provided more detail concerning some of the popular techniques and methodologies. The intention was to provide the reader with an insight into the typical functionality of these aids and to enable the reader to use some of them.

The five forces model and the strategic relevance and impact grid are popular techniques that have been successfully used in IS strategy formulation in many organisations and consequently were discussed in some detail. Four methodologies were included in Chapter 10. The Critical Success Factors methodology is widely available and has been applied to IS/IT with good effect. Being simple in concept though powerful in nature, CSF methodology is a valuable SISP approach. It was explained that many organisations use consultancy firms to undertake strategy activities and it was therefore felt appropriate to include outlines of the approaches developed by three of the leading international consultancy firms in this area. Together, the four methodologies illustrated how the scope and focus of methodologies vary considerably.

One of the aims of this book has been to blend concepts with practical application. Drawing from those practical aspects raised in Chapter 9, Chapter 11 discussed further the composition of the SISP team and the way in which the SISP exercise should be undertaken. It was suggested that the success of a SISP exercise is based upon:

- The formulated strategy being a realistic challenge
- The realisation that a strategy is not operational planning
- The tailoring of the approach to cater for organisational uniqueness
- The strategy being reconciled with overall corporate objectives
- The involvement of all parties affected by the derived strategy

There are many organisational factors which colour the way in which a SISP exercise is best undertaken. It was explained that by using the organisation structure grid an indication of the best approach could be ascertained. Further guidance was given as to which methodologies and techniques were applicable in a given situation. This was based on the classification framework devised by the authors.

Much has been written about BPR and the aim of Chapter 12 was not to duplicate this but to explore the relationships between BPR and SISP and SCB. A brief outline of BPR was followed by a discussion of factors affecting the success of a BPR approach to strategy formulation. It was suggested that the relationship between BPR and SISP depended upon whether BPR was considered to be IS/IT enabled or IS/IT driven, the former resulting in a partnership and the latter in an overlapping exercise.

❑ *Viewpoint*

Six steps to the millennium
by Julia Vowler

Five years is a very short time in IT. During the next half of the 1990s the IT department as we know it will change fundamentally.

The newly published report *IT and Corporate Transformation*, which surveyed 200 companies and major public sector organisations, identifies six key directional shifts that IT managers should focus on if they want to still be in business in the next century.

- *Leading IT departments will become more closely integrated with the business during the next five years.*

This may seem like a truism, but, says the report, "Few of the IT departments we studied could reasonably claim they were wholly integrated with the business. But the leaders were moving strongly in that direction."

But for every IT department that gets closer to business, there are dozens more who find obstacles: management suspicion, corporate politics and technophobe managers. Without the application of visionary leadership and change management, nothing will happen.

- *The role of IT is shifting from business support to business transformation.*

Companies experimenting with modest re-engineering projects that transform individual business processes are now preparing to take on more ambitious re-engineering ventures. But companies can vary in the importance of the role they assign IT in re-engineering, from minor support role to key facilitator. To succeed in re-engineering, IT departments will have first to re-engineer themselves – and so will IT professionals.

- *IT departments are changing from a static centralised structure to a flexible, federal structure.*

Primarily, this means moving the delivery of IT into the business units. Within five years the central "soup to nuts" IT department will be gone. Instead it will deliver the crucial infrastructure, leaving the commodity services to the markeplace and the rapid development to the business units.

- *Inter-enterprise computing will become a competitive weapon.*

Already companies such as manufacturers are creating an information highway along the whole length of their distribution chain, in from their suppliers and out to their customers. IT managers will have to look beyond the walls constraining their own companies.

- *Vendors are becoming partners.*

The IT department and the vendor will find a business pay-off by becoming closer. Vendors are finding it difficult to transform fast-developing generic technologies into market-leading products, just as IT users are wary of being early adopters. Being partners will help both.

- *IT professionals will develop a stronger business focus but technical skills will remain important.*

The beard-and-sandals programmer will become an endangered species in internal IT, but will thrive in service and software houses. The new breed of IT professional will be more sympathetic to the business. IT people will be rewarded for the value they add to a business, which will require sophisticated metrics to measure.

This transformation of the IT department requires two key players – the IT director and the chief executive. The IT director must be "obsessed with business" while the chief executive must put the role of IT firmly on his own agenda. ∎

CASE STUDY 1: BRISTOL & WEST

Shipshape and Bristol fashion
by Bryan Betts

Workgroup computing is often seen as a way of automating existing processes and making them more efficient. But as the Bristol & West proved it can equally well be used to take a business into a whole new field of operations.

The task for the building society, one of the UK's largest, was to set up a new division which would sell a variety of financial services by telephone. The society already had branches mostly in the West Country but it wanted to reach new customers and the telephone promised to be the best way.

"We started with a blank sheet and asked 'What's our proposition?' and then asked how best we could meet that," says group operations director Ian Kennedy.

The aim was to use IT not only to automate the processes required in any banking operation, but to make possible a business that would otherwise be unfeasible. The result is Asset: a system that uses a combination of dynamic workflow management and document image processing.

This allows operators at the division's Bristol headquarters to carry out the whole business of managing accounts over the telephone or by post.

They have immediate access to customer details, correspondence and files on-screen, without the need to put the customer on hold while they visit filing cabinets or hunt for information through a traditional mainframe database.

Asset's core is a suite of telephone banking software developed by systems house AIT, which has been adapted by the society to suit its own particular aims and needs. "The primary point of the business was remote servicing," Kennedy explains. "We have a tailored system delivering a high level of service; we can give the customer exactly what he or she wants, transparently.

"We put a high value on our staff, both for service levels and the personal approach. AIT sells the function of integrated workflow, not our way of doing workflow: that's our competitive edge."

Workgroup computing traditionally creates job queues for each user managing these queues around timed deadlines. In the dynamic methodology adopted for Asset, few activities are sequential; instead each task leads to another with little similarity in the way things are processed.

"AIT based its workflow model on a tree with alternative paths which is much more flexible. Some early workflow examples were too rigid and structured," says Mary McSherry, head of service architecture, whose team specified the system.

Asset uses a task pool, sorted into task categories. Tasks are assigned priorities with older pending tasks being reprioritised to make sure they are done. On average, the system has 2,000 jobs on general workflow.

A free operator can either request the highest priority task from the pool or specify a task. A scanned form or letter then appears on the screen and the operator can look up the account details, compare the signature with the sample stored on the system, input the details from the form, and approve whatever actions are required such as sending out a letter or cheque.

"For the first couple of months people didn't trust the workflow system and they chose to specify jobs," says Kennedy. "Now they trust it."

Hardware for the system was recommended by AIT, and along with the workstations it incorporates a fault-tolerant Novell Netware local area network with six servers and a total of 10 Gbytes of online hard disc storage. A further 11 Gbytes are available on an optical disc jukebox which is used for storing scanned documents on non-erasable "write-once read-many" discs. Also linked into the workstations is the telephone system. "We have full computer-integrated telephony," Kennedy says. "It routes calls to operators by type: we use an 0800 number for recruiting new customers and an 0345 number for existing customers.

"The incoming post is scanned and all transactions passed through Asset. The scanning process is quite sensitive: you need to get the density and contrast right which takes trial and error. We have been going a year now and have 300,000 documents imaged."

Original paper copies are archived after scanning initially for a year but the aim is to reduce this to six months. The fault-tolerant hard-disc subsystem

▶

stores all the correspondence that has been accessed in the past two weeks. This may include letters older than two weeks if an operator has specifically requested them.

After this, the correspondence is moved onto the optical disc jukebox, and as the jukebox fills, the oldest disc is periodically archived and replaced with a blank one.

One function that isn't yet used is caller line identification (CLI), the system that allows a caller's telephone number to be identified before the call is answered. As Kennedy points out, not all telephone companies transfer the information across, so, for example, BT users will not receive the number of a Mercury user.

In addition, Kennedy says, experience in the US has shown that many people see CLI as intrusive. He also believes it may be a bit too technical for Asset's older customer base.

Asset also needs a lot of flexibility and involvement from different departments and personnel he says. "A lot of our work can be done by several people. We're working 24 hours a day 365 days a year, so you can't have a single personal account manager. The personal touch is delivered by the system, not by the individual operator.

"We can note the customer's style on their file, and give a satisfaction rating. There is room for notes, such as the correct way to pronounce their name, the customer's interests, whether they like to chat, and so on." But he stresses that the human side remains important. There is no use of voice mail, and all calls are answered by a person.

Tasks can also come from operators scheduling follow-up activities, or from queries forwarded to other operators, eg if special expertise or higher authority is needed.

Similarly, reports can show up high levels of task forwarding, perhaps indicating that an operator needs more training or assistance. Also, analysis of peak system load times and of how real data is processed can greatly improve the planning of staffing needs.

Bristol & West already had core systems running on mainframe computers, but according to group services director Kevin Flanagan, the new system needed to be differently orientated: "It's customer driven, not core-driven," he says. "On the core system, the screens are one account at a time. Asset starts with the customer first. We would expect that thinking to filter through to other areas of our business. too."

Flanagan says that, when starting out, "You have to be very clear and work through what you're going to achieve, for example the service levels expected by the customer. We had a choice: either the low-risk option of tailoring existing systems, or a higher-risk bespoke option. We chose the latter because it was more innovative and adaptable. It took a year to develop and we launched the system in January 1994. Since then it has been a process of continuous refinement."

As a result of Asset, Mary McSherry has become convinced of the value of software development via prototyping. Traditionally, a specification is created for a programme, teams of programmers are set to work, and months or years later the users are presented with a working system and the question "Is this what you wanted?".

Using prototyping, users are brought in right from the beginning to help decide how the system should look and work, with prototypes being created and discussed as the process goes on.

She notes a couple of warnings: "While prototyping gives enormous value in showing the users what the system will look like, you have to avoid tinkering it to death, and you have to be strict in setting an end point for the project." It also needs the commitment of the users, although in McSherry's experience they are very committed once they have become accustomed to the system.

The signs are that customers are impressed by the speed with which Asset can retrieve their details and respond to queries, and that operators are happy too.

The system had a very testing first year – when all of a certain bond issue matured on the same day, the daily incoming call rate leapt from the usual several hundred to over 2,000 calls – and there is a file of requests from account managers for things that would improve service.

Kevin Flanagan says that Bristol & West will use both protoyping and workflow management again, and is looking to implement something similar to Asset when it replaces its less flexible account-driven branch computing systems. ∎

Reprinted with permission from *Computer Weekly*, 15th June 1995.

CASE STUDY 2: ICI

Seeing eye to eye
by Julia Vowler

For a company as large and diverse as ICI, one of the UK's handful of truly world-class businesses, its IT structure is surprisingly simple. Even following the shedding of some businesses over the past few years, and the split with pharmaceuticals division Zeneca, ICI remains a highly diversified and decentralised organisation.

The company consists of five core businesses, from paints to explosives, each of which is itself a conglomerate of substantial businesses. This diversification has necessitated a similarly decentralised IT organisation to service each constituent ICI company, says group IS manager, Dr Richard Sykes.

"Each business has a significant IT resource and always has done," he says. This is partly for accounting reasons: each company is accountable for its own performance, and maximising return on assets, including IT, is key.

But it also makes sense because of the different markets each business operates in.

"The businesses need to have their own IT departments, which are very varied," says Sykes. "Some are quite small, for example at ICI Acrylics and ICI Polyurethanes. Some, for historical reasons, have substantial internal departments."

Each business requires different IT responses. ICI Paints, for example, is in the business of filling shelves at DIY stores with millions of cans of paint, whereas some of the chemical industries consist of only two plants selling to no more than a handful of big industrial customers.

But the diversification of IT within ICI is not total. Sykes is more than group IS director in name alone. In addition to the IT departments within individual businesses, ICI's corporate headquarters in Milbank, London, house the group IT function. This, says Sykes, has two roles.

"We provide services, such as global telecommunications and software development, which are available to all businesses. And we set the IT standards and policies for the company as a whole."

There is also a central purchasing department which can use ICI's huge size to obtain economies of scale in buying kit and software.

Despite the existence of central IT, Sykes is keen that it should be a help, not a burden, to ICI's businesses, and it rides with as light a rein as possible over the rest of the company.

"From having a staff of 40 in the central resource we now have only a handful who set standards in three key areas. These, by common consent, are the only areas where central IT has any degree of determination and responsibility over the businesses."

The first of the three areas is IT security. "No business is an island on this issue," observes Sykes.

The second is ensuring that the businesses can use ICI's international global telecommunications network and have a harmonised local area network (Lan) strategy to enable inter-business communication.

The third is to create a common office environment across ICI as a whole so that electronic documents can flow seamlessly throughout the company among the 18,000 of ICI's 67,000 employees who are connected to each other through E-mail. This is not new, however.

"We've had this for around 12 years, based on IBM's mainframe Profs system and Digital Equipment's All-ln-One," says Sykes. Both are linked to ICI's own electronic document transmission system.

Outside those few areas where a centrally derived standard operates, ICI also seeks to achieve consensus on other areas of IT.

▶

"There's also fairly good consensus on other underlying IT systems, such as accounting and manufacturing systems," says Sykes. "Although there is no corporate edict, there is strong consensus that a mix of SAP's mainframe R2 and client/server R3 packages, plus SAA's BPICS, cover most of what we need. Clearly, we'll have to see how this may change in the next two to three years as the products develop."

Because while financial data required for global consolidation can be collected easily enough from the different packages, there is no top down reason at the moment for standardising on only one.

"We do a lot of technical consulting, but because technical people can debate issues indefinitely, we apply an 80:20 rule to making the final choice," says Sykes. "My role is strategic leadership because the main drivers for IT choice always come from the businesses."

This is, in a nutshell, ICI's IT strategy. "I have a notice on my door, 'Business information management must be business shaped and business driven'," Sykes says.

As well as setting standards by consensus, the central IT function includes a corporate IT service available to businesses. ICI TASC (Telecommunications and Service Computing) consists of two businesses which each turn over £20m a year and which trade profitably within ICI and absorb no corporate subsidy.

The telecoms infrastructure covers North America, Asia Pacific and Europe, and interfaces with ICI Australia which has its own IT network and installations. Originally, ICI built its own telecoms network because it was reluctant to pay BT's tariffs.

"We developed the inhouse capability to buy raw bandwidth and use our own digital inter-site dialling. It was well ahead of the market and saved us money and gave us a great deal of flexibility," says Sykes.

But when Zeneca was split off, the telecoms network had to be split up as well. "By then, the telecoms market had changed completely, and had become increasingly sophisticated," says Sykes. "We went out to tender and gave the contract to Racal who beat BT very firmly, plus Mercury and AT&T."

The deal gave Racal ICI's network, together with ICI's 20 telecoms engineers, and slashed ICI's tariffs by 20%. "It was a win-win deal," says Sykes

The second arm of TASC is the software service side. This acts as an independent software house, which ICI's individual departments commission to write business applications. However, it cannot rely on a captive market within ICI.

"No ICI business has to use it, and it is also free to develop commercially marketable software to sell outside ICI," says Sykes.

However, buying in has become increasingly prevalent within ICI businesses, whether it is from the central software development organisation within TASC or from independent systems and software companies.

"Within a few years there will be 50:50 internal and external sourced systems," says Sykes.

Moreover, there is a wholesale shift away from legacy systems as individual businesses undertake business process redesign. This is underpinned by new packages such as SAA's BPICS accounting and manufacturing software which was chosen by ICI Paints last year as part of its outsourcing deal with Computer Sciences Corporation.

As ICI moves with the times away from inhouse development towards a far more diverse approach, the skills required change, too. Sykes is currently focusing attention on what overall skills those whose work is associated with IT should have.

The trend is clearly away from a large number of highly expert IT professionals capable of building their own systems, whether telecoms or applications. Instead the new emphasis is on the ability to see just how the application of IT can be used to solve business problems and lend competitive advantage to ICI.

"Throughout, the key issue is people skills,"

says Sykes, a founder member of the IT Skills Forum, a collection of top IT managers concerned about the looming problem of mapping IT to business requirements.

"We are seeing a significant shift to new IT competencies within ICI, and we are also seeing a change in attitude among those who are business people.

"Now we are looking for IT people who are business literate as well literate in IT, to take their place as part of the business team and develop IT strategies to underwrite business performance.

"We are looking for a different breed of IT player." ■

Reprinted with permission from *Computer Weekly*, 14th September 1995.

PART 4

Strategic MSS

'Our little systems have their day. They have their day and cease to be.'
Alfred Tennyson

CHAPTER 14

Combining SISP/SCB and MSS: Strategic MSS

14.1 INTRODUCTION

Part 2 introduced the concept of MSS and described the issues to be addressed within MSS development. One vital issue concerning the development of any IS project (which may be an MSS project) is whether it is in line with corporate objectives and mission. Alignment may occur between an IS project and corporate objectives and mission by chance or on management's intuition. However, this approach is risky and, given the demands placed on IS/IT investment to demonstrate value for money, is not advocated. On the other hand, the appropriate combination of SISP/SCB leads to the identification of IS projects that are aligned with corporate objectives and mission.

This chapter focuses on the interrelationships between the organisation, SISP/SCB and MSS. The most important relationship is that the output from SISP/SCB determines the organisational needs for MSS. Any MSS that results from SISP/SCB is aligned with corporate objectives and mission, and is, by inference, of value to the organisation. An MSS that is aligned is termed a *Strategic MSS*. It is important to note that any MSS has the potential to be a Strategic MSS, irrespective of whether it supports operational control, management control or strategic planning activities. The factor which determines whether or not an MSS is a Strategic MSS is its alignment with corporate objectives and mission.

It is worth stressing that the use of the term *strategic* with respect to MSS implies a broader category of CBIS than that considered within other work. In general, any MSS has the potential to be a Strategic MSS, irrespective of whether it supports operational control, management control or strategic planning activities. The factor which determines whether or not an MSS is a Strategic MSS is its alignment with corporate objectives and mission. More specifically, the Strategic Relevance And Impact Grid, which was described in Chapter 10, places each IS/IT aspect into one of four quadrants. Only one quadrant of the grid is labelled strategic, despite the fact that all four quadrants of the grid refer to MSS provisions that are aligned with corporate objectives and mission. Given the definition of Strategic MSS within this book, however, MSS that lie in any of the four quadrants of the Strategic Relevance And Impact Grid are classed as Strategic MSS provisions.

The structure of this chapter is as follows. Section 14.2 introduces three possible relationships between the organisation, SISP/SCB and MSS. Section 14.3 focuses on the principal relationship between SISP/SCB and MSS, where the specification of the latter forms part of the output of the former. Exploring this relationship in detail requires the application of several of the approaches discussed in both Parts 2 and 3 of this book. Sections 14.4 briefly examines two other relationships that exist between the organisation, SISP/SCB and MSS. These relationships occur because of the particular role of MSS as management support tools. Finally, Section 14.5 provides a summary of this chapter.

At the end of this chapter the reader should understand:

- *The ways that the organisation, SISP/SCB and MSS interrelate*
- *The ways in which Strategic MSS can be identified from SISP/SCB activities*
- *The role of MSS in organisational strategy management (planning and controlling)*
- *The role of MSS within SISP/SCB activities*

14.2   AN OVERVIEW OF RELATIONSHIPS BETWEEN ORGANISATION, SISP/SCB AND MSS

Figure 9.3 illustrates the use of an appropriate combination of SISP/SCB as the means by which a resulting IS strategy reflects the organisation's mission and strategy. SISP/SCB, organisational mission and organisational strategy influence, and are influenced by, each other. The IS strategy which results from SISP/SCB includes the identification of suitable IS projects for implementation.

Figure 14.1 extends the diagram presented in Figure 9.3 to highlight the possible relationships between MSS and SISP/SCB. Firstly, it shows that the IS provision of an IS strategy, produced from an appropriate combination of SISP/SCB, may include both Strategic MSS provision and the provision of other IS (such as DP and inter-organisation systems). Thus, a relationship may exist between SISP/SCB and Strategic MSS provision, where the requirements for Strategic MSS form part of the IS provision component of the IS strategy which results from SISP/SCB. The output from effective SISP/SCB never results in MSS that are not strategic, if we use this term in the manner described in the previous section.

Relationships also exist between MSS provision and both the organisational strategy and mission. MSS may provide current organisational strategy support and current mission support by supporting management activities at various levels of the organisation. They support the planning of, and the monitoring and controlling of, operations towards the achievement of organisational strategy and mission. Some MSS may support the management of the mission and organisational strategy themselves. For example, the provision of external information by an MSS, regarding competitors and general economic and demographic trends, may trigger developments in overall mission and/or organisational strategy.

Finally, both SISP and SCB involve many management decisions, including how many participants to involve in a SISP process, what methodology to adopt, and what techniques to employ. MSS can be developed to aid both SISP activities and the SCB process.

The next section examines in more detail the relationship between SISP/SCB and the Strategic MSS provision identified within the IS strategy. Several SISP techniques are used to show particular ways by which the requirements for Strategic MSS can be identified.

Fig 14.1 The relationships between the organisational strategy and mission, SISP/SCB and MSS

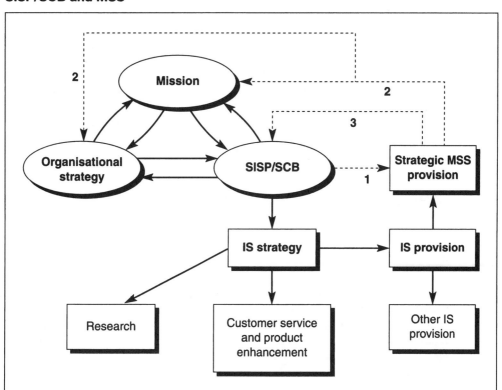

There are three relationships, as illustrated by the numbers on the diagram above. Firstly, SISP/SCB activities may result in an IS strategy. The IS strategy may prescribe an IS provision, a subset of which may be Strategic MSS. Secondly, MSS can be used to support organisational strategy and mission management (planning and controlling). Thirdly, MSS can be used to support SISP/SCB activities. The second and third relationships occur due to the role of MSS in supporting information handling and decision making tasks of management.

14.3   STRATEGIC MSS AS A RESULT OF SISP/SCB

Both SISP and SCB exist within an organisation, but the relative amounts will differ depending on factors such as the size of the organisation and the business environment. As illustrated in Figure 9.4, SCB is concerned with the behavioural aspects surrounding strategy formulation such as communication, vision, motivation and ownership. SISP is concerned with the mechanistic aspects of strategy formulation.

14.3.1 Strategic MSS resulting from SCB

Strategic MSS may result from the SCB process. Improvements in strategic thinking, through SCB, lead to improvements in strategy formulation in general, and in the identification of Strategic MSS in particular. There is no formula that can be applied to ensure improved strategy formulation. However, management can put into place a more conducive working environment for supporting strategic thinking amongst staff by, for example:

- Opening the channels for communicating mission and organisational strategy from the senior management to all staff, and for ideas and visions to be communicated from all staff to appropriate management.
- Encouraging staff to be forward-looking and to think strategically, and to communicate their ideas and visions to interested parties and stakeholders.
- Encouraging ownership of ideas and visions, and the responsibility of sharing ideas and visions.

14.3.2 Strategic MSS results from SISP: a general overview

SISP provides a structured way of identifying IS, which may be Strategic MSS, which support and enhance organisational strategy. The following paragraphs relate MSS issues to the major components of a SISP activity (as detailed in Section 9.5.2) in turn.

Defining the scope of the SISP exercise It is important to have a SISP team that has the combined knowledge and skills to embrace all aspects of information needs, IS and IT. A SISP team whose members have knowledge in a few specialist areas of IS/IT may be inclined to favour applications based on their views, albeit unconsciously. MSS knowledge and skills need to form part of the combined knowledge and skills of the team.

Understanding and interpreting the business requirements

This component includes a review of existing IS/IT and the identification of potential IS/IT applications. MSS that are in current use may serve to provide useful insight into the nature of any further MSS implementations and the environment within which they are to be embedded. For example, an existing MSS providing active decision making support may not be used by the intended manager. This may be due to various reasons, including:

- The manager's perception of the MSS as a tool not considered to be for management use.
- The manager's inadequate knowledge about the functionality of, and the possible advantages of using, the MSS.
- The unsuitable interaction method provided by the MSS.
- Current organisational policy does not enforce or persuade the manager to use it.

These individual issues associated with the use of a particular MSS may signal not only that future development of the existing system may be warranted or that non-technical issues need to be addressed surrounding the use of the MSS within the organisation, but also more general concerns about the implementation of future MSS within the organisation. The perception of the MSS by the manager and the absence of enforcement or persuasion may signify a view amongst potential and existing MSS users that senior management are not committed to the use of MSS in general. This perception (albeit correct or incorrect) must be rectified as it has a great bearing on all future MSS developments and their success.

Corporate strategy, once established, must be assessed with respect to potential MSS provision. Corporate CSFs could provide a starting point for this, where information needs are linked to each CSF in turn, and MSS to support those information needs identified (this is described more comprehensively in Section 14.3.2 below with respect to the use of the CSF technique within SISP methodologies). A SISP team should look further afield at new developments in IS/IT, and assess their potential to contribute to the support of the identified information needs. For example, advances in neural networks should be assessed to see if they can support active decision making where more traditional approaches (such as Rule-based models) are less effective. The greater potential for systems integration, in terms of hardware, software and communications networks, increases the possibilities for the SISP teams to consider physical MSS implementations, each of which offers a variety of interrelated functionality.

In addition to focusing on existing corporate MSS, the SISP team should also consider other existing IS, such as inter-organisation systems and DP systems. These systems provide a useful source of data. It may be possible to exploit this data for management decision making within the context of overall corporate strategy.

Defining the organisational needs and the underpinning systems architecture

The particular requirements for MSS need to be identified at this point. MSS requirements may be concerned predominantly with non-technical issues surrounding an existing MSS, such as commitment, education and training. Some requirements may be concerned with the development of existing MSS to ensure that they are used more effectively or have additional functionality, whereas others may relate to the development of new applications systems. Feasibility issues (as described in Chapter 7) regarding the provision of new MSS implementations or the enhancement of existing MSS implementations, may be assessed to some degree at this stage to ensure that any MSS project established at the next stage is both realistic and comprehensive in its treatment of non-technical as well as technical influences.

Formulate the information, IS and IT strategies

This is where the projects are defined, together with their relationships with other IS and their underlying IT requirements. Ordering of all the IS projects identified is an important activity within this stage of SISP. The SISP team should take into account the following issues when ordering any IS projects:

- The dependency of one project on another system's effective implementation – an IS project should not be embarked upon unless a system, upon which the project depends, is operating effectively.
- The priority of IS projects, as indicated by the priority of the corporate CSFs with which it is associated.
- The project risk – starting with a less risky project with a good likelihood of success can serve to instill confidence in the development team and help in gaining user commitment to future projects; success does breed success!
- The affinity of the target user base to computerised systems – starting with a project where a user exists who will assess the system fairly may lead to gaining a general internal ambassador for computerised systems within the company.

The last two issues are particularly relevant to MSS where many benefits are intangible or uncertain, and where costs are also uncertain. Choosing an initial project where benefits are most likely to be achieved and the MSS is welcomed can be very helpful in gaining support for future MSS developments. The Connoisseur Foods case study, described in Alter (1980), demonstrates the significant effect that an initial MSS can have on future implementations.

Present the final output to the client

The final deliverables will be determined by the scope of the SISP activity laid down at the outset. It may be the case that an IS development budget was fixed at the commencement of SISP activity. In this case, only those projects of sufficiently high priority which in combination are not expected to exceed the budget are presented (estimation of financial resources is particularly problematic with respect to MSS, however, as already described in Chapter 7). Often, all projects are presented for overall review and subsequent selection by the client, with possible recommendations as to the preferred subset being made by the SISP team.

14.3.3 Establishing strategic MSS: the role of SISP techniques/methodologies

As described in Part 3 of this book, SISP methodologies exist to guide the activities involved in a SISP exercise. A SISP methodology comprises one or more SISP techniques. Most of these techniques are used to determine IS, including Strategic MSS, opportunities. The following paragraphs examine how several of the SISP methodologies/techniques described in Chapters 9 and 10 support the identification of Strategic MSS functionality.

SWOT Analysis

SWOT analysis was described briefly in Chapter 9. An appraisal of a company's strengths and weaknesses may include a description of current IS/IT provision and related issues (such as human resource issues). Opportunities and threats may also refer to potential future IS/IT provision and associated issues. When looking towards capitalising on strengths, reducing weakness, seizing opportunities and minimising threats, IS solutions should be considered, some of which may be Strategic MSS.

During the SISP activity at Business Link Leicestershire (BLL, see the case study in Chapter 15), a SWOT analysis was the first technique employed. This enabled the consultants to gain an overall picture of the company within which SISP/SCB activities were taking place. Various strengths, weaknesses, opportunities and threats were enumerated, including:

- *Strengths* – a highly committed and experienced workforce.
- *Weaknesses* – marketing not pro-active, isolated patches of computer literate personnel.
- *Opportunities* – short-term IT budget set at a good rate.
- *Threats* – longer-term government changes in funding available for Business Links in general and operating practices.

IS/IT provision can help BLL to capitalise on its strengths, overcome its weaknesses, seize opportunities and reduce threats. For example, the above combination of SWOT elements indicates the requirement of MSS functionality that supports pro-active marketing decisions (such as which existing or potential customers to target, what services to offer to which customers, etc.). Human resource issues, such as specific MSS training, and general computer literacy training and education, need to be addressed as an integral part of this MSS provision. Present availability of funds but potential funding problems in the future indicate that MSS investment should be made sooner rather than later.

CSF Technique

SWOT analysis can help identify potential Strategic MSS functionality and associated projects, but does not provide any guidance as to their relative priority. The CSF technique may not only aid the identification of several Strategic MSS projects, but also help in assigning a priority level to each project.

The CSF technique, and its relationships with the CSF methodology, were described in detail in Chapter 10. Strategic MSS functionality may be identified from reviewing the information needs associated with each of the organisational CSFs established using the CSF technique. Organisational CSFs may, however, be too general to derive specific information needs. A hierarchy of CSFs (similar to the CSF/KPI hierarchy technique explained with respect to MSS design in Chapter 7) may need to be specified before particular information needs can be identified.

Within the SISP activity at BLL, the CSF technique was used in conjunction with other techniques, such as SWOT analysis, for assessing IS provision to support corporate objectives. A set of seven organisational CSFs were identified from the corporate strategy document. These were then reviewed, and contributing CSFs determined. For each contributing CSF, potential assistance via IS was considered. This led to the identification of the required Strategic MSS functionality. Some aspects of this functionality had already been uncovered as a result of SWOT analysis. An assessment of the relative importance of each organisational CSF to corporate achievement can be used to attach priority levels to each identified aspect of Strategic MSS functionality.

For example, one of the seven organisational CSFs at BLL was concerned with corporate image enhancement, and the spread of awareness and image enhancement of BLL's products and services, both within the locality and at national level. Four contributing CSFs were then identified that related to this CSF:

- Identifying different needs of both existing and potential customers.
- Communicating quickly and easily with potential and existing customers.
- Having a flagship product that will enhance BLL's view at both local and national level.
- Creating a quality image, by ensuring services are clear, effective and efficient, and identified with BLL, by ensuring problems are owned by an employee of BLL from start to finish, and by the high quality packaging of services and products.

Each of these contributing CSFs was discussed with regard to possible IS provision. The Strategic MSS functionality that was uncovered from this investigation included:

- MSS functionality to support pro-active marketing.
- E-mail, with Internet access, and/or Videoconferencing system(s), to communicate with existing or potential customers quickly and easily.
- Use of Teleconferencing systems as part of the 'Centre of Excellence' flagship service concept (originally identified by the CEO of BLL) for client management to use within group meetings where participants are remotely located.

- Document preparation systems to enhance the quality of information prepared by BLL on behalf of a client.

Note that the support of pro-active marketing was also identified as a result of the SWOT analysis. The high importance of this particular CSF to BLL's corporate strategy led to the provision of this MSS functionality being given high priority at BLL.

Strategic Relevance And Impact Grid and its adaptations

This technique, described in detail in Chapter 10, provides a way of viewing existing IS/MSS provision in the context of corporate strategy and mission, and where future developments with regard to this provision are required. A Strategic Relevance And Impact Grid can be used to establish the worth of current IS/MSS provision as perceived by employees within an organisation. Assessing this perception against another Strategic Relevance And Impact Grid, which establishes the worth of current IS/MSS provision from the SISP team's perspective, enables differences in views to be identified. This leads to the specification of ways by which the employees' views of current IS/MSS provision can be changed to those of the SISP team. In addition, potential IS provision, identified using other techniques such as SWOT analysis and CSF technique, can also be placed on a Strategic Relevance And Impact Grid to indicate their potential contribution to corporate strategy.

The Strategic Relevance And Impact Grid was used in all the above ways within the SISP activity at BLL. One existing IS within BLL was Link Track, a client tracking system developed by Initiative Software. Due to a variety of predominantly non-technical factors, Link Track was viewed as being in the factory quadrant of the grid: although necessary for sustaining current business, the use of Link Track within BLL was not considered vital to future company success. However, given the mission of BLL and the functionality provided by Link Track, the system was assessed by the SISP team as being in the strategic quadrant of the grid. This assessment reflects Link Track's vital role not only in maintaining current business but also in supporting future operations. Indeed, Link Track provided the underlying ability to support the pro-active marketing of services and products to both potential and existing customers. The problem lay not with the limitations of Link Track, rather with how it had been introduced to employees and configured to the needs of BLL. A project was specified that served to change the attitudes of employees towards Link Track and to enhance the IS/MSS functionality of Link Track to support BLL corporate strategy more comprehensively.

Another existing MSS provision was an internal e-mail facility. This was used very occasionally by BLL staff for information communication. In terms of the Strategic Relevance And Impact Grid, the e-mail facility was viewed as a support facility, where it was considered vital for neither current business activities nor future business activities. The SISP team however viewed e-mail as lying in the strategic quadrant of the grid, as communication between clients and BLL (via Internet access), and within BLL in support of client's needs, is vital to both current and future business (as shown by the Strategic MSS provision identified by applying the CSF technique). This laid the foundations of a Strategic MSS project concerned with the linking of the internal e-mail facility to the Internet and for ensuring employees were in a position to exploit the opportunities provided by e-mail facilities.

Other Techniques for the Support of Strategic MSS Determination

The techniques mentioned individually in the preceding subsections are only a few of the many SISP techniques that are available to aid identification of IS in general, and Strategic MSS in particular. For instance, Porter's Five Forces Model, as discussed in Chapter 10, can be used to aid identification of suitable IS provision (which may, or may not, include the identification of Strategic MSS functionality). Each of the Five Forces are assessed, with respect to overall corporate strategy, to see if IS/MSS can be used to combat a threat or take advantage of an opportunity. Value Chain Analysis (described briefly in Chapter 9, and in Chapter 10 as a component of the METHOD/1 approach) can be used to identify IS opportunities with respect to a company's strategically important business activities. The assessment of technology support activities associated with each of the primary activities and their linkages may lead to the identification of Strategic MSS. Looking at the value chain of a core product or service alongside that of its suppliers can lead to the identification of inter-organisation systems that provide MSS functionality to both parties. This may also occur when the value chain of a company's core product or service is viewed alongside that of its customers.

14.4 RELATIONSHIPS DUE TO THE SUPPORT ROLE OF MSS

14.4.1 Relationships between strategic MSS, and organisational strategy and mission

As stated in Section 14.2, relationships exist between Strategic MSS provision and both the organisational strategy and mission. This is due to the special role that MSS play with regard to management activities within an organisation. Firstly, MSS may provide current organisational strategy support and current mission support by supporting management activities at various levels of the organisation. For example, senior management may have access to an MSS that enables them to monitor and control corporate operations that are vital to organisational success. Often, a Briefing Book facility or a set of hierarchically interlinked as-needed pre-defined information reports with drill down capabilities is provided (as described in Chapter 5). An iconic interface with hotspots and traffic light colour coding is often employed, providing management with a very easy to use method of interacting directly with the MSS. The CSF/KPI hierarchy diagramming technique for designing these MSS (see Chapter 7) can follow directly from the organisational CSFs identified during a SISP exercise.

A Strategic MSS may not only aid monitoring and controlling of organisational CSFs associated with current organisational strategy and mission, but also aid decision making with respect to corporate strategic planning. External information may be available, via appropriate external databases, regarding competitors and general economic and demographic trends. Upon retrieving this information via an MSS that provides passive decision making support, strategists can assess current strategy in the light of changes and trends. This may lead to a re-assessment of organisational mission and strategy, and in turn require a new appraisal of IS strategy via SCB/SISP activities.

Strategic planning involves many decisions, typically made by a group. MSS that provide active support for group decision making, such as Decision Rooms, are therefore of potential benefit to these decisions. Communication between members of the group may be facilitated by communication support capabilities such as e-mail, Tele-conferencing and Chat facilities. Many documents may need to be prepared during the course of strategic planning activities, including the resultant corporate strategic plan. These documents may be created using document preparation systems, both for individual and joint authoring.

Moormann and Lochte-Holtgreven (1993) describe a prototype MSS, called Strat-Consult, which aims to provide an integrated set of facilities to support strategic planning activities. It comprises a set of interrelated modules, each of which provides support for some aspect of strategic planning activity. For example, 'external database access', 'SWOT analysis' and 'Decision Tree Technique' are modules of the prototype system. A menu hierarchy is provided for module selection. The use of a particular module may result in an output which can form the input to one or more modules used at a later stage. Module results are therefore stored by StratConsult in appropriate data files for use within subsequent modules.

StratConsult provides a basis upon which more generic MSS (or development packages) can be provided to support strategic planning activities. Eventually, this MSS could provide a set of interdependent modules, which is then tailored to a company's specific needs. Underlying support for module interrelationships could be provided via the definition and support of data structures that capture module inputs and outputs. An interrelationship would exist between two modules when the data structure of one of a module's outputs is the same as the data structure of one of the other module's inputs. The definition of new data structures should be easily achieved. Thus, new strategic planning modules could be added rapidly by

- describing new input and output data structures for the module and/or linking input and outputs to existing data structures, and
- by storing the module in the correct computer workspace area.

Any new module should be reflected automatically within the overall MSS menu hierarchy, when the above procedure has been undertaken effectively. A particular company may only require a subset of the modules provided by the system. Thus, only the required subset is provided for that particular company and the MSS menu automatically reflects this partial provision. Furthermore, some ordering of module usage may need to be specified to reflect the strategic planning approach of a particular company. A method by which sequences can be captured and used to control module usage should be provided as part of this system.

At present, there is conflicting evidence as to whether current MSS implementations always provide effective support for corporate strategic planning, monitoring and controlling. For instance, Holohan (1992) studied several MSS which were used within business performance appraisal. The majority of these systems were found to focus on supporting the monitoring and controlling of one aspect of the corporation, rather than overall business activity. Little support was provided within these systems for aiding the formulation of new corporate strategy. In a very recent survey of 97 of the top 800 Irish organisations, Finnegan et al. (1995) found that current MSS support for external information needs was perceived as poor. Rather, the marketing function within the organisation was considered to be the best source of external information. Sources of information that are current, objective, public and proactive were considered most valuable, such as journals and publicly available reports. Finnegan et al.'s study confirms Holohan's view of current MSS, but provides additional insight into the most appropriate provision of external information to suit management requirements. Different findings on current MSS provision for external information support is presented by Edwards and Peppard (1993). Their analysis of 23 cases of MSS supporting business performance appraisal showed nearly half provided external information retrieval functions for the monitoring of the external and competitive environment. However, although this paper shows MSS that have embraced external information sourcing within their functionality, the worth of these facilities, relative to other sources of external information, is not assessed.

14.4.2 Relationships between strategic MSS and SISP/SCB activities

There are many decisions to be made during SISP/SCB activities, including those concerning:

- the most appropriate composition of the SISP team
- the choice of methodology and techniques to employ
- the most effective method of opening up channels of communication to allow the flow of ideas and visions from staff to occur openly and freely
- the most appropriate method by which the success of the SISP/SCB process can be measured.

As decision making support tools, MSS can be developed to aid management decision making within both SISP and SCB activities. In addition, a large quantity of information may need to be collated and analysed during SISP/SCB activities. Information preparation and information handling activities may also be facilitated by MSS.

A review of IT support for SISP activities is provided by Sambamurphy et. al. (1993). In this paper, several organisational factors were considered to influence the overall approach to SISP, namely:

- The organisation's reliance on IS/IT – is IS/IT fundamental to organisational strategy achievement?
- The organisation's heterogeneity of markets between its SBUs.
- The SISP team's existing knowledge and experience in SISP.
- The level of existing agreement between SISP team members.

Within this review, issues relating to MSS provision are highlighted. For example, if an organisation's reliance on IS/IT is high, then there are more issues to bear in mind when considering IS/IT within the corporation than when reliance on IS/IT is low. In addition, the organisation has more likelihood of not knowing all the issues to bear in mind when the reliance on IS/IT is high. Thus, information acquisition with regard to SISP is different when organisational reliance on IS/IT is high to when it is low. Specifically, when reliance on IS/IT is high, the acquisition of information needs to be focused, otherwise information overload may occur. MSS that enable the summarising of information before dissemination to selected SISP team members could prove very beneficial. An iterative, trial and error approach to uncovering all the issues of relevance is also needed. *Ad hoc* querying of both individuals (using support facilities such as e-mail and Videoconferencing) and databases may prove particularly useful to support this approach. When reliance on IS/IT is low, less information is needed and the information needed is more clearly defined a priori. Thus, MSS that enable the scanning of pre-defined information reports may be adequate support in this case.

Apart from information acquisition and distribution issues, Sambamurphy et. al. also examine the impact on the aforementioned organisational factors on the level and nature of debate and argumentation needed to be built into the IT planning process. This has implications for the MSS provision for group decision making, in terms of the facilities provided. Essentially, where potential conflict between members' views is low, the focus of MSS facilities is expected to be on the development of consensus regarding an appropriate IS/IT strategy. However, as the potential conflict between the views of the SISP team members increases, the MSS must also embrace support for the explicit identification and analysis of different member's assumptions. Negotiation and compromise become key components of any SISP activities and need to be reflected within any MSS provision.

Aspects of SISP could be supported by an integrated MSS, similar to the StratConsult system which was provided for corporate strategic planning support. A comprehensive MSS for supporting SISP activities should include modules to aid:

- planning for SISP activity
- the activities and associated techniques employed within SISP activity, which may be embraced within a named SISP methodology
- post-SISP activity

Pre-SISP activity involves the choice of the SISP team and the techniques/methodologies to employ. In order to facilitate the choice of team structure, an MSS module could be provided which embraces a Rule-based model of the decision situation. The person whose responsibility it is to select the team can use this module to verify the soundness of the proposed team. On receiving answers to a series of questions, the MSS provides an estimation of the quality of the proposal, highlighting strengths and weaknesses in the current human profile (for example, the absence of a executive sponsor, the need for greater experience via a consultant, etc.)

Selection of the appropriate techniques/methodologies could also be aided by another MSS module. The module could provide an automated version of the selection approach described in Section 11.4. For each proposed methodology, the user is requested for a value, or set of values (when considering the constituency criterion), for each of the structural complexity criterion in turn. A value for each of the applications complexity criterion also needs to be provided, although the majority of these should remain the same across each methodology to be considered. The MSS module could process the information, and graphically depict either the Complexity grid (as illustrated in Figure 11.3) and the Spatial Profile (as illustrated in Figure 11.4) for a particular methodology. Overlaying different methodologies either on the same Complexity Grid, with appropriate labelling, or on a Spatial Profile diagram, using colour to distinguish the graph for each methodology, allows comparisons to be drawn. This can facilitate methodology selection. Interestingly, this approach to evaluating SISP methodologies also permits experimentation with the composition of the SISP team. As well as pointing out similar weaknesses to that established within the previously described Rule-based MSS module, it may also lead to the re-use of the SISP team selection module, due to the methodology issues now apparent. It is expected that these two MSS modules will be used in tandem to ensure that the most effective combination of SISP team and SISP methodology is selected for the situation in question.

Having established the composition of the SISP team and the SISP methodology to be utilised, actual SISP activity can progress. The integrated MSS should facilitate progression through the required SISP activities, by providing appropriate underlying support modules. Indeed, the system may also permit the user to specify, in a suitably formal language, the exact way in which the MSS is to support the current SISP methodology. Such a SISP methodology support specification needs to identify the set of support modules which is to be used, a subset of which may support recognised SISP techniques, together with any ordering imposed on modules, any module iteration and optionality of module application. In total, the specification delimits and prescribes the use of named MSS modules for the chosen SISP methodology. Figures 14.2 and 14.3 illustrate, in combination, the manner in which a SISP methodology support specification could lead to the configuration of the underlying MSS modules for supporting a particular SISP methodology.

Each SISP technique may be supported by one or more modules within the integrated MSS. For instance, a SWOT analysis module may be provided. This may be fairly passive in support, simply allowing the recording of Strengths, Weaknesses, Opportunities and Threats that have been identified by the SISP team. Alternatively, it

Fig 14.2 A possible methodology support specification for a SISP exercise

iteration of:
>> SWOT analysis (*output* SWOT);
>> CSF analysis (*input* corporate CSFs; *output* corporate information needs,
>>> *output* priorities);
>> Assess New IS (*input* SWOT, *input* corporate information needs,
>>> *output* new systems);
>> Assess Existing IS (*output* existing systems);
>> Strategic Relevance And Impact Grid Analysis (*input* new systems, *input*
>>> existing systems, *output* IS projects);
>> Assess IS Projects (*input* IS projects, *input* priorities, *input* budget, *output*
>>> assessed IS projects);
iteration end

Key
; = sequence

A SISP methodology support specification, such as that illustrated in the example above, identifies the particular SISP activity/technique support modules to be utilised, together with their ordering, iteration and optionality, within the SISP exercise of interest. For instance, 'SWOT analysis', 'CSF analysis', and 'Strategic Relevance And Impact Grid Analysis' are three support modules for SWOT analysis, CSF and Strategic Relevance And Impact Grid techniques respectively. The 'assess new IS' and 'assess existing IS' activity support modules fill in the gaps between the technique support modules to ensure more complete support of the SISP methodology in hand.

Fig 14.3 The SISP methodology specification's use in guiding MSS module usage

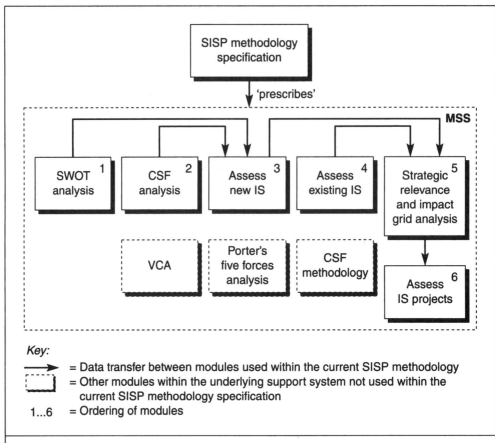

The SISP methodology specification, given in Figure 14.2, can be used to configure the underlying MSS. As shown in the above diagram, the MSS modules available to support the methodology are ordered and the data transfers required between modules are established from the specification. A comprehensive MSS should provide a variety of modules to support different SISP techniques and activities, a subset of which will be used within a particular SISP methodology application.

In total, a SISP methodology specification, such as that presented in Figure 14.2, identifies the set of underlying support modules required from an MSS to aid a particular SISP methodology, and the relationships between the modules (in terms of module ordering and data transfer).

may provide more guidance to the SISP team in terms of how to go about the activity. This may be provided by an active decision making support module which employs a Rule-based model based on the experiences and knowledge of recognised SISP experts.

The CSF technique may be supported by one or more MSS modules. For instance, a module may be provided that guides the user to consider and document organisational CSFs, possibly linking organisational CSFs to CSFs at a more specific level of detail, and the information needs that result from these more specific CSFs (either individually or in combination). Any gaps in the chain from organisational CSFs to information needs (for example, where information needs are not documented for a particular specific CSF and there is no explicit recognition from the user that this is meant to be the situation) should be highlighted to the user at appropriate times, thus ensuring information needs identification is complete based on the CSF technique. In addition, the Strategic Relevance And Impact Grid technique may also be supported by one or more MSS modules. Given that the existing systems within the company in question have already been enumerated and assessed, a module may provide a grid on which each existing system can be placed based on the general perception of that system held by corporate personnel. Another grid may also be provided upon which each existing system is placed based on the SISP team's views of the system. New systems can also be positioned on the same grid. From this, the MSS module can guide the user to consider all aspects of change within the list of resultant IS projects, which could range from a change of view within the company regarding an existing IS to the implementation of a new IS which will have substantial impact on corporate activities.

An MSS module may be explicitly tied to other MSS modules so that the requisite support can be provided. This may be due to one or both of the following reasons:

1. A SISP technique or activity may be available both on a standalone basis, or as part of a particular SISP methodology. Thus, a module which supports this SISP technique or activity may be referred to by another module which supports a methodology that has this technique or activity as one of its components.
2. Information sourcing may need to be available within several SISP activities. For example, MSS modules that provide access to external databanks may need to be available to all MSS modules that need to investigate external issues, for example modules that support Porter's five forces model, CSF methodology, SWOT analysis, and the 'determining new systems' activity.

Indeed, it is possible that MSS modules will be available that are never referred to explicitly within a SISP methodology support specification, but are used within one or more of the modules that are explicitly referenced.

The output of a SISP exercise is typically a written document that includes an explanation of the process employed, the results at both intermediate stages and at the end of the SISP exercise and any recommendations. This document needs to be prepared using appropriate document preparation systems, either by an individual or by a group using Joint Authoring Systems. Much of the input to the document, in terms of the overall process and results, can be provided by the recording of the progression through the activities and the results of each activity by the MSS described in previous paragraphs. Indeed, one or more of the modules within this MSS may facilitate document preparation.

Finally, SISP activity is a group activity, involving many decisions. An MSS, such as that proposed above, may need to be available within a group setting, such as through a Decision Room environment. Aspects such as the prioritising of CSFs, which results in the 'priorities' output, may not be easily determined from previous corporate strategic planning activities. Thus, debate on this issue may need to take place between SISP team members. Furthermore, the identification of IS projects may require some form of brainstorming on the part of SISP team members, where this is guided by the support system's identification of information needs. Integrating the underlying support system for SISP activity into a Decision Room environment extends the support available to the SISP team to include groups decision making techniques, such as voting, brainstorming and NGT (refer to Chapter 6 for a general discussion of the Decision Room concept and the associated group decision making techniques).

14.5   SUMMARY

This chapter has examined the possible relationships between:

- the organisation's mission and strategy,
- SISP/SCB
- MSS.

One very important relationship is that the output from SISP/SCB activities determines the organisational needs for MSS. Any MSS that results from effective SISP/SCB is aligned with corporate objectives and mission, and is, by inference, of value to the organisation. Within this book, an MSS that is aligned is termed a *Strategic MSS*.

Two other relationships exist: one between Strategic MSS provision and the organisation's mission and strategy, and the other between Strategic MSS provision and SISP/SCB activities. These are a consequence of the supportive role that MSS play. Specifically, MSS are designed to support the information handling and decision making activities of management. These activities occur within strategic management tasks in general, and SISP/SCB activities in particular. The nature of current MSS functionality to support general strategic planning and controlling tasks, and the effectiveness of this support, was discussed. A possible approach to supporting SISP activities in particular via MSS functionality was proposed. This support was based on the configuration of an MSS which comprised a library of MSS modules, that together support the preparation for, and documenting of, SISP activity as well as the actual SISP activity itself.

In summary, this chapter has provided a description of how MSS and SISP/SCB can be integrated to provide Strategic MSS provisions for an organisation, and how Strategic MSS themselves can support organisational strategy management and SISP/SCB activities. Based on these relationships, the knowledge gained from Part 2 concerning MSS design and development, and the knowledge of both SISP/SCB activities and SISP approaches, techniques and tools, readers are well equipped to identify, design and develop Strategic MSS.

References

Alter S L (1980) *Decision Support Systems*. Addison-Wesley.

Edwards C and Peppard J W (1993) A Taxonomy of Executive Information Systems: let the 4 Cs penetrate the Fog. *Information Management and Computer Security* Vol 1 No 2. pp. 4–10.

Finnegan P, Murphy C and O'Riordan J (1995) External Information and the Management Hierarchy: Implications for the IS Field. *Proceedings of the 13th International Association of Management (AoM) Conference: Information Systems Group, Vancouver, Canada.* pp. 1–10.

Holohan J (1992) Use of Executive Information Systems in measuring Business Performance. *Journal of Information Technology* Vol 7 No 3. pp. 177–186.

Moormann J and Lochte-Holtgreven M (1993) An Approach for an Integrated DSS for Strategic Planning. *Decision Support Systems* Vol 10. pp. 401–411.

Sambamurphy V, Venkataraman S and DeSanctis G (1993) The Design of Information Technology Planning Systems for Various Organisational Contexts. *European Journal of Information Systems* Vol 2 No 1. pp. 23–35.

Review questions

1 What is the principal relationship between organisational mission and strategy, SISP/SCB activities and/or MSS, that allows us to determine Strategic MSS for a particular company? Why does this relationship result in Strategic MSS?

2 What are the other important relationships that exist between organisational mission and strategy, SISP/SCB activities and/or MSS. Why do these relationships exist?

3 How can the following SISP techniques be used to identify MSS requirements: SWOT analysis, CSF technique, Strategic Relevance And Impact Grid?

4 Describe two types of MSS functionality that could be provided to support a company's strategic management (i.e. strategic planning and controlling) activities?

5 Why do we not know whether current MSS implementations are, in general, effective in their support of strategic management activities? List, and justify, factors that you believe might result in improved MSS implementations to support strategic management activities.

6 Describe three types of MSS functionality that could be provided to support a company's SISP/SCB activities.

Project idea

With a company, conduct an audit of their current MSS provision and their approach to SISP/SCB. From your investigations:

- Identify whether some or all of the company's current MSS provision are indeed Strategic MSS (or were when first specified). In other words, did each MSS result from an organisational need, related to the organisational strategy and mission at that time, or from an individual or other need?
- Establish how current decisions are made concerning MSS provision. Do MSS result from a SISP/SCB activity, or are they the result of individual executive requirements, or do they result from some other requirement?

You should present your findings to the company's IT management, with recommendations as to how the selection of MSS provision could be improved (possibly via the use of appropriate SISP/SCB activities).

CHAPTER 15

Conclusion

15.1 STRATEGIC MSS

This book has provided a new insight into the identification and use of information systems to support managerial decision making within organisations. There are many new concepts in the book based on original research undertaken by the authors. The combination and integration of two topics hitherto considered in isolation is a valuable addition to work in this area. New perspectives have been provided on MSS and SISP.

15.1.1 A new perspective on MSS

- MSS is defined as a computerised information system (CBIS).
- The focus is on the functionality of the MSS rather than being product oriented. This radical view overcomes many of the problems associated with current use and misuse of terminology.
- The scope and characteristics of computer technology are considered in addition to several current offerings.
- MSS can provide both both passive and active decision making support. Both types are of value given the right situation.
- MSS requires an integrated development approach. Some standard systems analysis and design techniques, such as Data Flow Diagramming, are either inappropriate or offer restricted support.

15.1.2 A new perspective on SISP

- SISP is the mechanistic element of strategy formulation whilst SCB is the behavioural element.
- Alignment of IS is achieved through the appropriate combination of SISP and SCB.
- The strategy team profile has a significant impact on the level and acceptance of the resultant IS strategy.
- SISP is supported by a three-layered approach of methodologies, techniques and tools.
- Classification and selection methods are needed to select the appropriate approach for undertaking a strategy formulation exercise.
- BPR interrelates with SISP and SCB but does not replace them.

15.1.3 New relationships

- SISP/SCB determines the organisational need for MSS.
- Given the supportive role of MSS, MSS can support SISP/SCB activities as well as mission and organisational strategy management activities.
- An MSS that is aligned with corporate objectives and the mission is a Strategic MSS.

15.2 AND FINALLY ...

Throughout the book emphasis has been placed upon conceptual ideas which have some practical meaning. The complex area of MSS is key in the effective management of organisations. The authors believe that any development of this subject should provide practical benefit. For this reason several unabridged real world case studies have been included. The reader has the opportunity to reflect on these case studies and consider how concepts introduced previously might impact on these practical situations. The provision of a book that balances concepts and practice should be of value to practitioners, academics and students alike.

In 1775 Samuel Johnson wrote, "Knowledge is of two kinds. We know a subject ourselves, or we know where we can find information upon it." In today's society dominated by complex structures, demands for faster and faster service and increasing interaction between people across the globe it is increasingly likely we do not have knowledge of the subject. Access to information is no longer desirable, it is essential. The ubiquitous computer symbolises the advent of the information age. This is the age where information dissemination is key to the success and very survival of organisations. It is an age where informed decision making is crucial. Thus it is time for strategic management support systems to come of age.

CASE STUDY: BUSINESS LINK LEICESTERSHIRE

Business Link Leicestershire (BLL) was formally opened in September 1993 as part of a Department of Trade and Industry (DTI) initiative to provide a One Stop Shop (OSS) for business support services. The main emphasis of BLL activities is on the provision of quality information, counselling and diagnostic consultancy, with access to training and advice. BLL's target customer base is all Small and Medium Enterprises (SMEs), considered as businesses of maximum 250 employees, within Leicestershire. These form approximately 99.9% of Leicestershire's total companies. The aim, towards which BLL strives via its service provision, is the increased economic wealth of Leicestershire.

BLL's mission statement is, "To ensure the delivery of the best business support services to smaller and growing enterprises for the creation of wealth in Leicestershire."

The company has several partners, including Leicestershire County Council and Leicester City Council, the DTI in the East Midlands, Leicestershire TEC, and the local branch of the Chamber of Commerce and Industry. Most of the partners provide a portion of the core funding required to support day-to-day operations at BLL, the remainder being provided by the DTI. Other additional funds come from gaining contracts that are periodically put out to tender principally by the DTI. The majority of these contracts are of a short-term nature, lasting for one or two years with no guarantee of renewal. Some of the contracts won by BLL require subsidised customer contributions, for example customers paying a subsidised amount towards a particular business service, with the DTI providing the balance. BLL does not perform any independent revenue-generating activity at present.

The company employs 12 staff directly. However, there are approximately 60 staff associated with BLL, many of whom are self-employed and work principally from home.

▶

Other personnel are employees of the partners, but provide services that are within the remit of BLL and are therefore located within BLL's central office in Leicester. In addition to the central office, there are two operational satellite offices within the locality with four more at pilot stage. The satellites provide a subset of the services that are catered for at the central office.

Aspects of BLL's environment are dynamic, even though BLL's mission remains stable. The unpredictability in what contracts are to be available and their relative short-term nature makes it difficult to predict what finances will actually be available even a few months ahead. The company has to react to any Invitation To Tender very quickly, as timescales between notification and tender submissions are commonly a matter of a few weeks. Even the core funding from partners is uncertain. The formal agreement can be cancelled at any time by any partner, and comes up for renewal in April 1996 with no guarantee. The focus of services provided to customers needs to change in accordance with changes in customer requirements. Legislation, grants and political outlook, at local, national and European levels, will influence the mix of customer services provided by BLL.

Overall SISP approach

BLL commissioned the authors of this book as external consultants to develop a new IS/IT strategy to cover the period from the beginning of April 1995 to the end of September 1996. The previous strategy was predominantly technical in focus. It did not embrace the information systems and information management aspects expected within any properly balanced IS/IT strategic plan. The new IS/IT strategic plan had to be available within six weeks of project initiation. To achieve this, a substantial amount of time was needed to be devoted by the consultants throughout the project.

The general approach undertaken by the authors was of a top-down nature, where the strategy was driven from the overall mission of the business. An overall path for strategy

development activities was mapped out at a very general level at the outset of the project. Within this path, there were opportunities for the inclusion of the bottom-up approach, where suggestions concerning IS/IT applications were made from employees directly rather than stemming from the mission, and the middle-out approach, where new IS/IT opportunities were considered with respect to BLL activities. A proprietary SISP methodology was not adopted, rather an evolutionary tool-kit approach was adopted with regard to technique selection, so that techniques were chosen as the project progressed rather than pre-determined. Hence a bespoke methodology was used. As shown in Section 11.4, this approach had inherent flexibility which was essential for this assignment, but required a considerable amount of IS and business knowledge and experience to be effective, and hence the heavy reliance on consultant input. The overall path to strategy development was also re-considered at many points during the project and resulted in omitting and adding activities when appropriate.

The following section describes the SISP activities carried out at BLL in greater detail and discusses key issues of these activities of particular relevance.

SISP activities and key issues

A business appraisal was first conducted to familiarise the consultants with the BLL ethos and environment. This involved interviewing key members of the company and reviewing key corporate documentation, such as the Corporate Strategic Planning Document. Having the mission of the company and the corporate strategic plan formally written down was extremely beneficial as SISP activities could concentrate on IS/IT without having the additional burden of identifying what the business was trying to achieve. The business appraisal culminated in the development of a SWOT analysis, which included both IS/IT specific issues and general corporate strengths, weaknesses, opportunities and threats.

▶

Based on the mission and corporate strategic plan, several business CSFs were identified. These related to issues such as customer service, finance and corporate image. The business CSFs were then analysed in terms of their impact on the success of BLL's key Business Units (BUs), via an Information Needs Matrix. This allowed each business CSF to be analysed regarding its overall range of effect across BU activities. It also confirmed that the BU managers' perspectives of the critical factors to their respective BU's success were in line with those critical factors to the business as a whole. From the business CSFs, activities and associated information needs were established leading to a portfolio of possible IT/IS projects. A Value-Chain Analysis (VCA), with respect to the core process of customer information service provision, was also undertaken. Principally, the results of the VCA confirmed the subset of information and activity needs related to customer service already established, but did additionally highlight the importance of effective MSS development.

Given the dynamic nature of BLL's environment, particularly with respect to funding arrangements, the emphasis of the business CSFs was not on the individual contracts and their success factors, but on those more general factors that apply equally to all contracts or, indeed, to all organisational activities. These included issues such as:

- the quality of customer service provision
- the enhancement of image and awareness of BLL, and its services and products
- the development of chargeable services to customers to lessen the financial dependence of the company on government grants

Thus, when determining BLL's information needs and associated activities, the focus was principally on supporting the general aspects of company operations that persist. For instance, clients will always need advice, whether it be oriented towards new or existing businesses. Training sessions will need professional-quality support in terms of easy-to-use presentation software and hardware, irrespective of the actual topic of the training. Despite different services offered to clients over time, BLL will always want to track and analyse details of clients, and the details of activities performed by BLL for clients.

Up to this point within SISP activities, BLL's existing IS/IT systems had not been investigated. This was to ensure that an open mind was maintained throughout the initial stages of SISP, rather than being influenced by any existing implementations. Having established BLL's requirements, the existing IS/IT systems were appraised. The Strategic Relevance And Impact Grid was used to analyse the portfolio of the current IS/IT provision, associating each system to one of the four quadrants based on attitude of employees towards the system. Indeed, the principal message from this analysis was that the current systems were considered support or factory systems rather than turnaround or strategic systems. A second strategic grid was then constructed to highlight the way in which current systems should be viewed within BLL. This was performed by the consultants, and provided an independent, objective view of current provision, backed up by the information on BLL's IS/IT requirements resulting from previous SISP activities. A subset of current systems was now placed in the turnaround or strategic categories. In most cases, the only changes needed within current IS/IT systems with strategic potential was a change in emphasis or minor enhancements in their functionality, and/or a change in people's perceptions of their importance to the company. The dual application of the Strategic Grid was extremely powerful in highlighting the importance of perception in IS/IT success, in general, and in externalising and communicating the problems of IS/IT perception to BLL's Chief Executive.

Finally, the existing IS/IT systems and proposed new IS/IT projects were pooled together to provide a Strategic Grid showing the entire portfolio of systems needed at BLL. At this point, an outline operational plan was developed, which outlined the activities needed for each project on a quarter-by-quarter basis. Non-technical, as well as technical, issues were included within the activity breakdown, and financial costs in terms of development, IT platforms, software, communications, procedures development, and staffing and training were estimated per quarter for each project. The consultants were concerned that not only the critical projects were put into place, but also that a strategic culture was developed within the company. Strategic culture promotes ownership of the IS/IT strategy by all staff. It promotes motivation towards IS/IT usage and encourages staff to be innovative and visionary in its usage. The culture must be aligned to the dynamic context of BLL and must be a receptive culture with willingness and support from the top. The management style must be able to embrace participation, disagreement and criticism as well as re-appraisal and re-organisation. For such a culture to flourish, the staff must be empowered. Thus, approximately 10% of the budget was allocated to issues such as staff training and procedures development. Staff training and procedures were seen not only to enable the systems, as initially developed, to operate effectively but also to put into effect new requirements as changes within the environment dictate.

Projects were separated into two categories: those that were mandatory to develop as failure to implement these systems would result in BLL's very survival being threatened, and those that were desirable in that their implementation could aid the increased prosperity of BLL, but their non-adoption would not threaten BLL's survival. The desirable systems' list provided BLL's Board of Directors with some element of choice over which projects were to proceed. This also allowed some flexibility in the level of finances made available for the strategic IS/IT plan, which was necessary as the original budget was not 100% guaranteed.

Identified strategic MSS

As explained in Chapter 14, any MSS that results from SISP/SCB is aligned with the corporate mission and is of value to the organisation. Such MSS are termed Strategic MSS. The required Strategic MSS functionality identified through the strategy exercise at BLL included:

- provision of flexible and summarised information regarding client tracking
- support for pro-active marketing
- e-mail and video conferencing facilities to communicate with existing and potential customers quickly and easily and to facilitate internal communication
- use of teleconferencing systems for client management to use within group meetings where participants were geographically dispersed
- document preparation systems to facilitate the quality of information for client consumption
- effective access to external information sources for client support and internal operations and market awareness
- resource management support
- reporting of key performance indicators in flexible formats to satisfy the needs of BLL management, partners and funding agencies

Sustaining strategic progress

Using the SISP/SCB continuum described in Section 9.4 it is possible to identify what the problems were in BLL regarding effective use of IS/IT and what overall philosophy should be adopted in order to improve. As previously discussed, the technically oriented plan existed and was being implemented and staff tended to view IS/IT as simply operational applications, many of which were not essential to run BLL. This results in a misalignment of SISP and SCB with SISP located to the far left and SCB to the far right and so it is inevitable that problems occurred in the strategic use of IS/IT. As has been already explained, BLL is a small, volatile organisation with a fairly complex organisational structure. Some staff are keen and capable of acting effectively on their own initiative whilst others need a little more

▶

direction which leads to a mixed workforce. This profile places BLL left of centre on the continuum which indicates that the company needs to adopt a philosophy where strategic culture is more predominant than strategic planning but that a strategic plan should be in place. Furthermore, the strategic plan should be flexible and high level allowing the company to respond effectively to the challenges in its dynamic environment. In this way IS, and in particular MSS, could be developed, introduced and enhanced to sustain the corporate mission of BLL. ∎

Project idea

As part of the British Government's strategy on privatisation many organisations within the public utilities sector were removed from direct government control and shares in them were issued publicly through the Stock Exchange. Measures were taken to introduce direct competition to eliminate monopolistic situations. As a result of this policy British Gas was privatised and is in the process of undergoing a fundamental change in the way its operates. Government policy effectively means that anyone will be allowed to use the gas network to sell to its clients. British Gas has responded to this challenge by restructuring its whole UK operation.

Old structure of the organisation
The Gas Business division was responsible for all activities within the UK excluding exploration and production. The division was divided into 12 regions each with many largely autonomous functions. Each regions ran an integrated set of activities which included:

- the maintenance of a mains network
- the supply and sale of gas to domestic, commercial and industrial customers
- the retailing of gas appliances
- the installation, servicing and repair of gas appliances
- a regulatory Gas Safety service

A number of the functions were under central control including IS/IT. However this was a relatively recent development (1992) and nearly all IS/IT was developed regionally. Use of these systems was restricted to the region where development took place.

Rationale for the new organisational structure
- There is a statutory requirement to split the gas transportation business from other trading activities.
- There is a need to reduce operating costs to respond to the competitive pressures as British Gas's monopoly is removed.

New structure of the organisation
The UK Gas Business will have five business units. Each business unit will be largely autonomous and have responsibility for its own supporting activities such as personnel and IS/IT. The business units are:

- Transco – This is responsible for the gas pipeline network and the shipment of gas for British Gas and other gas customers to the gas consumer. It is also responsible for regulatory safety aspects of gas transportation.
- Public Gas Supply – This is responsible for the selling of gas to the domestic market defined as consumers using less that 2500 therms per annum.
- Business Gas – This is responsible for selling gas to the non-domestic market defined as consumers using greater than 2500 therms per annum.
- Retail – This is responsible for the operation of Energy Centre outlets and marketing of appliances.
- Service – This is responsible for the installation, servicing and repair of appliances.

Business goals

- By April 1998 British Gas's monopoly over the supply and distribution of natural gas will end. British Gas is therefore striving to take advantage of its current position and place itself ahead of its future competitors.
- To segment the company in order to increase efficiency and maintain the more profitable elements of its business.

Public Gas Supply (PGS)

PGS buys and sells gas to Britain's 18 million homes which use less than 2500 therms per annum. Competition in the domestic gas supply market will be phased in from 1996, with full competition planned for 1998. PGS purchases gas from any supplier and ships it via Transco. Currently, PGS has little or no competition from other gas suppliers in the UK. Its main competition is from other forms of energy, mainly solid fuels, electricity and petrol.

PGS is organised into several functional sections in order to service its customers who are divided into eight areas covering the UK. Each section is headed by a director reporting to the managing director. The functional sections are:

Function	Responsibilities
● Supply	Gas purchase, transportation and storage purchase, daily operations
● Business Development	Market development, market research, competitor evaluation, tariffs and pricing, OFGAS liaison, public relations
● Finance	Financial management, business planning, financial services
● IS	Systems development, management of bill production centres, data centre operations
● Customer Operations	Sales, customer enquiries and advice, meter readings, billing, payments and debt collection
● Support Services	Employee relations, staff development and training, purchasing, legal services

Tasks

1. Find out as much as you can from newspaper items, business and computer trade magazines about the transition of British Gas.
2. List the disadvantages and advantages of the original regional approach to information systems development.
3. Define what you believe should be PGS's strategic objectives over the next ten years.
4. Develop a strategic plan for IS to support these objectives.
5. Comment on the individual IS needs of the six sections.
6. List and justify what you believe are the strategic MSS for PGS.

INDEX